THE ODYSSEY

HOMER
THE ODYSSEY

Translated by ROBERT FITZGERALD

ANCHOR PRESS
Doubleday
NEW YORK

For my sons and daughters

Contents

Book One 11
A GODDESS INTERVENES

Book Two 27
A HERO'S SON AWAKENS

Book Three 41
THE LORD OF THE WESTERN APPROACHES

Book Four 57
THE RED-HAIRED KING AND HIS LADY

Book Five 83
SWEET NYMPH AND OPEN SEA

Book Six 99
THE PRINCESS AT THE RIVER

Book Seven 109
GARDENS AND FIRELIGHT

Book Eight 121
THE SONGS OF THE HARPER

Book Nine 139
NEW COASTS AND POSEIDON'S SON

Book Ten 157
THE GRACE OF THE WITCH

Book Eleven   175
A GATHERING OF SHADES

Book Twelve   197
SEA PERILS AND DEFEAT

Book Thirteen   215
ONE MORE STRANGE ISLAND

Book Fourteen   231
HOSPITALITY IN THE FOREST

Book Fifteen   249
HOW THEY CAME TO ITHAKA

Book Sixteen   269
FATHER AND SON

Book Seventeen   287
THE BEGGAR AT THE MANOR

Book Eighteen   311
BLOWS AND A QUEEN'S BEAUTY

Book Nineteen   327
RECOGNITIONS AND A DREAM

Book Twenty   347
SIGNS AND A VISION

Book Twenty-one   361
THE TEST OF THE BOW

Book Twenty-two   377
DEATH IN THE GREAT HALL

Book Twenty-three *395*
THE TRUNK OF THE OLIVE TREE

Book Twenty-four *409*
WARRIORS, FAREWELL

PostScript *429*

BOOK ONE

A Goddess Intervenes

LINES 1 – 10

Sing in me, Muse, and through me tell the story   1
of that man skilled in all ways of contending,
the wanderer, harried for years on end,
after he plundered the stronghold
on the proud height of Troy.

                    He saw the townlands
and learned the minds of many distant men,
and weathered many bitter nights and days
in his deep heart at sea, while he fought only
to save his life, to bring his shipmates home.   10
But not by will nor valor could he save them,
for their own recklessness destroyed them all—
children and fools, they killed and feasted on
the cattle of Lord Hêlios, the Sun,
and he who moves all day through heaven
took from their eyes the dawn of their return.

Of these adventures, Muse, daughter of Zeus,
tell us in our time, lift the great song again.

Begin when all the rest who left behind them
headlong death in battle or at sea   20
had long ago returned, while he alone still hungered
for home and wife. Her ladyship Kalypso
clung to him in her sea-hollowed caves—
a nymph, immortal and most beautiful,
who craved him for her own.

           And when long years and seasons
wheeling brought around that point of time
ordained for him to make his passage homeward,
trials and dangers, even so, attended him
even in Ithaka, near those he loved.   30
Yet all the gods had pitied Lord Odysseus,
all but Poseidon, raging cold and rough
against the brave king till he came ashore
at last on his own land.

           But now that god
had gone far off among the sunburnt races,
most remote of men, at earth's two verges,
in sunset lands and lands of the rising sun,
to be regaled by smoke of thighbones burning,
haunches of rams and bulls, a hundred fold.   40
He lingered delighted at the banquet side.

In the bright hall of Zeus upon Olympos
the other gods were all at home, and Zeus,
the father of gods and men, made conversation.
For he had meditated on Aigísthos, dead
by the hand of Agamémnon's son, Orestês,
and spoke his thought aloud before them all:

"My word, how mortals take the gods to task!
All their afflictions come from us, we hear.
And what of their own failings? Greed and folly   50
double the suffering in the lot of man.
See how Aigísthos, for his double portion,
stole Agamémnon's wife and killed the soldier
on his homecoming day. And yet Aigísthos
knew that his own doom lay in this. We gods
had warned him, sent down Hermês Argeïphontês,

our most observant courier, to say:
'Don't kill the man, don't touch his wife,
or face a reckoning with Orestês
the day he comes of age and wants his patrimony.'   60
Friendly advice—but would Aigísthos take it?
Now he has paid the reckoning in full."

The grey-eyed goddess Athena replied to Zeus:

"O Majesty, O Father of us all,
that man is in the dust indeed, and justly.
So perish all who do what he had done.
But my own heart is broken for Odysseus,
the master mind of war, so long a castaway
upon an island in the running sea;
a wooded island, in the sea's middle,   70
and there's a goddess in the place, the daughter
of one whose baleful mind knows all the deeps
of the blue sea—Atlas, who holds the columns
that bear from land the great thrust of the sky.
His daughter will not let Odysseus go,
poor mournful man; she keeps on coaxing him
with her beguiling talk, to turn his mind
from Ithaka. But such desire is in him
merely to see the hearthsmoke leaping upward
from his own island, that he longs to die.   80
Are you not moved by this, Lord of Olympos?
Had you no pleasure from Odysseus' offerings
beside the Argive ships, on Troy's wide seaboard?
O Zeus, what do you hold against him now?"

To this the summoner of cloud replied:

"My child, what strange remarks you let escape you.
Could I forget that kingly man, Odysseus?
There is no mortal half so wise; no mortal
gave so much to the lords of open sky.
Only the god who laps the land in water,   90
Poseidon, bears the fighter an old grudge
since he poked out the eye of Polyphêmos,
brawniest of the Kyklopês. Who bore
that giant lout? Thoösa, daughter of Phorkys,

an offshore sea lord: for this nymph had lain
with Lord Poseidon in her hollow caves.
Naturally, the god, after the blinding—
mind you, he does not kill the man;
he only buffets him away from home.
But come now, we are all at leisure here,   100
let us take up this matter of his return
that he may sail. Poseidon must relent,
for being quarrelsome will get him nowhere,
one god, flouting the will of all the gods."

The grey-eyed goddess Athena answered him:

"O Majesty, O Father of us all,
if it now please the blissful gods
that wise Odysseus reach his home again,
let the Wayfinder, Hermês, cross the sea
to the island of Ogýgia; let him tell   110
our fixed intent to the nymph with pretty braids,
and let the steadfast man depart for home.
For my part, I shall visit Ithaka
to put more courage in the son, and rouse him
to call an assembly of the islanders,
Akhaian gentlemen with flowing hair.
He must warn off that wolf pack of the suitors
who prey upon his flocks and dusky cattle.
I'll send him to the mainland then, to Sparta
by the sand beach of Pylos; let him find   120
news of his dear father where he may
and win his own renown about the world."

She bent to tie her beautiful sandals on,
ambrosial, golden, that carry her over water
or over endless land on the wings of the wind,
and took the great haft of her spear in hand—
that bronzeshod spear this child of Power can use
to break in wrath long battle lines of fighters.

Flashing down from Olympos' height she went
to stand in Ithaka, before the Manor,   130

just at the doorsill of the court. She seemed
a family friend, the Taphian captain, Mentês,
waiting, with a light hand on her spear.
Before her eyes she found the lusty suitors
casting dice inside the gate, at ease
on hides of oxen—oxen they had killed.
Their own retainers made a busy sight
with houseboys, mixing bowls of water and wine,
or sopping water up in sponges, wiping
tables to be placed about in hall,   140
or butchering whole carcasses for roasting.

Long before anyone else, the prince Telémakhos
now caught sight of Athena—for he, too,
was sitting there, unhappy among the suitors,
a boy, daydreaming. What if his great father
came from the unknown world and drove these men
like dead leaves through the place, recovering
honor and lordship in his own domains?
Then he who dreamed in the crowd gazed out at Athena.

Straight to the door he came, irked with himself   150
to think a visitor had been kept there waiting,
and took her right hand, grasping with his left
her tall bronze-bladed spear. Then he said warmly:

"Greetings, stranger! Welcome to our feast.
There will be time to tell your errand later."

He led the way, and Pallas Athena followed
into the lofty hall. The boy reached up
and thrust her spear high in a polished rack
against a pillar, where tough spear on spear
of the old soldier, his father, stood in order.   160
Then, shaking out a splendid coverlet,
he seated her on a throne with footrest—all
finely carved—and drew his painted armchair
near her, at a distance from the rest.
To be amid the din, the suitors' riot,
would ruin his guest's appetite, he thought,

and he wished privacy to ask for news
about his father, gone for years.
                              A maid
brought them a silver finger bowl and filled it   170
out of a beautiful spouting golden jug,
then drew a polished table to their side.
The larder mistress with her tray came by
and served them generously. A carver lifted
cuts of each roast meat to put on trenchers
before the two. He gave them cups of gold,
and these the steward as he went his rounds
filled and filled again.
                              Now came the suitors,
young bloods trooping in to their own seats   180
on thrones or easy chairs. Attendants poured
water over their fingers, while the maids
piled baskets full of brown loaves near at hand,
and houseboys brimmed the bowls with wine.
Now they laid hands upon the ready feast
and thought of nothing more. Not till desire
for food and drink had left them were they mindful
of dance and song, that are the grace of feasting.
A herald gave a shapely cithern harp
to Phêmios, whom they compelled to sing—   190
and what a storm he plucked upon the strings
for prelude! High and clear the song arose.

Telémakhos now spoke to grey-eyed Athena,
his head bent close, so no one else might hear:

"Dear guest, will this offend you, if I speak?
It is easy for these men to like these things,
harping and song; they have an easy life,
scot free, eating the livestock of another—
a man whose bones are rotting somewhere now,
white in the rain on dark earth where they lie,   200
or tumbling in the groundswell of the sea.
If he returned, if these men ever saw him,
faster legs they'd pray for, to a man,
and not more wealth in handsome robes' or gold.
But he is lost; he came to grief and perished,

and there's no help for us in someone's hoping
he still may come; that sun has long gone down.
But tell me now, and put it for me clearly—
who are you? Where do you come from? Where's your home
and family? What kind of ship is yours,   210
and what course brought you here? Who are your sailors?
I don't suppose you walked here on the sea.
Another thing—this too I ought to know—
is Ithaka new to you, or were you ever
a guest here in the old days? Far and near
friends knew this house; for he whose home it was
had much acquaintance in the world."

                    To this
the grey-eyed goddess answered:

                              "As you ask,   220
I can account most clearly for myself.
Mentês I'm called, son of the veteran
Ankhíalos; I rule seafaring Taphos.
I came by ship, with a ship's company,
sailing the winedark sea for ports of call
on alien shores—to Témesê, for copper,
bringing bright bars of iron in exchange.
My ship is moored on a wild strip of coast
in Reithron Bight, under the wooded mountain.
Years back, my family and yours were friends,   230
as Lord Laërtês knows; ask when you see him.
I hear the old man comes to town no longer,
stays up country, ailing, with only one
old woman to prepare his meat and drink
when pain and stiffness take him in the legs
from working on his terraced plot, his vineyard.
As for my sailing here—
The tale was that your father had come home,
therefore I came. I see the gods delay him.
But never in this world is Odysseus dead—   240
only detained somewhere on the wide sea,
upon some island, with wild islanders;
savages, they must be, to hold him captive.

Well, I will forecast for you, as the gods
put the stong feeling in me—I see it all,
and I'm no prophet, no adept in bird-signs.
He will not, now, be long away from Ithaka,
his father's dear land; though he be in chains
he'll scheme a way to come; he can do anything.

But tell me this now, make it clear to me: 250
You must be, by your looks, Odysseus' boy?
The way your head is shaped, the fine eyes—yes,
how like him! We took meals like this together
many a time, before he sailed for Troy
with all the lords of Argos in the ships.
I have not seen him since, nor has he seen me."

And thoughtfully Telémakhos replied:

"Friend, let me put it in the plainest way.
My mother says I am his son; I know not
surely. Who has known his own engendering?   260
I wish at least I had some happy man
as father, growing old in his own house—
but unknown death and silence are the fate
of him that, since you ask, they call my father."

Then grey-eyed Athena said:

                              "The gods decreed
no lack of honor in this generation:
such is the son Penélopê bore in you.
But tell me now, and make this clear to me:
what gathering, what feast is this? Why here?   270
A wedding? Revel? At the expense of all?
Not that, I think. How arrogant they seem,
these gluttons, making free here in your house!
A sensible man would blush to be among them."

To this Telémakhos answered:

"Friend, now that you ask about these matters,
our house was always princely, a great house,
as long as he of whom we speak remained here.

But evil days the gods have brought upon it,
making him vanish, as they have, so strangely.   280
Were his death known, I could not feel such pain—
if he had died of wounds in Trojan country
or in the arms of friends, after the war.
They would have made a tomb for him, the Akhaians,
and I should have all honor as his son.
Instead, the whirlwinds got him, and no glory.
He's gone, no sign, no word of him; and I inherit
trouble and tears—and not for him alone,
the gods have laid such other burdens on me.
For now the lords of the islands,   290
Doulíkhion and Samê, wooded Zakynthos,
and rocky Ithaka's young lords as well,
are here courting my mother; and they use
our house as if it were a house to plunder.
Spurn them she dare not, though she hates that marriage,
nor can she bring herself to choose among them.
Meanwhile they eat their way through all we have,
and when they will, they can demolish me."

Pallas Athena was disturbed, and said:

"Ah, bitterly you need Odysseus, then!   300
High time he came back to engage these upstarts.
I wish we saw him standing helmeted
there in the doorway, holding shield and spear,
looking the way he did when I first knew him.
That was at our house, where he drank and feasted
after he left Ephyra, homeward bound
from a visit to the son of Mérmeris, Ilos.
He took his fast ship down the gulf that time
for a fatal drug to dip his arrows in
and poison the bronze points; but young Ilos   310
turned him away, fearing the gods' wrath.
My father gave it, for he loved him well.
I wish these men could meet the man of those days!
They'd know their fortune quickly: a cold bed.
Aye! but it lies upon the gods' great knees
whether he can return and force a reckoning
in his own house, or not.

                              If I were you,
I should take steps to make these men disperse.
Listen, now, and attend to what I say: 320
at daybreak call the islanders to assembly,
and speak your will, and call the gods to witness:
the suitors must go scattering to their homes.
Then here's a course for you, if you agree:
get a sound craft afloat with twenty oars
and go abroad for news of your lost father—
perhaps a traveller's tale, or rumored fame
issued from Zeus abroad in the world of men.
Talk to that noble sage at Pylos, Nestor,
then go to Meneláos, the red-haired king   330
at Sparta, last man home of all the Akhaians.
If you should learn your father is alive
and coming home, you could hold out a year.
Or if you learn that he is dead and gone,
then you can come back to your own dear country
and raise a mound for him, and burn his gear,
with all the funeral honors due the man,
and give your mother to another husband.

When you have done all this, or seen it done,
it will be time to ponder   340
concerning these contenders in your house—
how you should kill them, outright or by guile.
You need not bear this insolence of theirs,
you are a child no longer. Have you heard
what glory young Orestês won
when he cut down that two-faced man, Aigísthos,
for killing his illustrious father?
Dear friend, you are tall and well set up, I see;
be brave—you, too—and men in times to come
will speak of you respectfully.   350
                         Now I must join my ship;
my crew will grumble if I keep them waiting.
Look to yourself; remember what I told you."

Telémakhos replied:

                              "Friend, you have done me
kindness, like a father to his son,
and I shall not forget your counsel ever.
You must get back to sea, I know, but come
take a hot bath, and rest; accept a gift
to make your heart lift up when you embark—   360
some precious thing, and beautiful, from me,
a keepsake, such as dear friends give their friends."

But the grey-eyed goddess Athena answered him:

"Do not delay me, for I love the sea ways.
As for the gift your heart is set on giving,
let me accept it on my passage home,
and you shall have a choice gift in exchange."

With this Athena left him
as a bird rustles upward, off and gone.
But as she went she put new spirit in him,   370
a new dream of his father, clearer now,
so that he marvelled to himself
divining that a god had been his guest.
Then godlike in his turn he joined the suitors.

The famous minstrel still sang on before them,
and they sat still and listened, while he sang
that bitter song, the Homecoming of Akhaians—
how by Athena's will they fared from Troy;
and in her high room careful Penélopê,
Ikários' daughter, heeded the holy song.   380
She came, then, down the long stairs of her house,
this beautiful lady, with two maids in train
attending her as she approached the suitors;
and near a pillar of the roof she paused,
her shining veil drawn over across her cheeks,
the two girls close to her and still,
and through her tears spoke to the noble minstrel:

"Phêmios, other spells you know, high deeds
of gods and heroes, as the poets tell them;

let these men hear some other; let them sit   390
silent and drink their wine. But sing no more
this bitter tale that wears my heart away.
It opens in me again the wound of longing
for one incomparable, ever in my mind—
his fame all Hellas knows, and midland Argos."

But Telémakhos intervened and said to her:

"Mother, why do you grudge our own dear minstrel
joy of song, wherever his thought may lead?
Poets are not to blame, but Zeus who gives
what fate he pleases to adventurous men.   400
Here is no reason for reproof: to sing
the news of the Danaans! Men like best
a song that rings like morning on the ear.
But you must nerve yourself and try to listen.
Odysseus was not the only one at Troy
never to know the day of his homecoming.
Others, how many others, lost their lives!"

The lady gazed in wonder and withdrew,
her son's clear wisdom echoing in her mind.
But when she had mounted to her rooms again   410
with her two handmaids, then she fell to weeping
for Odysseus, her husband. Grey-eyed Athena
presently cast a sweet sleep on her eyes.

Meanwhile the din grew loud in the shadowy hall
as every suitor swore to lie beside her,
but Telémakhos turned now and spoke to them:

"You suitors of my mother! Insolent men,
now we have dined, let us have entertainment
and no more shouting. There can be no pleasure
so fair as giving heed to a great minstrel   420
like ours, whose voice itself is pure delight.
At daybreak we shall sit down in assembly
and I shall tell you—take it as you will—
you are to leave this hall. Go feasting elsewhere,
consume your own stores. Turn and turn about,

use one another's houses. If you choose
to slaughter one man's livestock and pay nothing,
this is rapine; and by the eternal gods
I beg Zeus you shall get what you deserve:
a slaughter here, and nothing paid for it!"   430

By now their teeth seemed fixed in their under-lips,
Telémakhos' bold speaking stunned them so.
Antínoös, Eupeithês' son, made answer:

"Telémakhos, no doubt the gods themselves
are teaching you this high and mighty manner.
Zeus forbid you should be king in Ithaka,
though you are eligible as your father's son."

Telémakhos kept his head and answered him:

"Antínoös, you may not like my answer,
but I would happily be king, if Zeus   440
conferred the prize. Or do you think it wretched?
I shouldn't call it bad at all. A king
will be respected, and his house will flourish.
But there are eligible men enough,
heaven knows, on the island, young and old,
and one of them perhaps may come to power
after the death of King Odysseus.
All I insist on is that I rule our house
and rule the slaves my father won for me."

Eurýmakhos, Pólybos' son, replied: 450

"Telémakhos, it is on the gods' great knees
who will be king in sea-girt Ithaka.
But keep your property, and rule your house,
and let no man, against your will, make havoc
of your possessions, while there's life on Ithaka.
But now, my brave young friend,
a question or two about the stranger.
Where did your guest come from? Of what country?
Where does he say his home is, and his family?
Has he some message of your father's coming,   460

or business of his own, asking a favor?
He left so quickly that one hadn't time
to meet him, but he seemed a gentleman."

Telémakhos made answer, cool enough:

"Eurýmakhos, there's no hope for my father.   470
I would not trust a message, if one came,
nor any forecaster my mother invites
to tell by divination of time to come.
My guest, however, was a family friend,
Mentês, son of Ankhíalos.
He rules the Taphian people of the sea."

So said Telémakhos, though in his heart
he knew his visitor had been immortal.
But now the suitors turned to play again
with dance and haunting song. They stayed till nightfall,   480
indeed black night came on them at their pleasure,
and half asleep they left, each for his home.

Telémakhos' bedroom was above the court,
a kind of tower, with a view all round;
here he retired to ponder in the silence,
while carrying brands of pine alight beside him
Eurýkleia went padding, sage and old.
Her father had been Ops, Peisênor's son,
and she had been a purchase of Laërtês
when she was still a blossoming girl. He gave   490
the price of twenty oxen for her, kept her
as kindly in his house as his own wife,
though, for the sake of peace, he never touched her.
No servant loved Telémakhos as she did,
she who had nursed him in his infancy.
So now she held the light, as he swung open
the door of his neat freshly painted chamber.
There he sat down, pulling his tunic off,
and tossed it into the wise old woman's hands.
She folded it and smoothed it, and then hung it   500
beside the inlaid bed upon a bar;

then, drawing the door shut by its silver handle
she slid the catch in place and went away.
And all night long, wrapped in the finest fleece,
he took in thought the course Athena gave him.

BOOK TWO

A Hero's Son Awakens

LINES 1 – 18

When primal Dawn spread on the eastern sky   1
her fingers of pink light, Odysseus' true son
stood up, drew on his tunic and his mantle,
slung on a sword-belt and a new-edged sword,
tied his smooth feet into good rawhide sandals,
and left his room, a god's brilliance upon him.
He found the criers with clarion voices and told them
to muster the unshorn Akhaians in full assembly.
The call sang out, and the men came streaming in;
and when they filled the assembly ground, he entered,   10
spear in hand, with two quick hounds at heel;
Athena lavished on him a sunlit grace
that held the eye of the multitude. Old men
made way for him as he took his father's chair.

Now Lord Aigýptios, bent down and sage with years,
opened the assembly. This man's son
had served under the great Odysseus, gone
in the decked ships with him to the wild horse country

of Troy—a spearman, Ántiphos by name.
The ravenous Kyklops in the cave destroyed him   20
last in his feast of men. Three other sons
the old man had, and one, Eurýnomos,
went with the suitors; two farmed for their father;
but even so the old man pined, remembering
the absent one, and a tear welled up as he spoke:

"Hear me, Ithakans! Hear what I have to say.
No meeting has been held here since our king,
Odysseus, left port in the decked ships.
Who finds occasion for assembly, now?
one of the young men? one of the older lot?   30
Has he had word our fighters are returning—
news to report if he got wind of it—
or is it something else, touching the realm?
The man has vigor, I should say; more power to him.
Whatever he desires, may Zeus fulfill it."

The old man's words delighted the son of Odysseus,
who kept his chair no longer but stood up,
eager to speak, in the midst of all the men.
The crier, Peisênor, master of debate,
brought him the staff and placed it in his hand;   40
then the boy touched the old man's shoulder, and said:

"No need to wonder any more, Sir,
who called this session. The distress is mine.
As to our troops returning, I have no news—
news to report if I got wind of it—
nor have I public business to propose;
only my need, and the trouble of my house—
the troubles.

                              My distinguished father is lost,
who ruled among you once, mild as a father,   50
and there is now this greater evil still:
my home and all I have are being ruined.
Mother wanted no suitors, but like a pack
they came—sons of the best men here among them—
lads with no stomach for an introduction

to Ikários, her father across the sea;
he would require a wedding gift, and give her
to someone who found favor in her eyes.
No; these men spend their days around our house
killing our beeves and sheep and fatted goats,   60
carousing, soaking up our good dark wine,
not caring what they do. They squander everything.
We have no strong Odysseus to defend us,
and as to putting up a fight ourselves—
we'd only show our incompetence in arms.
Expel them, yes, if I only had the power;
the whole thing's out of hand, insufferable.
My house is being plundered: is this courtesy?
Where is your indignation? Where is your shame?
Think of the talk in the islands all around us,   70
and fear the wrath of the gods,
or they may turn, and send you some devilry.
Friends, by Olympian Zeus and holy Justice
that holds men in assembly and sets them free,
make an end of this! Let me lament in peace
my private loss. Or did my father, Odysseus,
ever do injury to the armed Akhaians?
Is this your way of taking it out on me,
giving free rein to these young men?
I might as well—might better—see my treasure   80
and livestock taken over by you all;
then, if you fed on them, I'd have some remedy,
and when we met, in public, in the town,
I'd press my claim; you might make restitution.
This way you hurt me when my hands are tied."

And in hot anger now he threw the staff to the ground,
his eyes grown bright with tears. A wave of sympathy
ran through the crowd, all hushed; and no one there
had the audacity to answer harshly
except Antínoös, who said: 90

                    "What high and mighty
talk, Telémakhos! No holding you!
You want to shame us, and humiliate us,

but you should know the suitors are not to blame—
it is your own dear, incomparably cunning mother.
For three years now—and it will soon be four—
she has been breaking the hearts of the Akhaians,
holding out hope to all, and sending promises
to each man privately—but thinking otherwise.

Here is an instance of her trickery: 100
she had her great loom standing in the hall
and the fine warp of some vast fabric on it;
we were attending her, and she said to us:
'Young men, my suitors, now my lord is dead,
let me finish my weaving before I marry,
or else my thread will have been spun in vain.
It is a shroud I weave for Lord Laërtês,
when cold death comes to lay him on his bier.
The country wives would hold me in dishonor
if he, with all his fortune, lay unshrouded.'   110
We have men's hearts; she touched them; we agreed.
So every day she wove on the great loom—
but every night by torchlight she unwove it;
and so for three years she deceived the Akhaians.
But when the seasons brought the fourth around,
one of her maids, who knew the secret, told us;
we found her unraveling the splendid shroud.
She had to finish then, although she hated it.

Now here is the suitors' answer—
you and all the Akhaians, mark it well: 120
dismiss your mother from the house, or make her marry
the man her father names and she prefers.
Does she intend to keep us dangling forever?
She may rely too long on Athena's gifts—
talent in handicraft and a clever mind;
so cunning—history cannot show the like
among the ringleted ladies of Akhaia,
Mykênê with her coronet, Alkmênê, Tyro.
Wits like Penélopê's never were before,
but this time—well, she made poor use of them.   130
For here are suitors eating up your property

as long as she holds out—a plan some god
put in her mind. She makes a name for herself,
but you can feel the loss it means for you.
Our own affairs can wait; we'll never go anywhere else,
until she takes an Akhaian to her liking."

But clear-headed Telémakhos replied:

"Antínoös, can I banish against her will
the mother who bore me and took care of me?
My father is either dead or far away,   140
but dearly I should pay for this
at Ikários' hands, if ever I sent her back.
The powers of darkness would requite it, too,
my mother's parting curse would call hell's furies
to punish me, along with the scorn of men.
No: I can never give the word for this.
But if your hearts are capable of shame,
leave my great hall, and take your dinner elsewhere,
consume your own stores. Turn and turn about,
use one another's houses. If you choose   150
to slaughter one man's livestock and pay nothing,
this is rapine; and by the eternal gods
I beg Zeus you shall get what you deserve:
a slaughter here, and nothing paid for it!"

Now Zeus who views the wide world sent a sign to him,
launching a pair of eagles from a mountain crest
in gliding flight down the soft blowing wind,
wing-tip to wing-tip quivering taut, companions,
till high above the assembly of many voices
they wheeled, their dense wings beating, and in havoc   160
dropped on the heads of the crowd—a deathly omen—
wielding their talons, tearing cheeks and throats;
then veered away on the right hand through the city.
Astonished, gaping after the birds, the men
felt their hearts flood, foreboding things to come.
And now they heard the old lord Halithersês,
son of Mastor, keenest among the old
at reading birdflight into accurate speech;
in his anxiety for them, he rose and said:

"Hear me, Ithakans! Hear what I have to say,   170
and may I hope to open the suitors' eyes
to the black wave towering over them. Odysseus
will not be absent from his family long:
he is already near, carrying in him
a bloody doom for all these men, and sorrow
for many more on our high seamark, Ithaka.
Let us think how to stop it; let the suitors
drop their suit; they had better, without delay.
I am old enough to know a sign when I see one,
and I say all has come to pass for Odysseus   180
as I foretold when the Argives massed on Troy,
and he, the great tactician, joined the rest.
My forecast was that after nineteen years,
many blows weathered, all his shipmates lost,
himself unrecognized by anyone,
he would come home. I see this all fulfilled."

But Pólybos' son, Eurýmakhos, retorted:

"Old man, go tell the omens for your children
at home, and try to keep them out of trouble.
I am more fit to interpret this than you are.   190
Bird life aplenty is found in the sunny air,
not all of it significant. As for Odysseus,
he perished far from home. You should have perished with him—
then we'd be spared this nonsense in assembly,
as good as telling Telémakhos to rage on;
do you think you can gamble on a gift from him?
Here is what I foretell, and it's quite certain:
if you, with what you know of ancient lore,
encourage bitterness in this young man,
it means, for him, only the more frustration—   200
he can do nothing whatever with two eagles—
and as for you, old man, we'll fix a penalty
that you will groan to pay.
Before the whole assembly I advise Telémakhos
to send his mother to her father's house;
let them arrange her wedding there, and fix
a portion suitable for a valued daughter.
Until he does this, courtship is our business,

vexing though it may be; we fear no one,
certainly not Telémakhos, with his talk;   210
and we care nothing for your divining, uncle,
useless talk; you win more hatred by it.
We'll share his meat, no thanks or fee to him,
as long as she delays and maddens us.
It is a long, long time we have been waiting
in rivalry for this beauty. We could have gone
elsewhere and found ourselves very decent wives."

Clear-headed Telémakhos replied to this:

"Eurýmakhos, and noble suitors all,
I am finished with appeals and argument.   220
The gods know, and the Akhaians know, these things.
But give me a fast ship and a crew of twenty
who will see me through a voyage, out and back.
I'll go to sandy Pylos, then to Sparta,
for news of Father since he sailed from Troy—
some traveller's tale, perhaps, or rumored fame
issued from Zeus himself into the world.
If he's alive, and beating his way home,
I might hold out for another weary year;
but if they tell me that he's dead and gone,   230
then I can come back to my own dear country
and raise a mound for him, and burn his gear,
with all the funeral honors that befit him,
and give my mother to another husband."

The boy sat down in silence. Next to stand
was Mentor, comrade in arms of the prince Odysseus,
an old man now. Odysseus left him authority
over his house and slaves, to guard them well.
In his concern, he spoke to the assembly:

"Hear me, Ithakans! Hear what I have to say.   240
Let no man holding scepter as a king
be thoughtful, mild, kindly, or virtuous;
let him be cruel, and practice evil ways;
it is so clear that no one here remembers
how like a gentle father Odysseus ruled you.

I find it less revolting that the suitors
carry their malice into violent acts;
at least they stake their lives
when they go pillaging the house of Odysseus—
their lives upon it, he will not come again.　　　　250
What sickens me is to see the whole community
sitting still, and never a voice or a hand raised
against them—a mere handful compared with you."

Leókritos, Euênor's son, replied to him:

"Mentor, what mischief are you raking up?
Will this crowd risk the sword's edge over a dinner?
Suppose Odysseus himself indeed
came in and found the suitors at his table:
he might be hot to drive them out. What then?
Never would he enjoy his wife again—　　　　260
the wife who loves him well; he'd only bring down
abject death on himself against those odds.
Madness, to talk of fighting in either case.
Now let all present go about their business!
Halithersês and Mentor will speed the traveller;
they can help him: they were his father's friends.
I rather think he will be sitting here
a long time yet, waiting for news on Ithaka;
that seafaring he spoke of is beyond him."

On this note they were quick to end their parley.　　　　270
The assembly broke up; everyone went home—
the suitors home to Odysseus' house again.
But Telémakhos walked down along the shore
and washed his hands in the foam of the grey sea,
then said this prayer:

　　　　　　　　"O god of yesterday,
guest in our house, who told me to take ship
on the hazy sea for news of my lost father,
listen to me, be near me:
the Akhaians only wait, or hope to hinder me,　　　　280
the damned insolent suitors most of all."

Athena was nearby and came to him,
putting on Mentor's figure and his tone,
the warm voice in a lucid flight of words:

"You'll never be fainthearted or a fool,
Telémakhos, if you have your father's spirit;
he finished what he cared to say,
and what he took in hand he brought to pass.
The sea routes will yield their distances
to his true son, Penélopê's true son,—   290
I doubt another's luck would hold so far.
The son is rare who measures with his father,
and one in a thousand is a better man,
but you will have the sap and wit
and prudence—for you get that from Odysseus—
to give you a fair chance of winning through.
So never mind the suitors and their ways,
there is no judgment in them, neither do they
know anything of death and the black terror
close upon them—doom's day on them all.   300
You need not linger over going to sea.
I sailed beside your father in the old days,
I'll find a ship for you, and help you sail her.
So go on home, as if to join the suitors,
but get provisions ready in containers—
wine in two-handled jugs and barley meal,
the staying power of oarsmen,
in skin bags, watertight. I'll go the rounds
and call a crew of volunteers together.
Hundreds of ships are beached on sea-girt Ithaka;   310
let me but choose the soundest, old or new,
we'll rig her and take her out on the broad sea."

This was the divine speech Telémakhos heard
from Athena, Zeus's daughter. He stayed no longer,
but took his heartache home,
and found the robust suitors there at work,
skinning goats and roasting pigs in the courtyard.
Antínoös came straight over, laughing at him,
and took him by the hand with a bold greeting:

"High-handed Telémakhos, control your temper!   320
Come on, get over it, no more grim thoughts,
but feast and drink with me, the way you used to.
The Akhaians will attend to all you ask for—
ship, crew, and crossing to the holy land
of Pylos, for the news about your father."

Telémakhos replied with no confusion:

"Antínoös, I cannot see myself again
taking a quiet dinner in this company.
Isn't it enough that you could strip my house
under my very nose when I was young?   330
Now that I know, being grown, what others say,
I understand it all, and my heart is full.
I'll bring black doom upon you if I can—
either in Pylos, if I go, or in this country.
And I will go, go all the way, if only
as someone's passenger. I have no ship,
no oarsmen: and it suits you that I have none."

Calmly he drew his hand from Antínoös' hand.
At this the suitors, while they dressed their meat,
began to exchange loud mocking talk about him.   340
One young toplofty gallant set the tone:

                    "Well, think of that!
Telémakhos has a mind to murder us.
He's going to lead avengers out of Pylos,
or Sparta, maybe; oh, he's wild to do it.
Or else he'll try the fat land of Ephyra—
he can get poison there, and bring it home,
doctor the wine jar and dispatch us all."

Another took the cue:

                    "Well now, who knows?   350
He might be lost at sea, just like Odysseus,
knocking around in a ship, far from his friends.
And what a lot of trouble that would give us,
making the right division of his things!

We'd keep his house as dowry for his mother—
his mother and the man who marries her."

That was the drift of it. Telémakhos
went on through to the storeroom of his father,
a great vault where gold and bronze lay piled
along with chests of clothes, and fragrant oil.   360
And there were jars of earthenware in rows
holding an old wine,
mellow, unmixed, and rare; cool stood the jars
against the wall, kept for whatever day
Odysseus, worn by hardships, might come home.
The double folding doors were tightly locked
and guarded, night and day, by the serving woman,
Eurýkleia, grand-daughter of Peisênor,
in all her duty vigilant and shrewd.
Telémakhos called her to the storeroom, saying: 370

"Nurse, get a few two-handled travelling jugs
filled up with wine—the second best, not that
you keep for your unlucky lord and king,
hoping he may have slipped away from death
and may yet come again—royal Odysseus.
Twelve amphorai will do; seal them up tight.
And pour out barley into leather bags—
twenty bushels of barley meal ground fine.
Now keep this to yourself! Collect these things,
and after dark, when mother has retired   380
and gone upstairs to bed, I'll come for them.
I sail to sandy Pylos, then to Sparta,
to see what news there is of Father's voyage."

His loving nurse Eurýkleia gave a cry,
and tears sprang to her eyes as she wailed softly:

"Dear child, whatever put this in your head?
Why do you want to go so far in the world—
and you our only darling? Lord Odysseus
died in some strange place, far from his homeland.
Think how, when you have turned your back, these men   390
will plot to kill you and share all your things!

Stay with your own, dear, do. Why should you suffer
hardship and homelessness on the wild sea?"

But seeing all clear, Telémakhos replied:

"Take heart, Nurse, there's a god behind this plan.
And you must swear to keep it from my mother,
until the eleventh day, or twelfth, or till
she misses me, or hears that I am gone.
She must not tear her lovely skin lamenting."

So the old woman vowed by all the gods,   400
and vowed again, to carry out his wishes;
then she filled up the amphorai with wine
and sifted barley meal into leather bags.
Telémakhos rejoined the suitors.
                              Meanwhile
the goddess with grey eyes had other business:
disguised as Telémakhos, she roamed the town
taking each likely man aside and telling him:
"Meet us at nightfall at the ship!" Indeed,
she asked Noêmon, Phronios' wealthy son,   410
to lend her a fast ship, and he complied.
Now when at sundown shadows crossed the lanes
she dragged the cutter to the sea and launched it,
fitted out with tough seagoing gear,
and tied it up, away at the harbor's edge.
The crewmen gathered, sent there by the goddess.
Then it occurred to the grey-eyed goddess Athena
to pass inside the house of the hero Odysseus,
showering a sweet drowsiness on the suitors,
whom she had presently wandering in their wine;   420
and soon, as they could hold their cups no longer,
they straggled off to find their beds in town,
eyes heavy-lidded, laden down with sleep.
Then to Telémakhos the grey-eyed goddess
appeared again with Mentor's form and voice,
calling him out of the lofty emptied hall:

"Telémakhos, your crew of fighting men
is ready at the oars, and waiting for you;
come on, no point in holding up the sailing."

And Pallas Athena turned like the wind, running   430
ahead of him. He followed in her footsteps
down to the seaside, where they found the ship,
and oarsmen with flowing hair at the water's edge.
Telémakhos, now strong in the magic, cried:

"Come with me, friends, and get our rations down!
They are all packed at home, and my own mother
knows nothing!—only one maid was told."

He turned and led the way, and they came after,
carried and stowed all in the well-trimmed ship
as the dear son of Odysseus commanded.   440
Telémakhos then stepped aboard; Athena
took her position aft, and he sat by her.
The two stroke oars cast off the stern hawsers
and vaulted over the gunnels to their benches.
Grey-eyed Athena stirred them a following wind,
soughing from the north-west on the winedark sea,
and as he felt the wind, Telémakhos
called to all hands to break out mast and sail.
They pushed the fir mast high and stepped it firm
amidships in the box, made fast the forestays,   450
then hoisted up the white sail on its halyards
until the wind caught, booming in the sail;
and a flushing wave sang backward from the bow
on either side, as the ship got way upon her,
holding her steady course.
Now they made all secure in the fast black ship,
and, setting out the winebowls all a-brim,
they made libation to the gods,

                         the undying, the ever-new,
most of all to the grey-eyed daughter of Zeus.   460
And the prow sheared through the night into the dawn.

BOOK THREE
The Lord of the Western Approaches

LINES 1 – 13

The sun rose on the flawless brimming sea   1
into a sky all brazen—all one brightening
for gods immortal and for mortal men
on plowlands kind with grain.
                         And facing sunrise
the voyagers now lay off Pylos town,
compact stronghold of Neleus. On the shore
black bulls were being offered by the people
to the blue-maned god who makes the islands tremble:
nine congregations, each five hundred strong,   10
led out nine bulls apiece to sacrifice,
taking the tripes to eat, while on their altars
thighbones in fat lay burning for the god.
Here they put in, furled sail, and beached the ship;
but Telémakhos hung back in disembarking,
so that Athena turned and said:

"Not the least shyness, now, Telémakhos.
You came across the open sea for this—
to find out where the great earth hides your father
and what the doom was that he came upon.   20
Go to old Nestor, master charioteer,
so we may broach the storehouse of his mind.
Ask him with courtesy, and in his wisdom
he will tell you history and no lies."

But clear-headed Telémakhos replied:

"Mentor, how can I do it, how approach him?
I have no practice in elaborate speeches, and
for a young man to interrogate an old man
seems disrespectful—"

                      But the grey-eyed goddess said: 30

"Reason and heart will give you words, Telémakhos;
and a spirit will counsel others. I should say
the gods were never indifferent to your life."

She went on quickly, and he followed her
to where the men of Pylos had their altars.
Nestor appeared enthroned among his sons,
while friends around them skewered the red beef
or held it scorching. When they saw the strangers
a hail went up, and all that crowd came forward
calling out invitations to the feast.   40
Peisístratos in the lead, the young prince,
caught up their hands in his and gave them places
on curly lambskins flat on the sea sand
near Thrasymêdês, his brother, and his father;
he passed them bits of the food of sacrifice,
and, pouring wine in a golden cup,
he said to Pallas Athena, daughter of Zeus:

"Friend, I must ask you to invoke Poseidon:
you find us at this feast, kept in his honor.
Make the appointed offering then, and pray,   50
and give the honeyed winecup to your friend

so he may do the same. He, too,
must pray to the gods on whom all men depend,
but he is just my age, you are the senior,
so here, I give the goblet first to you."

And he put the cup of sweet wine in her hand.
Athena liked his manners, and the equity
that gave her precedence with the cup of gold,
so she besought Poseidon at some length:

"Earthshaker, listen and be well disposed.   60
Grant your petitioners everything they ask:
above all, honor to Nestor and his sons;
second, to every man of Pylos town
a fair gift in exchange for this hekatomb;
third, may Telémakhos and I perform
the errand on which last night we put to sea."

This was the prayer of Athena—
granted in every particular by herself.
She passed the beautiful wine cup to Telémakhos,
who tipped the wine and prayed as she had done.   70
Meanwhile the spits were taken off the fire,
portions of crisp meat for all. They feasted,
and when they had eaten and drunk their fill, at last
they heard from Nestor, prince of charioteers:

"Now is the time," he said, "for a few questions,
now that our young guests have enjoyed their dinner.
Who are you, strangers? Where are you sailing from,
and where to, down the highways of sea water?
Have you some business here? or are you, now,
reckless wanderers of the sea, like those corsairs   80
who risk their lives to prey on other men?"

Clear-headed Telémakhos responded cheerfully,
for Athena gave him heart. By her design
his quest for news about his father's wandering
would bring him fame in the world's eyes. So he said:

"Nestor, pride of Akhaians, Neleus' son,
you ask where we are from, and I can tell you:

our home port is under Mount Neion, Ithaka.
We are not here on Ithakan business, though,
but on my own. I want news of my father,   90
Odysseus, known for his great heart, and I
will comb the wide world for it. People say
he fought along with you when Troy was taken.
As to the other men who fought that war,
we know where each one died, and how he died;
but Zeus allotted my father death and mystery.
No one can say for sure where he was killed,
whether some hostile landsmen or the sea,
the stormwaves on the deep sea, got the best of him.
And this is why I come to you for help.   100
Tell me of his death, sir, if perhaps
you witnessed it, or have heard some wanderer
tell the tale. The man was born for trouble.
Spare me no part of it for kindness' sake,
but put the scene before me as you saw it.
If ever Odysseus my noble father
served you by promise kept or work accomplished
in the land of Troy, where you Akhaians suffered,
recall those things for me the way they were."

Then Nestor, prince of charioteers, made answer: 110

"Dear friend, you take me back to all the trouble
we went through in that country, we Akhaians:
rough days aboard ship on the cloudy sea
cruising away for pillage after Akhilleus;
rough days of battle around Priam's town.
Our losses, then—so many good men gone:
Arês' great Aias lies there, Akhilleus lies there,
Patróklos, too, the wondrous counselor,
and my own strong and princely son, Antílokhos—
fastest man of them all, and a born fighter.   120
Other miseries, and many, we endured there.
Could any mortal man tell the whole story?
Not if you stayed five years or six to hear
how hard it was for the flower of the Akhaians;
you'd go home weary, and the tale untold.
Think: we were there nine years, and we tried everything,

all stratagems against them,
up to the bitter end that Zeus begrudged us.
And as to stratagems, no man would claim
Odysseus' gift for those. He had no rivals,   130
your father, at the tricks of war.
                              Your father?
Well, I must say I marvel at the sight of you:
your manner of speech couldn't be more like his;
one would say No; no boy could speak so well.
And all that time at Ilion, he and I
were never at odds in council or assembly—
saw things the same way, had one mind between us
in all the good advice we gave the Argives.
But when we plundered Priam's town and tower   140
and took to the ships, God scattered the Akhaians.
He had a mind to make homecoming hard for them,
seeing they would not think straight nor behave,
or some would not. So evil days came on them,
and she who had been angered,
Zeus's dangerous grey-eyed daughter, did it,
starting a fight between the sons of Atreus.
First they were fools enough to call assembly
at sundown, unheard of hour;
the Akhaian soldiers turned out, soaked with wine,   150
to hear talk, talk about it from their commanders:
Meneláos harangued them to get organized—
time to ride home on the sea's broad back, he said;
but Agamémnon wouldn't hear of it. He wanted
to hold the troops, make sacrifice, a hekatomb,
something to pacify Athena's rage.
Folly again, to think that he could move her.
Will you change the will of the everlasting gods
in a night or a day's time?
The two men stood there hammering at each other   160
until the army got to its feet with a roar,
and no decision, wanting it both ways.
That night no one slept well, everyone cursing
someone else. Here was the bane from Zeus.
At dawn we dragged our ships to the lordly water,
stowed aboard all our plunder

and the slave women in their low hip girdles.
But half the army elected to stay behind
with Agamémnon as their corps commander;
the other half embarked and pulled away.   170
We made good time, the huge sea smoothed before us,
and held our rites when we reached Ténedos,
being wild for home. But Zeus, not willing yet,
now cruelly set us at odds a second time,
and one lot turned, put back in the rolling ships,
under command of the subtle captain, Odysseus;
their notion was to please Lord Agamémnon.
Not I. I fled, with every ship I had;
I knew fate had some devilment brewing there.
Diomêdês roused his company and fled, too,   180
and later Meneláos, the red-haired captain,
caught up with us at Lesbos,
while we mulled over the long sea route, unsure
whether to lay our course northward of Khios,
keeping the Isle of Psyria off to port,
or inside Khios, coasting by windy Mimas.
We asked for a sign from heaven, and the sign came
to cut across the open sea to Euboia,
and lose no time putting our ills behind us.
The wind freshened astern, and the ships ran   190
before the wind on paths of the deep sea fish,
making Geraistos before dawn. We thanked Poseidon
with many a charred thighbone for that crossing.
On the fourth day, Diomêdês' company
under full sail put in at Argos port,
and I held on for Pylos. The fair wind,
once heaven set it blowing, never failed.

So this, dear child, was how I came from Troy,
and saw no more of the others, lost or saved.
But you are welcome to all I've heard since then   200
at home; I have no reason to keep it from you.
The Myrmidon spearfighters returned, they say,
under the son of lionhearted Akhilleus;
and so did Poias' great son, Philoktêtês.
Idómeneus brought his company back to Krete;

the sea took not a man from him, of all
who lived through the long war.
And even as far away as Ithaka
you've heard of Agamémnon—how he came
home, how Aigísthos waited to destroy him   210
but paid a bitter price for it in the end.
That is a good thing, now, for a man to leave
a son behind him, like the son who punished
Aigísthos for the murder of his great father.
You, too, are tall and well set-up, I see;
be brave, you too, so men in times to come
will speak well of you."

                                    Then Telémakhos said:

"Nestor, pride of Akhaians, Neleus' son,
that was revenge, and far and wide the Akhaians   220
will tell the tale in song for generations.
I wish the gods would buckle his arms on me!
I'd be revenged for outrage
on my insidious and brazen enemies.
But no such happy lot was given to me
or to my father. Still, I must hold fast."

To this Lord Nestor of Gerênia said:

"My dear young friend, now that you speak of it,
I hear a crowd of suitors for your mother
lives with you, uninvited, making trouble.   230
Now tell me how you take this. Do the people
side against you, hearkening to some oracle?
Who knows, your father might come home some day
alone or backed by troops, and have it out with them.
If grey-eyed Athena loved you
the way she did Odysseus in the old days,
in Troy country, where we all went through so much—
never have I seen the gods help any man
as openly as Athena did your father—
well, as I say, if she cared for you that way,   240
there would be those to quit this marriage game."

But prudently Telémakhos replied:

"I can't think what you say will ever happen, sir.
It is a dazzling hope. But not for me.
It could not be—even if the gods willed it."

At this grey-eyed Athena broke in, saying:

"What strange talk you permit yourself, Telémakhos.
A god could save the man by simply wishing it—
from the farthest shore in the world.
If I were he, I should prefer to suffer   250
years at sea, and then be safe at home;
better that than a knife at my hearthside
where Agamémnon found it—killed by adulterers.
Though as for death, of course all men must suffer it:
the gods may love a man, but they can't help him
when cold death comes to lay him on his bier."

Telémakhos replied:

"Mentor, grievously though we miss my father, why
go on as if that homecoming could happen?
You know the gods had settled it already,   260
years ago, when dark death came for him.
But there is something else I imagine Nestor
can tell us, knowing as he does the ways of men.
They say his rule goes back over three generations,
so long, so old, it seems death cannot touch him.
Nestor, Neleus' son, true sage, say how
did the Lord of the Great Plains, Agamémnon, die?
What was the trick Aigísthos used
to kill the better man? And Meneláos,
where was he? Not at Argos in Akhaia,   270
but blown off course, held up in some far country,
is that what gave the killer nerve to strike?"

Lord Nestor of Gerênia made answer:

"Well, now, my son, I'll tell you the whole story.
You know, yourself, what would have come to pass
if red-haired Meneláos, back from Troy,
had caught Aigísthos in that house alive.

There would have been no burial mound for him,
but dogs and carrion birds to huddle on him
in the fields beyond the wall, and not a soul   280
bewailing him, for the great wrong he committed.
While we were hard-pressed in the war at Troy
he stayed safe inland in the grazing country,
making light talk to win Agamémnon's queen.
But the Lady Klytaimnéstra, in the first days,
rebuffed him, being faithful still;
then, too, she had at hand as her companion
a minstrel Agamémnon left attending her,
charged with her care, when he took ship for Troy.
Then came the fated hour when she gave in.   290
Her lover tricked the poet and marooned him
on a bare island for the seabirds' picking,
and took her home, as he and she desired.
Many thighbones he burned on the gods' altars
and many a woven and golden ornament
hung to bedeck them, in his satisfaction;
he had not thought life held such glory for him.

Now Meneláos and I sailed home together
on friendly terms, from Troy,
but when we came off Sunion Point in Attika,   300
the ships still running free, Onêtor's son
Phrontis, the steersman of Meneláos' ship,
fell over with a death grip on the tiller:
some unseen arrow from Apollo hit him.
No man handled a ship better than he did
in a high wind and sea, so Meneláos
put down his longing to get on, and landed
to give this man full honor in funeral.
His own luck turned then. Out on the winedark sea
in the murmuring hulls again, he made Cape Malea,   310
but Zeus who views the wide world sent a gloom
over the ocean, and a howling gale
came on with seas increasing, mountainous,
parting the ships and driving half toward Krete
where the Kydonians live by Iardanos river.
Off Gortyn's coastline in the misty sea there

a reef, a razorback, cuts through the water,
and every westerly piles up a pounding
surf along the left side, going toward Phaistos—
big seas buffeted back by the narrow stone.   320
They were blown here, and fought in vain for sea room;
the ships kept going in to their destruction,
slammed on the reef. The crews were saved. But now
those five that weathered it got off to southward,
taken by wind and current on to Egypt;
and there Meneláos stayed. He made a fortune
in sea traffic among those distant races,
but while he did so, the foul crime was planned
and carried out in Argos by Aigísthos,
who ruled over golden Mykênai seven years.   330
Seven long years, with Agamémnon dead,
he held the people down, before the vengeance.
But in the eighth year, back from exile in Attika,
Orestês killed the snake who killed his father.
He gave his hateful mother and her soft man
a tomb together, and proclaimed the funeral day
a festal day for all the Argive people.
That day Lord Meneláos of the great war cry
made port with all the gold his ships could carry.
And this should give you pause, my son: 340
don't stay too long away from home, leaving
your treasure there, and brazen suitors near;
they'll squander all you have or take it from you,
and then how will your journey serve?
I urge you, though, to call on Meneláos,
he being but lately home from distant parts
in the wide world. A man could well despair
of getting home at all, if the winds blew him
over the Great South Sea—that weary waste,
even the wintering birds delay   350
one winter more before the northward crossing.
Well, take your ship and crew and go by water,
or if you'd rather go by land, here are
horses, a car, and my own sons for company
as far as the ancient land of Lakedaimon
and Meneláos, the red-haired captain there.

Ask him with courtesy, and in his wisdom
he will tell you history and no lies."

While Nestor talked, the sun went down the sky
and gloom came on the land,
and now the grey-eyed goddess Athena said: 360

"Sir, this is all most welcome and to the point,
but why not slice the bulls' tongues now, and mix
libations for Poseidon and the gods?
Then we can all retire; high time we did;
the light is going under the dark world's rim,
better not linger at the sacred feast."

When Zeus's daughter spoke, they turned to listen,
and soon the squires brought water for their hands,
while stewards filled the winebowls and poured out
a fresh cup full for every man. The company   370
stood up to fling the tongues and a shower of wine
over the flames, then drank their thirst away.
Now finally Telémakhos and Athena
bestirred themselves, turning away to the ship,
but Nestor put a hand on each, and said:

"Now Zeus forbid, and the other gods as well,
that you should spend the night on board, and leave me
as though I were some pauper without a stitch,
no blankets in his house, no piles of rugs,
no sleeping soft for host or guest! Far from it!   380
I have all these, blankets and deep-piled rugs,
and while I live the only son of Odysseus
will never make his bed on a ship's deck—
no, not while sons of mine are left at home
to welcome any guest who comes to us."

The grey-eyed goddess Athena answered him:

"You are very kind, sir, and Telémakhos
should do as you ask. That is the best thing.
He will go with you, and will spend the night
under your roof. But I must join our ship   390
and talk to the crew, to keep their spirits up,

since I'm the only senior in the company.
The rest are boys who shipped for friendship's sake,
no older than Telémakhos, any of them.
Let me sleep out, then, by the black hull's side,
this night at least. At daybreak I'll be off
to see the Kaukonians about a debt they owe me,
an old one and no trifle. As for your guest,
send him off in a car, with one of your sons,
and give him thoroughbreds, a racing team."   400

Even as she spoke, Athena left them—seeming
a seahawk, in a clap of wings,—and all
the Akhaians of Pylos town looked up astounded.
Awed then by what his eyes had seen, the old man
took Telémakhos' hand and said warmly:

"My dear child, I can have no fears for you,
no doubt about your conduct or your heart,
if, at your age, the gods are your companions.
Here we had someone from Olympos—clearly
the glorious daughter of Zeus, his third child,   410
who held your father dear among the Argives.
O, Lady, hear me! Grant an illustrious name
to me and to my children and my dear wife!
A noble heifer shall be yours in sacrifice,
one that no man has ever yoked or driven;
my gift to you—her horns all sheathed in gold."

So he ended, praying; and Athena heard him.
Then Nestor of Gerênia led them all,
his sons and sons-in-law, to his great house;
and in they went to the famous hall of Nestor,   420
taking their seats on thrones and easy chairs,
while the old man mixed water in a wine bowl
with sweet red wine, mellowed eleven years
before his housekeeper uncapped the jar.
He mixed and poured his offering, repeating
prayers to Athena, daughter of royal Zeus.
The others made libation, and drank deep,
then all the company went to their quarters,
and Nestor of Gerênia showed Telémakhos

under the echoing eastern entrance hall   430
to a fine bed near the bed of Peisístratos,
captain of spearmen, his unmarried son.
Then he lay down in his own inner chamber
where his dear faithful wife had smoothed his bed.

When Dawn spread out her finger tips of rose,
Lord Nestor of Gerênia, charioteer,
left his room for a throne of polished stone,
white and gleaming as though with oil, that stood
before the main gate of the palace; Neleus here
had sat before him—masterful in kingship,   440
Neleus, long ago a prey to death, gone down
to the night of the underworld.
So Nestor held his throne and scepter now,
lord of the western approaches to Akhaia.
And presently his sons came out to join him,
leaving the palace: Ekhéphron and Stratíos,
Perseus and Arêtós and Thrasymêdês,
and after them the prince Peisístratos,
bringing Telémakhos along with him.
Seeing all present, the old lord Nestor said: 450

"Dear sons, here is my wish, and do it briskly
to please the gods, Athena first of all,
my guest in daylight at our holy feast.
One of you must go for a young heifer
and have the cowherd lead her from the pasture.
Another call on Lord Telémakhos' ship
to invite his crewmen, leaving two behind;
and someone else again send for the goldsmith,
Laerkês, to gild the horns.
The rest stay here together. Tell the servants   460
a ritual feast will be prepared in hall.
Tell them to bring seats, firewood and fresh water."

Before he finished, they were about these errands.
The heifer came from pasture,
the crewmen of Telémakhos from the ship,
the smith arrived, bearing the tools of his trade—
hammer and anvil, and the precision tongs

he handled fiery gold with,—and Athena
came as a god comes, numinous, to the rites.

The smith now gloved each horn in a pure foil   470
beaten out of the gold that Nestor gave him—
a glory and delight for the goddess' eyes—
while Ekhéphron and Stratíos held the horns.
Arêtós brought clear lustral water
in a bowl quivering with fresh-cut flowers,
a basket of barley in his other hand.
Thrasymêdês, who could stand his ground in war,
stood ready, with a sharp two-bladed axe,
for the stroke of sacrifice, and Perseus
held a bowl for the blood. And now Nestor,   480
strewing the barley grains, and water drops,
pronounced his invocation to Athena
and burned a pinch of bristles from the victim.
When prayers were said and all the grain was scattered
great-hearted Thrasymêdês in a flash
swung the axe, at one blow cutting through
the neck tendons. The heifer's spirit failed.
Then all the women gave a wail of joy—
daughters, daughters-in-law, and the Lady Eurydíkê,
Klyménos' eldest daughter. But the men   490
still held the heifer, shored her up
from the wide earth where the living go their ways,
until Peisístratos cut her throat across,
the black blood ran, and life ebbed from her marrow.
The carcass now sank down, and they disjointed
shoulder and thigh bone, wrapping them in fat,
two layers, folded, with raw strips of flesh.
These offerings Nestor burned on the split-wood fire
and moistened with red wine. His sons took up
five-tined forks in their hands, while the altar flame   500
ate through the bones, and bits of tripe went round.
Then came the carving of the quarters, and they spitted
morsels of lean meat on the long sharp tines
and broiled them at arm's length upon the fire.

Polykástê, a fair girl, Nestor's youngest,
had meanwhile given a bath to Telémakhos—
bathing him first, then rubbing him with oil.
She held fine clothes and a cloak to put around him
when he came godlike from the bathing place;
then out he went to take his place with Nestor.   510
When the best cuts were broiled and off the spits,
they all sat down to banquet. Gentle squires
kept every golden wine cup brimming full.
And so they feasted to their heart's content,
until the prince of charioteers commanded:

"Sons, harness the blood mares for Telémakhos;
hitch up the car, and let him take the road."

They swung out smartly to do the work, and hooked
the handsome horses to a chariot shaft.
The mistress of the stores brought up provisions   520
of bread and wine, with victuals fit for kings,
and Telémakhos stepped up on the painted car.
Just at his elbow stood Peisístratos,
captain of spearmen, reins in hand. He gave
a flick to the horses, and with streaming manes
they ran for the open country. The tall town
of Pylos sank behind them in the distance,
as all day long they kept the harness shaking.

The sun was low and shadows crossed the lanes
when they arrived at Phêrai. There Dióklês,   530
son of Ortílokhos whom Alpheios fathered,
welcomed the young men, and they slept the night.
But up when the young Dawn's finger tips of rose
opened in the east, they hitched the team
once more to the painted car,
and steered out eastward through the echoing gate,
whipping their fresh horses into a run.
That day they made the grainlands of Lakedaimon,
where, as the horses held to a fast clip,
they kept on to their journey's end. Behind them   540
the sun went down and all the roads grew dark.

BOOK FOUR

The Red-Haired King and His Lady

By vales and sharp ravines in Lakedaímon   1
the travellers drove to Meneláos' mansion,
and found him at a double wedding feast
for son and daughter.
                              Long ago at Troy
he pledged her to the heir of great Akhilleus,
breaker of men—a match the gods had ripened;
so he must send her with a chariot train
to the town and glory of the Myrmidons.
And that day, too, he brought Alektor's daughter   10
to marry his tall scion, Megapénthês,
born of a slave girl during the long war—
for the gods had never after granted Helen
a child to bring into the sunlit world
after the first, rose-lipped Hermionê,
a girl like the pale-gold goddess Aphroditê.

Down the great hall in happiness they feasted,
neighbors of Meneláos, and his kin,

for whom a holy minstrel harped and sang;
and two lithe tumblers moved out on the song   20
with spins and handsprings through the company.
Now when Telémakhos and Nestor's son
pulled up their horses at the main gate,
one of the king's companions in arms, Eteóneus,
going outside, caught sight of them. He turned
and passed through court and hall to tell the master,
stepping up close to get his ear. Said he:

"Two men are here—two strangers, Meneláos,
but nobly born Akhaians, they appear.
What do you say, shall we unhitch their team,   30
or send them on to someone free to receive them?"

The red-haired captain answered him in anger:

"You were no idiot before, Eteóneus,
but here you are talking like a child of ten.
Could we have made it home again—and Zeus
give us no more hard roving!—if other men
had never fed us, given us lodging?
                              Bring
these men to be our guests: unhitch their team!"

Eteóneus left the long room like an arrow,   40
calling equerries after him, on the run,
outside, they freed the sweating team from harness,
stabled the horses, tied them up, and showered
bushels of wheat and barley in the feed box;
then leaned the chariot pole
against the gleaming entry wall of stone
and took the guests in. What a brilliant place
that mansion of the great prince seemed to them!
A-glitter everywhere, as though with fiery
points of sunlight, lusters of the moon.   50
The young men gazed in joy before they entered
into a room of polished tubs to bathe.
Maidservants gave them baths, anointed them,
held out fresh tunics, cloaked them warm; and soon
they took tall thrones beside the son of Atreus.

Here a maid tipped out water for their hands
from a golden pitcher into a silver bowl,
and set a polished table near at hand;
the larder mistress with her tray of loaves
and savories came, dispensing all her best,   60
and then a carver heaped their platters high
with various meats, and put down cups of gold.
Now said the red-haired captain, Meneláos,
gesturing:

                         "Welcome; and fall to; in time,
when you have supped, we hope to hear your names,
forbears and families—in your case, it seems,
no anonymities, but lordly men.
Lads like yourself are not base born."

                         At this,   70
he lifted in his own hands the king's portion,
a chine of beef, and set it down before them.
Seeing all ready then, they took their dinner;
but when they had feasted well,
Telémakhos could not keep still, but whispered,
his head bent close, so the others might not hear:

"My dear friend, can you believe your eyes?—
the murmuring hall, how luminous it is
with bronze, gold, amber, silver, and ivory!
This is the way the court of Zeus must be,   80
inside, upon Olympos. What a wonder!"

But splendid Meneláos had overheard him
and spoke out on the instant to them both:

"Young friends, no mortal man can vie with Zeus.
His home and all his treasures are for ever.
But as for men, it may well be that few
have more than I. How painfully I wandered
before I brought it home! Seven years at sea,
Kypros, Phoinikia, Egypt, and still farther
among the sun-burnt races.   90
I saw the men of Sidon and Arabia
and Libya, too, where lambs are horned at birth.

In every year they have three lambing seasons,
so no man, chief or shepherd, ever goes
hungry for want of mutton, cheese, or milk—
all year at milking time there are fresh ewes.

But while I made my fortune on those travels
a stranger killed my brother, in cold blood,—
tricked blind, caught in the web of his deadly queen.
What pleasure can I take, then, being lord   100
over these costly things?
You must have heard your fathers tell my story,
whoever your fathers are; you must know of my life,
the anguish I once had, and the great house
full of my treasure, left in desolation.
How gladly I should live one third as rich
to have my friends back safe at home!—my friends
who died on Troy's wide seaboard, far
from the grazing lands of Argos.
But as things are, nothing but grief is left me   110
for those companions. While I sit at home
sometimes hot tears come, and I revel in them,
or stop before the surfeit makes me shiver.
And there is one I miss more than the other
dead I mourn for; sleep and food alike
grow hateful when I think of him. No soldier
took on so much, went through so much, as Odysseus.
That seems to have been his destiny, and this mine—
to feel each day the emptiness of his absence,
ignorant, even, whether he lived or died.   120
How his old father and his quiet wife,
Penélopê, must miss him still!
And Telémakhos, whom he left as a new-born child."

Now hearing these things said, the boy's heart rose
in a long pang for his father, and he wept,
holding his purple mantle with both hands
before his eyes. Meneláos knew him now,
and so fell silent with uncertainty
whether to let him speak and name his father
in his own time, or to inquire, and prompt him.   130

And while he pondered, Helen came
out of her scented chamber, a moving grace
like Artemis, straight as a shaft of gold.
Beside her came Adrastê, to place her armchair,
Alkippê, with a rug of downy wool,
and Phylo, bringing a silver basket, once
given by Alkandrê, the wife of Pólybos,
in the treasure city, Thebes of distant Egypt.
He gave two silver bathtubs to Meneláos
and a pair of tripods, with ten pure gold bars,   140
and she, then, made these beautiful gifts to Helen:
a golden distaff, and the silver basket
rimmed in hammered gold, with wheels to run on.
So Phylo rolled it in to stand beside her,
heaped with fine spun stuff, and cradled on it
the distaff swathed in dusky violet wool.
Reclining in her light chair with its footrest,
Helen gazed at her husband and demanded:

"Meneláos, my lord, have we yet heard
our new guests introduce themselves? Shall I   150
dissemble what I feel? No, I must say it.
Never, anywhere, have I seen so great a likeness
in man or woman—but it is truly strange!
This boy must be the son of Odysseus,
Telémakhos, the child he left at home
that year the Akhaian host made war on Troy—
daring all for the wanton that I was."

And the red-haired captain, Meneláos, answered:

"My dear, I see the likeness as well as you do.
Odysseus' hands and feet were like this boy's;   160
his head, and hair, and the glinting of his eyes.
Not only that, but when I spoke, just now,
of Odysseus' years of toil on my behalf
and all he had to endure—the boy broke down
and wept into his cloak."

                              Now Nestor's son,
Peisístratos, spoke up in answer to him:

"My lord marshal, Meneláos, son of Atreus,
this is that hero's son as you surmise,
but he is gentle, and would be ashamed   170
to clamor for attention before your grace
whose words have been so moving to us both.
Nestor, Lord of Gerênia, sent me with him
as guide and escort; he had wished to see you,
to be advised by you or assisted somehow.
A father far from home means difficulty
for an only son, with no one else to help him;
so with Telémakhos:
his father left the house without defenders."

The king with flaming hair now spoke again: 180

"His son, in my house! How I loved the man!
And how he fought through hardship for my sake!
I swore I'd cherish him above all others
if Zeus, who views the wide world, gave us passage
homeward across the sea in the fast ships.
I would have settled him in Argos, brought him
over with herds and household out of Ithaka,
his child and all his people. I could have cleaned out
one of my towns to be his new domain.
And so we might have been together often   190
in feasts and entertainments, never parted
till the dark mist of death lapped over one of us.
But God himself must have been envious,
to batter the bruised man so that he alone
should fail in his return."

A twinging ache of grief rose up in everyone,
and Helen of Argos wept, the daughter of Zeus,
Telémakhos and Meneláos wept,
and tears came to the eyes of Nestor's son—
remembering, for his part, Antílokhos,   200
whom the son of shining Dawn had killed in battle.
But thinking of that brother, he broke out:

"O son of Atreus, when we spoke of you
at home, and asked about you, my old father

would say you had the clearest mind of all.
If it is not too much to ask, then, let us not
weep away these hours after supper;
I feel we should not: Dawn will soon be here!
You understand, I would not grudge a man
right mourning when he comes to death and doom: 210
what else can one bestow on the poor dead?—
a lock of hair sheared, and a tear let fall.
For that matter, I, too,
lost someone in the war at Troy—my brother,
and no mean soldier, whom you must have known,
although I never did,—Antílokhos.
He ranked high as a runner and fighting man."

The red-haired captain Meneláos answered:

"My lad, what you have said is only sensible,
and you did well to speak. Yes, that was worthy   220
a wise man and an older man than you are:
you speak for all the world like Nestor's son.
How easily one can tell the man whose father
had true felicity, marrying and begetting!
And that was true of Nestor, all his days,
down to his sleek old age in peace at home,
with clever sons, good spearmen into the bargain.
Come, we'll shake off this mourning mood of ours
and think of supper. Let the men at arms
rinse our hands again! There will be time   230
for a long talk with Telémakhos in the morning."

The hero Meneláos' companion in arms,
Asphalion, poured water for their hands,
and once again they touched the food before them.
But now it entered Helen's mind
to drop into the wine that they were drinking
an anodyne, mild magic of forgetfulness.
Whoever drank this mixture in the wine bowl
would be incapable of tears that day—
though he should lose mother and father both,   240
or see, with his own eyes, a son or brother
mauled by weapons of bronze at his own gate.

The opiate of Zeus's daughter bore
this canny power. It had been supplied her
by Polydamna, mistress of Lord Thôn,
in Egypt, where the rich plantations grow
herbs of all kinds, maleficent and healthful;
and no one else knows medicine as they do,
Egyptian heirs of Paian, the healing god.
She drugged the wine, then, had it served, and said—   250
taking again her part in the conversation—

"O Meneláos, Atreus' royal son,
and you that are great heroes' sons, you know
how Zeus gives all of us in turn
good luck and bad luck, being all powerful.
So take refreshment, take your ease in hall,
and cheer the time with stories. I'll begin.
Not that I think of naming, far less telling,
every feat of that rugged man, Odysseus,
but here is something that he dared to do   260
at Troy, where you Akhaians endured the war.
He had, first, given himself an outrageous beating
and thrown some rags on—like a household slave—
then slipped into that city of wide lanes
among his enemies. So changed, he looked
as never before upon the Akhaian beachhead,
but like a beggar, merged in the townspeople;
and no one there remarked him. But I knew him—
even as he was, I knew him,
and questioned him. How shrewdly he put me off!   270
But in the end I bathed him and anointed him,
put a fresh cloak around him, and swore an oath
not to give him away as Odysseus to the Trojans,
till he got back to camp where the long ships lay.
He spoke up then, and told me
all about the Akhaians, and their plans—
then sworded many Trojans through the body
on his way out with what he learned of theirs.
The Trojan women raised a cry—but my heart
sang—for I had come round, long before,   280
to dreams of sailing home, and I repented

the mad day Aphroditê
drew me away from my dear fatherland,
forsaking all—child, bridal bed, and husband—
a man without defect in form or mind."

Replied the red-haired captain, Meneláos:

"An excellent tale, my dear, and most becoming.
In my life I have met, in many countries,
foresight and wit in many first rate men,
but never have I seen one like Odysseus   290
for steadiness and a stout heart. Here, for instance,
is what he did—had the cold nerve to do—
inside the hollow horse, where we were waiting,
picked men all of us, for the Trojan slaughter,
when all of a sudden, you came by—I dare say
drawn by some superhuman
power that planned an exploit for the Trojans;
and Deïphobos, that handsome man, came with you.
Three times you walked around it, patting it everywhere,
and called by name the flower of our fighters,   300
making your voice sound like their wives, calling.
Diomêdês and I crouched in the center
along with Odysseus; we could hear you plainly;
and listening, we two were swept
by waves of longing—to reply, or go.
Odysseus fought us down, despite our craving,
and all the Akhaians kept their lips shut tight,
all but Antiklos. Desire moved his throat
to hail you, but Odysseus' great hands clamped
over his jaws, and held. So he saved us all,   310
till Pallas Athena led you away at last."

Then clear-headed Telémakhos addressed him:

"My lord marshal, Meneláos, son of Atreus,
all the more pity, since these valors
could not defend him from annihilation—
not if his heart were iron in his breast.
But will you not dismiss us for the night now?
Sweet sleep will be a pleasure, drifting over us."

He said no more, but Helen called the maids
and sent them to make beds, with purple rugs   320
piled up, and sheets outspread, and fleecy
coverlets, in the porch inside the gate.
The girls went out with torches in their hands,
and presently a squire led the guests—
Telémakhos and Nestor's radiant son—
under the entrance colonnade, to bed.
Then deep in the great mansion, in his chamber,
Meneláos went to rest, and Helen,
queenly in her long gown, lay beside him.

When the young Dawn with finger tips of rose   330
made heaven bright, the deep-lunged man of battle
stood up, pulled on his tunic and his mantle,
slung on a swordbelt and a new edged sword,
tied his smooth feet into fine rawhide sandals
and left his room, a god's brilliance upon him.
He sat down by Telémakhos, asking gently:

"Telémakhos, why did you come, sir, riding
the sea's broad back to reach old Lakedaimon?
A public errand or private? Why, precisely?"

Telémakhos replied: 340

"My lord marshal Meneláos, son of Atreus,
I came to hear what news you had of Father.
My house, my good estates are being ruined.
Each day my mother's bullying suitors come
to slaughter flocks of mine and my black cattle;
enemies crowd our home. And this is why
I come to you for news of him who owned it.
Tell me of his death, sir, if perhaps
you witnessed it, or have heard some wanderer
tell the tale. The man was born for trouble.   350
Spare me no part for kindness' sake; be harsh;
but put the scene before me as you saw it.
If ever Odysseus my noble father
served you by promise kept or work accomplished
in the land of Troy, where you Akhaians suffered,
recall those things for me the way they were."

Stirred now to anger, Meneláos said:

"Intolerable—that soft men, as those are,
should think to lie in that great captain's bed.
Fawns in a lion's lair! As if a doe   360
put down her litter of sucklings there, while she
quested a glen or cropped some grassy hollow.
Ha! Then the lord returns to his own bed
and deals out wretched doom on both alike.
So will Odysseus deal out doom on these.
O Father Zeus, Athena, and Apollo!
I pray he comes as once he was, in Lesbos,
when he stood up to wrestle Philomeleidès—
champion and Island King—
and smashed him down. How the Akhaians cheered!   370
If only that Odysseus met the suitors,
they'd have their consummation, a cold bed!
Now for your questions, let me come to the point.
I would not misreport it for you; let me
tell you what the Ancient of the Sea,
who is infallible, said to me—every word.

During my first try at a passage homeward
the gods detained me, tied me down to Egypt—
for I had been too scant in hekatombs,
and gods will have the rules each time remembered.   380
There is an island washed by the open sea
lying off Nile mouth—seamen call it Pharos—
distant a day's sail in a clean hull
with a brisk land breeze behind. It has a harbor,
a sheltered bay, where shipmasters
take on dark water for the outward voyage.
Here the gods held me twenty days becalmed.
No winds came up, seaward escorting winds
for ships that ride the sea's broad back, and so
my stores and men were used up; we were failing   390
had not one goddess intervened in pity—
Eidothea, daughter of Proteus,
the Ancient of the Sea. How I distressed her!
I had been walking out alone that day—

my sailors, thin-bellied from the long fast,
were off with fish hooks, angling on the shore—
then she appeared to me, and her voice sang:

'What fool is here, what drooping dunce of dreams?
Or can it be, friend, that you love to suffer?
How can you linger on this island, aimless   400
and shiftless, while your people waste away?'

To this I quickly answered:

                              'Let me tell you,
goddess, whatever goddess you may be,
these doldrums are no will of mine. I take it
the gods who own broad heaven are offended.
Why don't you tell me—since the gods know everything—
who has me pinned down here?
How am I going to make my voyage home?'

Now she replied in her immortal beauty: 410

'I'll put it for you clearly as may be, friend.
The Ancient of the Salt Sea haunts this place,
immortal Proteus of Egypt; all the deeps
are known to him; he serves under Poseidon,
and is, they say, my father.
If you could take him by surprise and hold him,
he'd give you course and distance for your sailing
homeward across the cold fish-breeding sea.
And should you wish it, noble friend, he'd tell you
all that occurred at home, both good and evil,   420
while you were gone so long and hard a journey.'

To this I said:

                              'But you, now—you must tell me
how I can trap this venerable sea-god.
He will elude me if he takes alarm;
no man—god knows—can quell a god with ease.'

That fairest of unearthly nymphs replied:

'I'll tell you this, too, clearly as may be.
When the sun hangs at high noon in heaven,

the Ancient glides ashore under the Westwind,   430
hidden by shivering glooms on the clear water,
and rests in caverns hollowed by the sea.
There flippered seals, brine children, shining come
from silvery foam in crowds to lie around him,
exhaling rankness from the deep sea floor.
Tomorrow dawn I'll take you to those caves
and bed you down there. Choose three officers
for company—brave men they had better be—
the old one has strange powers, I must tell you.
He goes amid the seals to check their number,   440
and when he sees them all, and counts them all,
he lies down like a shepherd with his flock.
Here is your opportunity: at this point
gather yourselves, with all your heart and strength,
and tackle him before he bursts away.
He'll make you fight—for he can take the forms
of all the beasts, and water, and blinding fire;
but you must hold on, even so, and crush him
until he breaks the silence. When he does,
he will be in that shape you saw asleep.   450
Relax your grip, then, set the Ancient free,
and put your questions, hero:
Who is the god so hostile to you,
and how will you go home on the fish-cold sea.'

At this she dove under a swell and left me.
Back to the ships in the sandy cove I went,
my heart within me like a high surf running;
but there I joined my men once more
at supper, as the sacred Night came on,
and slept at last beside the lapping water.   460
When Dawn spread out her finger tips of rose
I started, by the sea's wide level ways,
praying the gods for help, and took along
three lads I counted on in any fight.
Meanwhile the nereid swam from the lap of Ocean
laden with four sealskins, new flayed
for the hoax she thought of playing on her father.
In the sand she scooped out hollows for our bodies
and sat down, waiting. We came close to touch her,

and, bedding us, she threw the sealskins over us—   470
a strong disguise; oh, yes, terribly strong
as I recall the stench of those damned seals.
Would any man lie snug with a sea monster?
But here the nymph, again, came to our rescue,
dabbing ambrosia under each man's nose—
a perfume drowning out the bestial odor.
So there we lay with beating hearts all morning
while seals came shoreward out of ripples, jostling
to take their places, flopping on the sand.
At noon the Ancient issued from the sea   480
and held inspection, counting off the sea-beasts.
We were the first he numbered; he went by,
detecting nothing. When at last he slept
we gave a battlecry and plunged for him,
locking our hands behind him. But the old one's
tricks were not knocked out of him; far from it.
First he took on a whiskered lion's shape,
a serpent then; a leopard; a great boar;
then sousing water; then a tall green tree.
Still we hung on, by hook or crook, through everything,   490
until the Ancient saw defeat, and grimly
opened his lips to ask me:

                        'Son of Atreus,
who counselled you to this? A god: what god?
Set a trap for me, overpower me—why?'

He bit it off, then, and I answered:

                        'Old one,
you know the reason—why feign not to know?
High and dry so long upon this island
I'm at my wits' end, and my heart is sore.   500
You gods know everything; now you can tell me:
which of the immortals chained me here?
And how will I get home on the fish-cold sea?'

He made reply at once:

                        'You should have paid
honor to Zeus and the other gods, performing

a proper sacrifice before embarking:
that was your short way home on the winedark sea.
You may not see your friends, your own fine house,
or enter your own land again,   510
unless you first remount the Nile in flood
and pay your hekatomb to the gods of heaven.
Then, and then only,
the gods will grant the passage you desire.'

Ah, how my heart sank, hearing this—
hearing him send me back on the cloudy sea
in my own track, the long hard way of Egypt.
Nevertheless, I answered him and said:

'Ancient, I shall do all as you command.
But tell me, now, the others—   520
had they a safe return, all those Akhaians
who stayed behind when Nestor and I left Troy?
Or were there any lost at sea—what bitterness!—
any who died in camp, after the war?'

To this he said:

                              'For you to know these things
goes beyond all necessity, Meneláos.
Why must you ask?—you should not know my mind,
and you will grieve to learn it, I can tell you.
Many there were who died, many remain,   530
but two high officers alone were lost—
on the passage home, I mean; you saw the war.
One is alive, a castaway at sea;
the other, Aias, perished with all hands—
though first Poseidon landed him on Gyrai
promontory, and saved him from the ocean.
Despite Athena's hate, he had lived on,
but the great sinner in his insolence
yelled that the gods' will and the sea were beaten,
and this loud brag came to Poseidon's ears.   540
He swung the trident in his massive hands
and in one shock from top to bottom split
that promontory, toppling into the sea

the fragment where the great fool sat.
So the vast ocean had its will with Aias,
drunk in the end on salt spume as he drowned.
Meanwhile your brother left that doom astern
in his decked ships—the Lady Hera saved him;
but as he came round Malea
a fresh squall caught him, bearing him away   550
over the cold sea, groaning in disgust,
to the Land's End of Argos, where Thyestês
lived in the days of old, and then his son,
Aigísthos. Now, again, return seemed easy:
the high gods wound the wind into the east,
and back he sailed, this time to his own coast.
He went ashore and kissed the earth in joy,
hot tears blinding his eyes at sight of home.
But there were eyes that watched him from a height—
a lookout, paid two bars of gold to keep   560
vigil the year round for Aigísthos' sake,
that he should be forewarned, and Agamémnon's
furious valor sleep unroused.
Now this man with his news ran to the tyrant,
who made his crooked arrangements in a flash,
stationed picked men at arms, a score of men
in hiding; set a feast in the next room;
then he went out with chariots and horses
to hail the king and welcome him to evil.
He led him in to banquet, all serene,   570
and killed him, like an ox felled at the trough;
and not a man of either company
survived that ambush in Aigísthos' house.'

Before the end my heart was broken down.
I slumped on the trampled sand and cried aloud,
caring no more for life or the light of day,
and rolled there weeping, till my tears were spent.
Then the unerring Ancient said at last:

'No more, no more; how long must you persist?
Nothing is gained by grieving so. How soon   580
can you return to Argos? You may take him

alive there still—or else meanwhile Orestês
will have despatched him. You'll attend the feast.'

At this my heart revived, and I recovered
the self command to question him once more:

'Of two companions now I know. The third?
Tell me his name, the one marooned at sea;
living, you say, or dead? Even in pain
I wish to hear.'

And this is all he answered: 590

'Laërtês' son, whose home is Ithaka.
I saw him weeping, weeping on an island.
The nymph Kalypso has him, in her hall.
No means of faring home are left him now;
no ship with oars, and no ship's company
to pull him on the broad back of the sea.
As to your own destiny, prince Meneláos,
you shall not die in the bluegrass land of Argos;
rather the gods intend you for Elysion
with golden Rhadamanthos at the world's end,   600
where all existence is a dream of ease.
Snowfall is never known there, neither long
frost of winter, nor torrential rain,
but only mild and lulling airs from Ocean
bearing refreshment for the souls of men—
the West Wind always blowing.
                              For the gods
hold you, as Helen's lord, a son of Zeus.'

At this he dove under a swell and left me,
and I went back to the ship with my companions,   610
feeling my heart's blood in me running high;
but in the long hull's shadow, near the sea,
we supped again as sacred Night came on
and slept at last beside the lapping water.

When Dawn spread out her finger tips of rose,
in first light we launched on the courtly breakers,

setting up masts and yards in the well-found ships;
went all on board, and braced on planks athwart
oarsmen in line dipped oars in the grey sea.
Soon I drew in to the great stream fed by heaven   620
and, laying by, slew bulls in the proper number,
until the immortal gods were thus appeased;
then heaped a death mound on that shore against
all-quenching time for Agamémnon's honor,
and put to sea once more. The gods sent down
a sternwind for a racing passage homeward.

So ends the story. Now you must stay with me
and be my guest eleven or twelve days more.
I'll send you on your way with gifts, and fine ones:
three chariot horses, and a polished car;   630
a hammered cup, too, so that all your days,
tipping the red wine for the deathless gods,
you will remember me."

                              Telémakhos answered:

"Lord, son of Atreus, no, you must not keep me.
Not that a year with you would be too long:
I never could be homesick here—I find
your tales and all you say so marvellous.
But time hangs heavy on my shipmates' hands
at holy Pylos, if you make me stay.   640
As for your gift, now, let it be some keepsake.
Horses I cannot take to Ithaka;
let me bestow them back on you, to serve
your glory here. My lord, you rule wide country,
rolling and rich with clover, galingale
and all the grains: red wheat and hoary barley.
At home we have no level runs or meadows,
but highland, goat land—prettier than plains, though.
Grasses, and pasture land, are hard to come by
upon the islands tilted in the sea,   650
and Ithaka is the island of them all."

At this the deep-lunged man of battle smiled.
Then he said kindly, patting the boy's hand:

"You come of good stock, lad. That was well spoken.
I'll change the gift, then—as indeed I can.
Let me see what is costliest and most beautiful
of all the precious things my house contains:
a wine bowl, mixing bowl, all wrought of silver,
but rimmed with hammered gold. Let this be yours.
It is Hephaistos' work, given me by Phaidimos,   660
captain and king of Sidon. He received me
during my travels. Let it be yours, I say."

This was their discourse on that morning. Meanwhile
guests were arriving at the great lord's house,
bringing their sheep, and wine, the ease of men,
with loaves their comely kerchiefed women sent,
to make a feast in hall.
                            At that same hour,
before the distant manor of Odysseus,
the suitors were competing at the discus throw   670
and javelin, on a measured field they used,
arrogant lords at play. The two best men,
Antínoös and Eurýmakhos, presided.
Now Phronios' son, Noêmon, came to see them
with a question for Antínoös. He said:

"Do any of us know, or not, Antínoös,
what day Telémakhos will be home from Pylos?
He took my ship, but now I need it back
to make a cruise to Elis, where the plains are.
I have a dozen mares at pasture there   680
with mule colts yet unweaned. My notion is
to bring one home and break him in for labor."

His first words made them stare—for they knew well
Telémakhos could not have gone to Pylos,
but inland with his flocks, or to the swineherd.
Eupeithês' son, Antínoös, quickly answered:

"Tell the story straight. He sailed? Who joined him—
a crew he picked up here in Ithaka,
or his own slaves? He might have done it that way.
And will you make it clear   690

whether he took the ship against your will?
Did he ask for it, did you lend it to him?"

Now said the son of Phronios in reply:

"Lent it to him, and freely. Who would not,
when a prince of that house asked for it, in trouble?
Hard to refuse the favor, it seems to me.
As for his crew, the best men on the island,
after ourselves, went with him. Mentor I noted
going aboard—or a god who looked like Mentor.
The strange thing is, I saw Lord Mentor here   700
in the first light yesterday—although he sailed
five days ago for Pylos."

                                   Turning away,
Noêmon took the path to his father's house,
leaving the two men there, baffled and hostile.
They called the rest in from the playing field
and made them all sit down, so that Antínoös
could speak out from the stormcloud of his heart,
swollen with anger; and his eyes blazed:

"A bad business. Telémakhos had the gall   710
to make that crossing, though we said he could not.
So the young cub rounds up a first rate crew
in spite of all our crowd, and puts to sea.
What devilment will he be up to next time?—
Zeus blast the life out of him before he's grown!
Just give me a fast ship and twenty men;
I'll intercept him, board him in the strait
between the crags of Samê and this island.
He'll find his sea adventure after his father
swamping work in the end!"   720

                              They all cried "Aye!"
and "After him!" and trailed back to the manor.

Now not much time went by before Penélopê
learned what was afoot among the suitors.
Medôn the crier told her. He had been
outside the wall, and heard them in the court

conspiring. Into the house and up the stairs
he ran to her with his news upon his tongue—
but at the door Penélopê met him, crying:

"Why have they sent you up here now? To tell   730
the maids of King Odysseus—'Leave your spinning:
Time to go down and slave to feed those men?'
I wish this were the last time they came feasting,
courting me or consorting here! The last!
Each day you crowd this house like wolves
to eat away my brave son's patrimony.
When you were boys, did your own fathers tell you
nothing of what Odysseus was for them?
In word and act impeccable, disinterested
toward all the realm—though it is king's justice   740
to hold one man abhorred and love another;
no man alive could say Odysseus wronged him.
But your own hearts—how different!—and your deeds!
How soon are benefactions all forgotten!"

Now Medôn, the alert and cool man, answered:

"I wish that were the worst of it, my Lady,
but they intend something more terrible—
may Zeus forfend and spare us!
They plan to drive the keen bronze through Telémakhos
when he comes home. He sailed away, you know,   750
to hallowed Pylos and old Lakedaimon
for news about his father."

                              Her knees failed,
and her heart failed as she listened to the words,
and all her power of speech went out of her.
Tears came; but the rich voice could not come.
Only after a long while she made answer:

"Why has my child left me? He had no need
of those long ships on which men shake out sail
to tug like horses, breasting miles of sea.   760
Why did he go? Must he, too, be forgotten?"

Then Medôn, the perceptive man, replied:

"A god moved him—who knows?—or his own heart
sent him to learn, at Pylos, if his father
roams the wide world still, or what befell him."

He left her then, and went down through the house.
And now the pain around her heart benumbed her;
chairs were a step away, but far beyond her;
she sank down on the doorsill of the chamber,
wailing, and all her women young and old   770
made a low murmur of lament around her,
until at last she broke out through her tears:

"Dearest companions, what has Zeus given me?
Pain—more pain than any living woman.
My lord, my lion heart, gone, long ago—
the bravest man, and best, of the Danaans,
famous through Hellas and the Argive midlands—
and now the squalls have blown my son, my dear one,
an unknown boy, southward. No one told me.
O brute creatures, not one soul would dare   780
to wake me from my sleep; you knew
the hour he took the black ship out to sea!
If I had seen that sailing in his eyes
he should have stayed with me, for all his longing,
stayed—or left me dead in the great hall.
Go, someone, now, and call old Dolios,
the slave my father gave me before I came,
my orchard keeper—tell him to make haste
and put these things before Laërtês; he
may plan some kind of action; let him come   790
to cry shame on these ruffians who would murder
Odysseus' son and heir, and end his line!"

The dear old nurse, Eurýkleia, answered her:

"Sweet mistress, have my throat cut without mercy
or what you will; it's true, I won't conceal it,
I knew the whole thing; gave him his provisions;
grain and sweet wine I gave, and a great oath
to tell you nothing till twelve days went by,
or till you heard of it yourself, or missed him;

he hoped you would not tear your skin lamenting.   800
Come, bathe and dress your loveliness afresh,
and go to the upper rooms with all your maids
to ask help from Athena, Zeus's daughter.
She it will be who saves this boy from death.
Spare the old man this further suffering;
the blissful gods cannot so hate his line,
heirs of Arkeisios; one will yet again
be lord of the tall house and the far fields."

She hushed her weeping in this way, and soothed her.
The Lady Penélopê arose and bathed,   810
dressing her body in her freshest linen,
filled a basket with barley, and led her maids
to the upper rooms, where she besought Athena:

"Tireless child of Zeus, graciously hear me!
If ever Odysseus burned at our altar fire
thighbones of beef or mutton in sacrifice,
remember it for my sake! Save my son!
Shield him, and make the killers go astray!"

She ended with a cry, and the goddess heard her.
Now voices rose from the shadowy hall below   820
where the suitors were assuring one another:

"Our so-long-courted Queen is even now
of a mind to marry one of us, and knows
nothing of what is destined for her son."

Of what was destined they in fact knew nothing,
but Antínoös addressed them in a whisper:

"No boasting—are you mad?—and no loud talk:
someone might hear it and alarm the house.
Come along now, be quiet, this way; come,
we'll carry out the plan our hearts are set on."   830

Picking out twenty of the strongest seamen,
he led them to a ship at the sea's edge,
and down they dragged her into deeper water,
stepping a mast in her, with furled sails,

and oars a-trail from thongs looped over thole pins,
ready all; then tried the white sail, hoisting,
while men at arms carried their gear aboard.
They moored the ship some way off shore, and left her
to take their evening meal there, waiting for night to come.

Penélopê at that hour in her high chamber   840
lay silent, tasting neither food nor drink,
and thought of nothing but her princely son—
could he escape, or would they find and kill him?—
her mind turning at bay, like a cornered lion
in whom fear comes as hunters close the ring.
But in her sick thought sweet sleep overtook her,
and she dozed off, her body slack and still.

Now it occurred to the grey-eyed goddess Athena
to make a figure of dream in a woman's form—
Iphthimê, great Ikários' other daughter,   850
whom Eumêlos of Phêrai took as bride.
The goddess sent this dream to Odysseus' house
to quiet Penélopê and end her grieving.
So, passing by the strap-slit through the door,
the image came a-gliding down the room
to stand at her bedside and murmur to her:

"Sleepest thou, sorrowing Penélopê?
The gods whose life is ease no longer suffer thee
to pine and weep, then; he returns unharmed,
thy little one; no way hath he offended."   860

Then pensive Penélopê made this reply,
slumbering sweetly in the gates of dream:

"Sister, hast thou come hither? Why? Aforetime
never wouldst come, so far away thy dwelling.
And am I bid be done with all my grieving?
But see what anguish hath my heart and soul!
My lord, my lion heart, gone, long ago—
the bravest man, and best, of the Danaans,
famous through Hellas and the Argive midlands—
and now my son, my dear one, gone seafaring,   870
a child, untrained in hardship or in council.

Aye, 'tis for him I weep, more than his father!
Aye, how I tremble for him, lest some blow
befall him at men's hands or on the sea!
Cruel are they and many who plot against him,
to take his life before he can return."

Now the dim phantom spoke to her once more:

"Lift up thy heart, and fear not overmuch.
For by his side one goes whom all men else
invoke as their defender, one so powerful—   880
Pallas Athena; in thy tears she pitied thee
and now hath sent me that I so assure thee."

Then said Penélopê the wise:

                              "If thou art
numinous and hast ears for divine speech,
O tell me, what of Odysseus, man of woe?
Is he alive still somewhere, seeth he day light still?
Or gone in death to the sunless underworld?"

The dim phantom said only this in answer:

"Of him I may not tell thee in this discourse,   890
alive or dead. And empty words are evil."

The wavering form withdrew along the doorbolt
into a draft of wind, and out of sleep
Penélopê awoke, in better heart
for that clear dream in the twilight of the night.

Meanwhile the suitors had got under way,
planning the death plunge for Telémakhos.
Between the Isles of Ithaka and Samê
the sea is broken by an islet, Asteris,
with access to both channels from a cove.   900
In ambush here that night the Akhaians lay.

BOOK FIVE

Sweet Nymph and Open Sea

LINES 1 – 16

Dawn came up from the couch of her reclining,
leaving her lord Tithonos' brilliant side
with fresh light in her arms for gods and men.
And the master of heaven and high thunder, Zeus,
went to his place among the gods assembled
hearing Athena tell Odysseus' woe.
For she, being vexed that he was still sojourning
in the sea chambers of Kalypso, said:

"O Father Zeus and gods in bliss forever,
let no man holding scepter as a king   10
think to be mild, or kind, or virtuous;
let him be cruel, and practice evil ways,
for those Odysseus ruled cannot remember
the fatherhood and mercy of his reign.
Meanwhile he lives and grieves upon that island
in thralldom to the nymph; he cannot stir,
cannot fare homeward, for no ship is left him,
fitted with oars—no crewmen or companions

to pull him on the broad back of the sea.
And now murder is hatched on the high sea   20
against his son, who sought news of his father
in the holy lands of Pylos and Lakedaimon."

To this the summoner of cloud replied:

"My child, what odd complaints you let escape you.
Have you not, you yourself, arranged this matter—
as we all know—so that Odysseus
will bring these men to book, on his return?
And are you not the one to give Telémakhos
a safe route for sailing? Let his enemies
encounter no one and row home again."   30

He turned then to his favorite son and said:

"Hermês, you have much practice on our missions,
go make it known to the softly-braided nymph
that we, whose will is not subject to error,
order Odysseus home; let him depart.
But let him have no company, gods or men,
only a raft that he must lash together,
and after twenty days, worn out at sea,
he shall make land upon the garden isle,
Skhería, of our kinsmen, the Phaiákians.   40
Let these men take him to their hearts in honor
and berth him in a ship, and send him home,
with gifts of garments, gold, and bronze—
so much he had not counted on from Troy
could he have carried home his share of plunder.
His destiny is to see his friends again
under his own roof, in his father's country."

No words were lost on Hermês the Wayfinder,
who bent to tie his beautiful sandals on,
ambrosial, golden, that carry him over water   50
or over endless land in a swish of the wind,
and took the wand with which he charms asleep—
or when he wills, awake—the eyes of men.
So wand in hand he paced into the air,
shot from Pieria down, down to sea level,

and veered to skim the swell. A gull patrolling
between the wave crests of the desolate sea
will dip to catch a fish, and douse his wings;
no higher above the whitecaps Hermês flew
until the distant island lay ahead,   60
then rising shoreward from the violet ocean
he stepped up to the cave. Divine Kalypso,
the mistress of the isle, was now at home.
Upon her hearthstone a great fire blazing
scented the farthest shores with cedar smoke
and smoke of thyme, and singing high and low
in her sweet voice, before her loom a-weaving,
she passed her golden shuttle to and fro.
A deep wood grew outside, with summer leaves
of alder and black poplar, pungent cypress.   70
Ornate birds here rested their stretched wings—
horned owls, falcons, cormorants—long-tongued
beachcombing birds, and followers of the sea.
Around the smoothwalled cave a crooking vine
held purple clusters under ply of green;
and four springs, bubbling up near one another
shallow and clear, took channels here and there
through beds of violets and tender parsley.
Even a god who found this place
would gaze, and feel his heart beat with delight: 80
so Hermês did; but when he had gazed his fill
he entered the wide cave. Now face to face
the magical Kalypso recognized him,
as all immortal gods know one another
on sight—though seeming strangers, far from home.
But he saw nothing of the great Odysseus,
who sat apart, as a thousand times before,
and racked his own heart groaning, with eyes wet
scanning the bare horizon of the sea.
Kalypso, lovely nymph, seated her guest   90
in a bright chair all shimmering, and asked:

"O Hermês, ever with your golden wand,
what brings you to my island?
Your awesome visits in the past were few.
Now tell me what request you have in mind;

for I desire to do it, if I can,
and if it is a proper thing to do.
But wait a while, and let me serve my friend."

She drew a table of ambrosia near him
and stirred a cup of ruby-colored nectar—   100
food and drink for the luminous Wayfinder,
who took both at his leisure, and replied:

"Goddess to god, you greet me, questioning me?
Well, here is truth for you in courtesy.
Zeus made me come, and not my inclination;
who cares to cross that tract of desolation,
the bitter sea, all mortal towns behind
where gods have beef and honors from mankind?
But it is not to be thought of—and no use—
for any god to elude the will of Zeus.   110

He notes your friend, most ill-starred by renown
of all the peers who fought for Priam's town—
nine years of war they had, before great Troy was down.
Homing, they wronged the goddess with grey eyes,
who made a black wind blow and the seas rise,
in which his troops were lost, and all his gear,
while easterlies and current washed him here.
Now the command is: send him back in haste.
His life may not in exile go to waste.
His destiny, his homecoming, is at hand,   120
when he shall see his dearest, and walk on his own land."

That goddess most divinely made
shuddered before him, and her warm voice rose:

"Oh you vile gods, in jealousy supernal!
You hate it when we choose to lie with men—
immortal flesh by some dear mortal side.
So radiant Dawn once took to bed Orion
until you easeful gods grew peevish at it,
and holy Artemis, Artemis throned in gold,
hunted him down in Delos with her arrows.   130
Then Dêmêtêr of the tasseled tresses yielded
to Iasion, mingling and making love

in a furrow three times plowed; but Zeus found out
and killed him with a white-hot thunderbolt.
So now you grudge me, too, my mortal friend.
But it was I who saved him—saw him straddle
his own keel board, the one man left afloat
when Zeus rent wide his ship with chain lightning
and overturned him in the winedark sea.
Then all his troops were lost, his good companions,   140
but wind and current washed him here to me.
I fed him, loved him, sang that he should not die
nor grow old, ever, in all the days to come.
But now there's no eluding Zeus's will.
If this thing be ordained by him, I say
so be it, let the man strike out alone
on the vast water. Surely I cannot 'send' him.
I have no long-oared ships, no company
to pull him on the broad back of the sea.
My counsel he shall have, and nothing hidden,   150
to help him homeward without harm."

To this the Wayfinder made answer briefly:

"Thus you shall send him, then. And show more grace
in your obedience, or be chastised by Zeus."

The strong god glittering left her as he spoke,
and now her ladyship, having given heed
to Zeus's mandate, went to find Odysseus
in his stone seat to seaward—tear on tear
brimming his eyes. The sweet days of his life time
were running out in anguish over his exile,   160
for long ago the nymph had ceased to please.
Though he fought shy of her and her desire,
he lay with her each night, for she compelled him.
But when day came he sat on the rocky shore
and broke his own heart groaning, with eyes wet
scanning the bare horizon of the sea.
Now she stood near him in her beauty, saying:

"O forlorn man, be still.
Here you need grieve no more; you need not feel

your life consumed here; I have pondered it,   170
and I shall help you go.
Come and cut down high timber for a raft
or flatboat; make her broad-beamed, and decked over,
so you can ride her on the misty sea.
Stores I shall put aboard for you—bread, water,
and ruby-colored wine, to stay your hunger—
give you a seacloak and a following wind
to help you homeward without harm—provided
the gods who rule wide heaven wish it so.
Stronger than I they are, in mind and power."   180

For all he had endured, Odysseus shuddered.
But when he spoke, his words went to the mark:

"After these years, a helping hand? O goddess,
what guile is hidden here?
A raft, you say, to cross the Western Ocean,
rough water, and unknown? Seaworthy ships
that glory in god's wind will never cross it.
I take no raft you grudge me out to sea.
Or yield me first a great oath, if I do,
to work no more enchantment to my harm."   190

At this the beautiful nymph Kalypso smiled
and answered sweetly, laying her hand upon him:

"What a dog you are! And not for nothing learned,
having the wit to ask this thing of me!
My witness then be earth and sky
and dripping Styx that I swear by—
the gay gods cannot swear more seriously—
I have no further spells to work against you.
But what I shall devise, and what I tell you,
will be the same as if your need were mine.   200
Fairness is all I think of. There are hearts
made of cold iron—but my heart is kind."

Swiftly she turned and led him to her cave,
and they went in, the mortal and immortal.
He took the chair left empty now by Hermês,

where the divine Kalypso placed before him
victuals and drink of men; then she sat down
facing Odysseus, while her serving maids
brought nectar and ambrosia to her side.
Then each one's hands went out on each one's feast   210
until they had had their pleasure; and she said:

"Son of Laërtês, versatile Odysseus,
after these years with me, you still desire
your old home? Even so, I wish you well.
If you could see it all, before you go—
all the adversity you face at sea—
you would stay here, and guard this house, and be
immortal—though you wanted her forever,
that bride for whom you pine each day.
Can I be less desirable than she is?   220
Less interesting? Less beautiful? Can mortals
compare with goddesses in grace and form?"

To this the strategist Odysseus answered:

"My lady goddess, here is no cause for anger.
My quiet Penélopê—how well I know—
would seem a shade before your majesty,
death and old age being unknown to you,
while she must die. Yet, it is true, each day
I long for home, long for the sight of home.
If any god has marked me out again   230
for shipwreck, my tough heart can undergo it.
What hardship have I not long since endured
at sea, in battle! Let the trial come."

Now as he spoke the sun set, dusk drew on,
and they retired, this pair, to the inner cave
to revel and rest softly, side by side.

When Dawn spread out her finger tips of rose
Odysseus pulled his tunic and his cloak on,
while the sea nymph dressed in a silvery gown
of subtle tissue, drew about her waist   240
a golden belt, and veiled her head, and then
took thought for the great-hearted hero's voyage.

A brazen axehead first she had to give him,
two-bladed, and agreeable to the palm
with a smooth-fitting haft of olive wood;
next a well-polished adze; and then she led him
to the island's tip where bigger timber grew—
besides the alder and poplar, tall pine trees,
long dead and seasoned, that would float him high.
Showing him in that place her stand of timber   250
the loveliest of nymphs took her way home.
Now the man fell to chopping; when he paused
twenty tall trees were down. He lopped the branches,
split the trunks, and trimmed his puncheons true.
Meanwhile Kalypso brought him an auger tool
with which he drilled through all his planks, then drove
stout pins to bolt them, fitted side by side.
A master shipwright, building a cargo vessel,
lays down a broad and shallow hull; just so
Odysseus shaped the bottom of his craft.   260
He made his decking fast to close-set ribs
before he closed the side with longer planking,
then cut a mast pole, and a proper yard,
and shaped a steering oar to hold her steady.
He drove long strands of willow in all the seams
to keep out waves, and ballasted with logs.
As for a sail, the lovely nymph Kalypso
brought him a cloth so he could make that, too.
Then he ran up his rigging—halyards, braces—
and hauled the boat on rollers to the water.   270

This was the fourth day, when he had all ready;
on the fifth day, she sent him out to sea.
But first she bathed him, gave him a scented cloak,
and put on board a skin of dusky wine
with water in a bigger skin, and stores—
boiled meats and other victuals—in a bag.
Then she conjured a warm landbreeze to blowing—
joy for Odysseus when he shook out sail!
Now the great seaman, leaning on his oar,
steered all the night unsleeping, and his eyes   280
picked out the Pleiadês, the laggard Ploughman,

and the Great Bear, that some have called the Wain,
pivoting in the sky before Orion;
of all the night's pure figures, she alone
would never bathe or dip in the Ocean stream.
These stars the beautiful Kalypso bade him
hold on his left hand as he crossed the main.
Seventeen nights and days in the open water
he sailed, before a dark shoreline appeared;
Skhería then came slowly into view   290
like a rough shield of bull's hide on the sea.

But now the god of earthquake, storming home
over the mountains of Asia from the Sunburned land,
sighted him far away. The god grew sullen
and tossed his great head, muttering to himself:

"Here is a pretty cruise! While I was gone
the gods have changed their minds about Odysseus.
Look at him now, just offshore of that island
that frees him from the bondage of his exile!
Still I can give him a rough ride in, and will."   300

Brewing high thunderheads, he churned the deep
with both hands on his trident—called up wind
from every quarter, and sent a wall of rain
to blot out land and sea in torrential night.
Hurricane winds now struck from the South and East
shifting North West in a great spume of seas,
on which Odysseus' knees grew slack, his heart
sickened, and he said within himself:

"Rag of man that I am, is this the end of me?
I fear the goddess told it all too well—   310
predicting great adversity at sea
and far from home. Now all things bear her out:
the whole rondure of heaven hooded so
by Zeus in woeful cloud, and the sea raging
under such winds. I am going down, that's sure.
How lucky those Danaans were who perished
on Troy's wide seaboard, serving the Atreidai!
Would God I, too, had died there—met my end

that time the Trojans made so many casts at me
when I stood by Akhilleus after death.   320
I should have had a soldier's burial
and praise from the Akhaians—not this choking
waiting for me at sea, unmarked and lonely."

A great wave drove at him with toppling crest
spinning him round, in one tremendous blow,
and he went plunging overboard, the oar-haft
wrenched from his grip. A gust that came on howling
at the same instant broke his mast in two,
hurling his yard and sail far out to leeward.
Now the big wave a long time kept him under,   330
helpless to surface, held by tons of water,
tangled, too, by the seacloak of Kalypso.
Long, long, until he came up spouting brine,
with streamlets gushing from his head and beard;
but still bethought him, half-drowned as he was,
to flounder for the boat and get a handhold
into the bilge—to crouch there, foiling death.
Across the foaming water, to and fro,
the boat careered like a ball of tumbleweed
blown on the autumn plains, but intact still.   340
So the winds drove this wreck over the deep,
East Wind and North Wind, then South Wind and West,
coursing each in turn to the brutal harry.

But Ino saw him—Ino, Kadmos' daughter,
slim-legged, lovely, once an earthling girl,
now in the seas a nereid, Leukothea.
Touched by Odysseus' painful buffeting
she broke the surface, like a diving bird,
to rest upon the tossing raft and say:

"O forlorn man, I wonder   350
why the Earthshaker, Lord Poseidon, holds
this fearful grudge—father of all your woes.
He will not drown you, though, despite his rage.
You seem clear-headed still; do what I tell you.
Shed that cloak, let the gale take your craft,
and swim for it—swim hard to get ashore

upon Skhería, yonder,
where it is fated that you find a shelter.
Here: make my veil your sash; it is not mortal;
you cannot, now, be drowned or suffer harm.   360
Only, the instant you lay hold of earth,
discard it, cast it far, far out from shore
in the winedark sea again, and turn away."

After she had bestowed her veil, the nereid
dove like a gull to windward
where a dark waveside closed over her whiteness.
But in perplexity Odysseus
said to himself, his great heart laboring:

"O damned confusion! Can this be a ruse
to trick me from the boat for some god's pleasure?   370
No I'll not swim; with my own eyes I saw
how far the land lies that she called my shelter.
Better to do the wise thing, as I see it.
While this poor planking holds, I stay aboard;
I may ride out the pounding of the storm,
or if she cracks up, take to the water then;
I cannot think it through a better way."

But even while he pondered and decided,
the god of earthquake heaved a wave against him
high as a rooftree and of awful gloom.   380
A gust of wind, hitting a pile of chaff,
will scatter all the parched stuff far and wide;
just so, when this gigantic billow struck
the boat's big timbers flew apart. Odysseus
clung to a single beam, like a jockey riding,
meanwhile stripping Kalypso's cloak away;
then he slung round his chest the veil of Ino
and plunged headfirst into the sea. His hands
went out to stroke, and he gave a swimmer's kick.
But the strong Earthshaker had him under his eye,   390
and nodded as he said:

                    "Go on, go on;
wander the high seas this way, take your blows,
before you join that race the gods have nurtured.

Nor will you grumble, even then, I think,
for want of trouble."

                             Whipping his glossy team
he rode off to his glorious home at Aigai.
But Zeus's daughter Athena countered him:
she checked the course of all the winds but one,   400
commanding them, "Be quiet and go to sleep."
Then sent a long swell running under a norther
to bear the prince Odysseus, back from danger,
to join the Phaiákians, people of the sea.

Two nights, two days, in the solid deep-sea swell
he drifted, many times awaiting death,
until with shining ringlets in the East
the dawn confirmed a third day, breaking clear
over a high and windless sea; and mounting
a rolling wave he caught a glimpse of land.   410
What a dear welcome thing life seems to children
whose father, in the extremity, recovers
after some weakening and malignant illness:
his pangs are gone, the gods have delivered him.
So dear and welcome to Odysseus
the sight of land, of woodland, on that morning.
It made him swim again, to get a foothold
on solid ground. But when he came in earshot
he heard the trampling roar of sea on rock,
where combers, rising shoreward, thudded down   420
on the sucking ebb—all sheeted with salt foam.
Here were no coves or harborage or shelter,
only steep headlands, rockfallen reefs and crags.
Odysseus' knees grew slack, his heart faint,
a heaviness came over him, and he said:

"A cruel turn, this. Never had I thought
to see this land, but Zeus has let me see it—
and let me, too, traverse the Western Ocean—
only to find no exit from these breakers.
Here are sharp rocks off shore, and the sea a smother   430
rushing around them; rock face rising sheer
from deep water; nowhere could I stand up

on my two feet and fight free of the welter.
No matter how I try it, the surf may throw me
against the cliffside; no good fighting there.
If I swim down the coast, outside the breakers,
I may find shelving shore and quiet water—
but what if another gale comes on to blow?
Then I go cursing out to sea once more.
Or then again, some shark of Amphitritê's   440
may hunt me, sent by the genius of the deep.
I know how he who makes earth tremble hates me."

During this meditation a heavy surge
was taking him, in fact, straight on the rocks.
He had been flayed there, and his bones broken,
had not grey-eyed Athena instructed him:
he gripped a rock-ledge with both hands in passing
and held on, groaning, as the surge went by,
to keep clear of its breaking. Then the backwash
hit him, ripping him under and far out.   450
An octopus, when you drag one from his chamber,
comes up with suckers full of tiny stones:
Odysseus left the skin of his great hands
torn on that rock-ledge as the wave submerged him.
And now at last Odysseus would have perished,
battered inhumanly, but he had the gift
of self-possession from grey-eyed Athena.
So, when the backwash spewed him up again,
he swam out and along, and scanned the coast
for some landspit that made a breakwater.   460
Lo and behold, the mouth of a calm river
at length came into view, with level shores
unbroken, free from rock, shielded from wind—
by far the best place he had found.
But as he felt the current flowing seaward
he prayed in his heart:

                              "O hear me, lord of the stream:
how sorely I depend upon your mercy!
derelict as I am by the sea's anger.
Is he not sacred, even to the gods,   470
the wandering man who comes, as I have come,

in weariness before your knees, your waters?
Here is your servant; lord, have mercy on me."

Now even as he prayed the tide at ebb
had turned, and the river god made quiet water,
drawing him in to safety in the shallows.
His knees buckled, his arms gave way beneath him,
all vital force now conquered by the sea.
Swollen from head to foot he was, and seawater
gushed from his mouth and nostrils. There he lay,   480
scarce drawing breath, unstirring, deathly spent.
In time, as air came back into his lungs
and warmth around his heart, he loosed the veil,
letting it drift away on the estuary
downstream to where a white wave took it under
and Ino's hands received it. Then the man
crawled to the river bank among the reeds
where, face down, he could kiss the soil of earth,
in his exhaustion murmuring to himself:

"What more can this hulk suffer? What comes now?   490
In vigil through the night here by the river
how can I not succumb, being weak and sick,
to the night's damp and hoarfrost of the morning?
The air comes cold from rivers before dawn.
But if I climb the slope and fall asleep
in the dark forest's undergrowth—supposing
cold and fatigue will go, and sweet sleep come—
I fear I make the wild beasts easy prey."

But this seemed best to him, as he thought it over.
He made his way to a grove above the water   500
on open ground, and crept under twin bushes
grown from the same spot—olive and wild olive—
a thicket proof against the stinging wind
or Sun's blaze, fine soever the needling sunlight;
nor could a downpour wet it through, so dense
those plants were interwoven. Here Odysseus
tunnelled, and raked together with his hands
a wide bed—for a fall of leaves was there,
enough to save two men or maybe three

on a winter night, a night of bitter cold.   510
Odysseus' heart laughed when he saw his leaf-bed,
and down he lay, heaping more leaves above him.

A man in a distant field, no hearthfires near,
will hide a fresh brand in his bed of embers
to keep a spark alive for the next day;
so in the leaves Odysseus hid himself,
while over him Athena showered sleep
that his distress should end, and soon, soon.
In quiet sleep she sealed his cherished eyes.

BOOK SIX

The Princess at the River

LINES 1 – 15

Far gone in weariness, in oblivion,   1
the noble and enduring man slept on;
but Athena in the night went down the land
of the Phaiákians, entering their city.
In days gone by, these men held Hypereia,
a country of wide dancing grounds, but near them
were overbearing Kyklopês, whose power
could not be turned from pillage. So the Phaiákians
migrated thence under Nausíthoös
to settle a New World across the sea,   10
Skhería Island. That first captain walled
their promontory, built their homes and shrines,
and parcelled out the black land for the plow.
But he had gone down long ago to Death.
Alkínoös ruled, and Heaven gave him wisdom,
so on this night the goddess, grey-eyed Athena,
entered the palace of Alkínoös
to make sure of Odysseus' voyage home.
She took her way to a painted bedchamber

where a young girl lay fast asleep—so fine   20
in mould and feature that she seemed a goddess—
the daughter of Alkínoös, Nausikaa.
On either side, as Graces might have slept,
her maids were sleeping. The bright doors were shut,
but like a sudden stir of wind, Athena
moved to the bedside of the girl, and grew
visible as the shipman Dymas' daughter,
a girl the princess' age, and her dear friend.
In this form grey-eyed Athena said to her:

"How so remiss, and yet thy mother's daughter?   30
leaving thy clothes uncared for, Nausikaa,
when soon thou must have store of marriage linen,
and put thy minstrelsy in wedding dress!
Beauty, in these, will make the folk admire,
and bring thy father and gentle mother joy.
Let us go washing in the shine of morning!
Beside thee will I drub, so wedding chests
will brim by evening. Maidenhood must end!
Have not the noblest born Phaiákians
paid court to thee, whose birth none can excel?   40
Go beg thy sovereign father, even at dawn,
to have the mule cart and the mules brought round
to take thy body-linen, gowns and mantles.
Thou shouldst ride, for it becomes thee more,
the washing pools are found so far from home."

On this word she departed, grey-eyed Athena,
to where the gods have their eternal dwelling—
as men say—in the fastness of Olympos.
Never a tremor of wind, or a splash of rain,
no errant snowflake comes to stain that heaven,   50
so calm, so vaporless, the world of light.
Here, where the gay gods live their days of pleasure,
the grey-eyed one withdrew, leaving the princess.

And now Dawn took her own fair throne, awaking
the girl in the sweet gown, still charmed by dream.
Down through the rooms she went to tell her parents,
whom she found still at home: her mother seated

near the great hearth among her maids—and twirling
out of her distaff yarn dyed like the sea—;
her father at the door, bound for a council   60
of princes on petition of the gentry.
She went up close to him and softly said:

"My dear Papà, could you not send the mule cart
around for me—the gig with pretty wheels?
I must take all our things and get them washed
at the river pools; our linen is all soiled.
And you should wear fresh clothing, going to council
with counselors and first men of the realm.
Remember your five sons at home: though two
are married, we have still three bachelor sprigs;   70
they will have none but laundered clothes each time
they go to the dancing. See what I must think of!"

She had no word to say of her own wedding,
though her keen father saw her blush. Said he:

"No mules would I deny you, child, nor anything.
Go along, now; the grooms will bring your gig
with pretty wheels and the cargo box upon it."

He spoke to the stableman, who soon brought round
the cart, low-wheeled and nimble;
harnessed the mules, and backed them in the traces.   80
Meanwhile the girl fetched all her soiled apparel
to bundle in the polished wagon box.
Her mother, for their luncheon, packed a hamper
with picnic fare, and filled a skin of wine,
and, when the princess had been handed up,
gave her a golden bottle of olive oil
for softening girls' bodies, after bathing.
Nausikaa took the reins and raised her whip,
lashing the mules. What jingling! What a clatter!
But off they went in a ground-covering trot,   90
with princess, maids, and laundry drawn behind.
By the lower river where the wagon came
were washing pools, with water all year flowing
in limpid spillways that no grime withstood.

The girls unhitched the mules, and sent them down
along the eddying stream to crop sweet grass.
Then sliding out the cart's tail board, they took
armloads of clothing to the dusky water,
and trod them in the pits, making a race of it.
All being drugged, all blemish rinsed away,   100
they spread them, piece by piece, along the beach
whose pebbles had been laundered by the sea;
then took a dip themselves, and, all anointed
with golden oil, ate lunch beside the river
while the bright burning sun dried out their linen.
Princess and maids delighted in that feast;
then, putting off their veils,
they ran and passed a ball to a rhythmic beat,
Nausikaa flashing first with her white arms.

So Artemis goes flying after her arrows flown   110
down some tremendous valley-side—

                            Taÿgetos, Erymanthos—
chasing the mountain goats or ghosting deer,
with nymphs of the wild places flanking her;
and Lêto's heart delights to see them running,
for, taller by a head than nymphs can be,
the goddess shows more stately, all being beautiful.
So one could tell the princess from the maids.

Soon it was time, she knew, for riding homeward—
mules to be harnessed, linen folded smooth—   120
but the grey-eyed goddess Athena made her tarry,
so that Odysseus might behold her beauty
and win her guidance to the town.

                            It happened
when the king's daughter threw her ball off line
and missed, and put it in the whirling stream,—
at which they all gave such a shout, Odysseus
awoke and sat up, saying to himself:

"Now, by my life, mankind again! But who?
Savages, are they, strangers to courtesy?   130
Or gentle folk, who know and fear the gods?
That was a lusty cry of tall young girls—

most like the cry of nymphs, who haunt the peaks,
and springs of brooks, and inland grassy places.
Or am I amid people of human speech?
Up again, man; and let me see for myself."

He pushed aside the bushes, breaking off
with his great hand a single branch of olive,
whose leaves might shield him in his nakedness;
so came out rustling, like a mountain lion,   140
rain-drenched, wind-buffeted, but in his might at ease,
with burning eyes—who prowls among the herds
or flocks, or after game, his hungry belly
taking him near stout homesteads for his prey.
Odysseus had this look, in his rough skin
advancing on the girls with pretty braids;
and he was driven on by hunger, too.
Streaked with brine, and swollen, he terrified them,
so that they fled, this way and that. Only
Alkínoös' daughter stood her ground, being given   150
a bold heart by Athena, and steady knees.

She faced him, waiting. And Odysseus came,
debating inwardly what he should do:
embrace this beauty's knees in supplication?
or stand apart, and, using honeyed speech,
inquire the way to town, and beg some clothing?
In his swift reckoning, he thought it best
to trust in words to please her—and keep away;
he might anger the girl, touching her knees.
So he began, and let the soft words fall: 160

"Mistress: please: are you divine, or mortal?
If one of those who dwell in the wide heaven,
you are most near to Artemis, I should say—
great Zeus's daughter—in your grace and presence.
If you are one of earth's inhabitants,
how blest your father, and your gentle mother,
blest all your kin. I know what happiness
must send the warm tears to their eyes, each time
they see their wondrous child go to the dancing!
But one man's destiny is more than blest—   170

he who prevails, and takes you as his bride.
Never have I laid eyes on equal beauty
in man or woman. I am hushed indeed.
So fair, one time, I thought a young palm tree
at Delos near the altar of Apollo—
I had troops under me when I was there
on the sea route that later brought me grief—
but that slim palm tree filled my heart with wonder:
never came shoot from earth so beautiful.
So now, my lady, I stand in awe so great   180
I cannot take your knees. And yet my case is desperate:
twenty days, yesterday, in the winedark sea,
on the ever-lunging swell, under gale winds,
getting away from the Island of Ogýgia.
And now the terror of Storm has left me stranded
upon this shore—with more blows yet to suffer,
I must believe, before the gods relent.
Mistress, do me a kindness!
After much weary toil, I come to you,
and you are the first soul I have seen—I know   190
no others here. Direct me to the town,
give me a rag that I can throw around me,
some cloth or wrapping that you brought along.
And may the gods accomplish your desire:
a home, a husband, and harmonious
converse with him—the best thing in the world
being a strong house held in serenity
where man and wife agree. Woe to their enemies,
joy to their friends! But all this they know best."

Then she of the white arms, Nausikaa, replied: 200

"Stranger, there is no quirk or evil in you
that I can see. You know Zeus metes out fortune
to good and bad men as it pleases him.
Hardship he sent to you, and you must bear it.
But now that you have taken refuge here
you shall not lack for clothing, or any other
comfort due to a poor man in distress.
The town lies this way, and the men are called
Phaiákians, who own the land and city.

I am daughter to the Prince Alkínoös,   210
by whom the power of our people stands."

Turning, she called out to her maids-in-waiting:

"Stay with me! Does the sight of a man scare you?
Or do you take this one for an enemy?
Why, there's no fool so brash, and never will be,
as to bring war or pillage to this coast,
for we are dear to the immortal gods,
living here, in the sea that rolls forever,
distant from other lands and other men.
No: this man is a castaway, poor fellow;   220
we must take care of him. Strangers and beggars
come from Zeus: a small gift, then, is friendly.
Give our new guest some food and drink, and take him
into the river, out of the wind, to bathe."

They stood up now, and called to one another
to go on back. Quite soon they led Odysseus
under the river bank, as they were bidden;
and there laid out a tunic, and a cloak,
and gave him olive oil in the golden flask.
"Here," they said, "go bathe in the flowing water."   230
But heard now from that kingly man, Odysseus:

"Maids," he said, "keep away a little; let me
wash the brine from my own back, and rub on
plenty of oil. It is long since my anointing.
I take no bath, however, where you can see me—
naked before young girls with pretty braids."

They left him, then, and went to tell the princess.
And now Odysseus, dousing in the river,
scrubbed the coat of brine from back and shoulders
and rinsed the clot of sea-spume from his hair;   240
got himself all rubbed down, from head to foot,
then he put on the clothes the princess gave him.
Athena lent a hand, making him seem
taller, and massive too, with crisping hair
in curls like petals of wild hyacinth,
but all red-golden. Think of gold infused

on silver by a craftsman, whose fine art
Hephaistos taught him, or Athena: one
whose work moves to delight: just so she lavished
beauty over Odysseus' head and shoulders.   250
Then he went down to sit on the sea beach
in his new splendor. There the girl regarded him,
and after a time she said to the maids beside her:

"My gentlewomen, I have a thing to tell you.
The Olympian gods cannot be all averse
to this man's coming here among our islanders.
Uncouth he seemed, I thought so, too, before;
but now he looks like one of heaven's people.
I wish my husband could be fine as he
and glad to stay forever on Skhería!   260

But have you given refreshment to our guest?"

At this the maids, all gravely listening, hastened
to set out bread and wine before Odysseus,
and ah! how ravenously that patient man
took food and drink, his long fast at an end.

The princess Nausikaa now turned aside
to fold her linens; in the pretty cart
she stowed them, put the mule team under harness,
mounted the driver's seat, and then looked down
to say with cheerful prompting to Odysseus: 270

"Up with you now, friend; back to town we go;
and I shall send you in before my father
who is wondrous wise; there in our house with him
you'll meet the noblest of the Phaiákians.
You have good sense, I think; here's how to do it:
while we go through the countryside and farmland
stay with my maids, behind the wagon, walking
briskly enough to follow where I lead.
But near the town—well, there's a wall with towers
around the Isle, and beautiful ship basins   280
right and left of the causeway of approach;
seagoing craft are beached beside the road
each on its launching ways. The agora,

with fieldstone benches bedded in the earth,
lies either side Poseidon's shrine—for there
men are at work on pitch-black hulls and rigging,
cables and sails, and tapering of oars.
The archer's craft is not for the Phaiákians,
but ship designing, modes of oaring cutters
in which they love to cross the foaming sea.   290
From these fellows I will have no salty talk,
no gossip later. Plenty are insolent.
And some seadog might say, after we passed:
'Who is this handsome stranger trailing Nausikaa?
Where did she find him? Will he be her husband?
Or is she being hospitable to some rover
come off his ship from lands across the sea—
there being no lands nearer. A god, maybe?
a god from heaven, the answer to her prayer,
descending now—to make her his forever?   300
Better, if she's roamed and found a husband
somewhere else: none of our own will suit her,
though many come to court her, and those the best.'
This is the way they might make light of me.
And I myself should hold it shame
for any girl to flout her own dear parents,
taking up with a man, before her marriage.

Note well, now, what I say, friend, and your chances
are excellent for safe conduct from my father.
You'll find black poplars in a roadside park   310
around a meadow and fountain—all Athena's—
but Father has a garden in the place—
this within earshot of the city wall.
Go in there and sit down, giving us time
to pass through town and reach my father's house.
And when you can imagine we're at home,
then take the road into the city, asking
directions to the palace of Alkínoös.
You'll find it easily: any small boy
can take you there; no family has a mansion   320
half so grand as he does, being king.
As soon as you are safe inside, cross over

and go straight through into the mégaron
to find my mother. She'll be there in firelight
before a column, with her maids in shadow,
spinning a wool dyed richly as the sea.
My father's great chair faces the fire, too;
there like a god he sits and takes his wine.
Go past him; cast yourself before my mother,
embrace her knees—and you may wake up soon   330
at home rejoicing, though your home be far.
On Mother's feeling much depends; if she
looks on you kindly, you shall see your friends
under your own roof in your father's country."

At this she raised her glistening whip, lashing
the team into a run; they left the river
cantering beautifully, then trotted smartly.
But then she reined them in, and spared the whip,
so that her maids could follow with Odysseus.
The sun was going down when they went by   340
Athena's grove. Here, then, Odysseus rested,
and lifted up his prayer to Zeus's daughter:

"Hear me, unwearied child of royal Zeus!
O listen to me now—thou so aloof
while the Earthshaker wrecked and battered me.
May I find love and mercy among these people."

He prayed for that, and Pallas Athena heard him—
although in deference to her father's brother
she would not show her true form to Odysseus,
at whom Poseidon smoldered on   350
until the kingly man came home to his own shore.

BOOK SEVEN

Gardens and Firelight

LINES 1 – 15

As Lord Odysseus prayed there in the grove   1
the girl rode on, behind her strapping team,
and came late to the mansion of her father,
where she reined in at the courtyard gate. Her brothers
awaited her like tall gods in the court,
circling to lead the mules away and carry
the laundered things inside. But she withdrew
to her own bedroom, where a fire soon shone,
kindled by her old nurse, Eurymedousa.
Years ago, from a raid on the continent,   10
the rolling ships had brought this woman over
to be Alkínoös' share—fit spoil for him
whose realm hung on his word as on a god's.
And she had schooled the princess, Nausikaa,
whose fire she tended now, making her supper.

Odysseus, when the time had passed, arose
and turned into the city. But Athena
poured a sea fog around him as he went—

her love's expedient, that no jeering sailor
should halt the man or challenge him for luck.   20
Instead, as he set foot in the pleasant city,
the grey-eyed goddess came to him, in figure
a small girl child, hugging a water jug.
Confronted by her, Lord Odysseus asked:

"Little one, could you take me to the house
of that Alkínoös, king among these people?
You see, I am a poor old stranger here;
my home is far away; here there is no one
known to me, in countryside or city."

The grey-eyed goddess Athena replied to him: 30

"Oh yes, good grandfer, sir, I know, I'll show you
the house you mean; it is quite near my father's.
But come now, hush, like this, and follow me.
You must not stare at people, or be inquisitive.
They do not care for strangers in this neighborhood;
a foreign man will get no welcome here.
The only things they trust are the racing ships
Poseidon gave, to sail the deep blue sea
like white wings in the sky, or a flashing thought."

Pallas Athena turned like the wind, running   40
ahead of him, and he followed in her footsteps.
And no seafaring men of Phaiákia
perceived Odysseus passing through their town:
the awesome one in pigtails barred their sight
with folds of sacred mist. And yet Odysseus
gazed out marvelling at the ships and harbors,
public squares, and ramparts towering up
with pointed palisades along the top.
When they were near the mansion of the king,
grey-eyed Athena in the child cried out: 50

"Here it is, grandfer, sir—that mansion house
you asked to see. You'll find our king and queen
at supper, but you must not be dismayed;
go in to them. A cheerful man does best
in every enterprise—even a stranger.

You'll see our lady just inside the hall—
her name is Arêtê; her grandfather
was our good king Alkínoös's father—
Nausithoös by name, son of Poseidon
and Periboia. That was a great beauty,   60
the daughter of Eurymedon, commander
of the Gigantês in the olden days,
who led those wild things to their doom and his.
Poseidon then made love to Periboia,
and she bore Nausíthoös, Phaiákia's lord,
whose sons in turn were Rhêxênor and Alkínoös.
Rhêxênor had no sons; even as a bridegroom
he fell before the silver bow of Apollo,
his only child a daughter, Arêtê.
When she grew up, Alkínoös married her   70
and holds her dear. No lady in the world,
no other mistress of a man's household,
is honored as our mistress is, and loved,
by her own children, by Alkínoös,
and by the people. When she walks the town
they murmur and gaze, as though she were a goddess.
No grace or wisdom fails in her; indeed
just men in quarrels come to her for equity.
Supposing, then, she looks upon you kindly,
the chances are that you shall see your friends   80
under your own roof, in your father's country."

At this the grey-eyed goddess Athena left him
and left that comely land, going over sea
to Marathon, to the wide roadways of Athens
and her retreat in the stronghold of Erekhtheus.
Odysseus, now alone before the palace,
meditated a long time before crossing
the brazen threshold of the great courtyard.
High rooms he saw ahead, airy and luminous
as though with lusters of the sun and moon,   90
bronze-paneled walls, at several distances,
making a vista, with an azure molding
of lapis lazuli. The doors were golden
guardians of the great room. Shining bronze

plated the wide doorsill; the posts and lintel
were silver upon silver; golden handles
curved on the doors, and golden, too, and silver
were sculptured hounds, flanking the entrance way,
cast by the skill and ardor of Hephaistos
to guard the prince Alkínoös's house—   100
undying dogs that never could grow old.
Through all the rooms, as far as he could see,
tall chairs were placed around the walls, and strewn
with fine embroidered stuff made by the women.
Here were enthroned the leaders of Phaiákia
drinking and dining, with abundant fare.
Here, too, were boys of gold on pedestals
holding aloft bright torches of pitch pine
to light the great rooms, and the night-time feasting.
And fifty maids-in-waiting of the household   110
sat by the round mill, grinding yellow corn,
or wove upon their looms, or twirled their distaffs,
flickering like the leaves of a poplar tree;
while drops of oil glistened on linen weft.
Skillful as were the men of Phaiákia
in ship handling at sea, so were these women
skilled at the loom, having this lovely craft
and artistry as talents from Athena.

To left and right, outside, he saw an orchard
closed by a pale—four spacious acres planted   120
with trees in bloom or weighted down for picking:
pear trees, pomegranates, brilliant apples,
luscious figs, and olives ripe and dark.
Fruit never failed upon these trees: winter
and summer time they bore, for through the year
the breathing Westwind ripened all in turn—
so one pear came to príme, and then another,
and so with apples, figs, and the vine's fruit
empurpled in the royal vineyard there.
Currants were dried at one end, on a platform   130
bare to the sun, beyond the vintage arbors
and vats the vintners trod; while near at hand
were new grapes barely formed as the green bloom fell,

or half-ripe clusters, faintly coloring.
After the vines came rows of vegetables
of all the kinds that flourish in every season,
and through the garden plots and orchard ran
channels from one clear fountain, while another
gushed through a pipe under the courtyard entrance
to serve the house and all who came for water.   140
These were the gifts of heaven to Alkínoös.

Odysseus, who had borne the barren sea,
stood in the gateway and surveyed this bounty.
He gazed his fill, then swiftly he went in.
The lords and nobles of Phaiákia
were tipping wine to the wakeful god, to Hermês—
a last libation before going to bed—
but down the hall Odysseus went unseen,
still in the cloud Athena cloaked him in,
until he reached Arêtê, and the king.   150
He threw his great hands round Arêtê's knees,
whereon the sacred mist curled back;
they saw him; and the diners hushed amazed
to see an unknown man inside the palace.
Under their eyes Odysseus made his plea:

"Arêtê, admirable Rhêxênor's daughter,
here is a man bruised by adversity, thrown
upon your mercy and the king your husband's,
begging indulgence of this company—
may the gods' blessing rest on them! May life   160
be kind to all! Let each one leave his children
every good thing this realm confers upon him!
But grant me passage to my father land.
My home and friends lie far. My life is pain."

He moved, then, toward the fire, and sat him down
amid the ashes. No one stirred or spoke
until Ekhenêos broke the spell—an old man,
eldest of the Phaiákians, an oracle,
versed in the laws and manners of old time.
He rose among them now and spoke out kindly: 170

"Alkínoös, this will not pass for courtesy:
a guest abased in ashes at our hearth?
Everyone here awaits your word; so come, then,
lift the man up; give him a seat of honor,
a silver-studded chair. Then tell the stewards
we'll have another wine bowl for libation
to Zeus, lord of the lightning—advocate
of honorable petitioners. And supper
may be supplied our friend by the larder mistress."

Alkínoös, calm in power, heard him out,   180
then took the great adventurer by the hand
and led him from the fire. Nearest his throne
the son whom he loved best, Laódamas,
had long held place; now the king bade him rise
and gave his shining chair to Lord Odysseus.
A serving maid poured water for his hands
from a gold pitcher into a silver bowl,
and spread a polished table at his side;
the mistress of provisions came with bread
and other victuals, generous with her store.   190
So Lord Odysseus drank, and tasted supper.
Seeing this done, the king in majesty
said to his squire:

                              "A fresh bowl, Pontónoös;
we make libation to the lord of lightning,
who seconds honorable petitioners."

Mixing the honey-hearted wine, Pontónoös
went on his rounds and poured fresh cups for all,
whereof when all had spilt they drank their fill.
Alkínoös then spoke to the company: 200

"My lords and leaders of Phaíakia:
hear now, all that my heart would have me say.
Our banquet's ended, so you may retire;
but let our seniors gather in the morning
to give this guest a festal day, and make
fair offerings to the gods. In due course we
shall put our minds upon the means at hand

to take him safely, comfortably, well
and happily, with speed, to his own country,
distant though it may lie. And may no trouble   210
come to him here or on the way; his fate
he shall pay out at home, even as the Spinners
spun for him on the day his mother bore him.
If, as may be, he is some god, come down
from heaven's height, the gods are working strangely:
until now, they have shown themselves in glory
only after great hekatombs—those figures
banqueting at our side, throned like ourselves.
Or if some traveller met them when alone
they bore no least disguise; we are their kin; Gigantês,   220
Kyklopês, rank no nearer gods than we."

Odysseus' wits were ready, and he replied:

"Alkínoös, you may set your mind at rest.
Body and birth, a most unlikely god
am I, being all of earth and mortal nature.
I should say, rather, I am like those men
who suffer the worst trials that you know,
and miseries greater yet, as I might tell you—
hundreds; indeed the gods could send no more.
You will indulge me if I finish dinner—?   230
grieved though I am to say it. There's no part
of man more like a dog than brazen Belly,
crying to be remembered—and it must be—
when we are mortal weary and sick at heart;
and that is my condition. Yet my hunger
drives me to take this food, and think no more
of my afflictions. Belly must be filled.
Be equally impelled, my lords, tomorrow
to berth me in a ship and send me home!
Rough years I've had; now may I see once more   240
my hall, my lands, my people before I die!"

Now all who heard cried out assent to this:
the guest had spoken well; he must have passage.
Then tipping wine they drank their thirst away,

and one by one went homeward for the night.
So Lord Odysseus kept his place alone
with Arêtê and the king Alkínoös
beside him, while the maids went to and fro
clearing away the wine cups and the tables.
Presently the ivory-skinned lady   250
turned to him—for she knew his cloak and tunic
to be her own fine work, done with her maids—
and arrowy came her words upon the air:

"Friend, I, for one, have certain questions for you.
Who are you, and who has given you this clothing?
Did you not say you wandered here by sea?"

The great tactician carefully replied:

"Ah, majesty, what labor it would be
to go through the whole story! All my years
of misadventures, given by those on high!   260
But this you ask about is quickly told:
in mid-ocean lies Ogýgia, the island
haunt of Kalypso, Atlas' guileful daughter,
a lovely goddess and a dangerous one.
No one, no god or man, consorts with her;
but supernatural power brought me there
to be her solitary guest: for Zeus
let fly with his bright bolt and split my ship,
rolling me over in the winedark sea.
There all my shipmates, friends were drowned, while I   270
hung on the keelboard of the wreck and drifted
nine full days. Then in the dead of night
the gods brought me ashore upon Ogýgia
into her hands. The enchantress in her beauty
fed and caressed me, promised me I should be
immortal, youthful, all the days to come;
but in my heart I never gave consent
though seven years detained. Immortal clothing
I had from her, and kept it wet with tears.
Then came the eighth year on the wheel of heaven   280
and word to her from Zeus, or a change of heart,
so that she now commanded me to sail,

sending me out to sea on a craft I made
with timber and tools of hers. She gave me stores,
victuals and wine, a cloak divinely woven,
and made a warm land breeze come up astern.
Seventeen days I sailed in the open water
before I saw your country's shore, a shadow
upon the sea rim. Then my heart rejoiced—
pitiable as I am! For blows aplenty   290
awaited me from the god who shakes the earth.
Cross gales he blew, making me lose my bearings,
and heaved up seas beyond imagination—
huge and foundering seas. All I could do
was hold hard, groaning under every shock,
until my craft broke up in the hurricane.
I kept afloat and swam your sea, or drifted,
taken by wind and current to this coast
where I went in on big swells running landward.
But cliffs and rock shoals made that place forbidding,   300
so I turned back, swimming off shore, and came
in the end to a river, to auspicious water,
with smooth beach and a rise that broke the wind.
I lay there where I fell till strength returned.
Then sacred night came on, and I went inland
to high ground and a leaf bed in a thicket.
Heaven sent slumber in an endless tide
submerging my sad heart among the leaves.
That night and next day's dawn and noon I slept;
the sun went west; and then sweet sleep unbound me,   310
when I became aware of maids—your daughter's—
playing along the beach; the princess, too,
most beautiful. I prayed her to assist me,
and her good sense was perfect; one could hope
for no behavior like it from the young,
thoughtless as they most often are. But she
gave me good provender and good red wine,
a river bath, and finally this clothing.
There is the bitter tale. These are the facts."

But in reply Alkínoös observed: 320

"Friend, my child's good judgment failed in this—
not to have brought you in her company home.
Once you approached her, you became her charge."

To this Odysseus tactfully replied:

"Sir, as to that, you should not blame the princess.
She did tell me to follow with her maids,
but I would not. I felt abashed, and feared
the sight would somehow ruffle or offend you.
All of us on this earth are plagued by jealousy."

Alkínoös' answer was a declaration: 330

"Friend, I am not a man for trivial anger:
better a sense of measure in everything.
No anger here. I say that if it should please
our father Zeus, Athena, and Apollo—
seeing the man you are, seeing your thoughts
are my own thoughts—my daughter should be yours
and you my son-in-law, if you remained.
A home, lands, riches you should have from me
if you could be contented here. If not,
by Father Zeus, let none of our men hold you!   340
On the contrary, I can assure you now
of passage late tomorrow: while you sleep
my men will row you through the tranquil night
to your own land and home or where you please.
It may be, even, far beyond Euboia—
called most remote by seamen of our isle
who landed there, conveying Rhadamanthos
when he sought Tityos, the son of Gaia.
They put about, with neither pause nor rest,
and entered their home port the selfsame day.   350
But this you, too, will see: what ships I have,
how my young oarsmen send the foam a-scudding!"

Now joy welled up in the patient Lord Odysseus
who said devoutly in the warmest tones:

"O Father Zeus, let all this be fulfilled
as spoken by Alkínoös! Earth of harvests
remember him! Return me to my homeland!"

In this manner they conversed with one another;
but the great lady called her maids, and sent them
to make a kingly bed, with purple rugs   360
piled up, and sheets outspread, and fleecy
coverlets, in an eastern colonnade.
The girls went out with torches in their hands,
swift at their work of bedmaking; returning
they whispered at the lord Odysseus' shoulder:

"Sir, you may come; your bed has been prepared."

How welcome the word "bed" came to his ears!
Now, then, Odysseus laid him down and slept
in luxury under the Porch of Morning,
while in his inner chamber Alkínoös   370
retired to rest where his dear consort lay.

BOOK EIGHT

The Songs of the Harper

LINES 1 – 16

Under the opening fingers of the dawn   1
Alkínoös, the sacred prince, arose,
and then arose Odysseus, raider of cities.
As the king willed, they went down by the shipways
to the assembly ground of the Phaiákians.
Side by side the two men took their ease there
on smooth stone benches. Meanwhile Pallas Athena
roamed through the byways of the town, contriving
Odysseus' voyage home—in voice and feature
the crier of the king Alkínoös   10
who stopped and passed the word to every man:

"Phaiákian lords and counselors, this way!
Come to assembly: learn about the stranger,
the new guest at the palace of Alkínoös—
a man the sea drove, but a comely man;
the gods' own light is on him."

                              She aroused them,
and soon the assembly ground and seats were filled

with curious men, a throng who peered and saw
the master mind of war, Laërtês' son.   20
Athena now poured out her grace upon him,
head and shoulders, height and mass—a splendor
awesome to the eyes of the Phaiákians;
she put him in a fettle to win the day,
mastering every trial they set to test him.
When all the crowd sat marshalled, quieted,
Alkínoös addressed the full assembly:

"Hear me, lords and captains of the Phaiákians!
Hear what my heart would have me say!
Our guest and new friend—nameless to me still—   30
comes to my house after long wandering
in Dawn lands, or among the Sunset races.
Now he appeals to me for conveyance home.
As in the past, therefore, let us provide
passage, and quickly, for no guest of mine
languishes here for lack of it. Look to it:
get a black ship afloat on the noble sea,
and pick our fastest sailer; draft a crew
of two and fifty from our younger townsmen—
men who have made their names at sea. Loop oars   40
well to your tholepins, lads, then leave the ship,
come to our house, fall to, and take your supper:
we'll furnish out a feast for every crewman.
These are your orders. As for my older peers
and princes of the realm, let them foregather
in festival for our friend in my great hall;
and let no man refuse. Call in our minstrel,
Demódokos, whom God made lord of song,
heart-easing, sing upon what theme he will."

He turned, led the procession, and those princes   50
followed, while his herald sought the minstrel.
Young oarsmen from the assembly chose a crew
of two and fifty, as the king commanded,
and these filed off along the waterside
to where the ship lay, poised above open water.
They hauled the black hull down to ride the sea,
rigging a mast and spar in the black ship,

with oars at trail from corded rawhide, all
seamanly; then tried the white sail, hoisting,
and moored her off the beach. Then going ashore   60
the crew went up to the great house of Alkínoös.
Here the enclosures, entrance ways, and rooms
were filled with men, young men and old, for whom
Alkínoös had put twelve sheep to sacrifice,
eight tuskers and a pair of shambling oxen.
These, now, they flayed and dressed to make their banquet.
The crier soon came, leading that man of song
whom the Muse cherished; by her gift he knew
the good of life, and evil—
for she who lent him sweetness made him blind.   70
Pontónoös fixed a studded chair for him
hard by a pillar amid the banqueters,
hanging the taut harp from a peg above him,
and guided up his hands upon the strings;
placed a bread basket at his side, and poured
wine in a cup, that he might drink his fill.
Now each man's hand went out upon the banquet.

In time, when hunger and thirst were turned away,
the Muse brought to the minstrel's mind a song
of heroes whose great fame rang under heaven: 80
the clash between Odysseus and Akhilleus,
how one time they contended at the godfeast
raging, and the marshal, Agamémnon,
felt inward joy over his captains' quarrel;
for such had been foretold him by Apollo
at Pytho—hallowed height—when the Akhaian
crossed that portal of rock to ask a sign—
in the old days when grim war lay ahead
for Trojans and Danaans, by God's will.
So ran the tale the minstrel sang. Odysseus   90
with massive hand drew his rich mantel down
over his brow, cloaking his face with it,
to make the Phaiákians miss the secret tears
that started to his eyes. How skillfully
he dried them when the song came to a pause!
threw back his mantle, spilt his gout of wine!

But soon the minstrel plucked his note once more
to please the Phaiákian lords, who loved the song;
then in his cloak Odysseus wept again.
His tears flowed in the mantle unperceived: 100
only Alkínoös, at his elbow, saw them,
and caught the low groan in the man's breathing.
At once he spoke to all the seafolk round him:

"Hear me, lords and captains of the Phaiákians.
Our meat is shared, our hearts are full of pleasure
from the clear harp tone that accords with feasting;
now for the field and track; we shall have trials
in the pentathlon. Let our guest go home
and tell his friends what champions we are
at boxing, wrestling, broadjump and foot racing."   110

On this he led the way and all went after.
The crier unslung and pegged the shining harp
and, taking Demódokos's hand,
led him along with all the rest—Phaiákian
peers, gay amateurs of the great games.
They gained the common, where a crowd was forming,
and many a young athlete now came forward
with seaside names like Tipmast, Tiderace, Sparwood,
Hullman, Sternman, Beacher and Pullerman,
Bluewater, Shearwater, Runningwake, Boardalee,   120
Seabelt, son of Grandfleet Shipwrightson;
Seareach stepped up, son of the Launching Master,
rugged as Arês, bane of men; his build
excelled all but the Prince Laódamas;
and Laódamas made entry with his brothers,
Halios and Klytóneus, sons of the king.
The runners, first, must have their quarter mile.
All lined up tense; then Go! and down the track
they raised the dust in a flying bunch, strung out
longer and longer behind Prince Klytóneus.   130
By just so far as a mule team, breaking ground,
will distance oxen, he left all behind
and came up to the crowd, an easy winner.
Then they made room for wrestling—grinding bouts
that Seareach won, pinning the strongest men;

then the broadjump; first place went to Seabelt;
Sparwood gave the discus the mightiest fling,
and Prince Laódamas outboxed them all.
Now it was he, the son of Alkínoös,
who said when they had run through these diversions: 140

"Look here, friends, we ought to ask the stranger
if he competes in something. He's no cripple;
look at his leg muscles and his forearms.
Neck like a bollard; strong as a bull, he seems;
and not old, though he may have gone stale under
the rough times he had. Nothing like the sea
for wearing out the toughest man alive."

Then Seareach took him up at once, and said:

"Laódamas, you're right, by all the powers.
Go up to him, yourself, and put the question."   150

At this, Alkínoös' tall son advanced
to the center ground, and there addressed Odysseus:

"Friend, Excellency, come join our competition,
if you are practiced, as you seem to be.
While a man lives he wins no greater honor
than footwork and the skill of hands can bring him.
Enter our games, then; ease your heart of trouble.
Your journey home is not far off, remember;
the ship is launched, the crew all primed for sea."

Odysseus, canniest of men, replied: 160

"Laódamas, why do you young chaps challenge me?
I have more on my mind than track and field—
hard days, and many, have I seen, and suffered.
I sit here at your field meet, yes; but only
as one who begs your king to send him home."

Now Seareach put his word in, and contentiously:

"The reason being, as I see it, friend,
you never learned a sport, and have no skill
in any of the contests of fighting men.

You must have been the skipper of some tramp   170
that crawled from one port to the next, jam full
of chaffering hands: a tallier of cargoes,
itching for gold—not, by your looks, an athlete."

Odysseus frowned, and eyed him coldly, saying:

"That was uncalled for, friend, you talk like a fool.
The gods deal out no gift, this one or any—
birth, brains, or speech—to every man alike.
In looks a man may be a shade, a specter,
and yet be master of speech so crowned with beauty
that people gaze at him with pleasure. Courteous,   180
sure of himself, he can command assemblies,
and when he comes to town, the crowds gather.
A handsome man, contrariwise, may lack
grace and good sense in everything he says.
You now, for instance, with your fine physique—
a god's, indeed—you have an empty noddle.
I find my heart inside my ribs aroused
by your impertinence. I am no stranger
to contests, as you fancy. I rated well
when I could count on youth and my two hands.   190
Now pain has cramped me, and my years of combat
hacking through ranks in war, and the bitter sea.
Aye. Even so I'll give your games a trial.
You spoke heart-wounding words. You shall be answered."

He leapt out, cloaked as he was, and picked a discus,
a rounded stone, more ponderous than those
already used by the Phaiákian throwers,
and, whirling, let it fly from his great hand
with a low hum. The crowd went flat on the ground—
all those oar-pulling, seafaring Phaiákians—   200
under the rushing noise. The spinning disk
soared out, light as a bird, beyond all others.
Disguised now as a Phaiákian, Athena
staked it and called out:

                          "Even a blind man,
friend, could judge this, finding with his fingers
one discus, quite alone, beyond the cluster.

Congratulations; this event is yours;
not a man here can beat you or come near you."

That was a cheering hail, Odysseus thought,   210
seeing one friend there on the emulous field,
so, in relief, he turned among the Phaiákians
and said:

                    "Now come alongside that one, lads.
The next I'll send as far, I think, or farther.
Anyone else on edge for competition
try me now. By heaven, you angered me.
Racing, wrestling, boxing—I bar nothing
with any man except Laódamas,
for he's my host. Who quarrels with his host?   220
Only a madman—or no man at all—
would challenge his protector among strangers,
cutting the ground away under his feet.
Here are no others I will not engage,
none but I hope to know what he is made of.
Inept at combat, am I? Not entirely.
Give me a smooth bow; I can handle it,
and I might well be first to hit my man
amid a swarm of enemies, though archers
in company around me drew together.   230
Philoktêtês alone, at Troy, when we
Akhaians took the bow, used to outshoot me.
Of men who now eat bread upon the earth
I hold myself the best hand with a bow—
conceding mastery to the men of old,
Heraklês, or Eurýtos of Oikhalía,
heroes who vied with gods in bowmanship.
Eurýtos came to grief, it's true; old age
never crept over him in his long hall;
Apollo took his challenge ill, and killed him.   240
What then, the spear? I'll plant it like an arrow.
Only in sprinting, I'm afraid, I may
be passed by someone. Roll of the sea waves
wearied me, and the victuals in my ship
ran low; my legs are flabby."

                When he finished,
the rest were silent, but Alkínoös answered:

"Friend, we take your challenge in good part,
for this man angered and affronted you
here at our peaceful games. You'd have us note   250
the prowess that is in you, and so clearly,
no man of sense would ever cry it down!
Come, turn your mind, now, on a thing to tell
among your peers when you are home again,
dining in hall, beside your wife and children:
I mean our prowess, as you may remember it,
for we, too, have our skills, given by Zeus,
and practiced from our father's time to this—
not in the boxing ring nor the palestra
conspicuous, but in racing, land or sea;   260
and all our days we set great store by feasting,
harpers, and the grace of dancing choirs,
changes of dress, warm baths, and downy beds.
O master dancers of the Phaiákians!
Perform now: let our guest on his return
tell his companions we excel the world
in dance and song, as in our ships and running.
Someone go find the gittern harp in hall
and bring it quickly to Demódokos!"

At the serene king's word, a squire ran   270
to bring the polished harp out of the palace,
and place was given to nine referees—
peers of the realm, masters of ceremony—
who cleared a space and smoothed a dancing floor.
The squire brought down, and gave Demódokos,
the clear-toned harp; and centering on the minstrel
magical young dancers formed a circle
with a light beat, and stamp of feet. Beholding,
Odysseus marvelled at the flashing ring.

Now to his harp the blinded minstrel sang   280
of Arês' dalliance with Aphroditê:
how hidden in Hephaistos' house they played

at love together, and the gifts of Arês,
dishonoring Hephaistos' bed—and how
the word that wounds the heart came to the master
from Hêlios, who had seen the two embrace;
and when he learned it, Lord Hephaistos went
with baleful calculation to his forge.
There mightily he armed his anvil block
and hammered out a chain, whose tempered links   290
could not be sprung or bent; he meant that they should hold.
Those shackles fashioned, hot in wrath Hephaistos
climbed to the bower and the bed of love,
pooled all his net of chain around the bed posts
and swung it from the rafters overhead—
light as a cobweb even gods in bliss
could not perceive, so wonderful his cunning.
Seeing his bed now made a snare, he feigned
a journey to the trim stronghold of Lemnos,
the dearest of earth's towns to him. And Arês?   300
Ah, golden Arês' watch had its reward
when he beheld the great smith leaving home.
How promptly to the famous door he came,
intent on pleasure with sweet Kythereia!
She, who had left her father's side but now,
sat in her chamber when her lover entered;
and tenderly he pressed her hand and said:

"Come and lie down, my darling, and be happy!
Hephaistos is no longer here, but gone
to see his grunting Sintian friends on Lemnos."   310

As she, too, thought repose would be most welcome,
the pair went in to bed—into a shower
of clever chains, the netting of Hephaistos.
So trussed, they could not move apart, nor rise,
at last they knew there could be no escape,
they were to see the glorious cripple now—
for Hêlios had spied for him, and told him;
so he turned back, this side of Lemnos Isle,
sick at heart, making his way homeward.

Now in the doorway of the room he stood   320
while deadly rage took hold of him; his voice,
hoarse and terrible, reached all the gods:

"O Father Zeus, O gods in bliss forever,
here is indecorous entertainment for you,
Aphroditê, Zeus's daughter,
caught in the act, cheating me, her cripple,
with Arês—devastating Arês.
Cleanlimbed beauty is her joy, not these
bandylegs I came into the world with:
no one to blame but the two gods who bred me!   330
Come see this pair entwining here
in my own bed! How hot it makes me burn!
I think they may not care to lie much longer,
pressing on one another, passionate lovers;
they'll have enough of bed together soon.
And yet the chain that bagged them holds them down
till Father sends me back my wedding gifts—
all that I poured out for his damned pigeon,
so lovely, and so wanton."

                    All the others   340
were crowding in, now, to the brazen house—
Poseidon who embraces earth, and Hermês
the runner, and Apollo, lord of Distance.
The goddesses stayed home for shame; but these
munificences ranged there in the doorway,
and irrepressible among them all
arose the laughter of the happy gods.
Gazing hard at Hephaistos' handiwork
the gods in turn remarked among themselves:

"No dash in adultery now."   350

                    "The tortoise tags the hare—
Hephaistos catches Arês—and Arês outran the wind."

"The lame god's craft has pinned him. Now shall he
pay what is due from gods taken in cuckoldry."

They made these improving remarks to one another,
but Apollo leaned aside to say to Hermês:

"Son of Zeus, beneficent Wayfinder,
would you accept a coverlet of chain, if only
you lay by Aphroditê's golden side?"

To this the Wayfinder replied, shining: 360

"Would I not, though, Apollo of distances!
Wrap me in chains three times the weight of these,
come goddesses and gods to see the fun;
only let me lie beside the pale-golden one!"

The gods gave way again to peals of laughter,
all but Poseidon, and he never smiled,
but urged Hephaistos to unpinion Arês,
saying emphatically, in a loud voice:

                              "Free him;
you will be paid, I swear; ask what you will;   370
he pays up every jot the gods decree."

To this the Great Gamelegs replied:

                              "Poseidon,
lord of the earth-surrounding sea, I should not
swear to a scoundrel's honor. What have I
as surety from you, if Arês leaves me
empty-handed, with my empty chain?"

The Earth-shaker for answer urged again:

"Hephaistos, let us grant he goes, and leaves
the fine unpaid; I swear, then, I shall pay it."   380

Then said the Great Gamelegs at last:

                              "No more;
you offer terms I cannot well refuse."

And down the strong god bent to set them free,
till disencumbered of their bond, the chain,

the lovers leapt away—he into Thrace,
while Aphroditê, laughter's darling, fled
to Kypros Isle and Paphos, to her meadow
and altar dim with incense. There the Graces
bathed and anointed her with golden oil—　　　　390
a bloom that clings upon immortal flesh alone—
and let her folds of mantle fall in glory.

So ran the song the minstrel sang.

　　　　　　　　　　　　　　Odysseus,
listening, found sweet pleasure in the tale,
among the Phaiákian mariners and oarsmen.
And next Alkínoös called upon his sons,
Halios and Laódamas, to show
the dance no one could do as well as they—
handling a purple ball carven by Pólybos.　　　　400
One made it shoot up under the shadowing clouds
as he leaned backward; bounding high in air
the other cut its flight far off the ground—
and neither missed a step as the ball soared.
The next turn was to keep it low, and shuttling
hard between them, while the ring of boys
gave them a steady stamping beat.
Odysseus now addressed Alkínoös:

"O majesty, model of all your folk,
your promise was to show me peerless dancers;　　　　410
here is the promise kept. I am all wonder."

At this Alkínoös in his might rejoicing
said to the seafarers of Phaiákia:

"Attend me now, Phaiákian lords and captains:
our guest appears a clear-eyed man and wise.
Come, let him feel our bounty as he should.
Here are twelve princes of the kingdom—lords
paramount, and I who make thirteen;
let each one bring a laundered cloak and tunic,
and add one bar of honorable gold.　　　　420
Heap all our gifts together; load his arms;
let him go joyous to our evening feast!

As for Seareach—why, man to man
he'll make amends, and handsomely; he blundered."

Now all as one acclaimed the king's good pleasure,
and each one sent a squire to bring his gifts.
Meanwhile Seareach found speech again, saying:

"My lord and model of us all, Alkínoös,
as you require of me, in satisfaction,
this broadsword of clear bronze goes to our guest.   430
Its hilt is silver, and the ringed sheath
of new-sawn ivory—a costly weapon."

He turned to give the broadsword to Odysseus,
facing him, saying blithely:

                              "Sir, my best
wishes, my respects; if I offended,
I hope the seawinds blow it out of mind.
God send you see your lady and your homeland
soon again, after the pain of exile."

Odysseus, the great tactician, answered: 440

"My hand, friend; may the gods award you fortune.
I hope no pressing need comes on you ever
for this fine blade you give me in amends."

He slung it, glinting silver, from his shoulder,
as the light shone from sundown. Messengers
were bearing gifts and treasure to the palace,
where the king's sons received them all, and made
a glittering pile at their grave mother's side;
then, as Alkínoös took his throne of power,
each went to his own high-backed chair in turn,   450
and said Alkínoös to Arêtê:

"Lady, bring here a chest, the finest one;
a clean cloak and tunic; stow these things;
and warm a cauldron for him. Let him bathe,
when he has seen the gifts of the Phaiákians,
and so dine happily to a running song.
My own wine-cup of gold intaglio

I'll give him, too; through all the days to come,
tipping his wine to Zeus or other gods
in his great hall, he shall remember me."   460

Then said Arêtê to her maids:

                    "The tripod:
stand the great tripod legs about the fire."

They swung the cauldron on the fire's heart,
poured water in, and fed the blaze beneath
until the basin simmered, cupped in flame.
The queen set out a rich chest from her chamber
and folded in the gifts—clothing and gold
given Odysseus by the Phaiákians;
then she put in the royal cloak and tunic,   470
briskly saying to her guest:

                    "Now here, sir,
look to the lid yourself, and tie it down
against light fingers, if there be any,
on the black ship tonight while you are sleeping."

Noble Odysseus, expert in adversity,
battened the lid down with a lightning knot
learned, once, long ago, from the Lady Kirkê.
And soon a call came from the Bathing Mistress
who led him to a hip-bath, warm and clear—   480
a happy sight, and rare in his immersions
after he left Kalypso's home—where, surely,
the luxuries of a god were ever his.
When the bath maids had washed him, rubbed him down,
put a fresh tunic and a cloak around him,
he left the bathing place to join the men
at wine in hall.

                    The princess Nausikaa,
exquisite figure, as of heaven's shaping,
waited beside a pillar as he passed   490
and said swiftly, with wonder in her look:

"Fare well, stranger; in your land remember me
who met and saved you. It is worth your thought."

The man of all occasions now met this:

"Daughter of great Alkínoös, Nausikaa,
may Zeus the lord of thunder, Hera's consort,
grant me daybreak again in my own country!
But there and all my days until I die
may I invoke you as I would a goddess,
princess, to whom I owe my life."   500

                            He left her
and went to take his place beside the king.

Now when the roasts were cut, the winebowls full,
a herald led the minstrel down the room
amid the deference of the crowd, and paused
to seat him near a pillar in the center—
whereupon that resourceful man, Odysseus,
carved out a quarter from his chine of pork,
crisp with fat, and called the blind man's guide:

"Herald! here, take this to Demódokos: 510
let him feast and be merry, with my compliments.
All men owe honor to the poets—honor
and awe, for they are dearest to the Muse
who puts upon their lips the ways of life."

Gentle Demódokos took the proffered gift
and inwardly rejoiced. When all were served,
every man's hand went out upon the banquet,
repelling hunger and thirst, until at length
Odysseus spoke again to the blind minstrel:

"Demódokos, accept my utmost praise.   520
The Muse, daughter of Zeus in radiance,
or else Apollo gave you skill to shape
with such great style your songs of the Akhaians—
their hard lot, how they fought and suffered war.
You shared it, one would say, or heard it all.

Now shift your theme, and sing that wooden horse
Epeios built, inspired by Athena—
the ambuscade Odysseus filled with fighters
and sent to take the inner town of Troy.
Sing only this for me, sing me this well,   530
and I shall say at once before the world
the grace of heaven has given us a song."

The minstrel stirred, murmuring to the god, and soon
clear words and notes came one by one, a vision
of the Akhaians in their graceful ships
drawing away from shore: the torches flung
and shelters flaring: Argive soldiers crouched
in the close dark around Odysseus: and
the horse, tall on the assembly ground of Troy.
For when the Trojans pulled it in, themselves,   540
up to the citadel, they sat nearby
with long-drawn-out and hapless argument—
favoring, in the end, one course of three:
either to stave the vault with brazen axes,
or haul it to a cliff and pitch it down,
or else to save it for the gods, a votive glory—
the plan that could not but prevail.
For Troy must perish, as ordained, that day
she harbored the great horse of timber; hidden
the flower of Akhaia lay, and bore   550
slaughter and death upon the men of Troy.
He sang, then, of the town sacked by Akhaians
pouring down from the horse's hollow cave,
this way and that way raping the steep city,
and how Odysseus came like Arês to
the door of Deïphobos, with Meneláos,
and braved the desperate fight there—
conquering once more by Athena's power.

The splendid minstrel sang it.

                              And Odysseus   560
let the bright molten tears run down his cheeks,
weeping the way a wife mourns for her lord
on the lost field where he has gone down fighting

the day of wrath that came upon his children.
At sight of the man panting and dying there,
she slips down to enfold him, crying out;
then feels the spears, prodding her back and shoulders,
and goes bound into slavery and grief.
Piteous weeping wears away her cheeks:
but no more piteous than Odysseus' tears,   570
cloaked as they were, now, from the company.
Only Alkínoös, at his elbow, knew—
hearing the low sob in the man's breathing—
and when he knew, he spoke:

"Hear me, lords and captains of Phaiákia!
And let Demódokos touch his harp no more.
His theme has not been pleasing to all here.
During the feast, since our fine poet sang,
our guest has never left off weeping. Grief
seems fixed upon his heart. Break off the song!   580
Let everyone be easy, host and guest;
there's more decorum in a smiling banquet!
We had prepared here, on our friend's behalf,
safe conduct in a ship, and gifts to cheer him,
holding that any man with a grain of wit
will treat a decent suppliant like a brother.
Now by the same rule, friend, you must not be
secretive any longer! Come, in fairness,
tell me the name you bore in that far country;
how were you known to family, and neighbors?   590
No man is nameless—no man, good or bad,
but gets a name in his first infancy,
none being born, unless a mother bears him!
Tell me your native land, your coast and city—
sailing directions for the ships, you know—
for those Phaiákian ships of ours
that have no steersman, and no steering oar,
divining the crew's wishes, as they do,
and knowing, as they do, the ports of call
about the world. Hidden in mist or cloud   600
they scud the open sea, with never a thought
of being in distress or going down.

There is, however, something I once heard
Nausíthoös, my father, say: Poseidon
holds it against us that our deep sea ships
are sure conveyance for all passengers.
My father said, some day one of our cutters
homeward bound over the cloudy sea
would be wrecked by the god, and a range of hills
thrown round our city. So, in his age, he said,   610
and let it be, or not, as the god please.
But come, now, put it for me clearly, tell me
the sea ways that you wandered, and the shores
you touched; the cities, and the men therein,
uncivilized, if such there were, and hostile,
and those godfearing who had kindly manners.
Tell me why you should grieve so terribly
over the Argives and the fall of Troy.
That was all gods' work, weaving ruin there
so it should make a song for men to come!   620
Some kin of yours, then, died at Ilion,
some first rate man, by marriage near to you,
next your own blood most dear?
Or some companion of congenial mind
and valor? True it is, a wise friend
can take a brother's place in our affection."

BOOK NINE

New Coasts and Poseidon's Son

LINES 1 – 17

Now this was the reply Odysseus made: 1

"Alkínoös, king and admiration of men,
how beautiful this is, to hear a minstrel
gifted as yours: a god he might be, singing!
There is no boon in life more sweet, I say,
than when a summer joy holds all the realm,
and banqueters sit listening to a harper
in a great hall, by rows of tables heaped
with bread and roast meat, while a steward goes
to dip up wine and brim your cups again.   10
Here is the flower of life, it seems to me!
But now you wish to know my cause for sorrow—
and thereby give me cause for more.

                       What shall I
say first? What shall I keep until the end?
The gods have tried me in a thousand ways.
But first my name: let that be known to you,

and if I pull away from pitiless death,
friendship will bind us, though my land lies far.

I am Laërtês' son, Odysseus.   20
                   Men hold me
formidable for guile in peace and war:
this fame has gone abroad to the sky's rim.
My home is on the peaked sea-mark of Ithaka
under Mount Neion's wind-blown robe of leaves,
in sight of other islands—Doulíkhion,
Samê, wooded Zakynthos—Ithaka
being most lofty in that coastal sea,
and northwest, while the rest lie east and south.
A rocky isle, but good for a boy's training;   30
I shall not see on earth a place more dear,
though I have been detained long by Kalypso,
loveliest among goddesses, who held me
in her smooth caves, to be her heart's delight,
as Kirkê of Aiaia, the enchantress,
desired me, and detained me in her hall.
But in my heart I never gave consent.
Where shall a man find sweetness to surpass
his own home and his parents? In far lands
he shall not, though he find a house of gold.   40

What of my sailing, then, from Troy?
                      What of those years
of rough adventure, weathered under Zeus?
The wind that carried west from Ilion
brought me to Ísmaros, on the far shore,
a strongpoint on the coast of the Kikonês.
I stormed that place and killed the men who fought.
Plunder we took, and we enslaved the women,
to make division, equal shares to all—
but on the spot I told them: 'Back, and quickly!   50
Out to sea again!' My men were mutinous,
fools, on stores of wine. Sheep after sheep
they butchered by the surf, and shambling cattle,
feasting,—while fugitives went inland, running
to call to arms the main force of Kikonês.

This was an army, trained to fight on horseback
or, where the ground required, on foot. They came
with dawn over that terrain like the leaves
and blades of spring. So doom appeared to us,
dark word of Zeus for us, our evil days.   60
My men stood up and made a fight of it—
backed on the ships, with lances kept in play,
from bright morning through the blaze of noon
holding our beach, although so far outnumbered;
but when the sun passed toward unyoking time,
then the Akhaians, one by one, gave way.
Six benches were left empty in every ship
that evening when we pulled away from death.
And this new grief we bore with us to sea:
our precious lives we had, but not our friends.   70
No ship made sail next day until some shipmate
had raised a cry, three times, for each poor ghost
unfleshed by the Kikonês on that field.

Now Zeus the lord of cloud roused in the north
a storm against the ships, and driving veils
of squall moved down like night on land and sea.
The bows went plunging at the gust; sails
cracked and lashed out strips in the big wind.
We saw death in that fury, dropped the yards,
unshipped the oars, and pulled for the nearest lee: 80
then two long days and nights we lay offshore
worn out and sick at heart, tasting our grief,
until a third Dawn came with ringlets shining.
Then we put up our masts, hauled sail, and rested,
letting the steersmen and the breeze take over.

I might have made it safely home, that time,
but as I came round Malea the current
took me out to sea, and from the north
a fresh gale drove me on, past Kythera.
Nine days I drifted on the teeming sea   90
before dangerous high winds. Upon the tenth
we came to the coastline of the Lotos Eaters,
who live upon that flower. We landed there

to take on water. All ships' companies
mustered alongside for the mid-day meal.
Then I sent out two picked men and a runner
to learn what race of men that land sustained.
They fell in, soon enough, with Lotos Eaters,
who showed no will to do us harm, only
offering the sweet Lotos to our friends—   100
but those who ate this honeyed plant, the Lotos,
never cared to report, nor to return:
they longed to stay forever, browsing on
that native bloom, forgetful of their homeland.
I drove them, all three wailing, to the ships,
tied them down under their rowing benches,
and called the rest: 'All hands aboard;
come, clear the beach and no one taste
the Lotos, or you lose your hope of home.'
Filing in to their places by the rowlocks   110
my oarsmen dipped their long oars in the surf,
and we moved out again on our sea faring.

In the next land we found were Kyklopês,
giants, louts, without a law to bless them.
In ignorance leaving the fruitage of the earth in mystery
to the immortal gods, they neither plow
nor sow by hand, nor till the ground, though grain—
wild wheat and barley—grows untended, and
wine-grapes, in clusters, ripen in heaven's rain.
Kyklopês have no muster and no meeting,   120
no consultation or old tribal ways,
but each one dwells in his own mountain cave
dealing out rough justice to wife and child,
indifferent to what the others do.
                         Well, then:
across the wide bay from the mainland
there lies a desert island, not far out,
but still not close inshore. Wild goats in hundreds
breed there; and no human being comes
upon the isle to startle them—no hunter   130
of all who ever tracked with hounds through forests
or had rough going over mountain trails.

The isle, unplanted and untilled, a wilderness,
pastures goats alone. And this is why:
good ships like ours with cheekpaint at the bows
are far beyond the Kyklopês. No shipwright
toils among them, shaping and building up
symmetrical trim hulls to cross the sea
and visit all the seaboard towns, as men do
who go and come in commerce over water.   140
This isle—seagoing folk would have annexed it
and built their homesteads on it: all good land,
fertile for every crop in season: lush
well-watered meads along the shore, vines in profusion,
prairie, clear for the plow, where grain would grow
chin high by harvest time, and rich sub-soil.
The island cove is landlocked, so you need
no hawsers out astern, bow-stones or mooring:
run in and ride there till the day your crews
chafe to be under sail, and a fair wind blows.   150
You'll find good water flowing from a cavern
through dusky poplars into the upper bay.
Here we made harbor. Some god guided us
that night, for we could barely see our bows
in the dense fog around us, and no moonlight
filtered through the overcast. No look-out,
nobody saw the island dead ahead,
nor even the great landward rolling billow
that took us in: we found ourselves in shallows,
keels grazing shore: so furled our sails   160
and disembarked where the low ripples broke.
There on the beach we lay, and slept till morning.

When Dawn spread out her finger tips of rose
we turned out marvelling, to tour the isle,
while Zeus's shy nymph daughters flushed wild goats
down from the heights—a breakfast for my men.
We ran to fetch our hunting bows and long-shanked
lances from the ships, and in three companies
we took our shots. Heaven gave us game a-plenty:
for every one of twelve ships in my squadron   170
nine goats fell to be shared; my lot was ten.

So there all day, until the sun went down,
we made our feast on meat galore, and wine—
wine from the ship, for our supply held out,
so many jars were filled at Ísmaros
from stores of the Kikonês that we plundered.
We gazed, too, at Kyklopês Land, so near,
we saw their smoke, heard bleating from their flocks.
But after sundown, in the gathering dusk,
we slept again above the wash of ripples.   180

When the young Dawn with finger tips of rose
came in the east, I called my men together
and made a speech to them:

                    'Old shipmates, friends,
the rest of you stand by; I'll make the crossing
in my own ship, with my own company,
and find out what the mainland natives are—
for they may be wild savages, and lawless,
or hospitable and god fearing men.'

At this I went aboard, and gave the word   190
to cast off by the stern. My oarsmen followed,
filing in to their benches by the rowlocks,
and all in line dipped oars in the grey sea.

As we rowed on, and nearer to the mainland,
at one end of the bay, we saw a cavern
yawning above the water, screened with laurel,
and many rams and goats about the place
inside a sheepfold—made from slabs of stone
earthfast between tall trunks of pine and rugged
towering oak trees.   200
                    A prodigious man
slept in this cave alone, and took his flocks
to graze afield—remote from all companions,
knowing none but savage ways, a brute
so huge, he seemed no man at all of those
who eat good wheaten bread; but he seemed rather
a shaggy mountain reared in solitude.
We beached there, and I told the crew

to stand by and keep watch over the ship;
as for myself I took my twelve best fighters   210
and went ahead. I had a goatskin full
of that sweet liquor that Euanthês' son,
Maron, had given me. He kept Apollo's
holy grove at Ísmaros; for kindness
we showed him there, and showed his wife and child,
he gave me seven shining golden talents
perfectly formed, a solid silver winebowl,
and then this liquor—twelve two-handled jars
of brandy, pure and fiery. Not a slave
in Maron's household knew this drink; only   220
he, his wife and the storeroom mistress knew;
and they would put one cupful—ruby-colored,
honey-smooth—in twenty more of water,
but still the sweet scent hovered like a fume
over the winebowl. No man turned away
when cups of this came round.
                              A wineskin full
I brought along, and victuals in a bag,
for in my bones I knew some towering brute
would be upon us soon—all outward power,   230
a wild man, ignorant of civility.

We climbed, then, briskly to the cave. But Kyklops
had gone afield, to pasture his fat sheep,
so we looked round at everything inside:
a drying rack that sagged with cheeses, pens
crowded with lambs and kids, each in its class:
firstlings apart from middlings, and the 'dewdrops,'
or newborn lambkins, penned apart from both.
And vessels full of whey were brimming there—
bowls of earthenware and pails for milking.   240
My men came pressing round me, pleading:

                              'Why not
take these cheeses, get them stowed, come back,
throw open all the pens, and make a run for it?
We'll drive the kids and lambs aboard. We say
put out again on good salt water!'

                         Ah,
how sound that was! Yet I refused. I wished
to see the caveman, what he had to offer—
no pretty sight, it turned out, for my friends.   250

We lit a fire, burnt an offering,
and took some cheese to eat; then sat in silence
around the embers, waiting. When he came
he had a load of dry boughs on his shoulder
to stoke his fire at suppertime. He dumped it
with a great crash into that hollow cave,
and we all scattered fast to the far wall.
Then over the broad cavern floor he ushered
the ewes he meant to milk. He left his rams
and he-goats in the yard outside, and swung   260
high overhead a slab of solid rock
to close the cave. Two dozen four-wheeled wagons,
with heaving wagon teams, could not have stirred
the tonnage of that rock from where he wedged it
over the doorsill. Next he took his seat
and milked his bleating ewes. A practiced job
he made of it, giving each ewe her suckling;
thickened his milk, then, into curds and whey,
sieved out the curds to drip in withy baskets,
and poured the whey to stand in bowls   270
cooling until he drank it for his supper.
When all these chores were done, he poked the fire,
heaping on brushwood. In the glare he saw us.

'Strangers,' he said, 'who are you? And where from?
What brings you here by sea ways—a fair traffic?
Or are you wandering rogues, who cast your lives
like dice, and ravage other folk by sea?'

We felt a pressure on our hearts, in dread
of that deep rumble and that mighty man.
But all the same I spoke up in reply: 280

'We are from Troy, Akhaians, blown off course
by shifting gales on the Great South Sea;
homeward bound, but taking routes and ways

uncommon; so the will of Zeus would have it.
We served under Agamémnon, son of Atreus—
the whole world knows what city
he laid waste, what armies he destroyed.
It was our luck to come here; here we stand,
beholden for your help, or any gifts
you give—as custom is to honor strangers.   290
We would entreat you, great Sir, have a care
for the gods' courtesy; Zeus will avenge
the unoffending guest.'

                            He answered this
from his brute chest, unmoved:

                            'You are a ninny,
or else you come from the other end of nowhere,
telling me, mind the gods! We Kyklopês
care not a whistle for your thundering Zeus
or all the gods in bliss; we have more force by far.   300
I would not let you go for fear of Zeus—
you or your friends—unless I had a whim to.
Tell me, where was it, now, you left your ship—
around the point, or down the shore, I wonder?'

He thought he'd find out, but I saw through this,
and answered with a ready lie:

                            'My ship?
Poseidon Lord, who sets the earth a-tremble,
broke it up on the rocks at your land's end.
A wind from seaward served him, drove us there.   310
We are survivors, these good men and I.'

Neither reply nor pity came from him,
but in one stride he clutched at my companions
and caught two in his hands like squirming puppies
to beat their brains out, spattering the floor.
Then he dismembered them and made his meal,
gaping and crunching like a mountain lion—
everything: innards, flesh, and marrow bones.
We cried aloud, lifting our hands to Zeus,
powerless, looking on at this, appalled;   320

but Kyklops went on filling up his belly
with manflesh and great gulps of whey,
then lay down like a mast among his sheep.
My heart beat high now at the chance of action,
and drawing the sharp sword from my hip I went
along his flank to stab him where the midriff
holds the liver. I had touched the spot
when sudden fear stayed me: if I killed him
we perished there as well, for we could never
move his ponderous doorway slab aside.   330
So we were left to groan and wait for morning.

When the young Dawn with finger tips of rose
lit up the world, the Kyklops built a fire
and milked his handsome ewes, all in due order,
putting the sucklings to the mothers. Then,
his chores being all dispatched, he caught
another brace of men to make his breakfast,
and whisked away his great door slab
to let his sheep go through—but he, behind,
reset the stone as one would cap a quiver.   340
There was a din of whistling as the Kyklops
rounded his flock to higher ground, then stillness.
And now I pondered how to hurt him worst,
if but Athena granted what I prayed for.
Here are the means I thought would serve my turn:

a club, or staff, lay there along the fold—
an olive tree, felled green and left to season
for Kyklops' hand. And it was like a mast
a lugger of twenty oars, broad in the beam—
a deep-sea-going craft—might carry: 350
so long, so big around, it seemed. Now I
chopped out a six foot section of this pole
and set it down before my men, who scraped it;
and when they had it smooth, I hewed again
to make a stake with pointed end. I held this
in the fire's heart and turned it, toughening it,
then hid it, well back in the cavern, under
one of the dung piles in profusion there.

Now came the time to toss for it: who ventured
along with me? whose hand could bear to thrust   360
and grind that spike in Kyklops' eye, when mild
sleep had mastered him? As luck would have it,
the men I would have chosen won the toss—
four strong men, and I made five as captain.

At evening came the shepherd with his flock,
his woolly flock. The rams as well, this time,
entered the cave: by some sheep-herding whim—
or a god's bidding—none were left outside.
He hefted his great boulder into place
and sat him down to milk the bleating ewes   370
in proper order, put the lambs to suck,
and swiftly ran through all his evening chores.
Then he caught two more men and feasted on them.
My moment was at hand, and I went forward
holding an ivy bowl of my dark drink,
looking up, saying:

                   'Kyklops, try some wine.
Here's liquor to wash down your scraps of men.
Taste it, and see the kind of drink we carried
under our planks. I meant it for an offering   380
if you would help us home. But you are mad,
unbearable, a bloody monster! After this,
will any other traveller come to see you?'

He seized and drained the bowl, and it went down
so fiery and smooth he called for more:

'Give me another, thank you kindly. Tell me,
how are you called? I'll make a gift will please you.
Even Kyklopês know the wine-grapes grow
out of grassland and loam in heaven's rain,
but here's a bit of nectar and ambrosia!'   390

Three bowls I brought him, and he poured them down.
I saw the fuddle and flush come over him,
then I sang out in cordial tones:

'Kyklops,
you ask my honorable name? Remember
the gift you promised me, and I shall tell you.
My name is Nohbdy: mother, father, and friends,
everyone calls me Nohbdy.'

                    And he said:

'Nohbdy's my meat, then, after I eat his friends.   400
Others come first. There's a noble gift, now.'

Even as he spoke, he reeled and tumbled backward,
his great head lolling to one side; and sleep
took him like any creature. Drunk, hiccuping,
he dribbled streams of liquor and bits of men.

Now, by the gods, I drove my big hand spike
deep in the embers, charring it again,
and cheered my men along with battle talk
to keep their courage up: no quitting now.
The pike of olive, green though it had been,   410
reddened and glowed as if about to catch.
I drew it from the coals and my four fellows
gave me a hand, lugging it near the Kyklops
as more than natural force nerved them; straight
forward they sprinted, lifted it, and rammed it
deep in his crater eye, and I leaned on it
turning it as a shipwright turns a drill
in planking, having men below to swing
the two-handled strap that spins it in the groove.
So with our brand we bored that great eye socket   420
while blood ran out around the red hot bar.
Eyelid and lash were seared; the pierced ball
hissed broiling, and the roots popped.

                    In a smithy
one sees a white-hot axehead or an adze
plunged and wrung in a cold tub, screeching steam—
the way they make soft iron hale and hard—:
just so that eyeball hissed around the spike.
The Kyklops bellowed and the rock roared round him,

and we fell back in fear. Clawing his face   430
he tugged the bloody spike out of his eye,
threw it away, and his wild hands went groping;
then he set up a howl for Kyklopês
who lived in caves on windy peaks nearby.
Some heard him; and they came by divers ways
to clump around outside and call:

        'What ails you,
Polyphêmos? Why do you cry so sore
in the starry night? You will not let us sleep.
Sure no man's driving off your flock? No man   440
has tricked you, ruined you?'

       Out of the cave
the mammoth Polyphêmos roared in answer:

'Nohbdy, Nohbdy's tricked me, Nohbdy's ruined me!'

To this rough shout they made a sage reply:

'Ah well, if nobody has played you foul
there in your lonely bed, we are no use in pain
given by great Zeus. Let it be your father,
Poseidon Lord, to whom you pray.'

       So saying   450
they trailed away. And I was filled with laughter
to see how like a charm the name deceived them.
Now Kyklops, wheezing as the pain came on him,
fumbled to wrench away the great doorstone
and squatted in the breach with arms thrown wide
for any silly beast or man who bolted—
hoping somehow I might be such a fool.
But I kept thinking how to win the game:
death sat there huge; how could we slip away?
I drew on all my wits, and ran through tactics,   460
reasoning as a man will for dear life,
until a trick came—and it pleased me well.
The Kyklops' rams were handsome, fat, with heavy
fleeces, a dark violet.

                                    Three abreast
I tied them silently together, twining
cords of willow from the ogre's bed;
then slung a man under each middle one
to ride there safely, shielded left and right.
So three sheep could convey each man. I took   470
the woolliest ram, the choicest of the flock,
and hung myself under his kinky belly,
pulled up tight, with fingers twisted deep
in sheepskin ringlets for an iron grip.
So, breathing hard, we waited until morning.

When Dawn spread out her finger tips of rose
the rams began to stir, moving for pasture,
and peals of bleating echoed round the pens
where dams with udders full called for a milking.
Blinded, and sick with pain from his head wound,   480
the master stroked each ram, then let it pass,
but my men riding on the pectoral fleece
the giant's blind hands blundering never found.
Last of them all my ram, the leader, came,
weighted by wool and me with my meditations.
The Kyklops patted him, and then he said:

'Sweet cousin ram, why lag behind the rest
in the night cave? You never linger so,
but graze before them all, and go afar
to crop sweet grass, and take your stately way   490
leading along the streams, until at evening
you run to be the first one in the fold.
Why, now, so far behind? Can you be grieving
over your Master's eye? That carrion rogue
and his accurst companions burnt it out
when he had conquered all my wits with wine.
Nohbdy will not get out alive, I swear.
Oh, had you brain and voice to tell
where he may be now, dodging all my fury!
Bashed by this hand and bashed on this rock wall   500
his brains would strew the floor, and I should have
rest from the outrage Nohbdy worked upon me.'

He sent us into the open, then. Close by,
I dropped and rolled clear of the ram's belly,
going this way and that to untie the men.
With many glances back, we rounded up
his fat, stiff-legged sheep to take aboard,
and drove them down to where the good ship lay.
We saw, as we came near, our fellows' faces
shining; then we saw them turn to grief   510
tallying those who had not fled from death.
I hushed them, jerking head and eyebrows up,
and in a low voice told them: 'Load this herd;
move fast, and put the ship's head toward the breakers.'
They all pitched in at loading, then embarked
and struck their oars into the sea. Far out,
as far off shore as shouted words would carry,
I sent a few back to the adversary:

'O Kyklops! Would you feast on my companions?
Puny, am I, in a Caveman's hands?   520
How do you like the beating that we gave you,
you damned cannibal? Eater of guests
under your roof! Zeus and the gods have paid you!'

The blind thing in his doubled fury broke
a hilltop in his hands and heaved it after us.
Ahead of our black prow it struck and sank
whelmed in a spuming geyser, a giant wave
that washed the ship stern foremost back to shore.
I got the longest boathook out and stood
fending us off, with furious nods to all   530
to put their backs into a racing stroke—
row, row, or perish. So the long oars bent
kicking the foam sternward, making head
until we drew away, and twice as far.
Now when I cupped my hands I heard the crew
in low voices protesting:

                                    'Godsake, Captain!
Why bait the beast again? Let him alone!'

'That tidal wave he made on the first throw
all but beached us.'   540

                    'All but stove us in!'

'Give him our bearing with your trumpeting,
he'll get the range and lob a boulder.'

                    'Aye
He'll smash our timbers and our heads together!'

I would not heed them in my glorying spirit,
but let my anger flare and yelled:

                 'Kyklops,
if ever mortal man inquire
how you were put to shame and blinded, tell him   550
Odysseus, raider of cities, took your eye:
Laërtês' son, whose home's on Ithaka!'

At this he gave a mighty sob and rumbled:

'Now comes the weird upon me, spoken of old.
A wizard, grand and wondrous, lived here—Télemos,
a son of Eurymos; great length of days
he had in wizardry among the Kyklopês,
and these things he foretold for time to come:
my great eye lost, and at Odysseus' hands.
Always I had in mind some giant, armed   560
in giant force, would come against me here.
But this, but you—small, pitiful and twiggy—
you put me down with wine, you blinded me.
Come back, Odysseus, and I'll treat you well,
praying the god of earthquake to befriend you—
his son I am, for he by his avowal
fathered me, and, if he will, he may
heal me of this black wound—he and no other
of all the happy gods or mortal men.'

Few words I shouted in reply to him: 570

'If I could take your life I would and take
your time away, and hurl you down to hell!
The god of earthquake could not heal you there!'

At this he stretched his hands out in his darkness
toward the sky of stars, and prayed Poseidon:

'O hear me, lord, blue girdler of the islands,
if I am thine indeed, and thou art father:
grant that Odysseus, raider of cities, never
see his home: Laërtês' son, I mean,
who kept his hall on Ithaka. Should destiny   580
intend that he shall see his roof again
among his family in his father land,
far be that day, and dark the years between.
Let him lose all companions, and return
under strange sail to bitter days at home.'

In these words he prayed, and the god heard him.
Now he laid hands upon a bigger stone
and wheeled around, titanic for the cast,
to let it fly in the black-prowed vessel's track.
But it fell short, just aft the steering oar,   590
and whelming seas rose giant above the stone
to bear us onward toward the island.
                                        There
as we ran in we saw the squadron waiting,
the trim ships drawn up side by side, and all
our troubled friends who waited, looking seaward.
We beached her, grinding keel in the soft sand,
and waded in, ourselves, on the sandy beach.
Then we unloaded all the Kyklops' flock
to make division, share and share alike,   600
only my fighters voted that my ram,
the prize of all, should go to me. I slew him
by the sea side and burnt his long thighbones
to Zeus beyond the stormcloud, Kronos' son,
who rules the world. But Zeus disdained my offering;
destruction for my ships he had in store
and death for those who sailed them, my companions.

Now all day long until the sun went down
we made our feast on mutton and sweet wine,
till after sunset in the gathering dark   610
we went to sleep above the wash of ripples.

When the young Dawn with finger tips of rose
touched the world, I roused the men, gave orders
to man the ships, cast off the mooring lines;
and filing in to sit beside the rowlocks
oarsmen in line dipped oars in the grey sea.
So we moved out, sad in the vast offing,
having our precious lives, but not our friends.

BOOK TEN

The Grace of the Witch

LINES 1 – 17

We made our landfall on Aiolia Island,   1
domain of Aiolos Hippotadês,
the wind king, dear to the gods who never die—
an isle adrift upon the sea, ringed round
with brazen ramparts on a sheer cliffside.
Twelve children had old Aiolos at home—
six daughters and six lusty sons—and he
gave girls to boys to be their gentle brides;
now those lords, in their parents' company,
sup every day in hall—a royal feast   10
with fumes of sacrifice and winds that pipe
'round hollow courts; and all the night they sleep
on beds of filigree beside their ladies.
Here we put in, lodged in the town and palace,
while Aiolos played host to me. He kept me
one full month to hear the tale of Troy,
the ships and the return of the Akhaians,
all which I told him point by point in order.
When in return I asked his leave to sail

and asked provisioning, he stinted nothing,   20
adding a bull's hide sewn from neck to tail
into a mighty bag, bottling storm winds;
for Zeus had long ago made Aiolos
warden of winds, to rouse or calm at will.
He wedged this bag under my afterdeck,
lashing the neck with shining silver wire
so not a breath got through; only the west wind
he lofted for me in a quartering breeze
to take my squadron spanking home.
                              No luck: 30
the fair wind failed us when our prudence failed.

Nine days and nights we sailed without event,
till on the tenth we raised our land. We neared it,
and saw men building fires along the shore;
but now, being weary to the bone, I fell
into deep slumber; I had worked the sheet
nine days alone, and given it to no one,
wishing to spill no wind on the homeward run.
But while I slept, the crew began to parley:
silver and gold, they guessed, were in that bag   40
bestowed on me by Aiolos' great heart;
and one would glance at his benchmate and say:

'It never fails. He's welcome everywhere:
hail to the captain when he goes ashore!
He brought along so many presents, plunder
out of Troy, that's it. How about ourselves—
his shipmates all the way? Nigh home we are
with empty hands. And who has gifts from Aiolos?
He has. I say we ought to crack that bag,
there's gold and silver, plenty, in that bag!'   50

Temptation had its way with my companions,
and they untied the bag.
                         Then every wind
roared into hurricane; the ships went pitching
west with many cries; our land was lost.
Roused up, despairing in that gloom, I thought:
'Should I go overside for a quick finish

or clench my teeth and stay among the living?"
Down in the bilge I lay, pulling my sea cloak
over my head, while the rough gale blew the ships   60
and rueful crews clear back to Aiolia.

We put ashore for water; then all hands
gathered alongside for a mid-day meal.
When we had taken bread and drink, I picked
one soldier, and one herald, to go with me
and called again on Aiolos. I found him
at meat with his young princes and his lady,
but there beside the pillars, in his portico,
we sat down silent at the open door.
The sight amazed them, and they all exclaimed: 70

'Why back again, Odysseus?'

                         'What sea fiend
rose in your path?'

                         'Did we not launch you well
for home, or for whatever land you chose?'

Out of my melancholy I replied:

'Mischief aboard and nodding at the tiller—
a damned drowse—did for me. Make good my loss,
dear friends! You have the power!'

                         Gently I pleaded,   80
but they turned cold and still. Said Father Aiolos:

'Take yourself out of this island, creeping thing—
no law, no wisdom, lays it on me now
to help a man the blessed gods detest—
out! Your voyage here was cursed by heaven!'

He drove me from the place, groan as I would,
and comfortless we went again to sea,
days of it, till the men flagged at the oars—
no breeze, no help in sight, by our own folly—
six indistinguishable nights and days   90
before we raised the Laistrygonian height
and far stronghold of Lamos. In that land
the daybreak follows dusk, and so the shepherd

homing calls to the cowherd setting out;
and he who never slept could earn two wages,
tending oxen, pasturing silvery flocks,
where the low night path of the sun is near
the sun's path by day. Here, then, we found
a curious bay with mountain walls of stone
to left and right, and reaching far inland,—   100
a narrow entrance opening from the sea
where cliffs converged as though to touch and close.
All of my squadron sheltered here, inside
the cavern of this bay.

              Black prow by prow
those hulls were made fast in a limpid calm
without a ripple, stillness all around them.
My own black ship I chose to moor alone
on the sea side, using a rock for bollard;
and climbed a rocky point to get my bearings.   110
No farms, no cultivated land appeared,
but puffs of smoke rose in the wilderness;
so I sent out two picked men and a herald
to learn what race of men this land sustained.

My party found a track—a wagon road
for bringing wood down from the heights to town;
and near the settlement they met a daughter
of Antiphatês the Laistrygon—a stalwart
young girl taking her pail to Artakía,
the fountain where these people go for water.   120
My fellows hailed her, put their questions to her:
who might the king be? ruling over whom?
She waved her hand, showing her father's lodge,
so they approached it. In its gloom they saw
a woman like a mountain crag, the queen—
and loathed the sight of her. But she, for greeting,
called from the meeting ground her lord and master,
Antiphatês, who came to drink their blood.
He seized one man and tore him on the spot,
making a meal of him; the other two   130
leaped out of doors and ran to join the ships.
Behind, he raised the whole tribe howling, countless

Laistrygonês—and more than men they seemed,
gigantic when they gathered on the sky line
to shoot great boulders down from slings; and hell's own
crashing rose, and crying from the ships,
as planks and men were smashed to bits—poor gobbets
the wildmen speared like fish and bore away.
But long before it ended in the anchorage—
havoc and slaughter—I had drawn my sword   140
and cut my own ship's cable. 'Men,' I shouted,
'man the oars and pull till your hearts break
if you would put this butchery behind!'
The oarsmen rent the sea in mortal fear
and my ship spurted out of range, far out
from that deep canyon where the rest were lost.
So we fared onward, and death fell behind,
and we took breath to grieve for our companions.

Our next landfall was on Aiaia, island
of Kirkê, dire beauty and divine,   150
sister of baleful Aiêtês, like him
fathered by Hêlios the light of mortals
on Persê, child of the Ocean stream.
                              We came
washed in our silent ship upon her shore,
and found a cove, a haven for the ship—
some god, invisible, conned us in. We landed,
to lie down in that place two days and nights,
worn out and sick at heart, tasting our grief.
But when Dawn set another day a-shining   160
I took my spear and broadsword, and I climbed
a rocky point above the ship, for sight
or sound of human labor. Gazing out
from that high place over a land of thicket,
oaks and wide watercourses, I could see
a smoke wisp from the woodland hall of Kirkê.
So I took counsel with myself: should I
go inland scouting out that reddish smoke?
No: better not, I thought, but first return
to waterside and ship, and give the men   170
breakfast before I sent them to explore.

Now as I went down quite alone, and came
a bowshot from the ship, some god's compassion
set a big buck in motion to cross my path—
a stag with noble antlers, pacing down
from pasture in the woods to the riverside,
as long thirst and the power of sun constrained him.
He started from the bush and wheeled: I hit him
square in the spine midway along his back
and the bronze point broke through it. In the dust   180
he fell and whinnied as life bled away.
I set one foot against him, pulling hard
to wrench my weapon from the wound, then left it,
butt-end on the ground. I plucked some withies
and twined a double strand into a rope—
enough to tie the hocks of my huge trophy;
then pickaback I lugged him to the ship,
leaning on my long spearshaft; I could not
haul that mighty carcass on one shoulder.
Beside the ship I let him drop, and spoke   190
gently and low to each man standing near:

'Come, friends, though hard beset, we'll not go down
into the House of Death before our time.
As long as food and drink remain aboard
let us rely on it, not die of hunger.'

At this those faces, cloaked in desolation
upon the waste sea beach, were bared;
their eyes turned toward me and the mighty trophy,
lighting, foreseeing pleasure, one by one.
So hands were washed to take what heaven sent us.   200
And all that day until the sun went down
we had our fill of venison and wine,
till after sunset in the gathering dusk
we slept at last above the line of breakers.
When the young Dawn with finger tips of rose
made heaven bright, I called them round and said:

'Shipmates, companions in disastrous time,
O my dear friends, where Dawn lies, and the West,
and where the great Sun, light of men, may go
under the earth by night, and where he rises—   210

of these things we know nothing. Do we know
any least thing to serve us now? I wonder.
All that I saw when I went up the rock
was one more island in the boundless main,
a low landscape, covered with woods and scrub,
and puffs of smoke ascending in mid-forest.'

They were all silent, but their hearts contracted,
remembering Antiphatês the Laistrygon
and that prodigious cannibal, the Kyklops.
They cried out, and the salt tears wet their eyes.   220
But seeing our time for action lost in weeping,
I mustered those Akhaians under arms,
counting them off in two platoons, myself
and my godlike Eurýlokhos commanding.
We shook lots in a soldier's dogskin cap
and his came bounding out—valiant Eurýlokhos!—
So off he went, with twenty-two companions
weeping, as mine wept, too, who stayed behind.

In the wild wood they found an open glade,
around a smooth stone house—the hall of Kirkê—   230
and wolves and mountain lions lay there, mild
in her soft spell, fed on her drug of evil.
None would attack—oh, it was strange, I tell you—
but switching their long tails they faced our men
like hounds, who look up when their master comes
with tidbits for them—as he will—from table.
Humbly those wolves and lions with mighty paws
fawned on our men—who met their yellow eyes
and feared them.

              In the entrance way they stayed   240
to listen there: inside her quiet house
they heard the goddess Kirkê.

              Low she sang
in her beguiling voice, while on her loom
she wove ambrosial fabric sheer and bright,
by that craft known to the goddesses of heaven.

No one would speak, until Politês—most
faithful and likable of my officers, said:

'Dear friends, no need for stealth: here's a young weaver
singing a pretty song to set the air   250
a-tingle on these lawns and paven courts.
Goddess she is, or lady. Shall we greet her?'

So reassured, they all cried out together,
and she came swiftly to the shining doors
to call them in. All but Eurýlokhos—
who feared a snare—the innocents went after her.
On thrones she seated them, and lounging chairs,
while she prepared a meal of cheese and barley
and amber honey mixed with Pramnian wine,
adding her own vile pinch, to make them lose   260
desire or thought of our dear father land.
Scarce had they drunk when she flew after them
with her long stick and shut them in a pigsty—
bodies, voices, heads, and bristles, all
swinish now, though minds were still unchanged.
So, squealing, in they went. And Kirkê tossed them
acorns, mast, and cornel berries—fodder
for hogs who rut and slumber on the earth.

Down to the ship Eurýlokhos came running
to cry alarm, foul magic doomed his men!   270
But working with dry lips to speak a word
he could not, being so shaken; blinding tears
welled in his eyes; foreboding filled his heart.
When we were frantic questioning him, at last
we heard the tale: our friends were gone. Said he:

'We went up through the oak scrub where you sent us,
Odysseus, glory of commanders,
until we found a palace in a glade,
a marble house on open ground, and someone
singing before her loom a chill, sweet song—   280
goddess or girl, we could not tell. They hailed her,
and then she stepped through shining doors and said,
"Come, come in!" Like sheep they followed her,
but I saw cruel deceit, and stayed behind.
Then all our fellows vanished. Not a sound,
and nothing stirred, although I watched for hours.'

When I heard this I slung my silver-hilted
broadsword on, and shouldered my long bow,
and said, 'Come, take me back the way you came.'
But he put both his hands around my knees   290
in desperate woe, and said in supplication:

'Not back there, O my lord! Oh, leave me here!
You, even you, cannot return, I know it,
I know you cannot bring away our shipmates;
better make sail with these men, quickly too,
and save ourselves from horror while we may.'

But I replied:

                        'By heaven, Eurýlokhos,
rest here then; take food and wine;
stay in the black hull's shelter. Let me go,   300
as I see nothing for it but to go.'

I turned and left him, left the shore and ship,
and went up through the woodland hushed and shady
to find the subtle witch in her long hall.
But Hermês met me, with his golden wand,
barring the way—a boy whose lip was downy
in the first bloom of manhood, so he seemed.
He took my hand and spoke as though he knew me:

    'Why take the inland path alone,
    poor seafarer, by hill and dale   310
    upon this island all unknown?
    Your friends are locked in Kirkê's pale;
    All are become like swine to see;
    and if you go to set them free
    you go to stay, and never more make sail
    for your old home upon Thaki.

    But I can tell you what to do
    to come unchanged from Kirkê's power
    and disenthrall your fighting crew:
    take with you to her bower   320
    as amulet, this plant I know—

it will defeat her horrid show,
so pure and potent is the flower;
no mortal herb was ever so.

Your cup with numbing drops of night
and evil, stilled of all remorse,
she will infuse to charm your sight;
but this great herb with holy force
will keep your mind and senses clear:
when she turns cruel, coming near   330
with her long stick to whip you out of doors,
then let your cutting blade appear,

Let instant death upon it shine,
and she will cower and yield her bed—
a pleasure you must not decline,
so may her lust and fear bestead
you and your friends, and break her spell;
but make her swear by heaven and hell
no witches' tricks, or else, your harness shed,
you'll be unmanned by her as well.'   340

He bent down glittering for the magic plant
and pulled it up, black root and milky flower—
a *molu* in the language of the gods—
fatigue and pain for mortals to uproot;
but gods do this, and everything, with ease.

Then toward Olympos through the island trees
Hermês departed, and I sought out Kirkê,
my heart high with excitement, beating hard.
Before her mansion in the porch I stood
to call her, all being still. Quick as a cat   350
she opened her bright doors and sighed a welcome;
then I strode after her with heavy heart
down the long hall, and took the chair she gave me,
silver-studded, intricately carved,
made with a low footrest. The lady Kirkê
mixed me a golden cup of honeyed wine,
adding in mischief her unholy drug.

I drank, and the drink failed. But she came forward
aiming a stroke with her long stick, and whispered:

'Down in the sty and snore among the rest!'   360

Without a word, I drew my sharpened sword
and in one bound held it against her throat.
She cried out, then slid under to take my knees,
catching her breath to say, in her distress:

'What champion, of what country, can you be?
Where are your kinsmen and your city?
Are you not sluggish with my wine? Ah, wonder!
Never a mortal man that drank this cup
but when it passed his lips he had succumbed.
Hale must your heart be and your tempered will.   370
Odysseus then you are, O great contender,
of whom the glittering god with golden wand
spoke to me ever, and foretold
the black swift ship would carry you from Troy.
Put up your weapon in the sheath. We two
shall mingle and make love upon our bed.
So mutual trust may come of play and love.'

To this I said:

                              'Kirkê, am I a boy,
that you should make me soft and doting now?   380
Here in this house you turned my men to swine;
now it is I myself you hold, enticing
into your chamber, to your dangerous bed,
to take my manhood when you have me stripped.
I mount no bed of love with you upon it.
Or swear me first a great oath, if I do,
you'll work no more enchantment to my harm.'

She swore at once, outright, as I demanded,
and after she had sworn, and bound herself,
I entered Kirkê's flawless bed of love.   390

Presently in the hall her maids were busy,
the nymphs who waited upon Kirkê: four,

whose cradles were in fountains, under boughs,
or in the glassy seaward-gliding streams.
One came with richly colored rugs to throw
on seat and chairback, over linen covers;
a second pulled the tables out, all silver,
and loaded them with baskets all of gold;
a third mixed wine as tawny-mild as honey
in a bright bowl, and set out golden cups.   400
The fourth came bearing water, and lit a blaze
under a cauldron. By and by it bubbled,
and when the dazzling brazen vessel seethed
she filled a bathtub to my waist, and bathed me,
pouring a soothing blend on head and shoulders,
warming the soreness of my joints away.
When she had done, and smoothed me with sweet oil,
she put a tunic and a cloak around me
and took me to a silver-studded chair
with footrest, all elaborately carven.   410
Now came a maid to tip a golden jug
of water into a silver finger bowl,
and draw a polished table to my side.
The larder mistress brought her tray of loaves
with many savory slices, and she gave
the best, to tempt me. But no pleasure came;
I huddled with my mind elsewhere, oppressed.

Kirkê regarded me, as there I sat
disconsolate, and never touched a crust.
Then she stood over me and chided me: 420

'Why sit at table mute, Odysseus?
Are you mistrustful of my bread and drink?
Can it be treachery that you fear again,
after the gods' great oath I swore for you?'

I turned to her at once, and said:

                              'Kirkê,
where is the captain who could bear to touch
this banquet, in my place? A decent man
would see his company before him first.

Put heart in me to eat and drink—you may,   430
by freeing my companions. I must see them.'

But Kirkê had already turned away.
Her long staff in her hand, she left the hall
and opened up the sty. I saw her enter,
driving those men turned swine to stand before me.
She stroked them, each in turn, with some new chrism;
and then, behold! their bristles fell away,
the coarse pelt grown upon them by her drug
melted away, and they were men again,
younger, more handsome, taller than before.   440
Their eyes upon me, each one took my hands,
and wild regret and longing pierced them through,
so the room rang with sobs, and even Kirkê
pitied that transformation. Exquisite
the goddess looked as she stood near me, saying:

'Son of Laërtês and the gods of old,
Odysseus, master mariner and soldier,
go to the sea beach and sea-breasting ship;
drag it ashore, full length upon the land;
stow gear and stores in rock-holes under cover;   450
return; be quick; bring all your dear companions.'

Now, being a man, I could not help consenting.
So I went down to the sea beach and the ship,
where I found all my other men on board,
weeping, in despair along the benches.
Sometimes in farmyards when the cows return
well fed from pasture to the barn, one sees
the pens give way before the calves in tumult,
breaking through to cluster about their mothers,
bumping together, bawling. Just that way   460
my crew poured round me when they saw me come—
their faces wet with tears as if they saw
their homeland, and the crags of Ithaka,
even the very town where they were born.
And weeping still they all cried out in greeting:

'Prince, what joy this is, your safe return!
Now Ithaka seems here, and we in Ithaka!
But tell us now, what death befell our friends?'

And, speaking gently, I replied:

'First we must get the ship high on the shingle,   470
and stow our gear and stores in clefts of rock
for cover. Then come follow me, to see
your shipmates in the magic house of Kirkê
eating and drinking, endlessly regaled.'

They turned back, as commanded, to this work;
only one lagged, and tried to hold the others:
Eurýlokhos it was, who blurted out:

'Where now, poor remnants? is it devil's work
you long for? Will you go to Kirkê's hall?
Swine, wolves, and lions she will make us all,   480
beasts of her courtyard, bound by her enchantment.
Remember those the Kyklops held, remember
shipmates who made that visit with Odysseus!
The daring man! They died for his foolishness!'

When I heard this I had a mind to draw
the blade that swung against my side and chop him,
bowling his head upon the ground—kinsman
or no kinsman, close to me though he was.
But others came between, saying, to stop me,

'Prince, we can leave him, if you say the word;   490
let him stay here on guard. As for ourselves,
show us the way to Kirkê's magic hall.'

So all turned inland, leaving shore and ship,
and Eurýlokhos—he, too, came on behind,
fearing the rough edge of my tongue. Meanwhile
at Kirkê's hands the rest were gently bathed,
anointed with sweet oil, and dressed afresh
in tunics and new cloaks with fleecy linings.
We found them all at supper when we came.
But greeting their old friends once more, the crew   500

could not hold back their tears; and now again
the rooms rang with sobs. Then Kirkê, loveliest
of all immortals, came to counsel me:

'Son of Laërtês and the gods of old,
Odysseus, master mariner and soldier,
enough of weeping fits. I know—I, too—
what you endured upon the inhuman sea,
what odds you met on land from hostile men.
Remain with me, and share my meat and wine;
restore behind your ribs those gallant hearts   510
that served you in the old days, when you sailed
from stony Ithaka. Now parched and spent,
your cruel wandering is all you think of,
never of joy, after so many blows.'

As we were men we could not help consenting.
So day by day we lingered, feasting long
on roasts and wine, until a year grew fat.
But when the passing months and wheeling seasons
brought the long summery days, the pause of summer,
my shipmates one day summoned me and said: 520

'Captain, shake off this trance, and think of home—
if home indeed awaits us,

                              if we shall ever see
your own well-timbered hall on Ithaka.'

They made me feel a pang, and I agreed.
That day, and all day long, from dawn to sundown,
we feasted on roast meat and ruddy wine,
and after sunset when the dusk came on
my men slept in the shadowy hall, but I
went through the dark to Kirkê's flawless bed   530
and took the goddess' knees in supplication,
urging, as she bent to hear:

                              'O Kirkê,
now you must keep your promise; it is time.
Help me make sail for home. Day after day
my longing quickens, and my company

give me no peace, but wear my heart away
pleading when you are not at hand to hear.'

The loveliest of goddesses replied:

'Son of Laërtês and the gods of old,   540
Odysseus, master mariner and soldier,
you shall not stay here longer against your will;
but home you may not go
unless you take a strange way round and come
to the cold homes of Death and pale Perséphonê.
You shall hear prophecy from the rapt shade
of blind Teirêsias of Thebes, forever
charged with reason even among the dead;
to him alone, of all the flitting ghosts,
Perséphonê has given a mind undarkened.'   550

At this I felt a weight like stone within me,
and, moaning, pressed my length against the bed,
with no desire to see the daylight more.
But when I had wept and tossed and had my fill
of this despair, at last I answered her:

'Kirkê, who pilots me upon this journey?
No man has ever sailed to the land of Death.'

That loveliest of goddesses replied:

'Son of Laërtês and the gods of old,
Odysseus, master of land ways and sea ways,   560
feel no dismay because you lack a pilot;
only set up your mast and haul your canvas
to the fresh blowing North; sit down and steer,
and hold that wind, even to the bourne of Ocean,
Perséphonê's deserted strand and grove,
dusky with poplars and the drooping willow.
Run through the tide-rip, bring your ship to shore,
land there, and find the crumbling homes of Death.
Here, toward the Sorrowing Water, run the streams
of Wailing, out of Styx, and quenchless Burning—   570
torrents that join in thunder at the Rock.
Here then, great soldier, setting foot obey me:

dig a well shaft a forearm square; pour out
libations round it to the unnumbered dead:
sweet milk and honey, then sweet wine, and last
clear water, scattering handfulls of white barley.
Pray now, with all your heart, to the faint dead;
swear you will sacrifice your finest heifer,
at home in Ithaka, and burn for them
her tenderest parts in sacrifice; and vow   580
to the lord Teirêsias, apart from all,
a black lamb, handsomest of all your flock—
thus to appease the nations of the dead.
Then slash a black ewe's throat, and a black ram,
facing the gloom of Erebos; but turn
your head away toward Ocean. You shall see, now
souls of the buried dead in shadowy hosts,
and now you must call out to your companions
to flay those sheep the bronze knife has cut down,
for offerings, burnt flesh to those below,   590
to sovereign Death and pale Perséphonê.
Meanwhile draw sword from hip, crouch down, ward off
the surging phantoms from the bloody pit
until you know the presence of Teirêsias.
He will come soon, great captain; be it he
who gives you course and distance for your sailing
homeward across the cold fish-breeding sea.'

As the goddess ended, Dawn came stitched in gold.
Now Kirkê dressed me in my shirt and cloak,
put on a gown of subtle tissue, silvery,   600
then wound a golden belt about her waist
and veiled her head in linen,
while I went through the hall to rouse my crew.
I bent above each one, and gently said:

'Wake from your sleep: no more sweet slumber. Come,
we sail: the Lady Kirkê so ordains it.'

They were soon up, and ready at that word;
but I was not to take my men unharmed
from this place, even from this. Among them all
the youngest was Elpênor—   610

no mainstay in a fight nor very clever—
and this one, having climbed on Kirkê's roof
to taste the cool night, fell asleep with wine.
Waked by our morning voices, and the tramp
of men below, he started up, but missed
his footing on the long steep backward ladder
and fell that height headlong. The blow smashed
the nape cord, and his ghost fled to the dark.
But I was outside, walking with the rest,
saying: 620

              'Homeward you think we must be sailing
to our own land; no, elsewhere is the voyage
Kirkê has laid upon me. We must go
to the cold homes of Death and pale Perséphonê
to hear Teirêsias tell of time to come.'

They felt so stricken, upon hearing this,
they sat down wailing loud, and tore their hair.
But nothing came of giving way to grief.
Down to the shore and ship at last we went,
bowed with anguish, cheeks all wet with tears,   630
to find that Kirkê had been there before us
and tied nearby a black ewe and a ram:
she had gone by like air.
For who could see the passage of a goddess
unless she wished his mortal eyes aware?

BOOK ELEVEN

A Gathering of Shades

LINES 1 – 17

We bore down on the ship at the sea's edge   1
and launched her on the salt immortal sea,
stepping our mast and spar in the black ship;
embarked the ram and ewe and went aboard
in tears, with bitter and sore dread upon us.
But now a breeze came up for us astern—
a canvas-bellying landbreeze, hale shipmate
sent by the singing nymph with sun-bright hair;
so we made fast the braces, took our thwarts,
and let the wind and steersman work the ship   10
with full sail spread all day above our coursing,
till the sun dipped, and all the ways grew dark
upon the fathomless unresting sea.
                              By night
our ship ran onward toward the Ocean's bourne,
the realm and region of the Men of Winter,
hidden in mist and cloud. Never the flaming
eye of Hêlios lights on those men
at morning, when he climbs the sky of stars,

nor in descending earthward out of heaven;   20
ruinous night being rove over those wretches.
We made the land, put ram and ewe ashore,
and took our way along the Ocean stream
to find the place foretold for us by Kirkê.
There Perimêdês and Eurýlokhos
pinioned the sacred beasts. With my drawn blade
I spaded up the votive pit, and poured
libations round it to the unnumbered dead:
sweet milk and honey, then sweet wine, and last
clear water; and I scattered barley down.   30
Then I addressed the blurred and breathless dead,
vowing to slaughter my best heifer for them
before she calved, at home in Ithaka,
and burn the choice bits on the altar fire;
as for Teirêsias, I swore to sacrifice
a black lamb, handsomest of all our flock.
Thus to assuage the nations of the dead
I pledged these rites, then slashed the lamb and ewe,
letting their black blood stream into the wellpit.
Now the souls gathered, stirring out of Erebos,   40
brides and young men, and men grown old in pain,
and tender girls whose hearts were new to grief;
many were there, too, torn by brazen lanceheads,
battle-slain, bearing still their bloody gear.
From every side they came and sought the pit
with rustling cries; and I grew sick with fear.
But presently I gave command to my officers
to flay those sheep the bronze cut down, and make
burnt offerings of flesh to the gods below—
to sovereign Death, to pale Perséphonê.   50
Meanwhile I crouched with my drawn sword to keep
the surging phantoms from the bloody pit
till I should know the presence of Teirêsias.

One shade came first—Elpênor, of our company,
who lay unburied still on the wide earth
as we had left him—dead in Kirkê's hall,
untouched, unmourned, when other cares compelled us.
Now when I saw him there I wept for pity
and called out to him:

'How is this, Elpênor,   60
how could you journey to the western gloom
swifter afoot than I in the black lugger?'

He sighed, and answered:

'Son of great Laërtês,
Odysseus, master mariner and soldier,
bad luck shadowed me, and no kindly power;
ignoble death I drank with so much wine.
I slept on Kirkê's roof, then could not see
the long steep backward ladder, coming down,
and fell that height. My neck bone, buckled under,   70
snapped, and my spirit found this well of dark.
Now hear the grace I pray for, in the name
of those back in the world, not here—your wife
and father, he who gave you bread in childhood,
and your own child, your only son, Telémakhos,
long ago left at home.
                        When you make sail
and put these lodgings of dim Death behind,
you will moor ship, I know, upon Aiaia Island;
there, O my lord, remember me, I pray,   80
do not abandon me unwept, unburied,
to tempt the gods' wrath, while you sail for home;
but fire my corpse, and all the gear I had,
and build a cairn for me above the breakers—
an unknown sailor's mark for men to come.
Heap up the mound there, and implant upon it
the oar I pulled in life with my companions.'

He ceased, and I replied:

'Unhappy spirit,
I promise you the barrow and the burial.'   90

So we conversed; and grimly, at a distance,
with my long sword between, guarding the blood,
while the faint image of the lad spoke on.
Now came the soul of Antikleía, dead,
my mother, daughter of Autólykos,
dead now, though living still when I took ship

for holy Troy. Seeing this ghost I grieved,
but held her off, through pang on pang of tears,
till I should know the presence of Teirêsias.
Soon from the dark that prince of Thebes came forward   100
bearing a golden staff; and he addressed me:

'Son of Laërtês and the gods of old,
Odysseus, master of land ways and sea ways,
why leave the blazing sun, O man of woe,
to see the cold dead and the joyless region?
Stand clear, put up your sword;
let me but taste of blood, I shall speak true.'

At this I stepped aside, and in the scabbard
let my long sword ring home to the pommel silver,
as he bent down to the sombre blood. Then spoke   110
the prince of those with gift of speech:

                              'Great captain,
a fair wind and the honey lights of home
are all you seek. But anguish lies ahead;
the god who thunders on the land prepares it,
not to be shaken from your track, implacable,
in rancor for the son whose eye you blinded.
One narrow strait may take you through his blows:
denial of yourself, restraint of shipmates.
When you make landfall on Thrinakia first   120
and quit the violet sea, dark on the land
you'll find the grazing herds of Hêlios
by whom all things are seen, all speech is known.
Avoid those kine, hold fast to your intent,
and hard seafaring brings you all to Ithaka.
But if you raid the beeves, I see destruction
for ship and crew. Though you survive alone,
bereft of all companions, lost for years,
under strange sail shall you come home, to find
your own house filled with trouble: insolent men   130
eating your livestock as they court your lady.
Aye, you shall make those men atone in blood!
But after you have dealt out death—in open
combat or by stealth—to all the suitors,
go overland on foot, and take an oar,

until one day you come where men have lived
with meat unsalted, never known the sea,
nor seen seagoing ships, with crimson bows
and oars that fledge light hulls for dipping flight.
The spot will soon be plain to you, and I   140
can tell you how: some passerby will say,
"What winnowing fan is that upon your shoulder?"
Halt, and implant your smooth oar in the turf
and make fair sacrifice to Lord Poseidon:
a ram, a bull, a great buck boar; turn back,
and carry out pure hekatombs at home
to all wide heaven's lords, the undying gods,
to each in order. Then a seaborne death
soft as this hand of mist will come upon you
when you are wearied out with rich old age,   150
your country folk in blessed peace around you.
And all this shall be just as I foretell.'

When he had done, I said at once,

                          'Teirêsias,
my life runs on then as the gods have spun it.
But come, now, tell me this; make this thing clear:
I see my mother's ghost among the dead
sitting in silence near the blood. Not once
has she glanced this way toward her son, nor spoken.
Tell me, my lord,   160
may she in some way come to know my presence?'

To this he answered:

                          'I shall make it clear
in a few words and simply. Any dead man
whom you allow to enter where the blood is
will speak to you, and speak the truth; but those
deprived will grow remote again and fade.'

When he had prophesied, Teirêsias' shade
retired lordly to the halls of Death;
but I stood fast until my mother stirred,   170
moving to sip the black blood; then she knew me
and called out sorrowfully to me:

'Child,
how could you cross alive into this gloom
at the world's end?—No sight for living eyes;
great currents run between, desolate waters,
the Ocean first, where no man goes a journey
without ship's timber under him.

                    Say, now,
is it from Troy, still wandering, after years,   180
that you come here with ship and company?
Have you not gone at all to Ithaka?
Have you not seen your lady in your hall?'

She put these questions, and I answered her:

'Mother, I came here, driven to the land of death
in want of prophecy from Teirêsias' shade;
nor have I yet coasted Akhaia's hills
nor touched my own land, but have had hard roving
since first I joined Lord Agamémnon's host
by sea for Ilion, the wild horse country,   190
to fight the men of Troy.
But come now, tell me this, and tell me clearly,
what was the bane that pinned you down in Death?
Some ravaging long illness, or mild arrows
a-flying down one day from Artemis?
Tell me of Father, tell me of the son
I left behind me; have they still my place,
my honors, or have other men assumed them?
Do they not say that I shall come no more?
And tell me of my wife: how runs her thought,   200
still with her child, still keeping our domains,
or bride again to the best of the Akhaians?'

To this my noble mother quickly answered:

'Still with her child indeed she is, poor heart,
still in your palace hall. Forlorn her nights
and days go by, her life used up in weeping.
But no man takes your honored place. Telémakhos
has care of all your garden plots and fields,
and holds the public honor of a magistrate,

feasting and being feasted. But your father   210
is country bound and comes to town no more.
He owns no bedding, rugs, or fleecy mantles,
but lies down, winter nights, among the slaves,
rolled in old cloaks for cover, near the embers.
Or when the heat comes at the end of summer,
the fallen leaves, all round his vineyard plot,
heaped into windrows, make his lowly bed.
He lies now even so, with aching heart,
and longs for your return, while age comes on him.
So I, too, pined away, so doom befell me,   220
not that the keen-eyed huntress with her shafts
had marked me down and shot to kill me; not
that illness overtook me—no true illness
wasting the body to undo the spirit;
only my loneliness for you, Odysseus,
for your kind heart and counsel, gentle Odysseus,
took my own life away.'

       I bit my lip,
rising perplexed, with longing to embrace her,
and tried three times, putting my arms around her,   230
but she went sifting through my hands, impalpable
as shadows are, and wavering like a dream.
Now this embittered all the pain I bore,
and I cried in the darkness:

       'O my mother,
will you not stay, be still, here in my arms,
may we not, in this place of Death, as well,
hold one another, touch with love, and taste
salt tears' relief, the twinge of welling tears?
Or is this all hallucination, sent   240
against me by the iron queen, Perséphonê,
to make me groan again?'

      My noble mother
answered quickly:

      'O my child—alas,
most sorely tried of men—great Zeus's daughter,
Perséphonê, knits no illusion for you.

All mortals meet this judgment when they die.
No flesh and bone are here, none bound by sinew,
since the bright-hearted pyre consumed them down—   250
the white bones long exanimate—to ash;
dreamlike the soul flies, insubstantial.

You must crave sunlight soon.
                  Note all things strange
seen here, to tell your lady in after days.'

So went our talk; then other shadows came,
ladies in company, sent by Perséphonê—
consorts or daughters of illustrious men—
crowding about the black blood.
                I took thought   260
how best to separate and question them,
and saw no help for it, but drew once more
the long bright edge of broadsword from my hip,
that none should sip the blood in company
but one by one, in order; so it fell
that each declared her lineage and name.

Here was great loveliness of ghosts! I saw
before them all, that princess of great ladies,
Tyro, Salmoneus' daughter, as she told me,
and queen to Krêtheus, a son of Aiolos.   270
She had gone daft for the river Enipeus,
most graceful of all running streams, and ranged
all day by Enipeus' limpid side,
whose form the foaming girdler of the islands,
the god who makes earth tremble, took and so
lay down with her where he went flooding seaward,
their bower a purple billow, arching round
to hide them in a sea-vale, god and lady.
Now when his pleasure was complete, the god
spoke to her softly, holding fast her hand: 280

'Dear mortal, go in joy! At the turn of seasons,
winter to summer, you shall bear me sons;
no lovemaking of gods can be in vain.
Nurse our sweet children tenderly, and rear them.

Home with you now, and hold your tongue, and tell
no one your lover's name—though I am yours,
Poseidon, lord of surf that makes earth tremble.'

He plunged away into the deep sea swell,
and she grew big with Pelias and Neleus,
powerful vassals, in their time, of Zeus.   290
Pelias lived on broad Iolkos seaboard
rich in flocks, and Neleus at Pylos.
As for the sons borne by that queen of women
to Krêtheus, their names were Aison, Pherês,
and Amytháon, expert charioteer.

Next after her I saw Antiopê,
daughter of Ásopos. She too could boast
a god for lover, having lain with Zeus
and borne two sons to him: Amphion and
Zêthos, who founded Thebes, the upper city,   300
and built the ancient citadel. They sheltered
no life upon that plain, for all their power,
without a fortress wall.

                                        And next I saw
Amphitrion's true wife, Alkmênê, mother,
as all men know, of lionish Heraklês,
conceived when she lay close in Zeus's arms;
and Megarê, high-hearted Kreon's daughter,
wife of Amphitrion's unwearying son.

I saw the mother of Oidipous, Epikastê,   310
whose great unwitting deed it was
to marry her own son. He took that prize
from a slain father; presently the gods
brought all to light that made the famous story.
But by their fearsome wills he kept his throne
in dearest Thebes, all through his evil days,
while she descended to the place of Death,
god of the locked and iron door. Steep down
from a high rafter, throttled in her noose,
she swung, carried away by pain, and left him   320
endless agony from a mother's Furies.

And I saw Khloris, that most lovely lady,
whom for her beauty in the olden time
Neleus wooed with countless gifts, and married.
She was the youngest daughter of Amphion,
son of Iasos. In those days he held
power at Orkhómenos, over the Minyai.
At Pylos then as queen she bore her children—
Nestor, Khromios, Periklýmenos,
and Pêro, too, who turned the heads of men   330
with her magnificence. A host of princes
from nearby lands came courting her; but Neleus
would hear of no one, not unless the suitor
could drive the steers of giant Íphiklos
from Phylakê—longhorns, broad in the brow,
so fierce that one man only, a diviner,
offered to round them up. But bitter fate
saw him bound hand and foot by savage herdsmen.
Then days and months grew full and waned, the year
went wheeling round, the seasons came again,   340
before at last the power of Iphiklos,
relenting, freed the prisoner, who foretold
all things to him. So Zeus's will was done.

And I saw Lêda, wife of Tyndareus,
upon whom Tyndareus had sired twins
indomitable: Kastor, tamer of horses,
and Polydeukês, best in the boxing ring.
Those two live still, though life-creating earth
embraces them: even in the underworld
honored as gods by Zeus, each day in turn   350
one comes alive, the other dies again.
Then after Lêda to my vision came
the wife of Aloeus, Iphimedeia,
proud that she once had held the flowing sea
and borne him sons, thunderers for a day,
the world-renowned Otos and Ephialtês.
Never were men on such a scale
bred on the plowlands and the grainlands, never
so magnificent any, after Orion.
At nine years old they towered nine fathoms tall,   360

nine cubits in the shoulders, and they promised
furor upon Olympos, heaven broken by battle cries,
the day they met the gods in arms.
                          With Ossa's
mountain peak they meant to crown Olympos
and over Ossa Pelion's forest pile
for footholds up the sky. As giants grown
they might have done it, but the bright son of Zeus
by Lêto of the smooth braid shot them down
while they were boys unbearded; no dark curls   370
clustered yet from temples to the chin.

Then I saw Phaidra, Prokris; and Ariadnê,
daughter of Minos, the grim king. Theseus took her
aboard with him from Krete for the terraced land
of ancient Athens; but he had no joy of her.
Artemis killed her on the Isle of Dia
at a word from Dionysos.
                          Maira, then,
and Klymênê, and that detested queen,
Eríphylê, who betrayed her lord for gold . . .   380
but how name all the women I beheld there,
daughters and wives of kings? The starry night
wanes long before I close.
                          Here, or aboard ship,
amid the crew, the hour for sleep has come.
Our sailing is the gods' affair and yours."

Then he fell silent. Down the shadowy hall
the enchanted banqueters were still. Only
the queen with ivory pale arms, Arêtê, spoke,
saying to all the silent men: 390

                          "Phaiákians,
how does he stand, now, in your eyes, this captain,
the look and bulk of him, the inward poise?
He is my guest, but each one shares that honor.
Be in no haste to send him on his way
or scant your bounty in his need. Remember
how rich, by heaven's will, your possessions are."

Then Ekhenêos, the old soldier, eldest
of all Phaiákians, added his word:

"Friends, here was nothing but our own thought spoken,   400
the mark hit square. Our duties to her majesty.
For what is to be said and done,
we wait upon Alkínoös' command."

At this the king's voice rang:

          "I so command—
as sure as it is I who, while I live,
rule the sea rovers of Phaiákia. Our friend
longs to put out for home, but let him be
content to rest here one more day, until
I see all gifts bestowed. And every man   410
will take thought for his launching and his voyage,
I most of all, for I am master here."

Odysseus, the great tactician, answered:

"Alkínoös, king and admiration of men,
even a year's delay, if you should urge it,
in loading gifts and furnishing for sea—
I too could wish it; better far that I
return with some largesse of wealth about me—
I shall be thought more worthy of love and courtesy
by every man who greets me home in Ithaka."   420

The king said:

          "As to that, one word, Odysseus:
from all we see, we take you for no swindler—
though the dark earth be patient of so many,
scattered everywhere, baiting their traps with lies
of old times and of places no one knows.
You speak with art, but your intent is honest.
The Argive troubles, and your own troubles,
you told as a poet would, a man who knows the world.
But now come tell me this: among the dead   430
did you meet any of your peers, companions
who sailed with you and met their doom at Troy?
Here's a long night—an endless night—before us,

and no time yet for sleep, not in this hall.
Recall the past deeds and the strange adventures.
I could stay up until the sacred Dawn
as long as you might wish to tell your story."

Odysseus the great tactician answered:

"Alkínoös, king and admiration of men,
there is a time for story telling; there is   440
also a time for sleep. But even so,
if, indeed, listening be still your pleasure,
I must not grudge my part. Other and sadder
tales there are to tell, of my companions,
of some who came through all the Trojan spears,
clangor and groan of war,
only to find a brutal death at home—
and a bad wife behind it.

                              After Perséphonê,
icy and pale, dispersed the shades of women,   450
the soul of Agamémnon, son of Atreus,
came before me, sombre in the gloom,
and others gathered round, all who were with him
when death and doom struck in Aegísthos' hall.
Sipping the black blood, the tall shade perceived me,
and cried out sharply, breaking into tears;
then tried to stretch his hands toward me, but could not,
being bereft of all the reach and power
he once felt in the great torque of his arms.
Gazing at him, and stirred, I wept for pity,   460
and spoke across to him:

                              'O son of Atreus,
illustrious Lord Marshal, Agamémnon,
what was the doom that brought you low in death?
Were you at sea, aboard ship, and Poseidon
blew up a wicked squall to send you under,
or were you cattle-raiding on the mainland
or in a fight for some strongpoint, or women,
when the foe hit you to your mortal hurt?'

But he replied at once: 470

'Son of Laërtês,
Odysseus, master of land ways and sea ways,
neither did I go down with some good ship
in any gale Poseidon blew, nor die
upon the mainland, hurt by foes in battle.
It was Aigísthos who designed my death,
he and my heartless wife, and killed me, after
feeding me, like an ox felled at the trough.
That was my miserable end—and with me
my fellows butchered, like so many swine   480
killed for some troop, or feast, or wedding banquet
in a great landholder's household. In your day
you have seen men, and hundreds, die in war,
in the bloody press, or downed in single combat,
but these were murders you would catch your breath at:
think of us fallen, all our throats cut, winebowl
brimming, tables laden on every side,
while blood ran smoking over the whole floor.
In my extremity I heard Kassandra,
Priam's daughter, piteously crying   490
as the traitress Klytaimnéstra made to kill her
along with me. I heaved up from the ground
and got my hands around the blade, but she
eluded me, that whore. Nor would she close
my two eyes as my soul swam to the underworld
or shut my lips. There is no being more fell,
more bestial than a wife in such an action,
and what an action that one planned!
The murder of her husband and her lord.
Great god, I thought my children and my slaves   500
at least would give me welcome. But that woman,
plotting a thing so low, defiled herself
and all her sex, all women yet to come,
even those few who may be virtuous.'

He paused then, and I answered:

'Foul and dreadful.
That was the way that Zeus who views the wide world
vented his hatred on the sons of Atreus—
intrigues of women, even from the start.

Myriads   510

died by Helen's fault, and Klytaimnestra
plotted against you half the world away.'

And he at once said:

'Let it be a warning

even to you. Indulge a woman never,
and never tell her all you know. Some things
a man may tell, some he should cover up.
Not that I see a risk for you, Odysseus,
of death at your wife's hands. She is too wise,
too clear-eyed, sees alternatives too well,   520
Penélopê, Ikários' daughter—
that young bride whom we left behind—think of it!—
when we sailed off to war. The baby boy
still cradled at her breast—now he must be
a grown man, and a lucky one. By heaven,
you'll see him yet, and he'll embrace his father
with old fashioned respect, and rightly.

My own

lady never let me glut my eyes
on my own son, but bled me to death first.   530
One thing I will advise, on second thought;
stow it away and ponder it.

Land your ship

in secret on your island; give no warning.
The day of faithful wives is gone forever.

But tell me, have you any word at all
about my son's life? Gone to Orkhómenos
or sandy Pylos, can he be? Or waiting
with Meneláos in the plain of Sparta?
Death on earth has not yet taken Orestês.'   540

But I could only answer:

'Son of Atreus,

why do you ask these questions of me? Neither
news of home have I, nor news of him,
alive or dead. And empty words are evil.'

So we exchanged our speech, in bitterness,
weighed down by grief, and tears welled in our eyes,
when there appeared the spirit of Akhilleus,
son of Peleus; then Patróklos' shade,
and then Antílokhos, and then Aias,   550
first among all the Danaans in strength
and bodily beauty, next to prince Akhilleus.
Now that great runner, grandson of Aíakhos,
recognized me and called across to me:

'Son of Laërtês and the gods of old,
Odysseus, master mariner and soldier,
old knife, what next? What greater feat remains
for you to put your mind on, after this?
How did you find your way down to the dark
where these dimwitted dead are camped forever,   560
the after images of used-up men?'

                                   I answered:

'Akhilleus, Peleus' son, strongest of all
among the Akhaians, I had need of foresight
such as Teirêsias alone could give
to help me, homeward bound for the crags of Ithaka.
I have not yet coasted Akhaia, not yet
touched my land; my life is all adversity.
But was there ever a man more blest by fortune
than you, Akhilleus? Can there ever be?   570
We ranked you with immortals in your lifetime,
we Argives did, and here your power is royal
among the dead men's shades. Think, then, Akhilleus:
you need not be so pained by death.'

                                   To this
he answered swiftly:

                                   'Let me hear no smooth talk
of death from you, Odysseus, light of councils.
Better, I say, to break sod as a farm hand
for some poor country man, on iron rations,   580
than lord it over all the exhausted dead.

Tell me, what news of the prince my son: did he
come after me to make a name in battle
or could it be he did not? Do you know
if rank and honor still belong to Peleus
in the towns of the Myrmidons? Or now, may be,
Hellas and Phthia spurn him, seeing old age
fetters him, hand and foot. I cannot help him
under the sun's rays, cannot be that man
I was on Troy's wide seaboard, in those days   590
when I made bastion for the Argives
and put an army's best men in the dust.
Were I but whole again, could I go now
to my father's house, one hour would do to make
my passion and my hands no man could hold
hateful to any who shoulder him aside.'

Now when he paused I answered:

                              'Of all that—
of Peleus' life, that is—I know nothing;
but happily I can tell you the whole story   600
of Neoptólemos, as you require.
In my own ship I brought him out from Skyros
to join the Akhaians under arms.

                              And I can tell you,
in every council before Troy thereafter
your son spoke first and always to the point;
no one but Nestor and I could out-debate him.
And when we formed against the Trojan line
he never hung back in the mass, but ranged
far forward of his troops—no man could touch him   610
for gallantry. Aye, scores went down before him
in hard fights man to man. I shall not tell
all about each, or name them all—the long
roster of enemies he put out of action,
taking the shock of charges on the Argives.
But what a champion his lance ran through
in Eurýpulos the son of Télephos! Keteians
in throngs around that captain also died—

all because Priam's gifts had won his mother
to send the lad to battle; and I thought   620
Memnon alone in splendor ever outshone him.

But one fact more: while our picked Argive crew
still rode that hollow horse Epeios built,
and when the whole thing lay with me, to open
the trapdoor of the ambuscade or not,
at that point our Danaan lords and soldiers
wiped their eyes, and their knees began to quake,
all but Neoptólemos. I never saw
his tanned cheek change color or his hand
brush one tear away. Rather he prayed me,   630
hand on hilt, to sortie, and he gripped
his tough spear, bent on havoc for the Trojans.
And when we had pierced and sacked Priam's tall city
he loaded his choice plunder and embarked
with no scar on him; not a spear had grazed him
nor the sword's edge in close work—common wounds
one gets in war. Arês in his mad fits
knows no favorites.'

                              But I said no more,
for he had gone off striding the field of asphodel,   640
the ghost of our great runner, Akhilleus Aiákidês,
glorying in what I told him of his son.

Now other souls of mournful dead stood by,
each with his troubled questioning, but one
remained alone, apart: the son of Télamon,
Aîas, it was—the great shade burning still
because I had won favor on the beachhead
in rivalry over Akhilleus' arms.
The Lady Thetis, mother of Akhilleus,
laid out for us the dead man's battle gear,   650
and Trojan children, with Athena,
named the Danaan fittest to own them. Would
god I had not borne the palm that day!
For earth took Aîas then to hold forever,
the handsomest and, in all feats of war,

noblest of the Danaans after Akhilleus.
Gently therefore I called across to him:

'Aîas, dear son of royal Télamon,
you would not then forget, even in death,
your fury with me over those accurst   660
calamitous arms?—and so they were, a bane
sent by the gods upon the Argive host.
For when you died by your own hand we lost
a tower, formidable in war. All we Akhaians
mourn you forever, as we do Akhilleus;
and no one bears the blame but Zeus.
He fixed that doom for you because he frowned
on the whole expedition of our spearmen.
My lord, come nearer, listen to our story!
Conquer your indignation and your pride.'   670

But he gave no reply, and turned away,
following other ghosts toward Erebos.
Who knows if in that darkness he might still
have spoken, and I answered?
                              But my heart
longed, after this, to see the dead elsewhere.

And now there came before my eyes Minos,
the son of Zeus, enthroned, holding a golden staff,
dealing out justice among ghostly pleaders
arrayed about the broad doorways of Death.   680

And then I glimpsed Orion, the huge hunter,
gripping his club, studded with bronze, unbreakable,
with wild beasts he had overpowered in life
on lonely mountainsides, now brought to bay
on fields of asphodel.
                              And I saw Títyos,
the son of Gaia, lying
abandoned over nine square rods of plain.
Vultures, hunched above him, left and right,
rifling his belly, stabbed into the liver,   690
and he could never push them off.

                                This hulk
had once committed rape of Zeus's mistress,
Lêto, in her glory, when she crossed
the open grass of Panopeus toward Pytho.

Then I saw Tántalos put to the torture:
in a cool pond he stood, lapped round by water
clear to the chin, and being athirst he burned
to slake his dry weasand with drink, though drink
he would not ever again. For when the old man   700
put his lips down to the sheet of water
it vanished round his feet, gulped underground,
and black mud baked there in a wind from hell.
Boughs, too, drooped low above him, big with fruit,
pear trees, pomegranates, brilliant apples,
luscious figs, and olives ripe and dark;
but if he stretched his hand for one, the wind
under the dark sky tossed the bough beyond him.

Then Sísyphos in torment I beheld
being roustabout to a tremendous boulder.   710
Leaning with both arms braced and legs driving,
he heaved it toward a height, and almost over,
but then a Power spun him round and sent
the cruel boulder bounding again to the plain.
Whereon the man bent down again to toil,
dripping sweat, and the dust rose overhead.
Next I saw manifest the power of Heraklês—
a phantom, this, for he himself has gone
feasting amid the gods, reclining soft
with Hêbê of the ravishing pale ankles,   720
daughter of Zeus and Hêra, shod in gold.
But, in my vision, all the dead around him
cried like affrighted birds; like Night itself
he loomed with naked bow and nocked arrow
and glances terrible as continual archery.
My hackles rose at the gold swordbelt he wore
sweeping across him: gorgeous intaglio
of savage bears, boars, lions with wildfire eyes,
swordfights, battle, slaughter, and sudden death—

the smith who had that belt in him, I hope   730
he never made, and never will make, another.
The eyes of the vast figure rested on me,
and of a sudden he said in kindly tones:

'Son of Laërtês and the gods of old,
Odysseus, master mariner and soldier,
under a cloud, you too? Destined to grinding
labors like my own in the sunny world?
Son of Kroníon Zeus or not, how many
days I sweated out, being bound in servitude
to a man far worse than I, a rough master!   740
He made me hunt this place one time
to get the watchdog of the dead: no more
perilous task, he thought, could be; but I
brought back thàt beast, up from the underworld;
Hermês and grey-eyed Athena showed the way.'

And Heraklês, down the vistas of the dead,
faded from sight; but I stood fast, awaiting
other great souls who perished in times past.
I should have met, then, god-begotten Theseus
and Peirithoös, whom both I longed to see,   750
but first came shades in thousands, rustling
in a pandemonium of whispers, blown together,
and the horror took me that Perséphonê
had brought from darker hell some saurian death's head.
I whirled then, made for the ship, shouted to crewmen
to get aboard and cast off the stern hawsers,
an order soon obeyed. They took their thwarts,
and the ship went leaping toward the stream of Ocean
first under oars, then with a following wind.

BOOK TWELVE

Sea Perils and Defeat

LINES 1 – 15

The ship sailed on, out of the Ocean Stream,   1
riding a long swell on the open sea
for the Island of Aiaia.
                          Summering Dawn
has dancing grounds there, and the Sun his rising;
but still by night we beached on a sand shelf
and waded in beyond the line of breakers
to fall asleep, awaiting the Day Star.

When the young Dawn with finger tips of rose
made heaven bright, I sent shipmates to bring   10
Elpênor's body from the house of Kirkê.
We others cut down timber on the foreland,
on a high point, and built his pyre of logs,
then stood by weeping while the flame burnt through
corse and equipment.
                     Then we heaped his barrow,
lifting a gravestone on the mound, and fixed
his light but unwarped oar against the sky.

These were our rites in memory of him. Soon, then,
knowing us back from the Dark Land, Kirkê came   20
freshly adorned for us, with handmaids bearing
loaves, roast meats, and ruby-colored wine.
She stood among us in immortal beauty
jesting:

        'Hearts of oak, did you go down
alive into the homes of Death? One visit
finishes all men but yourselves, twice mortall
Come, here is meat and wine, enjoy your feasting
for one whole day; and in the dawn tomorrow
you shall put out to sea. Sailing directions,   30
landmarks, perils, I shall sketch for you, to keep you
from being caught by land or water
in some black sack of trouble.'

      In high humor
and ready for carousal, we agreed;
so all that day until the sun went down
we feasted on roast meat and good red wine,
till after sunset, at the fall of night,
the men dropped off to sleep by the stern hawsers.
She took my hand then, silent in that hush,   40
drew me apart, made me sit down, and lay
beside me, softly questioning, as I told
all I had seen, from first to last.

       Then said the Lady Kirkê:

'So: all those trials are over.

      Listen with care
to this, now, and a god will arm your mind.
Square in your ship's path are Seirênês, crying
beauty to bewitch men coasting by;
woe to the innocent who hears that sound!   50
He will not see his lady nor his children
in joy, crowding about him, home from sea;
the Seirênês will sing his mind away
on their sweet meadow lolling. There are bones

of dead men rotting in a pile beside them
and flayed skins shrivel around the spot.
                                        Steer wide;
keep well to seaward; plug your oarsmen's ears
with beeswax kneaded soft; none of the rest
should hear that song.   60
                                But if you wish to listen,
let the men tie you in the lugger, hand
and foot, back to the mast, lashed to the mast,
so you may hear those harpies' thrilling voices;
shout as you will, begging to be untied,
your crew must only twist more line around you
and keep their stroke up, till the singers fade.
What then? One of two courses you may take,
and you yourself must weigh them. I shall not
plan the whole action for you now, but only   70
tell you of both.
                                Ahead are beetling rocks
and dark blue glancing Amphitritê, surging,
roars around them. Prowling Rocks, or Drifters,
the gods in bliss have named them—named them well.
Not even birds can pass them by, not even
the timorous doves that bear ambrosia
to Father Zeus; caught by downdrafts, they die
on rockwall smooth as ice.
                                Each time, the Father   80
wafts a new courier to make up his crew.

Still less can ships get searoom of these Drifters,
whose boiling surf, under high fiery winds,
carries tossing wreckage of ships and men.
Only one ocean-going craft, the far-famed
Argo, made it, sailing from Aiêta;
but she, too, would have crashed on the big rocks
if Hêra had not pulled her through, for love
of Iêson, her captain.
                                A second course   90
lies between headlands. One is a sharp mountain
piercing the sky, with stormcloud round the peak

dissolving never, not in the brightest summer,
to show heaven's azure there, nor in the fall.
No mortal man could scale it, nor so much
as land there, not with twenty hands and feet,
so sheer the cliffs are—as of polished stone.
Midway that height, a cavern full of mist
opens toward Erebos and evening. Skirting
this in the lugger, great Odysseus,   100
your master bowman, shooting from the deck,
would come short of the cavemouth with his shaft;
but that is the den of Skylla, where she yaps
abominably, a newborn whelp's cry,
though she is huge and monstrous. God or man,
no one could look on her in joy. Her legs—
and there are twelve—are like great tentacles,
unjointed, and upon her serpent necks
are borne six heads like nightmares of ferocity,
with triple serried rows of fangs and deep   110
gullets of black death. Half her length, she sways
her heads in air, outside her horrid cleft,
hunting the sea around that promontory
for dolphins, dogfish, or what bigger game
thundering Amphitritê feeds in thousands.
And no ship's company can claim
to have passed her without loss and grief; she takes,
from every ship, one man for every gullet.

The opposite point seems more a tongue of land
you'd touch with a good bowshot, at the narrows.   120
A great wild fig, a shaggy mass of leaves,
grows on it, and Kharybdis lurks below
to swallow down the dark sea tide. Three times
from dawn to dusk she spews it up
and sucks it down again three times, a whirling
maelstrom; if you come upon her then
the god who makes earth tremble could not save you.
No, hug the cliff of Skylla, take your ship
through on a racing stroke. Better to mourn
six men than lose them all, and the ship, too.'   130

So her advice ran; but I faced her, saying:

'Only instruct me, goddess, if you will,
how, if possible, can I pass Kharybdis,
or fight off Skylla when she raids my crew?'

Swiftly that loveliest goddess answered me:

'Must you have battle in your heart forever?
The bloody toil of combat? Old contender,
will you not yield to the immortal gods?
That nightmare cannot die, being eternal
evil itself—horror, and pain, and chaos;   140
there is no fighting her, no power can fight her,
all that avails is flight.
                          Lose headway there
along that rockface while you break out arms,
and she'll swoop over you, I fear, once more,
taking one man again for every gullet.
No, no, put all your backs into it, row on;
invoke Blind Force, that bore this scourge of men,
to keep her from a second strike against you.

Then you will coast Thrinákia, the island   150
where Hêlios' cattle graze, fine herds, and flocks
of goodly sheep. The herds and flocks are seven,
with fifty beasts in each.
                          No lambs are dropped,
or calves, and these fat cattle never die.
Immortal, too, their cowherds are—their shepherds—
Phaëthousa and Lampetía, sweetly braided
nymphs that divine Neaira bore
to the overlord of high noon, Hêlios.
These nymphs their gentle mother bred and placed   160
upon Thrinákia, the distant land,
in care of flocks and cattle for their father.

Now give those kine a wide berth, keep your thoughts
intent upon your course for home,
and hard seafaring brings you all to Ithaka.
But if you raid the beeves, I see destruction
for ship and crew.

Rough years then lie between
you and your homecoming, alone and old,
the one survivor, all companions lost.'   170

As Kirkê spoke, Dawn mounted her golden throne,
and on the first rays Kirkê left me, taking
her way like a great goddess up the island.
I made straight for the ship, roused up the men
to get aboard and cast off at the stern.
They scrambled to their places by the rowlocks
and all in line dipped oars in the grey sea.
But soon an off-shore breeze blew to our liking—
a canvas-bellying breeze, a lusty shipmate
sent by the singing nymph with sunbright hair.   180
So we made fast the braces, and we rested,
letting the wind and steersman work the ship.
The crew being now silent before me, I
addressed them, sore at heart:

                              'Dear friends,
more than one man, or two, should know those things
Kirkê foresaw for us and shared with me,
so let me tell her forecast: then we die
with our eyes open, if we are going to die,
or know what death we baffle if we can. Seirênês   190
weaving a haunting song over the sea
we are to shun, she said, and their green shore
all sweet with clover; yet she urged that I
alone should listen to their song. Therefore
you are to tie me up, tight as a splint,
erect along the mast, lashed to the mast,
and if I shout and beg to be untied,
take more turns of the rope to muffle me.'

I rather dwelt on this part of the forecast,
while our good ship made time, bound outward down   200
the wind for the strange island of Seirênês.
Then all at once the wind fell, and a calm
came over all the sea, as though some power
lulled the swell.

                                    The crew were on their feet
briskly, to furl the sail, and stow it; then,
each in place, they poised the smooth oar blades
and sent the white foam scudding by. I carved
a massive cake of beeswax into bits
and rolled them in my hands until they softened—   210
no long task, for a burning heat came down
from Hêlios, lord of high noon. Going forward
I carried wax along the line, and laid it
thick on their ears. They tied me up, then, plumb
amidships, back to the mast, lashed to the mast,
and took themselves again to rowing. Soon,
as we came smartly within hailing distance,
the two Seirênês, noting our fast ship
off their point, made ready, and they sang:

>   *This way, oh turn your bows,*   220
>   *Akhaia's glory,*
>   *As all the world allows—*
>   *Moor and be merry.*
>
>   *Sweet coupled airs we sing.*
>   *No lonely seafarer*
>   *Holds clear of entering*
>   *Our green mirror.*
>
>   *Pleased by each purling note*
>   *Like honey twining*
>   *From her throat and my throat,*   230
>   *Who lies a-pining?*
>
>   *Sea rovers here take joy*
>   *Voyaging onward,*
>   *As from our song of Troy*
>   *Greybeard and rower-boy*
>   *Goeth more learnèd.*
>
>   *All feats on that great field*
>   *In the long warfare,*
>   *Dark days the bright gods willed,*
>   *Wounds you bore there,*   240

Argos' old soldiery
    On Troy beach teeming,
Charmed out of time we see.
No life on earth can be
    Hid from our dreaming.

The lovely voices in ardor appealing over the water
made me crave to listen, and I tried to say
'Untie me!' to the crew, jerking my brows;
but they bent steady to the oars. Then Perimêdês
got to his feet, he and Eurýlokhos,   250
and passed more line about, to hold me still.
So all rowed on, until the Seirênês
dropped under the sea rim, and their singing
dwindled away.

                    My faithful company
rested on their oars now, peeling off
the wax that I had laid thick on their ears;
then set me free.

                    But scarcely had that island
faded in blue air than I saw smoke   260
and white water, with sound of waves in tumult—
a sound the men heard, and it terrified them.
Oars flew from their hands; the blades went knocking
wild alongside till the ship lost way,
with no oarblades to drive her through the water.

Well, I walked up and down from bow to stern,
trying to put heart into them, standing over
every oarsman, saying gently,

                    'Friends,
have we never been in danger before this?   270
More fearsome, is it now, than when the Kyklops
penned us in his cave? What power he had!
Did I not keep my nerve, and use my wits
to find a way out for us?

                    Now I say
by hook or crook this peril too shall be
something that we remember.

Heads up, lads!
We must obey the orders as I give them.
Get the oarshafts in your hands, and lay back   280
hard on your benches; hit these breaking seas.
Zeus help us pull away before we founder.

You at the tiller, listen, and take in
all that I say—the rudders are your duty;
keep her out of the combers and the smoke;
steer for that headland; watch the drift, or we
fetch up in the smother, and you drown us.'

That was all, and it brought them round to action.
But as I sent them on toward Skylla, I
told them nothing, as they could do nothing.   290
They would have dropped their oars again, in panic,
to roll for cover under the decking. Kirkê's
bidding against arms had slipped my mind,
so I tied on my cuirass and took up
two heavy spears, then made my way along
to the foredeck—thinking to see her first from there,
the monster of the grey rock, harboring
torment for my friends. I strained my eyes
upon that cliffside veiled in cloud, but nowhere
could I catch sight of her.   300
                        And all this time,
in travail, sobbing, gaining on the current,
we rowed into the strait—Skylla to port
and on our starboard beam Kharybdis, dire
gorge of the salt sea tide. By heaven! when she
vomited, all the sea was like a cauldron
seething over intense fire, when the mixture
suddenly heaves and rises.
                        The shot spume
soared to the landside heights, and fell like rain.   310

But when she swallowed the sea water down
we saw the funnel of the maelstrom, heard
the rock bellowing all around, and dark

sand raged on the bottom far below.
My men all blanched against the gloom, our eyes
were fixed upon that yawning mouth in fear
of being devoured.

>   Then Skylla made her strike,
whisking six of my best men from the ship.

I happened to glance aft at ship and oarsmen   320
and caught sight of their arms and legs, dangling
high overhead. Voices came down to me
in anguish, calling my name for the last time.

A man surfcasting on a point of rock
for bass or mackerel, whipping his long rod
to drop the sinker and the bait far out,
will hook a fish and rip it from the surface
to dangle wriggling through the air:

>   so these
were borne aloft in spasms toward the cliff.   330

She ate them as they shrieked there, in her den,
in the dire grapple, reaching still for me—
and deathly pity ran me through
at that sight—far the worst I ever suffered,
questing the passes of the strange sea.

>   We rowed on.
The Rocks were now behind; Kharybdis, too,
and Skylla dropped astern.

>   Then we were coasting
the noble island of the god, where grazed   340
those cattle with wide brows, and bounteous flocks
of Hêlios, lord of noon, who rides high heaven.

From the black ship, far still at sea, I heard
the lowing of the cattle winding home
and sheep bleating; and heard, too, in my heart
the words of blind Teirêsias of Thebes
and Kirkê of Aiaia: both forbade me
the island of the world's delight, the Sun.
So I spoke out in gloom to my companions:

'Shipmates, grieving and weary though you are,   350
listen: I had forewarning from Teirêsias
and Kirkê, too; both told me I must shun
this island of the Sun, the world's delight.
Nothing but fatal trouble shall we find here.
Pull away, then, and put the land astern.'

That strained them to the breaking point, and, cursing,
Eurýlokhos cried out in bitterness:

'Are you flesh and blood, Odysseus, to endure
more than a man can? Do you never tire?
God, look at you, iron is what you're made of.   360
Here we all are, half dead with weariness,
falling asleep over the oars, and you
say "No landing"—no firm island earth
where we could make a quiet supper. No:
pull out to sea, you say, with night upon us—
just as before, but wandering now, and lost.
Sudden storms can rise at night and swamp
ships without a trace.
                        Where is your shelter
if some stiff gale blows up from south or west—   370
the winds that break up shipping every time
when seamen flout the lord gods' will? I say
do as the hour demands and go ashore
before black night comes down.
                        We'll make our supper
alongside, and at dawn put out to sea.'

Now when the rest said 'Aye' to this, I saw
the power of destiny devising ill.
Sharply I answered, without hesitation:

'Eurýlokhos, they are with you to a man.   380
I am alone, outmatched.
                        Let this whole company
swear me a great oath: Any herd of cattle
or flock of sheep here found shall go unharmed;
no one shall slaughter out of wantonness
ram or heifer; all shall be content
with what the goddess Kirkê put aboard.'

They fell at once to swearing as I ordered,
and when the round of oaths had ceased, we found
a halfmoon bay to beach and moor the ship in,   390
with a fresh spring nearby. All hands ashore
went about skillfully getting up a meal.
Then, after thirst and hunger, those besiegers,
were turned away, they mourned for their companions
plucked from the ship by Skylla and devoured,
and sleep came soft upon them as they mourned.

In the small hours of the third watch, when stars
that shone out in the first dusk of evening
had gone down to their setting, a giant wind
blew from heaven, and clouds driven by Zeus   400
shrouded land and sea in a night of storm;
so, just as Dawn with finger tips of rose
touched the windy world, we dragged our ship
to cover in a grotto, a sea cave
where nymphs had chairs of rock and sanded floors.
I mustered all the crew and said:

                                 'Old shipmates,
our stores are in the ship's hold, food and drink;
the cattle here are not for our provision,
or we pay dearly for it.   410
                          Fierce the god is
who cherishes these heifers and these sheep:
Hêlios; and no man avoids his eye.'

To this my fighters nodded. Yes. But now
we had a month of onshore gales, blowing
day in, day out—south winds, or south by east.
As long as bread and good red wine remained
to keep the men up, and appease their craving,
they would not touch the cattle. But in the end,
when all the barley in the ship was gone,   420
hunger drove them to scour the wild shore
with angling hooks, for fishes and sea fowl,
whatever fell into their hands; and lean days
wore their bellies thin.

The storms continued.
So one day I withdrew to the interior
to pray the gods in solitude, for hope
that one might show me some way of salvation.
Slipping away, I struck across the island
to a sheltered spot, out of the driving gale.   430
I washed my hands there, and made supplication
to the gods who own Olympos, all the gods—
but they, for answer, only closed my eyes
under slow drops of sleep.

                    Now on the shore Eurýlokhos

made his insidious plea:

                    'Comrades,' he said,
'You've gone through everything; listen to what I say.
All deaths are hateful to us, mortal wretches,
but famine is the most pitiful, the worst   440
end that a man can come to.

                    Will you fight it?
Come, we'll cut out the noblest of these cattle
for sacrifice to the gods who own the sky;
and once at home, in the old country of Ithaka,
if ever that day comes—
we'll build a costly temple and adorn it
with every beauty for the Lord of Noon.
But if he flares up over his heifers lost,
wishing our ship destroyed, and if the gods   450
make cause with him, why, then I say: Better
open your lungs to a big sea once for all
than waste to skin and bones on a lonely island!'

Thus Eurýlokhos; and they murmured 'Aye!'
trooping away at once to round up heifers.
Now, that day tranquil cattle with broad brows
were grazing near, and soon the men drew up
around their chosen beasts in ceremony.
They plucked the leaves that shone on a tall oak—
having no barley meal—to strew the victims,   460
performed the prayers and ritual, knifed the kine
and flayed each carcass, cutting thighbones free
to wrap in double folds of fat. These offerings,

with strips of meat, were laid upon the fire.
Then, as they had no wine, they made libation
with clear spring water, broiling the entrails first;
and when the bones were burnt and tripes shared,
they spitted the carved meat.

                         Just then my slumber
left me in a rush, my eyes opened,   470
and I went down the seaward path. No sooner
had I caught sight of our black hull, than savory
odors of burnt fat eddied around me;
grief took hold of me, and I cried aloud:

'O Father Zeus and gods in bliss forever,
you made me sleep away this day of mischief!
O cruel drowsing, in the evil hour!
Here they sat, and a great work they contrived.'

Lampetía in her long gown meanwhile
had borne swift word to the Overlord of Noon: 480

'They have killed your kine.'

                      And the Lord Hêlios
burst into angry speech amid the immortals:

'O Father Zeus and gods in bliss forever,
punish Odysseus' men! So overweening,
now they have killed my peaceful kine, my joy
at morning when I climbed the sky of stars,
and evening, when I bore westward from heaven.
Restitution or penalty they shall pay—
and pay in full—or I go down forever   490
to light the dead men in the underworld.'

Then Zeus who drives the stormcloud made reply:

'Peace, Hêlios: shine on among the gods,
shine over mortals in the fields of grain.
Let me throw down one white-hot bolt, and make
splinters of their ship in the winedark sea.'

—Kalypso later told me of this exchange,
as she declared that Hermês had told her.

Well, when I reached the sea cave and the ship,
I faced each man, and had it out; but where   500
could any remedy be found? There was none.
The silken beeves of Hêlios were dead.
The gods, moreover, made queer signs appear:
cowhides began to crawl, and beef, both raw
and roasted, lowed like kine upon the spits.

Now six full days my gallant crew could feast
upon the prime beef they had marked for slaughter
from Hêlios' herd; and Zeus, the son of Kronos,
added one fine morning.
                              All the gales   510
had ceased, blown out, and with an offshore breeze
we launched again, stepping the mast and sail,
to make for the open sea. Astern of us
the island coastline faded, and no land
showed anywhere, but only sea and heaven,
when Zeus Kroníon piled a thunderhead
above the ship, while gloom spread on the ocean.
We held our course, but briefly. Then the squall
struck whining from the west, with gale force, breaking
both forestays, and the mast came toppling aft   520
along the ship's length, so the running rigging
showered into the bilge.
                              On the after deck
the mast had hit the steersman a slant blow
bashing the skull in, knocking him overside,
as the brave soul fled the body, like a diver.
With crack on crack of thunder, Zeus let fly
a bolt against the ship, a direct hit,
so that she bucked, in reeking fumes of sulphur,
and all the men were flung into the sea.   530
They came up 'round the wreck, bobbing a while
like petrels on the waves.
                              No more seafaring
homeward for these, no sweet day of return;
the god had turned his face from them.
                              I clambered
fore and aft my hulk until a comber

split her, keel from ribs, and the big timber
floated free; the mast, too, broke away.
A backstay floated dangling from it, stout   540
rawhide rope, and I used this for lashing
mast and keel together. These I straddled,
riding the frightful storm.
                              Nor had I yet
seen the worst of it: for now the west wind
dropped, and a southeast gale came on—one more
twist of the knife—taking me north again,
straight for Kharybdis. All that night I drifted,
and in the sunrise, sure enough, I lay
off Skylla mountain and Kharybdis deep.   550
There, as the whirlpool drank the tide, a billow
tossed me, and I sprang for the great fig tree,
catching on like a bat under a bough.
Nowhere had I to stand, no way of climbing,
the root and bole being far below, and far
above my head the branches and their leaves,
massed, overshadowing Kharybdis pool.
But I clung grimly, thinking my mast and keel
would come back to the surface when she spouted.
And ah! how long, with what desire, I waited!   560
till, at the twilight hour, when one who hears
and judges pleas in the marketplace all day
between contentious men, goes home to supper,
the long poles at last reared from the sea.

Now I let go with hands and feet, plunging
straight into the foam beside the timbers,
pulled astride, and rowed hard with my hands
to pass by Skylla. Never could I have passed her
had not the Father of gods and men, this time,
kept me from her eyes. Once through the strait,   570
nine days I drifted in the open sea
before I made shore, buoyed up by the gods,
upon Ogýgia Isle. The dangerous nymph
Kalypso lives and sings there, in her beauty,
and she received me, loved me.

                                    But why tell
the same tale that I told last night in hall
to you and to your lady? Those adventures
made a long evening, and I do not hold
with tiresome repetition of a story."   580

BOOK THIRTEEN

One More Strange Island

LINES 1 – 15

He ended it, and no one stirred or sighed   1
in the shadowy hall, spellbound as they all were,
until Alkínoös answered:

                   "When you came
here to my strong home, Odysseus, under
my tall roof, headwinds were left behind you.
Clear sailing shall you have now, homeward now,
however painful all the past.

                   My lords,
ever my company, sharing the wine of Council,   10
the songs of the blind harper, hear me further:
garments are folded for our guest and friend
in the smooth chest, and gold
in various shaping of adornment lies
with other gifts, and many, brought by our peers;
let each man add his tripod and deep-bellied
cauldron: we'll make levy upon the realm
to pay us for the loss each bears in this."

Alkínoös had voiced their own hearts' wish.
All gave assent, then home they went to rest;   20
but young Dawn's finger tips of rose, touching
the world, roused them to make haste to the ship,
each with his gift of noble bronze. Alkínoös,
their ardent king, stepping aboard himself,
directed the stowing under the cross planks,
not to cramp the long pull of the oarsmen.
Going then to the great hall, lords and crew
prepared for feasting.

              As the gods' anointed,
Alkínoös made offering on their behalf—an ox   30
to Zeus beyond the stormcloud, Kronos' son,
who rules the world. They burnt the great thighbones
and feasted at their ease on fresh roast meat,
as in their midst the godlike harper sang—
Demódokos, honored by all that realm.

              Only Odysseus
time and again turned craning toward the sun,
impatient for day's end, for the open sea.
Just as a farmer's hunger grows, behind
the bolted plow and share, all day afield,   40
drawn by his team of winedark oxen: sundown
is benison for him, sending him homeward
stiff in the knees from weariness, to dine;
just so, the light on the sea rim gladdened Odysseus,
and as it dipped he stood among the Phaiákians,
turned to Alkínoös, and said:

"O king and admiration of your people,
give me fare well, and stain the ground with wine;
my blessings on you all! This hour brings
fulfillment to the longing of my heart: 50
a ship for home, and gifts the gods of heaven
make so precious and so bountiful.

              After this voyage
god grant I find my own wife in my hall
with everyone I love best, safe and sound!
And may you, settled in your land, give joy
to wives and children; may the gods reward you
every way, and your realm be free of woe."

Then all the voices rang out, "Be it so!"
and "Well spoken!" and "Let our friend make sail!"   60
Whereon Alkínoös gave command to his crier:

"Fill the winebowl, Pontónoös: mix and serve:
go the whole round, so may this company
invoke our Father Zeus, and bless our friend,
seaborne tonight and bound for his own country."

Pontónoös mixed the honey-hearted wine
and went from chair to chair, filling the cups;
then each man where he sat poured out his offering
to the gods in bliss who own the sweep of heaven.
With gentle bearing Odysseus rose, and placed   70
his double goblet in Arêtê's hands,
saying:

                              "Great Queen, farewell;
be blest through all your days till age comes on you,
and death, last end for mortals, after age.
Now I must go my way. Live in felicity,
and make this palace lovely for your children,
your countrymen, and your king, Alkínoös."

Royal Odysseus turned and crossed the doorsill,
a herald at his right hand, sent by Alkínoös   80
to lead him to the sea beach and the ship.
Arêtê, too, sent maids in waiting after him,
one with a laundered great cloak and a tunic,
a second balancing the crammed sea chest,
a third one bearing loaves and good red wine.
As soon as they arrived alongside, crewmen
took these things for stowage under the planks,
their victualling and drink; then spread a rug
and linen cover on the after deck,
where Lord Odysseus might sleep in peace.   90
Now he himself embarked, lay down, lay still,
while oarsmen took their places at the rowlocks
all in order. They untied their hawser,
passing it through a drilled stone ring; then bent

forward at the oars and caught the sea
as one man, stroking.
                        Slumber, soft and deep
like the still sleep of death, weighed on his eyes
as the ship hove seaward.
                        How a four horse team   100
whipped into a run on a straightaway
consumes the road, surging and surging over it!
So ran that craft and showed her heels to the swell,
her bow wave riding after, and her wake
on the purple night-sea foaming.
                        Hour by hour
she held her pace; not even a falcon wheeling
downwind, swiftest bird, could stay abreast of her
in that most arrowy flight through open water,
with her great passenger—godlike in counsel,   110
he that in twenty years had borne such blows
in his deep heart, breaking through ranks in war
and waves on the bitter sea.
                        This night at last
he slept serene, his long-tried mind at rest.

When on the East the sheer bright star arose
that tells of coming Dawn, the ship made landfall
and came up islandward in the dim of night.
Phorkys, the old sea baron, has a cove
here in the realm of Ithaka; two points   120
of high rock, breaking sharply, hunch around it,
making a haven from the plunging surf
that gales at sea roll shoreward. Deep inside,
at mooring range, good ships can ride unmoored.
There, on the inmost shore, an olive tree
throws wide its boughs over the bay; nearby
a cave of dusky light is hidden
for those immortal girls, the Naiadês.
Within are winebowls hollowed in the rock
and amphorai; bees bring their honey here;   130
and there are looms of stone, great looms, whereon
the weaving nymphs make tissues, richly dyed
as the deep sea is; and clear springs in the cavern

flow forever. Of two entrances,
one on the north allows descent of mortals,
but beings out of light alone, the undying,
can pass by the south slit; no men come there.

This cove the sailors knew. Here they drew in,
and the ship ran half her keel's length up the shore,
she had such way on her from those great oarsmen.   140
Then from their benches forward on dry ground
they disembarked. They hoisted up Odysseus
unruffled on his bed, under his cover,
handing him overside still fast asleep,
to lay him on the sand; and they unloaded
all those gifts the princes of Phaiákia
gave him, when by Athena's heart and will
he won his passage home. They bore this treasure
off the beach, and piled it close around
the roots of the olive tree, that no one passing   150
should steal Odysseus' gear before he woke.
That done, they pulled away on the homeward track.

But now the god that shakes the islands, brooding
over old threats of his against Odysseus,
approached Lord Zeus to learn his will. Said he:

"Father of gods, will the bright immortals ever
pay me respect again, if mortals do not?—
Phaiákians, too, my own blood kin?
                          I thought
Odysseus should in time regain his homeland;   160
I had no mind to rob him of that day—
no, no; you promised it, being so inclined;
only I thought he should be made to suffer
all the way.
                          But now these islanders
have shipped him homeward, sleeping soft, and put him
on Ithaka, with gifts untold
of bronze and gold, and fine cloth to his shoulder.
Never from Troy had he borne off such booty
if he had got home safe with all his share."   170

Then Zeus who drives the stormcloud answered, sighing:

"God of horizons, making earth's underbeam
tremble, why do you grumble so?
The immortal gods show you no less esteem,
and the rough consequence would make them slow
to let barbs fly at their eldest and most noble.
But if some mortal captain, overcome
by his own pride of strength, cuts or defies you,
are you not always free to take reprisal?
Act as your wrath requires and as you will."   180

Now said Poseidon, god of earthquake:

                         "Aye,
god of the stormy sky, I should have taken
vengeance, as you say, and on my own;
but I respect, and would avoid, your anger.
The sleek Phaiákian cutter, even now,
has carried out her mission and glides home
over the misty sea. Let me impale her,
end her voyage, and end all ocean-crossing
with passengers, then heave a mass of mountain   190
in a ring around the city."

Now Zeus who drives the stormcloud said benignly:

"Here is how I should do it, little brother:
when all who watch upon the wall have caught
sight of the ship, let her be turned to stone—
an island like a ship, just off the bay.
Mortals may gape at that for generations!
But throw no mountain round the sea port city."

When he heard this, Poseidon, god of earthquake,
departed for Skhería, where the Phaiákians   200
are born and dwell. Their ocean-going ship
he saw already near, heading for harbor;
so up behind her swam the island-shaker
and struck her into stone, rooted in stone, at one
blow of his palm,
                         then took to the open sea.

Those famous ship handlers, the Phaiákians,
gazed at each other, murmuring in wonder;
you could have heard one say:

"Now who in thunder   210
has anchored, moored that ship in the seaway,
when everyone could see her making harbor?"

The god had wrought a charm beyond their thought.
But soon Alkínoös made them hush, and told them:

"This present doom upon the ship—on me—
my father prophesied in the olden time.
If we gave safe conveyance to all passengers
we should incur Poseidon's wrath, he said,
whereby one day a fair ship, manned by Phaiákians,
would come to grief at the god's hands; and great   220
mountains would hide our city from the sea.
So my old father forecast.

Use your eyes:
these things are even now being brought to pass.
Let all here abide by my decree:

We make
an end henceforth of taking, in our ships,
castaways who may land upon Skhería;
and twelve choice bulls we dedicate at once
to Lord Poseidon, praying him of his mercy   230
not to heave up a mountain round our city."

In fearful awe they led the bulls to sacrifice
and stood about the altar stone, those captains,
peers of Phaiákia, led by their king in prayer
to Lord Poseidon.

Meanwhile, on his island,
his father's shore, that kingly man, Odysseus,
awoke, but could not tell what land it was
after so many years away; moreover,
Pallas Athena, Zeus's daughter, poured   240
a grey mist all around him, hiding him

from common sight—for she had things to tell him
and wished no one to know him, wife or townsmen,
before the suitors paid up for their crimes.

The landscape then looked strange, unearthly strange
to the Lord Odysseus: paths by hill and shore,
glimpses of harbors, cliffs, and summer trees.
He stood up, rubbed his eyes, gazed at his homeland,
and swore, slapping his thighs with both his palms,
then cried aloud: 250

        "What am I in for now?
Whose country have I come to this time? Rough
savages and outlaws, are they, or
godfearing people, friendly to castaways?
Where shall I take these things? Where take myself,
with no guide, no directions? These should be
still in Phaiákian hands, and I uncumbered,
free to find some other openhearted
prince who might be kind and give me passage.
I have no notion where to store this treasure;   260
first-comer's trove it is, if I leave it here.

My lords and captains of Phaiákia
were not those decent men they seemed, not honorable,
landing me in this unknown country—no,
by god, they swore to take me home to Ithaka
and did not! Zeus attend to their reward,
Zeus, patron of petitioners, who holds
all other mortals under his eye; he takes
payment from betrayers!
        I'll be busy.   270
I can look through my gear. I shouldn't wonder
if they pulled out with part of it on board."

He made a tally of his shining pile—
tripods, cauldrons, cloaks, and gold—and found
he lacked nothing at all.
        And then he wept,
despairing, for his own land, trudging down

beside the endless wash of the wide, wide sea,
weary and desolate as the sea. But soon
Athena came to him from the nearby air,   280
putting a young man's figure on—a shepherd,
like a king's son, all delicately made.
She wore a cloak, in two folds off her shoulders,
and sandals bound upon her shining feet.
A hunting lance lay in her hands.

                              At sight of her
Odysseus took heart, and he went forward
to greet the lad, speaking out fair and clear:

"Friend, you are the first man I've laid eyes on
here in this cove. Greetings. Do not feel   290
alarmed or hostile, coming across me; only
receive me into safety with my stores.
Touching your knees I ask it, as I might
ask grace of a god.

                              O sir, advise me,
what is this land and realm, who are the people?
Is it an island all distinct, or part
of the fertile mainland, sloping to the sea?"

To this grey-eyed Athena answered:

                              "Stranger,   300
you must come from the other end of nowhere,
else you are a great booby, having to ask
what place this is. It is no nameless country.
Why, everyone has heard of it, the nations
over on the dawn side, toward the sun,
and westerners in cloudy lands of evening.
No one would use this ground for training horses,
it is too broken, has no breadth of meadow;
but there is nothing meager about the soil,
the yield of grain is wondrous, and wine, too,   310
with drenching rains and dewfall.

                              There's good pasture
for oxen and for goats, all kinds of timber,
and water all year long in the cattle ponds.
For these blessings, friend, the name of Ithaka

has made its way even as far as Troy—
and they say Troy lies far beyond Akhaia."

Now Lord Odysseus, the long-enduring,
laughed in his heart, hearing his land described
by Pallas Athena, daughter of Zeus who rules   320
the veering stormwind; and he answered her
with ready speech—not that he told the truth,
but, just as she did, held back what he knew,
weighing within himself at every step
what he made up to serve his turn.

Said he:

"Far away in Krete I learned of Ithaka—
in that broad island over the great ocean.
And here I am now, come myself to Ithaka!
Here is my fortune with me. I left my sons   330
an equal part, when I shipped out. I killed
Orsílokhos, the courier, son of Idómeneus.
This man could beat the best cross country runners
in Krete, but he desired to take away
my Trojan plunder, all I had fought and bled for,
cutting through ranks in war and the cruel sea.
Confiscation is what he planned; he knew
I had not cared to win his father's favor
as a staff officer in the field at Troy,
but led my own command.   340
I acted: I
hit him with a spearcast from a roadside
as he came down from the open country. Murky
night shrouded all heaven and the stars.
I made that ambush with one man at arms.
We were unseen. I took his life in secret,
finished him off with my sharp sword. That night
I found asylum on a ship off shore
skippered by gentlemen of Phoinikia; I gave
all they could wish, out of my store of plunder,   350
for passage, and for landing me at Pylos
or Elis Town, where the Epeioi are in power.

Contrary winds carried them willy-nilly
past that coast; they had no wish to cheat me,
but we were blown off course.

                         Here, then, by night
we came, and made this haven by hard rowing.
All famished, but too tired to think of food,
each man dropped in his tracks after the landing,
and I slept hard, being wearied out. Before   360
I woke today, they put my things ashore
on the sand here beside me where I lay,
then reimbarked for Sidon, that great city.
Now they are far at sea, while I am left
forsaken here."

                        At this the grey-eyed goddess
Athena smiled, and gave him a caress,
her looks being changed now, so she seemed a woman,
tall and beautiful and no doubt skilled
at weaving splendid things. She answered briskly: 370

"Whoever gets around you must be sharp
and guileful as a snake; even a god
might bow to you in ways of dissimulation.
You! You chameleon!
Bottomless bag of tricks! Here in your own country
would you not give your stratagems a rest
or stop spellbinding for an instant?

You play a part as if it were your own tough skin.

No more of this, though. Two of a kind, we are,
contrivers, both. Of all men now alive   380
you are the best in plots and story telling.
My own fame is for wisdom among the gods—
deceptions, too.

                  Would even you have guessed
that I am Pallas Athena, daughter of Zeus,
I that am always with you in times of trial,
a shield to you in battle, I who made
the Phaiákians befriend you, to a man?

Now I am here again to counsel with you—
but first to put away those gifts the Phaiákians   390
gave you at departure—I planned it so.
Then I can tell you of the gall and wormwood
it is your lot to drink in your own hall.
Patience, iron patience, you must show;
so give it out to neither man nor woman
that you are back from wandering. Be silent
under all injuries, even blows from men."

His mind ranging far, Odysseus answered:

"Can mortal man be sure of you on sight,
even a sage, O mistress of disguises?   400
Once you were fond of me—I am sure of that—
years ago, when we Akhaians made
war, in our generation, upon Troy.
But after we had sacked the shrines of Priam
and put to sea, God scattered the Akhaians;
I never saw you after that, never
knew you aboard with me, to act as shield
in grievous times—not till you gave me comfort
in the rich hinterland of the Phaiákians
and were yourself my guide into that city.   410

Hear me now in your father's name, for I
cannot believe that I have come to Ithaka.
It is some other land. You made that speech
only to mock me, and to take me in.
Have I come back in truth to my home island?"

To this the grey-eyed goddess Athena answered:

"Always the same detachment! That is why
I cannot fail you, in your evil fortune,
coolheaded, quick, well-spoken as you are!
Would not another wandering man, in joy,   420
make haste home to his wife and children? Not
you, not yet. Before you hear their story
you will have proof about your wife.

                              I tell you,
she still sits where you left her, and her days
and nights go by forlorn, in lonely weeping.
For my part, never had I despaired; I felt
sure of your coming home, though all your men
should perish; but I never cared to fight
Poseidon, Father's brother, in his baleful   430
rage with you for taking his son's eye.

Now I shall make you see the shape of Ithaka.
Here is the cove the sea lord Phorkys owns,
there is the olive spreading out her leaves
over the inner bay, and there the cavern
dusky and lovely, hallowed by the feet
of those immortal girls, the Naiadês—
the same wide cave under whose vault you came
to honor them with hekatombs—and there
Mount Neion, with his forest on his back!"   440

She had dispelled the mist, so all the island
stood out clearly. Then indeed Odysseus'
heart stirred with joy. He kissed the earth,
and lifting up his hands prayed to the nymphs:

"O slim shy Naiadês, young maids of Zeus,
I had not thought to see you ever again!
                              O listen smiling
to my gentle prayers, and we'll make offering
plentiful as in the old time, granted I
live, granted my son grows tall, by favor   450
of great Athena, Zeus's daughter,
who gives the winning fighter his reward!"

The grey-eyed goddess said directly:

                              "Courage;
and let the future trouble you no more.
We go to make a cache now, in the cave,
to keep your treasure hid. Then we'll consider
how best the present action may unfold."

The goddess turned and entered the dim cave,
exploring it for crannies, while Odysseus   460
carried up all the gold, the fire-hard bronze,
and well-made clothing the Phaiákians gave him.
Pallas Athena, daughter of Zeus the storm king,
placed them, and shut the cave mouth with a stone,
and under the old grey olive tree those two
sat down to work the suitors death and woe.
Grey-eyed Athena was the first to speak, saying:

"Son of Laërtês and the gods of old,
Odysseus, master of land ways and sea ways,
put your mind on a way to reach and strike   470
a crowd of brazen upstarts.

                                    Three long years
they have played master in your house: three years
trying to win your lovely lady, making
gifts as though betrothed. And she? Forever
grieving for you, missing your return,
she has allowed them all to hope, and sent
messengers with promises to each—
though her true thoughts are fixed elsewhere."

                              At this   480
the man of ranging mind, Odysseus, cried:

"So hard beset! An end like Agamémnon's
might very likely have been mine, a bad end,
bleeding to death in my own hall. You forestalled it,
goddess, by telling me how the land lies.
Weave me a way to pay them back! And you, too,
take your place with me, breathe valor in me
the way you did that night when we Akhaians
unbound the bright veil from the brow of Troy!
O grey-eyed one, fire my heart and brace me!   490
I'll take on fighting men three hundred strong
if you fight at my back, immortal lady!"

The grey-eyed goddess Athena answered him:

"No fear but I shall be there; you'll go forward
under my arm when the crux comes at last.

And I foresee your vast floor stained with blood,
spattered with brains of this or that tall suitor
who fed upon your cattle.

               Now, for a while,
I shall transform you; not a soul will know you,   500
the clear skin of your arms and legs shriveled,
your chestnut hair all gone, your body dressed
in sacking that a man would gag to see,
and the two eyes, that were so brilliant, dirtied—
contemptible, you shall seem to your enemies,
as to the wife and son you left behind.

But join the swineherd first—the overseer
of all your swine, a good soul now as ever,
devoted to Penélopê and your son.
He will be found near Raven's Rock and the well   510
of Arethousa, where the swine are pastured,
rooting for acorns to their hearts' content,
drinking the dark still water. Boarflesh grows
pink and fat on that fresh diet. There
stay with him, and question him, while I
am off to the great beauty's land of Sparta,
to call your son Telémakhos home again—
for you should know, he went to the wide land
of Lakedaimon, Meneláos' country,
to learn if there were news of you abroad."   520

Odysseus answered:

                  "Why not tell him, knowing
my whole history, as you do? Must he
traverse the barren sea, he too, and live
in pain, while others feed on what is his?"

At this the grey-eyed goddess Athena said:

"No need for anguish on that lad's account.
I sent him off myself, to make his name
in foreign parts—no hardship in the bargain,
taking his ease in Meneláos' mansion,   530
lapped in gold.

The young bucks here, I know,
lie in wait for him in a cutter, bent
on murdering him before he reaches home.
I rather doubt they will. Cold earth instead
will take in her embrace a man or two
of those who fed so long on what is his."

Speaking no more, she touched him with her wand,
shriveled the clear skin of his arms and legs,
made all his hair fall out, cast over him   540
the wrinkled hide of an old man, and bleared
both his eyes, that were so bright. Then she
clapped an old tunic, a foul cloak, upon him,
tattered, filthy, stained by greasy smoke,
and over that a mangy big buck skin.
A staff she gave him, and a leaky knapsack
with no strap but a loop of string.
                              Now then,
their colloquy at an end, they went their ways—
Athena toward illustrious Lakedaimon   550
far over sea, to join Odysseus' son.

BOOK FOURTEEN

Hospitality
in the Forest

LINES 1 – 17

He went up from the cove through wooded ground,   1
taking a stony trail into the high hills, where
the swineherd lived, according to Athena.
Of all Odysseus' field hands in the old days
this forester cared most for the estate;
and now Odysseus found him
in a remote clearing, sitting inside the gate
of a stockade he built to keep the swine
while his great lord was gone.

                            Working alone,   10
far from Penélopê and old Laërtês,
he had put up a fieldstone hut and timbered it
with wild pear wood. Dark hearts of oak he split
and trimmed for a high palisade around it,
and built twelve sties adjoining in this yard
to hold the livestock. Fifty sows with farrows
were penned in each, bedded upon the earth,
while the boars lay outside—fewer by far,

as those well-fatted were for the suitors' table,
fine pork, sent by the swineherd every day.   20
Three hundred sixty now lay there at night,
guarded by dogs—four dogs like wolves, one each
for the four lads the swineherd reared and kept
as under-herdsmen.
                          When Odysseus came,
the good servant sat shaping to his feet
oxhide for sandals, cutting the well-cured leather.
Three of his young men were afield, pasturing
herds in other woods; one he had sent
with a fat boar for tribute into town,   30
the boy to serve while the suitors got their fill.

The watch dogs, when they caught sight of Odysseus,
faced him, a snarling troop, and pelted out
viciously after him. Like a tricky beggar
he sat down plump, and dropped his stick. No use.
They would have rolled him in the dust and torn him
there by his own steading if the swineherd
had not sprung up and flung his leather down,
making a beeline for the open. Shouting,
throwing stone after stone,   40
he made them scatter; then turned to his lord
and said:

                          "You might have got a ripping, man!
Two shakes more and a pretty mess for me
you could have called it, if you had the breath.
As though I had not trouble enough already,
given me by the gods, my master gone,
true king that he was. I hang on here,
still mourning for him, raising pigs of his
to feed foreigners, and who knows where the man is,   50
in some far country among strangers! Aye—
if he is living still, if he still sees the light of day.

Come to the cabin. You're a wanderer too.
You must eat something, drink some wine, and tell me
where you are from and the hard times you've seen."

The forester now led him to his hut
and made a couch for him, with tips of fir
piled for a mattress under a wild goat skin,
shaggy and thick, his own bed covering.
                              Odysseus,   60
in pleasure at this courtesy, gently said:

"May Zeus and all the gods give you your heart's desire
for taking me in so kindly, friend."

                              Eumaios—
O my swineherd!—answered him:

                              "Tush, friend,
rudeness to a stranger is not decency,
poor though he may be, poorer than you.
                              All wanderers
and beggars come from Zeus. What we can give   70
is slight but well-meant—all we dare. You know
that is the way of slaves, who live in dread
of masters—new ones like our own.
                              I told you
the gods, long ago, hindered our lord's return.
He had a fondness for me, would have pensioned me
with acres of my own, a house, a wife
that other men admired and courted; all
gifts good-hearted kings bestow for service,
for a life work the bounty of god has prospered—   80
for it does prosper here, this work I do.
Had he grown old in his own house, my master
would have rewarded me. But the man's gone.
God curse the race of Helen and cut it down,
that wrung the strength out of the knees of many!
And he went, too—for the honor of Agemémnon
he took ship overseas for the wild horse country
of Troy, to fight the Trojans."

                              This being told,
he tucked his long shirt up inside his belt
and strode into the pens for two young porkers.   90
He slaughtered them and singed them at the fire,

flayed and quartered them, and skewered the meat
to broil it all; then gave it to Odysseus
hot on the spits. He shook out barley meal,
took a winebowl of ivy wood and filled it,
and sat down facing him, with a gesture, saying:

"There is your dinner, friend, the pork of slaves.
Our fat shoats are all eaten by the suitors,
cold-hearted men, who never spare a thought   100
for how they stand in the sight of Zeus. The gods
living in bliss are fond of no wrongdoing,
but honor discipline and right behavior.
Even the outcasts of the earth, who bring
piracy from the sea, and bear off plunder
given by Zeus in shiploads—even those men
deep in their hearts tremble for heaven's eye.
But the suitors, now, have heard some word, some oracle
of my lord's death, being so unconcerned
to pay court properly or to go about their business.   110
All they want is to prey on his estate,
proud dogs; they stop at nothing. Not a day
goes by, and not a night comes under Zeus,
but they make butchery of our beeves and swine—
not one or two beasts at a time, either.
As for swilling down wine, they drink us dry.
Only a great domain like his could stand it—
greater than any on the dusky mainland
or here in Ithaka. Not twenty heroes
in the whole world were as rich as he. I know: 120
I could count it all up: twelve herds in Elis,
as many flocks, as many herds of swine,
and twelve wide-ranging herds of goats, as well,
attended by his own men or by others—
out at the end of the island, eleven herds
are scattered now, with good men looking after them,
and every herdsman, every day, picks out
a prize ram to hand over to those fellows.
I too as overseer, keeper of swine,
must go through all my boars and send the best."   130

While he ran on, Odysseus with zeal
applied himself to the meat and wine, but inwardly
his thought shaped woe and ruin for the suitors.
When he had eaten all that he desired
and the cup he drank from had been filled again
with wine—a welcome sight—,
he spoke, and the words came light upon the air:

"Who is this lord who once acquired you,
so rich, so powerful, as you describe him?
You think he died for Agamémnon's honor.   140
Tell me his name: I may have met someone
of that description in my time. Who knows?
Perhaps only the immortal gods could say
if I should claim to have seen him: I have roamed
about the world so long."

                              The swineherd answered
as one who held a place of trust:

                              "Well, man,
his lady and his son will put no stock
in any news of him brought by a rover.   150
Wandering men tell lies for a night's lodging,
for fresh clothing; truth doesn't interest them.
Every time some traveller comes ashore
he has to tell my mistress his pretty tale,
and she receives him kindly, questions him,
remembering her prince, while the tears run
down her cheeks—and that is as it should be
when a woman's husband has been lost abroad.
I suppose you, too, can work your story up
at a moment's notice, given a shirt or cloak.   160
No: long ago wild dogs and carrion
birds, most like, laid bare his ribs on land
where life had left him. Or it may be, quick fishes
picked him clean in the deep sea, and his bones
lie mounded over in sand upon some shore.
One way or another, far from home he died,
a bitter loss, and pain, for everyone,
certainly for me. Never again shall I

have for my lot a master mild as he was
anywhere—not even with my parents   170
at home, where I was born and bred. I miss them
less than I do him—though a longing comes
to set my eyes on them in the old country.
No, it is the lost man I ache to think of—
Odysseus. And I speak the name respectfully,
even if he is not here. He loved me, cared for me.
I call him dear my lord, far though he be."

Now royal Odysseus, who had borne the long war,
spoke again:

                         "Friend, as you are so dead sure   180
he will not come—and so mistrustful, too—
let me not merely talk, as others talk,
but swear to it: your lord is now at hand.
And I expect a gift for this good news
when he enters his own hall. Till then I would not
take a rag, no matter what my need.
I hate as I hate Hell's own gate that weakness
that makes a poor man into a flatterer.
Zeus be my witness, and the table garnished
for true friends, and Odysseus' own hearth—   190
by heaven, all I say will come to pass!
He will return, and he will be avenged
on any who dishonor his wife and son."

Eumaios—O my swineherd!—answered him:

"I take you at your word, then: you shall have
no good news gift from me. Nor will Odysseus
enter his hall. But peace! drink up your wine.
Let us talk now of other things. No more
imaginings. It makes me heavy-hearted
when someone brings my master back to mind—   200
my own true master.

                  No, by heaven,
let us have no oaths! But if Odysseus
can come again god send he may! My wish
is that of Penélopê and old Laërtês
and Prince Telémakhos.

                              Ah, he's another
to be distressed about—Odysseus' child,
Telémakhos! By the gods' grace he grew
like a tough sapling, and I thought he'd be   210
no less a man than his great father—strong
and admirably made; but then someone,
god or man, upset him, made him rash,
so that he sailed away to sandy Pylos
to hear news of his father. Now the suitors
lie in ambush on his homeward track,
ready to cut away the last shoot of Arkêsios'
line, the royal stock of Ithaka.
                              No good
dwelling on it. Either he'll be caught   220
or else Kroníon's hand will take him through.

Tell me, now, of your own trials and troubles.
And tell me truly first, for I should know,
who are you, where do you hail from, where's your home
and family? What kind of ship was yours,
and what course brought you here? Who are your sailors?
I don't suppose you walked here on the sea."

To this the master of improvisation answered:

"I'll tell you all that, clearly as I may.
If we could sit here long enough, with meat   230
and good sweet wine, warm here, in peace and quiet
within doors, while the work of the world goes on—
I might take all this year to tell my story
and never end the tale of misadventures
that wore my heart out, by the gods' will.

My native land is the wide seaboard of Krete
where I grew up. I had a wealthy father,
and many other sons were born to him
of his true lady. My mother was a slave,
his concubine; but Kastor Hylákidês,   240
my father, treated me as a true born son.
High honor came to him in that part of Krete
for wealth and ease, and sons born for renown,

before the death-bearing Kêrês drew him down
to the underworld. His avid sons thereafter
dividing up the property by lot
gave me a wretched portion, a poor house.
But my ability won me a wife
of rich family. Fool I was never called,
nor turn-tail in a fight.   250

                    My strength's all gone,
but from the husk you may divine the ear
that stood tall in the old days. Misery owns me
now, but then great Arês and Athena
gave me valor and man-breaking power,
whenever I made choice of men-at-arms
to set a trap with me for my enemies.
Never, as I am a man, did I fear Death
ahead, but went in foremost in the charge,
putting a spear through any man whose legs   260
were not as fast as mine. That was my element,
war and battle. Farming I never cared for,
nor life at home, nor fathering fair children.
I reveled in long ships with oars; I loved
polished lances, arrows in the skirmish,
the shapes of doom that others shake to see.
Carnage suited me; heaven put those things
in me somehow. Each to his own pleasure!
Before we young Akhaians shipped for Troy
I led men on nine cruises in corsairs   270
to raid strange coasts, and had great luck, taking
rich spoils on the spot, and even more
in the division. So my house grew prosperous,
my standing therefore high among the Kretans.
Then came the day when Zeus who views the wide world
drew men's eyes upon that way accurst
that wrung the manhood from the knees of many!
Everyone pressed me, pressed King Idómeneus
to take command of ships for Ilion.
No way out; the country rang with talk of it.   280
So we Akhaians had nine years of war.
In the tenth year we sacked the inner city,
Priam's town, and sailed for home; but heaven

dispersed the Akhaians. Evil days for me
were stored up in the hidden mind of Zeus.
One month, no more, I stayed at home in joy
with children, wife, and treasure. Lust for action
drove me to go to sea then, in command
of ships and gallant seamen bound for Egypt.
Nine ships I fitted out; my men signed on   290
and came to feast with me, as good shipmates,
for six full days. Many a beast I slaughtered
in the gods' honor, for my friends to eat.
Embarking on the seventh, we hauled sail
and filled away from Krete on a fresh north wind
effortlessly, as boats will glide down stream.
All rigging whole and all hands well, we rested,
letting the wind and steersmen work the ships,
for five days; on the fifth we made the delta.
I brought my squadron in to the river bank   300
with one turn of the sweeps. There, heaven knows,
I told the men to wait and guard the ships
while I sent out patrols to rising ground.
But reckless greed carried them all away
to plunder the rich bottomlands; they bore off
wives and children, killed what men they found.

When this news reached the city, all who heard it
came at dawn. On foot they came, and horsemen,
filling the river plain with dazzle of bronze;
and Zeus lord of lightning   310
threw my men into blind panic: no one dared
stand against that host closing around us.
Their scything weapons left our dead in piles,
but some they took alive, into forced labor.
And I—ah, how I wish that I had died
in Egypt, on that field! So many blows
awaited me!— Well, Zeus himself inspired me;
I wrenched my dogskin helmet off my head,
dropped my spear, dodged out of my long shield,
ran for the king's chariot and swung on   320
to embrace and kiss his knees. He pulled me up,
took pity on me, placed me on the footboards,

and drove home with me crouching there in tears.
Aye—for the troops, in battle fury still,
made one pass at me after another, pricking me
with spears, hoping to kill me. But he saved me,
for fear of the great wrath of Zeus that comes
when men who ask asylum are given death.

Seven years, then, my sojourn lasted there,
and I amassed a fortune, going about   330
among the openhanded Egyptians.
But when the eighth came round, a certain
Phoinikian adventurer came too,
a plausible rat, who had already done
plenty of devilry in the world.

                              This fellow
took me in completely with his schemes,
and led me with him to Phoinikia,
where he had land and houses. One full year
I stayed there with him, to the month and day,   340
and when fair weather came around again
he took me in a deepsea ship for Libya,
pretending I could help in the cargo trade;
he meant, in fact, to trade me off, and get
a high price for me. I could guess the game
but had to follow him aboard. One day
on course due west, off central Krete, the ship
caught a fresh norther, and we ran southward
before the wind while Zeus piled ruin ahead.
When Krete was out of sight astern, no land   350
anywhere to be seen, but sky and ocean,
Kroníon put a dark cloud in the zenith
over the ship, and gloom spread on the sea.
With crack on crack of thunder, he let fly
a bolt against the ship, a direct hit,
so that she bucked, in sacred fumes of sulphur,
and all the men were flung into the water.
They came up round the wreck, bobbing a while
like petrels on the waves. No homecoming
for these, from whom the god had turned his face!   360

Stunned in the smother as I was, yet Zeus
put into my hands the great mast of the ship—
a way to keep from drowning. So I twined
my arms and legs around it in the gale
and stayed afloat nine days. On the tenth night,
a big surf cast me up in Thesprotia.
Pheidon the king there gave me refuge, nobly,
with no talk of reward. His son discovered me
exhausted and half dead with cold, and gave me
a hand to bear me up till he reached home   370
where he could clothe me in a shirt and cloak.
In that king's house I heard news of Odysseus,
who lately was a guest there, passing by
on his way home, the king said; and he showed me
the treasure that Odysseus had brought:
bronze, gold, and iron wrought with heavy labor—
in that great room I saw enough to last
Odysseus' heirs for ten long generations.
The man himself had gone up to Dodona
to ask the spelling leaves of the old oak   380
the will of God: how to return, that is,
to the rich realm of Ithaka, after so long
an absence—openly, or on the quiet.
And, tipping wine out, Pheidon swore to me
the ship was launched, the seamen standing by
to take Odysseus to his land at last.
But he had passage first for me: Thesprotians
were sailing, as luck had it, for Doulíkhion,
the grain-growing island; there, he said,
they were to bring me to the king, Akastos.   390
Instead, that company saw fit to plot
foul play against me; in my wretched life
there was to be more suffering.
                                    At sea, then,
when land lay far astern, they sprang their trap.
They'd make a slave of me that day, stripping
cloak and tunic off me, throwing around me
the dirty rags you see before you now.
At evening, off the fields of Ithaka,
they bound me, lashed me down under the decking   400

with stout ship's rope, while they all went ashore
in haste to make their supper on the beach.
The gods helped me to pry the lashing loose
until it fell away. I wound my rags
in a bundle round my head and eased myself
down the smooth lading plank into the water,
up to the chin, then swam an easy breast stroke
out and around, putting that crew behind,
and went ashore in underbrush, a thicket,
where I lay still, making myself small.   410
They raised a bitter yelling, and passed by
several times. When further groping seemed
useless to them, back to the ship they went
and out to sea again. The gods were with me,
keeping me hid; and with me when they brought me
here to the door of one who knows the world.
My destiny is yet to live awhile."

The swineherd bowed and said:

                              "Ah well, poor drifter,
you've made me sad for you, going back over it,   420
all your hard life and wandering. That tale
about Odysseus, though, you might have spared me;
you will not make me believe that.
Why must you lie, being the man you are,
and all for nothing?
                              I can see so well
what happened to my master, sailing home!
Surely the gods turned on him, to refuse him
death in the field, or in his friends' arms
after he wound up the great war at Troy.   430
They would have made a tomb for him, the Akhaians,
and paid all honor to his son thereafter. No,
stormwinds made off with him. No glory came to him.

I moved here to the mountain with my swine.
Never, now, do I go down to town
unless I am sent for by Penélopê
when news of some sort comes. But those who sit
around her go on asking the old questions—

a few who miss their master still,
and those who eat his house up, and go free.   440
For my part, I have had no heart for inquiry
since one year an Aitolian made a fool of me.
Exiled from land to land after some killing,
he turned up at my door; I took him in.
My master he had seen in Krete, he said,
lodged with Idómeneus, while the long ships,
leaky from gales, were laid up for repairs.
But they were all to sail, he said, that summer,
or the first days of fall—hulls laden deep
with treasure, manned by crews of heroes.   450
                                    This time
you are the derelict the Powers bring.
Well, give up trying to win me with false news
or flattery. If I receive and shelter you,
it is not for your tales but for your trouble,
and with an eye to Zeus, who guards a guest."

Then said that sly and guileful man, Odysseus:

"A black suspicious heart beats in you surely;
the man you are, not even an oath could change you.
Come then, we'll make a compact; let the gods   460
witness it from Olympos, where they dwell.
Upon your lord's homecoming, if he comes
here to this very hut, and soon—
then give me a new outfit, shirt and cloak,
and ship me to Doulíkhion—I thought it
a pleasant island. But if Odysseus
fails to appear as I predict, then Swish!
let the slaves pitch me down from some high rock,
so the next poor man who comes will watch his tongue."

The forester gave a snort and answered: 470

                        "Friend,
if I agreed to that, a great name
I should acquire in the world for goodness—
at one stroke and forever: your kind host
who gave you shelter and the hand of friendship,

only to take your life next day!
How confidently, after that, should I
address my prayers to Zeus, the son of Kronos!

It is time now for supper. My young herdsmen
should be arriving soon to set about it.   480
We'll make a quiet feast here at our hearth."

At this point in their talk the swine had come
up to the clearing, and the drovers followed
to pen them for the night—the porkers squealing
to high heaven, milling around the yard.
The swineherd then gave orders to his men:

"Bring in our best pig for a stranger's dinner.
A feast will do our hearts good, too; we know
grief and pain, hard scrabbling with our swine,
while the outsiders live on our labor."   490

                              Bronze
axe in hand, he turned to split up kindling,
while they drove in a tall boar, prime and fat,
planting him square before the fire. The gods,
as ever, had their due in the swineherd's thought,
for he it was who tossed the forehead bristles
as a first offering on the flames, calling
upon the immortal gods to let Odysseus
reach his home once more.

                    Then he stood up   500
and brained the boar with split oak from the woodpile.
Life ebbed from the beast; they slaughtered him,
singed the carcass, and cut out the joints.
Eumaios, taking flesh from every quarter,
put lean strips on the fat of sacrifice,
floured each one with barley meal, and cast it
into the blaze. The rest they sliced and skewered,
roasted with care, then took it off the fire
and heaped it up on platters. Now their chief,
who knew best the amenities, rose to serve,   510
dividing all that meat in seven portions—
one to be set aside, with proper prayers,

for the wood nymphs and Hermês, Maia's son;
the others for the company. Odysseus
he honored with long slices from the chine—
warming the master's heart. Odysseus looked at him
and said:

                    "May you be dear to Zeus
as you are dear to me for this, Eumaios,
favoring with choice cuts a man like me."   520

And—O my swineherd!—you replied, Eumaios:

"Bless you, stranger, fall to and enjoy it
for what it is. Zeus grants us this or that,
or else refrains from granting, as he wills;
all things are in his power."

                  He cut and burnt
a morsel for the gods who are young forever,
tipped out some wine, then put it in the hands
of Odysseus, the old soldier, raider of cities,
who sat at ease now with his meat before him.   530
As for the loaves, Mesaúlios dealt them out,
a yard boy, bought by the swineherd on his own,
unaided by his mistress or Laërtês,
from Taphians, while Odysseus was away.
Now all hands reached for that array of supper,
until, when hunger and thirst were turned away
Mesaúlios removed the bread and, heavy
with food and drink, they settled back to rest.

Now night had come on, rough, with no moon,
but a nightlong downpour setting in, the rainwind   540
blowing hard from the west. Odysseus
began to talk, to test the swineherd, trying
to put it in his head to take his cloak off
and lend it, or else urge the others to.
He knew the man's compassion.

                "Listen," he said,
"Eumaios, and you others, here's a wishful
tale that I shall tell. The wine's behind it,

vaporing wine, that makes a serious man
break down and sing, kick up his heels and clown,   550
or tell some story that were best untold.
But now I'm launched, I can't stop now.

                        Would god I felt
the hot blood in me that I had at Troy!
Laying an ambush near the walls one time,
Odysseus and Meneláos were commanders
and I ranked third. I went at their request.
We worked in toward the bluffs and battlements
and, circling the town, got into canebrakes,
thick and high, a marsh where we took cover,   560
hunched under arms.

                      The northwind dropped, and night
came black and wintry. A fine sleet descending
whitened the cane like hoarfrost, and clear ice
grew dense upon our shields. The other men,
all wrapt in blanket cloaks as well as tunics,
rested well, in shields up to their shoulders,
but I had left my cloak with friends in camp,
foolhardy as I was. No chance of freezing hard,
I thought, so I wore kilts and a shield only.   570
But in the small hours of the third watch, when stars
that rise at evening go down to their setting,
I nudged Odysseus, who lay close beside me;
he was alert then, listening, and I said:

'Son of Laërtês and the gods of old,
Odysseus, master mariner and soldier,
I cannot hold on long among the living.
The cold is making a corpse of me. Some god
inveigled me to come without a cloak.
No help for it now; too late.'   580

                      Next thing I knew
he had a scheme all ready in his mind—
and what a man he was for schemes and battles!
Speaking under his breath to me, he murmured:

'Quiet; none of the rest should hear you.'

                              Then,
propping his head on his forearm, he said:

'Listen, lads, I had an ominous dream,
the point being how far forward from our ships
and lines we've come. Someone should volunteer   590
to tell the corps commander, Agamémnon;
he may reinforce us from the base.'

                              At this,
Thoas jumped up, the young son of Andraimon,
put down his crimson cloak and headed off,
running shoreward.

                              Wrapped in that man's cloak
how gratefully I lay in the bitter dark
until the dawn came stitched in gold! I wish
I had that sap and fiber in me now!"   600

Then—O my swineherd!—you replied, Eumaios:

"That was a fine story, and well told,
not a word out of place, not a pointless word.
No, you'll not sleep cold for lack of cover,
or any other comfort one should give
to a needy guest. However, in the morning,
you must go flapping in the same old clothes.
Shirts and cloaks are few here; every man
has one change only. When our prince arrives,
the son of Odysseus, he will make you gifts—   610
cloak, tunic, everything—and grant you passage
wherever you care to go."

                              On this he rose
and placed the bed of balsam near the fire,
strewing sheepskins on top, and skins of goats.
Odysseus lay down. His host threw over him
a heavy blanket cloak, his own reserve
against the winter wind when it came wild.
So there Odysseus dropped off to sleep,
while herdsmen slept nearby. But not the swineherd: 620
not in the hut could he lie down in peace,

but now equipped himself for the night outside;
and this rejoiced Odysseus' heart, to see him
care for the herd so, while his lord was gone.
He hung a sharp sword from his shoulder, gathered
a great cloak round him, close, to break the wind,
and pulled a shaggy goatskin on his head.
Then, to keep at a distance dogs or men,
he took a sharpened lance, and went to rest
under a hollow rock where swine were sleeping   630
out of the wind and rain.

BOOK FIFTEEN

How They Came to Ithaka

LINES 1 – 11

South into Lakedaimon 1

into the land where greens are wide for dancing
Athena went, to put in mind of home
her great-hearted hero's honored son,
rousing him to return.

And there she found him

with Nestor's lad in the late night at rest
under the portico of Meneláos,
the famous king. Stilled by the power of slumber
the son of Nestor lay, but honeyed sleep   10
had not yet taken in her arms Telémakhos.
All through the starlit night, with open eyes,
he pondered what he had heard about his father,
until at his bedside grey-eyed Athena
towered and said:

"The brave thing now, Telémakhos,

would be to end this journey far from home.
All that you own you left behind

with men so lost to honor in your house
they may devour it all, shared out among them.   20
How will your journey save you then?
                              Go quickly
to the lord of the great war cry, Meneláos;
press him to send you back. You may yet find
the queen your mother in her rooms alone.
It seems her father and her kinsmen say
Eurýmakhos is the man for her to marry.
He has outdone the suitors, all the rest,
in gifts to her, and made his pledges double.
Check him, or he will have your lands and chattels   30
in spite of you.
                         You know a woman's pride
at bringing riches to the man she marries.
As to her girlhood husband, her first children,
he is forgotten, being dead—and they
no longer worry her.
                            So act alone.
Go back; entrust your riches to the servant
worthiest in your eyes, until the gods
make known what beauty you yourself shall marry.   40

This too I have to tell you: now take heed:
the suitors' ringleaders are hot for murder,
waiting in the channel between Ithaka
and Samê's rocky side; they mean to kill you
before you can set foot ashore. I doubt
they'll bring it off. Dark earth instead
may take to her cold bed a few brave suitors
who preyed upon your cattle.
                                  Bear well out
in your good ship, to eastward of the islands,   50
and sail again by night. Someone immortal
who cares for you will make a fair wind blow.
Touch at the first beach, go ashore, and send
your ship and crew around to port by sea,
while you go inland to the forester,
your old friend, loyal keeper of the swine.
Remain that night with him; send him to town

to tell your watchful mother Penélopê
that you are back from Pylos safe and sound."

With this Athena left him for Olympos.   60
He swung his foot across and gave a kick
and said to the son of Nestor:

                            "Open your eyes,
Peisístratos. Get our team into harness.
We have a long day's journey."

                            Nestor's son
turned over and answered him:

                            "It is still night,
and no moon. Can we drive now? We can not,
itch as we may for the road home. Dawn is near.   70
Allow the captain of spearmen, Meneláos,
time to pack our car with gifts and time
to speak a gracious word, sending us off.
A guest remembers all his days
that host who makes provision for him kindly."

The Dawn soon took her throne of gold, and Lord
Meneláos, clarion in battle,
rose from where he lay beside the beauty
of Helen with her shining hair. He strode
into the hall nearby.   80
                            Hearing him come,
Odysseus' son pulled on his snowy tunic
over the skin, gathered his long cape
about his breadth of shoulder like a captain,
the heir of King Odysseus. At the door
he stood and said:

                            "Lord Marshal, Meneláos,
send me home now to my own dear country:
longing has come upon me to go home."

The lord of the great war cry said at once: 90

"If you are longing to go home, Telémakhos,
I would not keep you for the world, not I.

I'd think myself or any other host
as ill-mannered for over-friendliness
as for hostility.

                    Measure is best in everything.
To send a guest packing, or cling to him
when he's in haste—one sin equals the other.
'Good entertaining ends with no detaining.'
Only let me load your car with gifts   100
and fine ones, you shall see.

                    I'll bid the women
set out breakfast from the larder stores;
honor and appetite—we'll attend to both
before a long day's journey overland.
Or would you care to try the Argive midlands
and Hellas, in my company? I'll harness
my own team, and take you through the towns.
Guests like ourselves no lord will turn away;
each one will make one gift, at least,   110
to carry home with us: tripod or cauldron
wrought in bronze, mule team, or golden cup."

Clearheaded Telémakhos replied:

                    "Lord Marshal
Meneláos, royal son of Atreus,
I must return to my own hearth. I left
no one behind as guardian of my property.
This going abroad for news of a great father—
heaven forbid it be my own undoing,
or any precious thing be lost at home."   120

At this the tall king, clarion in battle,
called to his lady and her waiting women
to give them breakfast from the larder stores.
Eteóneus, the son of Boethoös, came
straight from bed, from where he lodged nearby,
and Meneláos ordered a fire lit
for broiling mutton. The king's man obeyed.
Then down to the cedar chamber Meneláos
walked with Helen and Prince Megapénthês.

Amid the gold he had in that place lying   130
the son of Atreus picked a wine cup, wrought
with handles left and right, and told his son
to take a silver winebowl.
                              Helen lingered
near the deep coffers filled with gowns, her own
handiwork.
                              Tall goddess among women,
she lifted out one robe of state so royal,
adorned and brilliant with embroidery,
deep in the chest it shimmered like a star.   140
Now all three turned back to the door to greet
Telémakhos. And red-haired Meneláos
cried out to him:

                              "O prince Telémakhos,
may Hêra's Lord of Thunder see you home
and bring you to the welcome you desire!
Here are your gifts—perfect and precious things
I wish to make your own, out of my treasure."

And gently the great captain, son of Atreus,
handed him the goblet. Megapénthês   150
carried the winebowl glinting silvery
to set before him, and the Lady Helen
drew near, so that he saw her cheek's pure line.
She held the gown and murmured:

"I, too,
bring you a gift, dear child, and here it is;
remember Helen's hands by this; keep it
for your own bride, your joyful wedding day;
let your dear mother guard it in her chamber.
My blessing: may you come soon to your island,   160
home to your timbered hall."

                              So she bestowed it,
and happily he took it. These fine things
Peisístratos packed well in the wicker carrier,
admiring every one. Then Meneláos
led the two guests in to take their seats

on thrones and easy chairs in the great hall.
Now came a maid to tip a golden jug
of water over a silver finger bowl,
and draw the polished tables up beside them;   170
the larder mistress brought her tray of loaves,
with many savories to lavish on them;
viands were served by Eteóneus, and wine
by Meneláos' son. Then every hand
reached out upon good meat and drink to take them,
driving away hunger and thirst. At last,
Telémakhos and Nestor's son led out
their team to harness, mounted their bright car,
and drove down under the echoing entrance way,
while red-haired Meneláos, Atreus' son,   180
walked alongside with a golden cup—
wine for the wayfarers to spill at parting.
Then by the tugging team he stood, and spoke
over the horses' heads:

                             "Farewell, my lads.
Homage to Nestor, the benevolent king;
in my time he was fatherly to me,
when the flower of Akhaia warred on Troy."

Telémakhos made this reply:

"No fear   190
but we shall bear at least as far as Nestor
your messages, great king. How I could wish
to bring them home to Ithaka! If only
Odysseus were there, if he could hear me tell
of all the courtesy I have had from you,
returning with your finery and your treasure."

Even as he spoke, a beat of wings went skyward
off to the right—a mountain eagle, grappling
a white goose in his talons, heavy prey
hooked from a farmyard. Women and men-at-arms   200
made hubbub, running up, as he flew over,
but then he wheeled hard right before the horses—
a sight that made the whole crowd cheer, with hearts
lifting in joy. Peisístratos called out:

"Read us the sign, O Meneláos, Lord
Marshal of armies! Was the god revealing
something thus to you, or to ourselves?"

At this the old friend of the god of battle
groped in his mind for the right thing to say,
but regal Helen put in quickly: 210

"Listen:
I can tell you—tell what the omen means,
as light is given me, and as I see it
point by point fulfilled. The beaked eagle
flew from the wild mountain of his fathers
to take for prey the tame house bird. Just so,
Odysseus, back from his hard trials and wandering,
will soon come down in fury on his house.
He may be there today, and a black hour
he brings upon the suitors."   220

                    Telémakhos
gazed and said:

                         "May Zeus, the lord of Hêra,
make it so! In far-off Ithaka, all my life,
I shall invoke you as a goddess, lady."

He let the whip fall, and the restive mares
broke forward at a canter through the town
into the open country.

                         All that day
they kept their harness shaking, side by side,   230
until at sundown when the roads grew dim
they made a halt at Pherai. There Dióklês
son of Ortílokhos whom Alpheios fathered,
welcomed the young men, and they slept the night.
Up when the young Dawn's finger tips of rose
opened in the east, they hitched the team
once more to the painted car
and steered out westward through the echoing gate,
whipping their fresh horses into a run.

Approaching Pylos Height at that day's end,   240
Telémakhos appealed to the son of Nestor:

"Could you, I wonder, do a thing I'll tell you,
supposing you agree?
We take ourselves to be true friends—in age
alike, and bound by ties between our fathers,
and now by partnership in this adventure.
Prince, do not take me roundabout,
but leave me at the ship, else the old king
your father will detain me overnight
for love of guests, when I should be at sea."   250

The son of Nestor nodded, thinking swiftly
how best he could oblige his friend.
Here was his choice: to pull the team hard over
along the beach till he could rein them in
beside the ship. Unloading Meneláos'
royal keepsakes into the stern sheets,
he sang out:

                              "Now for action! Get aboard,
and call your men, before I break the news
at home in hall to father. Who knows better   260
the old man's heart than I? If you delay,
he will not let you go, but he'll descend on you
in person and imperious; no turning
back with empty hands for him, believe me,
once his blood is up."

                              He shook the reins
to the lovely mares with long manes in the wind,
guiding them full tilt toward his father's hall.
Telémakhos called in the crew, and told them:

"Get everything shipshape aboard this craft;   270
we pull out now, and put sea miles behind us."

The listening men obeyed him, climbing in
to settle on their benches by the rowlocks,
while he stood watchful by the stern. He poured out
offerings there, and prayers to Athena.

Now a strange man came up to him, an easterner
fresh from spilling blood in distant Argos,
a hunted man. Gifted in prophecy,
he had as forebear that Melampous, wizard
who lived of old in Pylos, mother city   280
of western flocks.

                    Melampous, a rich lord,
had owned a house unmatched among the Pylians,
until the day came when king Neleus, noblest
in that age, drove him from his native land.
And Neleus for a year's term sequestered
Melampous' fields and flocks, while he lay bound
hand and foot in the keep of Phylakos.
Beauty of Neleus' daughter put him there
and sombre folly the inbreaking Fury   290
thrust upon him. But he gave the slip
to death, and drove the bellowing herd of Iphiklos
from Phylakê to Pylos, there to claim
the bride that ordeal won him from the king.
He led her to his brother's house, and went on
eastward into another land, the bluegrass
plain of Argos. Destiny held for him
rule over many Argives. Here he married,
built a great manor house, fathered Antíphatês
and Mantios, commanders both, of whom   300
Antíphatês begot Oikleiês
and Oikleiês the firebrand Amphiaraos.
This champion the lord of stormcloud, Zeus,
and strong Apollo loved; nor had he ever
to cross the doorsill into dim old age.
A woman, bought by trinkets, gave him over
to be cut down in the assault on Thebes.
His sons were Alkmáon and Amphílokhos.
In the meantime Lord Mantios begot
Polypheidês, the prophet, and   310
Kleitos—famous name! For Dawn in silks
of gold carried off Kleitos for his beauty
to live among the gods. But Polypheidês,
high-hearted and exalted by Apollo

above all men for prophecy, withdrew
to Hyperesia when his father angered him.
He lived on there, foretelling to the world
the shape of things to come.

His son it was,
Theoklýmenos, who came upon Telémakhos   320
as he poured out the red wine in the sand
near his trim ship, with prayer to Athena;
and he called out, approaching:

"Friend, well met
here at libation before going to sea.
I pray you by the wine you spend, and by
your god, your own life, and your company;
enlighten me, and let the truth be known.
Who are you? Of what city and what parents?"

Telémakhos turned to him and replied: 330

"Stranger, as truly as may be, I'll tell you.
I am from Ithaka, where I was born;
my father is, or he once was, Odysseus.
But he's a long time gone, and dead, may be;
and that is what I took ship with my friends
to find out—for he left long years ago."

Said Theoklýmenos in reply:

"I too
have had to leave my home. I killed a cousin.
In the wide grazing lands of Argos live   340
many kinsmen of his and friends in power,
great among the Akhaians. These I fled.
Death and vengeance at my back, as Fate
has turned now, I came wandering overland.
Give me a plank aboard your ship, I beg,
or they will kill me. They are on my track."

Telémakhos made answer:

"No two ways
about it. Will I pry you from our gunnel

when you are desperate to get to sea?   350
Come aboard; share what we have, and welcome."

He took the bronze-shod lance from the man's hand
and laid it down full-length on deck; then swung
his own weight after it aboard the cutter,
taking position aft, making a place
for Theoklýmenos near him. The stern lines
were slacked off, and Telémakhos commanded:
"Rig the mast; make sail!" Nimbly they ran
to push the fir pole high and step it firm
amidships in the box, make fast the forestays,   360
and hoist aloft the white sail on its halyards.
A following wind came down from grey-eyed Athena,
blowing brisk through heaven, and so steady
the cutter lapped up miles of salt blue sea,
passing Krounoi abeam and Khalkis estuary
at sundown when the sea ways all grew dark.
Then by Athena's wind borne on the ship
rounded Pheai by night and coasted Elis,
the green domain of the Epeioi; thence
he put her head north toward the running pack   370
of islets, wondering if by sailing wide
he sheered off Death, or would be caught.

                              That night
Odysseus and the swineherd supped again
with herdsmen in their mountain hut. At ease
when appetite and thirst were turned away,
Odysseus, while he talked, observed the swineherd
to see if he were hospitable still—
if yet again the man would make him stay
under his roof, or send him off to town.   380

"Listen," he said, "Eumaios; listen, lads.
At daybreak I must go and try my luck
around the port. I burden you too long.
Direct me, put me on the road with someone.
Nothing else for it but to play the beggar
in populous parts. I'll get a cup or loaf,

maybe, from some householder. If I go
as far as the great hall of King Odysseus
I might tell Queen Penélopê my news.
Or I can drift inside among the suitors   390
to see what alms they give, rich as they are.
If they have whims, I'm deft in ways of service—
that I can say, and you may know for sure.
By grace of Hermês the Wayfinder, patron
of mortal tasks, the god who honors toil,
no man can do a chore better than I can.
Set me to build a fire, or chop wood,
cook or carve, mix wine and serve—or anything
inferior men attend to for the gentry."

Now you were furious at this, Eumaios,   400
and answered—O my swineherd!—

                         "Friend, friend,
how could this fantasy take hold of you?
You dally with your life, and nothing less,
if you feel drawn to mingle in that company—
reckless, violent, and famous for it
out to the rim of heaven. Slaves
they have, but not like you. No—theirs are boys
in fresh cloaks and tunics, with pomade
ever on their sleek heads, and pretty faces.   410
These are their minions, while their tables gleam
and groan under big roasts, with loaves and wine.
Stay with us here. No one is burdened by you,
neither myself nor any of my hands.
Wait here until Odysseus' son returns.
You shall have clothing from him, cloak and tunic,
and passage where your heart desires to go."

The noble and enduring man replied:

"May you be dear to Zeus for this, Eumaios,
even as you are to me. Respite from pain   420
you give me—and from homelessness. In life
there's nothing worse than knocking about the world,
no bitterness we vagabonds are spared
when the curst belly rages! Well, you master it

and me, making me wait for the king's son.
But now, come, tell me:
what of Odysseus' mother, and his father
whom he took leave of on the sill of age?
Are they under the sun's rays, living still,
or gone down long ago to lodge with Death?"   430

To this the rugged herdsman answered:

"Aye,
that I can tell you; it is briefly told.
Laërtês lives, but daily in his hall
prays for the end of life and soul's delivery,
heartbroken as he is for a son long gone
and for his lady. Sorrow, when she died,
aged and enfeebled him like a green tree stricken;
but pining for her son, her brilliant son,
wore out her life.   440
                      Would god no death so sad
might come to benefactors dear as she!
I loved always to ask and hear about her
while she lived, although she lived in sorrow.
For she had brought me up with her own daughter,
Princess Ktimenê, her youngest child.
We were alike in age and nursed as equals
nearly, till in the flower of our years
they gave her, married her, to a Samian prince,
taking his many gifts. For my own portion   450
her mother gave new clothing, cloak and sandals,
and sent me to the woodland. Well she loved me.
Ah, how I miss that family! It is true
the blissful gods prosper my work; I have
meat and drink to spare for those I prize;
but so removed I am, I have no speech
with my sweet mistress, now that evil days
and overbearing men darken her house.
Tenants all hanker for good talk and gossip
around their lady, and a snack in hall,   460
a cup or two before they take the road
to their home acres, each one bearing home
some gift to cheer his heart."

                         The great tactician
answered:

                              "You were still a child, I see,
when exiled somehow from your parents' land.
Tell me, had it been sacked in war, the city
of spacious ways in which they made their home,
your father and your gentle mother? Or   470
were you kidnapped alone, brought here by sea
huddled with sheep in some foul pirate squadron,
to this landowner's hall? He paid your ransom?"

The master of the woodland answered:

                              "Friend,
now that you show an interest in that matter,
attend me quietly, be at your ease,
and drink your wine. These autumn nights are long,
ample for story-telling and for sleep.
You need not go to bed before the hour;   480
sleeping from dusk to dawn's a dull affair.
Let any other here who wishes, though,
retire to rest. At daybreak let him breakfast
and take the king's own swine into the wilderness.
Here's a tight roof; we'll drink on, you and I,
and ease our hearts of hardships we remember,
sharing old times. In later days a man
can find a charm in old adversity,
exile and pain. As to your question, now:

A certain island, Syriê by name—   490
you may have heard the name—lies off Ortýgia
due west, and holds the sunsets of the year.
Not very populous, but good for grazing
sheep and kine; rich too in wine and grain.
No dearth is ever known there, no disease
wars on the folk, of ills that plague mankind;
but when the townsmen reach old age, Apollo
with his longbow of silver comes, and Artemis,
showering arrows of mild death.

Two towns   500
divide the farmlands of that whole domain,
and both were ruled by Ktêsios, my father,
Orménos' heir, and a great godlike man.

Now one day some of those renowned seafaring
men, sea-dogs, Phoinikians, came ashore
with bags of gauds for trading. Father had
in our household a woman of Phoinikia,
a handsome one, and highly skilled. Well, she
gave in to the seductions of those rovers.
One of them found her washing near the mooring   510
and lay with her, making such love to her
as women in their frailty are confused by,
even the best of them.

In due course, then,
he asked her who she was and where she hailed from:
and nodding toward my father's roof, she said:

'I am of Sidon town, smithy of bronze
for all the East. Arubas Pasha's daughter.
Taphian pirates caught me in a byway
and sold me into slavery overseas   520
in this man's home. He could afford my ransom.'

The sailor who had lain with her replied:

'Why not ship out with us on the run homeward,
and see your father's high-roofed hall again,
your father and your mother? Still in Sidon
and still rich, they are said to be.'

She answered:

'It could be done, that, if you sailors take
oath I'll be given passage home unharmed.'

Well, soon she had them swearing it all pat   530
as she desired, repeating every syllable,
whereupon she warned them:

                                    'Not a word
about our meeting here! Never call out to me
when any of you see me in the lane
or at the well. Some visitor might bear
tales to the old man. If he guessed the truth,
I'd be chained up, your lives would be in peril.
No: keep it secret. Hurry with your peddling,
and when your hold is filled with livestock, send   540
a message to me at the manor hall.
Gold I'll bring, whatever comes to hand,
and something else, too, as my passage fee—
the master's child, my charge: a boy so high,
bright for his age; he runs with me on errands.
I'd take him with me happily; his price
would be I know not what in sale abroad.'

Her bargain made, she went back to the manor.
But they were on the island all that year,
getting by trade a cargo of our cattle;   550
until, the ship at length being laden full,
ready for sea, they sent a messenger
to the Phoinikian woman. Shrewd he was,
this fellow who came round my father's hall,
showing a golden chain all strung with amber,
a necklace. Maids in waiting and my mother
passed it from hand to hand, admiring it,
engaging they would buy it. But that dodger,
as soon as he had caught the woman's eye
and nodded, slipped away to join the ship.   560
She took my hand and led me through the court
into the portico. There by luck she found
winecups and tables still in place—for Father's
attendant counselors had dined just now
before they went to the assembly. Quickly
she hid three goblets in her bellying dress
to carry with her, while I tagged along
in my bewilderment. The sun went down
and all the lanes grew dark as we descended,
skirting the harbor in our haste to where   570
those traders of Phoinikia held their ship.

All went aboard at once and put to sea,
taking the two of us. A favoring wind
blew from the power of heaven. We sailed on
six nights and days without event. Then Zeus
the Son of Kronos added one more noon—and sudden
arrows from Artemis pierced the woman's heart.
Stone-dead she dropped
into the sloshing bilge the way a tern
plummets; and the sailors heaved her over   580
as tender pickings for the seals and fish.
Now I was left in dread, alone, while wind
and current bore them on to Ithaka.
Laërtês purchased me. That was the way
I first laid eyes upon this land."

                              Odysseus,
the kingly man, replied:

                      "You rouse my pity,
telling what you endured when you were young.
But surely Zeus put good alongside ill: 590
torn from your own far home, you had the luck
to come into a kind man's service, generous
with food and drink. And a good life you lead,
unlike my own, all spent in barren roaming
from one country to the next, till now."

So the two men talked on, into the night,
leaving few hours for sleep before the Dawn
stepped up to her bright chair.

                      The ship now drifting
under the island lee, Telémakhos'   600
companions took in sail and mast, unshipped
the oars and rowed ashore. They moored her stern
by the stout hawser lines, tossed out the bow stones,
and waded in beyond the wash of ripples
to mix their wine and cook their morning meal.
When they had turned back hunger and thirst, Telémakhos
arose to give the order of the day.

"Pull for the town," he said, "and berth our ship,
while I go inland across country. Later,
this evening, after looking at my farms,   610
I'll join you in the city. When day comes
I hope to celebrate our crossing, feasting
everyone on good red meat and wine."

His noble passenger, Theoklýmenos,
now asked:

                    "What as to me, my dear young fellow,
where shall I go? Will I find lodging here
with some one of the lords of stony Ithaka?
Or go straight to your mother's hall and yours?"

Telémakhos turned round to him and said: 620

"I should myself invite you to our hall
if things were otherwise; there'd be no lack
of entertainment for you. As it stands,
no place could be more wretched for a guest
while I'm away. Mother will never see you;
she almost never shows herself at home
to the suitors there, but stays in her high chamber
weaving upon her loom. No, let me name
another man for you to go to visit:
Eurýmakhos, the honored son of Pólybos.   630
In Ithaka they are dazzled by him now—
the strongest of their princes, bent on making
mother and all Odysseus' wealth his own.
Zeus on Olympos only knows
if some dark hour for them will intervene."

The words were barely spoken, when a hawk,
Apollo's courier, flew up on the right,
clutching a dove and plucking her—so feathers
floated down to the ground between Telémakhos
and the moored cutter. Theoklýmenos   640
called him apart and gripped his hand, whispering:

"A god spoke in this bird-sign on the right.
I knew it when I saw the hawk fly over us.
There is no kinglier house than yours, Telémakhos,

here in the realm of Ithaka. Your family
will be in power forever."

                              The young prince,
clear in spirit, answered:

                              "Be it so,
friend, as you say. And may you know as well   650
the friendship of my house, and many gifts
from me, so everyone may call you fortunate."

He called a trusted crewman named Peiraios,
and said to him:

                              "Peiraios, son of Klýtios,
can I rely on you again as ever, most
of all the friends who sailed with me to Pylos?
Take this man home with you, take care of him,
treat him with honor, till I come."

                              To this   660
Peiraios the good spearman answered:

"Aye,
stay in the wild country while you will,
I shall be looking after him, Telémakhos.
He will not lack good lodging."

                              Down to the ship
he turned, and boarded her, and called the others
to cast off the stern lines and come aboard.
So men climbed in to sit beside the rowlocks.
Telémakhos now tied his sandals on   670
and lifted his tough spear from the ship's deck;
hawsers were taken in, and they shoved off
to reach the town by way of the open sea
as he commanded them—royal Odysseus'
own dear son, Telémakhos.
                              On foot
and swiftly he went up toward the stockade
where swine were penned in hundreds, and at night
the guardian of the swine, the forester,
slept under arms on duty for his masters.   680

BOOK SIXTEEN

Father and Son

LINES 1 — 12

But there were two men in the mountain hut—   1
Odysseus and the swineherd. At first light
blowing their fire up, they cooked their breakfast
and sent their lads out, driving herds to root
in the tall timber.
              When Telémakhos came,
the wolvish troop of watchdogs only fawned on him
as he advanced. Odysseus heard them go
and heard the light crunch of a man's footfall—
at which he turned quickly to say: 10

                  "Eumaios,
here is one of your crew come back, or maybe
another friend: the dogs are out there snuffling
belly down; not one has even growled.
I can hear footsteps—"

                But before he finished
his tall son stood at the door.

                    The swineherd
rose in surprise, letting a bowl and jug
tumble from his fingers. Going forward,   20
he kissed the young man's head, his shining eyes
and both hands, while his own tears brimmed and fell.
Think of a man whose dear and only son,
born to him in exile, reared with labor,
has lived ten years abroad and now returns:
how would that man embrace his son! Just so
the herdsman clapped his arms around Telémakhos
and covered him with kisses—for he knew
the lad had got away from death. He said:

"Light of my days, Telémakhos,   30
you made it back! When you took ship for Pylos
I never thought to see you here again.
Come in, dear child, and let me feast my eyes;
here you are, home from the distant places!
How rarely, anyway, you visit us,
your own men, and your own woods and pastures!
Always in the town, a man would think
you loved the suitors' company, those dogs!"

Telémakhos with his clear candor said:

"I am with you, Uncle. See now, I have come   40
because I wanted to see you first, to hear from you
if Mother stayed at home—or is she married
off to someone, and Odysseus' bed
left empty for some gloomy spider's weaving?"

Gently the forester replied to this:

"At home indeed your mother is, poor lady,
still in the women's hall. Her nights and days
are wearied out with grieving."

                    Stepping back
he took the bronze-shod lance, and the young prince   50
entered the cabin over the worn door stone.
Odysseus moved aside, yielding his couch,
but from across the room Telémakhos checked him:

"Friend, sit down; we'll find another chair
in our own hut. Here is the man to make one!"

The swineherd, when the quiet man sank down,
built a new pile of evergreens and fleeces—
a couch for the dear son of great Odysseus—
then gave them trenchers of good meat, left over
from the roast pork of yesterday, and heaped up   60
willow baskets full of bread, and mixed
an ivy bowl of honey-hearted wine.
Then he in turn sat down, facing Odysseus,
their hands went out upon the meat and drink
as they fell to, ridding themselves of hunger,
until Telémakhos paused and said:

                              "Oh, Uncle,
what's your friend's home port? How did he come?
Who were the sailors brought him here to Ithaka?
I doubt if he came walking on the sea."   70

And you replied, Eumaios—O my swineherd—

"Son, the truth about him is soon told.
His home land, and a broad land, too, is Krete,
but he has knocked about the world, he says,
for years, as the Powers wove his life. Just now
he broke away from a shipload of Thesprotians
to reach my hut. I place him in your hands.
Act as you will. He wishes your protection."

The young man said:

                              "Eumaios, my protection!   80
The notion cuts me to the heart. How can I
receive your friend at home? I am not old enough
or trained in arms. Could I defend myself
if someone picked a fight with me?
                              Besides,
mother is in a quandary, whether to stay with me
as mistress of our household, honoring
her lord's bed, and opinion in the town,

or take the best Akhaian who comes her way—
the one who offers most.   90

                              I'll undertake,
at all events, to clothe your friend for winter,
now he is with you. Tunic and cloak of wool,
a good broadsword, and sandals—these are his.
I can arrange to send him where he likes
or you may keep him in your cabin here.
I shall have bread and wine sent up; you need not
feel any pinch on his behalf.

                              Impossible
to let him stay in hall, among the suitors.   100
They are drunk, drunk on impudence, they might
injure my guest—and how could I bear that?
How could a single man take on those odds?
Not even a hero could.

                              The suitors are too strong."

At this the noble and enduring man, Odysseus,
addressed his son:

                              "Kind prince, it may be fitting
for me to speak a word. All that you say
gives me an inward wound as I sit listening.   110
I mean this wanton game they play, these fellows,
riding roughshod over you in your own house,
admirable as you are. But tell me,
are you resigned to being bled? The townsmen,
stirred up against you, are they, by some oracle?
Your brothers—can you say your brothers fail you?
A man should feel his kin, at least, behind him
in any clash, when a real fight is coming.
If my heart were as young as yours, if I were
son to Odysseus, or the man himself,   120
I'd rather have my head cut from my shoulders
by some slashing adversary, if I
brought no hurt upon that crew! Suppose
I went down, being alone, before the lot,
better, I say, to die at home in battle
than see these insupportable things, day after
day the stranger cuffed, the women slaves

dragged here and there, shame in the lovely rooms,
the wine drunk up in rivers, sheer waste
of pointless feasting, never at an end!"   130

Telémakhos replied:

                              "Friend, I'll explain to you.
There is no rancor in the town against me,
no fault of brothers, whom a man should feel
behind him when a fight is in the making;
no, no—in our family the First Born
of Heaven, Zeus, made single sons the rule.
Arkeísios had but one, Laërtês; he
in his turn fathered only one, Odysseus,
who left me in his hall alone, too young   140
to be of any use to him.
And so you see why enemies fill our house
in these days: all the princes of the islands,
Doulíkhion, Samê, wooded Zakýnthos,
Ithaka, too—lords of our island rock—
eating our house up as they court my mother.
She cannot put an end to it; she dare not
bar the marriage that she hates; and they
devour all my substance and my cattle,
and who knows when they'll slaughter me as well?   150
It rests upon the gods' great knees.
                              Uncle,
go down at once and tell the Lady Penélopê
that I am back from Pylos, safe and sound.
I stay here meanwhile. You will give your message
and then return. Let none of the Akhaians
hear it; they have a mind to do me harm."

To this, Eumaios, you replied:

                              "I know.
But make this clear, now—should I not likewise   160
call on Laërtês with your news? Hard hit
by sorrow though he was, mourning Odysseus,
he used to keep an eye upon his farm.
He had what meals he pleased, with his own folk.
But now no more, not since you sailed for Pylos;

he has not taken food or drink, I hear,
sitting all day, blind to the work of harvest,
groaning, while the skin shrinks on his bones."

Telémakhos answered:

                    "One more misery,   170
but we had better leave it so.
If men could choose, and have their choice, in everything,
we'd have my father home.
              Turn back
when you have done your errand, as you must,
not to be caught alone in the countryside.
But wait—you may tell Mother
to send our old housekeeper on the quiet
and quickly; she can tell the news to Grandfather."

The swineherd, roused, reached out to get his sandals,   180
tied them on, and took the road.

              Who else
beheld this but Athena? From the air
she walked, taking the form of a tall woman,
handsome and clever at her craft, and stood
beyond the gate in plain sight of Odysseus,
unseen, though, by Telémakhos, unguessed,
for not to everyone will gods appear.
Odysseus noticed her; so did the dogs,
who cowered whimpering away from her. She only   190
nodded, signing to him with her brows,
a sign he recognized. Crossing the yard,
he passed out through the gate in the stockade
to face the goddess. There she said to him:

"Son of Laërtês and the gods of old,
Odysseus, master of land ways and sea ways,
dissemble to your son no longer now.
The time has come: tell him how you together
will bring doom on the suitors in the town.
I shall not be far distant then, for I   200
myself desire battle."

Saying no more,
she tipped her golden wand upon the man,
making his cloak pure white, and the knit tunic
fresh around him. Lithe and young she made him,
ruddy with sun, his jawline clean, the beard
no longer grey upon his chin. And she
withdrew when she had done.

                         Then Lord Odysseus
reappeared—and his son was thunderstruck.   210
Fear in his eyes, he looked down and away
as though it were a god, and whispered:

                         "Stranger,
you are no longer what you were just now!
Your cloak is new; even your skin! You are
one of the gods who rule the sweep of heaven!
Be kind to us, we'll make you fair oblation
and gifts of hammered gold. Have mercy on us!"

The noble and enduring man replied:

"No god. Why take me for a god? No, no.   220
I am that father whom your boyhood lacked
and suffered pain for lack of. I am he."

Held back too long, the tears ran down his cheeks
as he embraced his son.

                         Only Telémakhos,
uncomprehending, wild
with incredulity, cried out:

                         "You cannot
be my father Odysseus! Meddling spirits
conceived this trick to twist the knife in me!   231
No man of woman born could work these wonders
by his own craft, unless a god came into it
with ease to turn him young or old at will.
I swear you were in rags and old,
and here you stand like one of the immortals!"

Odysseus brought his ranging mind to bear
and said:

"This is not princely, to be swept
away by wonder at your father's presence.
No other Odysseus will ever come,   240
for he and I are one, the same; his bitter
fortune and his wanderings are mine.
Twenty years gone, and I am back again
on my own island.

As for my change of skin,
that is a charm Athena, Hope of Soldiers,
uses as she will; she has the knack
to make me seem a beggar man sometimes
and sometimes young, with finer clothes about me.
It is no hard thing for the gods of heaven   250
to glorify a man or bring him low."

When he had spoken, down he sat.
Then, throwing
his arms around this marvel of a father
Telémakhos began to weep. Salt tears
rose from the wells of longing in both men,
and cries burst from both as keen and fluttering
as those of the great taloned hawk,
whose nestlings farmers take before they fly.
So helplessly they cried, pouring out tears,   260
and might have gone on weeping so till sundown,
had not Telémakhos said:

"Dear father! Tell me
what kind of vessel put you here ashore
on Ithaka? Your sailors, who were they?
I doubt you made it, walking on the sea!"

Then said Odysseus, who had borne the barren sea:

"Only plain truth shall I tell you, child.
Great seafarers, the Phaiákians, gave me passage
as they give other wanderers. By night   270
over the open ocean, while I slept,
they brought me in their cutter, set me down
on Ithaka, with gifts of bronze and gold
and stores of woven things. By the gods' will

these lie all hidden in a cave. I came
to this wild place, directed by Athena,
so that we might lay plans to kill our enemies.
Count up the suitors for me, let me know
what men at arms are there, how many men.
I must put all my mind to it, to see   280
if we two by ourselves can take them on
or if we should look round for help."

                              Telémakhos

replied:

                              "O Father, all my life your fame
as a fighting man has echoed in my ears—
your skill with weapons and the tricks of war—
but what you speak of is a staggering thing,
beyond imagining, for me. How can two men
do battle with a houseful in their prime?   290
For I must tell you this is no affair
of ten or even twice ten men, but scores,
throngs of them. You shall see, here and now.
The number from Doulíkhion alone
is fifty-two, picked men, with armorers,
a half dozen; twenty-four came from Samê,
twenty from Zakýnthos; our own island
accounts for twelve, high-ranked, and their retainers,
Medôn the crier, and the Master Harper,
besides a pair of handymen at feasts.   300
If we go in against all these
I fear we pay in salt blood for your vengeance.
You must think hard if you would conjure up
the fighting strength to take us through."

                              Odysseus
who had endured the long war and the sea
answered:

                              "I'll tell you now.
Suppose Athena's arm is over us, and Zeus
her father's, must I rack my brains for more?"   310

Clearheaded Telémakhos looked hard and said:

"Those two are great defenders, no one doubts it,
but throned in the serene clouds overhead;
other affairs of men and gods they have
to rule over."

                    And the hero answered:

"Before long they will stand to right and left of us
in combat, in the shouting, when the test comes—
our nerve against the suitors' in my hall.
Here is your part: at break of day tomorrow   320
home with you, go mingle with our princes.
The swineherd later on will take me down
the port-side trail—a beggar, by my looks,
hangdog and old. If they make fun of me
in my own courtyard, let your ribs cage up
your springing heart, no matter what I suffer,
no matter if they pull me by the heels
or practice shots at me, to drive me out.
Look on, hold down your anger. You may even
plead with them, by heaven! in gentle terms   330
to quit their horseplay—not that they will heed you,
rash as they are, facing their day of wrath.
Now fix the next step in your mind.
                    Athena,
counseling me, will give me word, and I
shall signal to you, nodding: at that point
round up all armor, lances, gear of war
left in our hall, and stow the lot away
back in the vaulted store room. When the suitors
miss those arms and question you, be soft   340
in what you say: answer:

                    'I thought I'd move them
out of the smoke. They seemed no longer those
bright arms Odysseus left us years ago
when he went off to Troy. Here where the fire's
hot breath came, they had grown black and drear.
One better reason, too, I had from Zeus:

suppose a brawl starts up when you are drunk,
you might be crazed and bloody one another,
and that would stain your feast, your courtship. Tempered   350
iron can magnetize a man.'
                                    Say that.
But put aside two broadswords and two spears
for our own use, two oxhide shields nearby
when we go into action. Pallas Athena
and Zeus All Provident will see you through,
bemusing our young friends.
                                    Now one thing more.
If son of mine you are and blood of mine,
let no one hear Odysseus is about.   360
Neither Laërtês, nor the swineherd here,
nor any slave, nor even Penélopê.
But you and I alone must learn how far
the women are corrupted; we should know
how to locate good men among our hands,
the loyal and respectful, and the shirkers
who take you lightly, as alone and young."

His admirable son replied:

                                    "Ah, Father,
even when danger comes I think you'll find   370
courage in me. I am not scatterbrained.
But as to checking on the field hands now,
I see no gain for us in that. Reflect,
you make a long toil, that way, if you care
to look men in the eye at every farm,
while these gay devils in our hall at ease
eat up our flocks and herds, leaving us nothing.

As for the maids I say, Yes: make distinction
between good girls and those who shame your house;
all that I shy away from is a scrutiny   380
of cottagers just now. The time for that
comes later—if in truth you have a sign
from Zeus the Stormking."

So their talk ran on,
while down the coast, and round toward Ithaka,
hove the good ship that had gone out to Pylos
bearing Telémakhos and his companions.
Into the wide bay waters, on to the dark land,
they drove her, hauled her up, took out the oars
and canvas for light-hearted squires to carry   390
homeward—as they carried, too, the gifts
of Meneláos round to Klýtios' house.
But first they sped a runner to Penélopê.
They knew that quiet lady must be told
the prince her son had come ashore, and sent
his good ship round to port; not one soft tear
should their sweet queen let fall.

                              Both messengers,
crewman and swineherd—reached the outer gate
in the same instant, bearing the same news,   400
and went in side by side to the king's hall.
He of the ship burst out among the maids:

"Your son's ashore this morning, O my Queen!"

But the swineherd calmly stood near Penélopê
whispering what her son had bade him tell
and what he had enjoined on her. No more.
When he had done, he left the place and turned
back to his steading in the hills.

                              By now,
sullen confusion weighed upon the suitors.   410
Out of the house, out of the court they went,
beyond the wall and gate, to sit in council.
Eurýmakhos, the son of Pólybos,
opened discussion:

                              "Friends, face up to it;
that young pup, Telémakhos, has done it;
he made the round trip, though we said he could not.
Well—now to get the best craft we can find
afloat, with oarsmen who can drench her bows,
and tell those on the island to come home."   420

He was yet speaking when Amphínomos,
craning seaward, spotted the picket ship
already in the roadstead under oars
with canvas brailed up; and this fresh arrival
made him chuckle. Then he told his friends:

"Too late for messages. Look, here they come
along the bay. Some god has brought them news,
or else they saw the cutter pass—and could not
overtake her."

                        On their feet at once,   430
the suitors took the road to the sea beach,
where, meeting the black ship, they hauled her in.
Oars and gear they left for their light-hearted
squires to carry, and all in company
made off for the assembly ground. All others,
young and old alike, they barred from sitting.
Eupeithês' son, Antínoös, made the speech:

"How the gods let our man escape a boarding,
that is the wonder.

                       We had lookouts posted   440
up on the heights all day in the sea wind,
and every hour a fresh pair of eyes;
at night we never slept ashore
but after sundown cruised the open water
to the southeast, patrolling until Dawn.
We were prepared to cut him off and catch him,
squelch him for good and all. The power of heaven
steered him the long way home.

Well, let this company plan his destruction,
and leave him no way out, this time. I see   450
our business here unfinished while he lives.
He knows, now, and he's no fool. Besides,
his people are all tired of playing up to us.
I say, act now, before he brings the whole
body of Akhaians to assembly—
and he would leave no word unsaid, in righteous
anger speaking out before them all

of how we plotted murder, and then missed him.
Will they commend us for that pretty work?
Take action now, or we are in for trouble;   460
we might be exiled, driven off our lands.
Let the first blow be ours.
If we move first, and get our hands on him
far from the city's eye, on path or field,
then stores and livestock will be ours to share;
the house we may confer upon his mother—
and on the man who marries her. Decide
otherwise you may—but if, my friends,
you want that boy to live and have his patrimony,
then we should eat no more of his good mutton,   470
come to this place no more.

                    Let each from his own hall
court her with dower gifts. And let her marry
the destined one, the one who offers most."

He ended, and no sound was heard among them,
sitting all hushed, until at last the son
of Nisos Aretíadês arose—
Amphínomos.

                  He led the group of suitors
who came from grainlands on Doulíkhion,   480
and he had lightness in his talk that pleased
Penélopê, for he meant no ill.
Now, in concern for them, he spoke:

                "O Friends
I should not like to kill Telémakhos.
It is a shivery thing to kill a prince
of royal blood.

                We should consult the gods.
If Zeus hands down a ruling for that act,
then I shall say, 'Come one, come all,' and go   490
cut him down with my own hand—
but I say Halt, if gods are contrary."

Now this proposal won them, and it carried.
Breaking their session up, away they went
to take their smooth chairs in Odysseus' house.

Meanwhile Penélopê the Wise,
decided, for her part, to make appearance
before the valiant young men.
                              She knew now
they plotted her child's death in her own hall,   500
for once more Medôn, who had heard them, told her.
Into the hall that lovely lady came,
with maids attending, and approached the suitors,
till near a pillar of the well-wrought roof
she paused, her shining veil across her cheeks,
and spoke directly to Antínoös:

                              "Infatuate,
steeped in evil! Yet in Ithaka they say
you were the best one of your generation
in mind and speech. Not so, you never were.   510
Madman, why do you keep forever knitting
death for Telémakhos? Have you no piety
toward men dependent on another's mercy?
Before Lord Zeus, no sanction can be found
for one such man to plot against another!
Or are you not aware that your own father
fled to us when the realm was up in arms
against him? He had joined the Taphian pirates
in ravaging Thesprotian folk, our friends.
Our people would have raided *him*, then—breached   520
his heart, butchered his herds to feast upon—
only Odysseus took him in, and held
the furious townsmen off. It is Odysseus'
house you now consume, his wife you court,
his son you kill, or try to kill. And me
you ravage now, and grieve. I call upon you
to make an end of it!—and your friends too!"

The son of Pólybos it was, Eurýmakhos,
who answered her with ready speech:

                              "My lady   530
Penélopê, wise daughter of Ikários,
you must shake off these ugly thoughts. I say

that man does not exist, nor will, who dares
lay hands upon your són Telémakhos,
while I live, walk the earth, and use my eyes.
The man's life blood, I swear,
will spurt and run out black around my lancehead!
For it is true of me, too, that Odysseus,
raider of cities, took me on his knees
and fed me often—tidbits and red wine.   540
Should not Telémakhos, therefore, be dear to me
above the rest of men? I tell the lad
he must not tremble for his life, at least
alone in the suitors' company. Heaven
deals death no man avoids."

                  Blasphemous lies
in earnest tones he told—the one who planned
the lad's destruction!
                Silently the lady
made her way to her glowing upper chamber,   550
there to weep for her dear lord, Odysseus,
until grey-eyed Athena
cast sweet sleep upon her eyes.

                At fall of dusk
Odysseus and his son heard the approach
of the good forester. They had been standing
over the fire with a spitted pig,
a yearling. And Athena coming near
with one rap of her wand made of Odysseus
an old old man again, with rags about him—   560
for if the swineherd knew his lord were there
he could not hold the news; Penélopê
would hear it from him.
                Now Telémakhos
greeted him first:

                "Eumaios, back again!
What was the talk in town? Are the tall suitors
home again, by this time, from their ambush,
or are they still on watch for my return?"

And you replied, Eumaios—O my swineherd: 570

"There was no time to ask or talk of that;
I hurried through the town. Even while I spoke
my message, I felt driven to return.
A runner from your friends turned up, a crier,
who gave the news first to your mother. Ah!
One thing I do know; with my own two eyes
I saw it. As I climbed above the town
to where the sky is cut by Hermês' ridge,
I saw a ship bound in for our own bay
with many oarsmen in it, laden down   580
with sea provisioning and two-edged spears,
and I surmised those were the men.
                                Who knows?"

Telémakhos, now strong with magic, smiled
across at his own father—but avoided
the swineherd's eye.
                      So when the pig was done,
the spit no longer to be turned, the table
garnished, everyone sat down to feast
on all the savory flesh he craved. And when   590
they had put off desire for meat and drink,
they turned to bed and took the gift of sleep.

BOOK SEVENTEEN

The Beggar at the Manor

LINES 1 – 15

When the young Dawn came bright into the East   1
spreading her finger tips of rose, Telémakhos
the king's son, tied on his rawhide sandals
and took the lance that bore his handgrip. Burning
to be away, and on the path to town,
he told the swineherd:

                              "Uncle, the truth is
I must go down myself into the city.
Mother must see me there, with her own eyes,
or she will weep and feel forsaken still,   10
and will not set her mind at rest. Your job
will be to lead this poor man down to beg.
Some householder may want to dole him out
a loaf and pint. I have my own troubles.
Am I to care for every last man who comes?
And if he takes it badly—well, so much
the worse for him. Plain truth is what I favor."

At once Odysseus the great tactician
spoke up briskly:

                "Neither would I myself   20
care to be kept here, lad. A beggar man
fares better in the town. Let it be said
I am not yet so old I must lay up
indoors and mumble, 'Aye, Aye' to a master.
Go on, then. As you say, my friend can lead me
as soon as I have had a bit of fire
and when the sun grows warmer. These old rags
could be my death, outside on a frosty morning,
and the town is distant, so they say."

                Telémakhos   30
with no more words went out, and through the fence,
and down hill, going fast on the steep footing,
nursing woe for the suitors in his heart.

Before the manor hall, he leaned his lance
against a great porch pillar and stepped in
across the door stone.
                Old Eurýkleia
saw him first, for that day she was covering
handsome chairs nearby with clean fleeces.
She ran to him at once, tears in her eyes;   40
and other maidservants of the old soldier
Odysseus gathered round to greet their prince,
kissing his head and shoulders.
                Quickly, then,
Penélopê the Wise, tall in her beauty
as Artemis or pale-gold Aphroditê,
appeared from her high chamber and came down
to throw her arms around her son. In tears
she kissed his head, kissed both his shining eyes,
then cried out, and her words flew: 50

                "Back with me!
Telémakhos, more sweet to me than sunlight!
I thought I should not see you again, ever,
after you took the ship that night to Pylos—
against my will, with not a word! you went

for news of your dear father. Tell me now
of everything you saw!"

But he made answer:

"Mother, not now. You make me weep. My heart
already aches—I came near death at sea.   60
You must bathe, first of all, and change your dress,
and take your maids to the highest room to pray.
Pray, and burn offerings to the gods of heaven,
that Zeus may put his hand to our revenge.

I am off now to bring home from the square
a guest, a passenger I had. I sent him
yesterday with all my crew to town.
Peiraios was to care for him, I said,
and keep him well, with honor, till I came."

She caught back the swift words upon her tongue.   70
Then softly she withdrew
to bathe and dress her body in fresh linen,
and make her offerings to the gods of heaven,
praying Almighty Zeus
to put his hand to their revenge.

Telémakhos
had left the hall, taken his lance, and gone
with two quick hounds at heel into the town,
Athena's grace in his long stride
making the people gaze as he came near.   80
And suitors gathered, primed with friendly words,
despite the deadly plotting in their hearts—
but these, and all their crowd, he kept away from.
Next he saw sitting some way off, apart,
Mentor, with Ántiphos and Halithérsês,
friends of his father's house in years gone by.
Near these men he sat down, and told his tale
under their questioning.

His crewman, young Peiraios,
guided through town, meanwhile, into the Square,   90
the Argive exile, Theoklýmenos.

Telémakhos lost no time in moving toward him;
but first Peiraios had his say:

                    "Telémakhos,
you must send maids to me, at once, and let me
turn over to you those gifts from Meneláos!"

The prince had pondered it, and said:

                    "Peiraios,
none of us knows how this affair will end.
Say one day our fine suitors, without warning,   100
draw upon me, kill me in our hall,
and parcel out my patrimony—I wish
you, and no one of them, to have those things.
But if my hour comes, if I can bring down
bloody death on all that crew,
you will rejoice to send my gifts to me—
and so will I rejoice!"

                              Then he departed,
leading his guest, the lonely stranger, home.

Over chair-backs in hall they dropped their mantles   110
and passed in to the polished tubs, where maids
poured out warm baths for them, anointed them,
and pulled fresh tunics, fleecy cloaks around them.
Soon they were seated at their ease in hall.
A maid came by to tip a golden jug
over their fingers into a silver bowl
and draw a gleaming table up beside them.
The larder mistress brought her tray of loaves
and savories, dispensing each.
                              In silence   120
across the hall, beside a pillar, propped
in a long chair, Telémakhos' mother
spun a fine wool yarn.
                    The young men's hands
went out upon the good things placed before them,
and only when their hunger and thirst were gone
did she look up and say:

"Telémakhos,
what am I to do now? Return alone
and lie again on my forsaken bed—   130
sodden how often with my weeping
since that day when Odysseus put to sea
to join the Atreidai before Troy?
                           Could you not
tell me, before the suitors fill our house,
what news you have of his return?"

He answered:

"Now that you ask a second time, dear Mother,
here is the truth.
                           We went ashore at Pylos   140
to Nestor, lord and guardian of the West,
who gave me welcome in his towering hall.
So kind he was, he might have been my father
and I his long-lost son—so truly kind,
taking me in with his own honored sons.
But as to Odysseus' bitter fate,
living or dead, he had no news at all
from anyone on earth, he said. He sent me
overland in a strong chariot
to Atreus' son, the captain, Meneláos.   150
And I saw Helen there, for whom the Argives
fought, and the Trojans fought, as the gods willed.
Then Meneláos of the great war cry
asked me my errand in that ancient land
of Lakedaimon. So I told our story,
and in reply he burst out:

                           'Intolerable!
That feeble men, unfit as those men are,
should think to lie in that great captain's bed,
fawns in the lion's lair! As if a doe   160
put down her litter of sucklings there, while she
sniffed at the glen or grazed a grassy hollow.
Ha! Then the lord returns to his own bed
and deals out wretched doom on both alike.

So will Odysseus deal out doom on these.
O Father Zeus, Athena, and Apollo!
I pray he comes as once he was, in Lesbos,
when he stood up to wrestle Philomeleidês—
champion and Island King—
and smashed him down. How the Akhaians cheered!   170
If that Odysseus could meet the suitors,
they'd have a quick reply, a stunning dowry!
Now for your questions, let me come to the point.
I would not misreport it for you; let me
tell you what the Ancient of the Sea,
that infallible seer, told me.

                              On an island
your father lies and grieves. The Ancient saw him
held by a nymph, Kalypso, in her hall;
no means of sailing home remained to him,   180
no ship with oars, and no ship's company
to pull him on the broad back of the sea.'

I had this from the lord marshal, Meneláos,
and when my errand in that place was done
I left for home. A fair breeze from the gods
brought me swiftly back to our dear island."

The boy's tale made her heart stir in her breast,
but this was not all. Mother and son now heard
Theoklýmenos, the diviner, say:

"He does not see it clear—   190
                    O gentle lady,
wife of Odysseus Laërtiadês,
listen to me, I can reveal this thing.
Zeus be my witness, and the table set
for strangers and the hearth to which I've come—
the lord Odysseus, I tell you,
is present now, already, on this island!
Quartered somewhere, or going about, he knows
what evil is afoot. He has it in him
to bring a black hour on the suitors. Yesterday,   200
still at the ship, I saw this in a portent.
I read the sign aloud, I told Telémakhos!"

The prudent queen, for her part, said:

> "Stranger,
> if only this came true—
> our love would go to you, with many gifts;
> aye, every man who passed would call you happy!"

So ran the talk between these three.
                    Meanwhile,
swaggering before Odysseus' hall,   210
the suitors were competing at the discus throw
and javelin, on the level measured field.
But when the dinner hour drew on, and beasts
were being driven from the fields to slaughter—
as beasts were, every day—Medôn spoke out:
Medôn, the crier, whom the suitors liked;
he took his meat beside them.

                    "Men," he said,
"each one has had his work-out and his pleasure,
come in to Hall now; time to make our feast.   220
Are discus throws more admirable than a roast
when the proper hour comes?"

                    At this reminder
they all broke up their games, and trailed away
into the gracious, timbered hall. There, first,
they dropped their cloaks on chairs; then came their ritual:
putting great rams and fat goats to the knife—
pigs and a cow, too.
                    So they made their feast.

During these hours, Odysseus and the swineherd   230
were on their way out of the hills to town.
The forester had got them started, saying:

"Friend, you have hopes, I know, of your adventure
into the heart of town today. My lord
wishes it so, not I. No, I should rather
you stood by here as guardian of our steading.
But I owe reverence to my prince, and fear

he'll make my ears burn later if I fail.
A master's tongue has a rough edge. Off we go.
Part of the day is past; nightfall will be   240
early, and colder, too."

                              Odysseus,
who had it all timed in his head, replied:

"I know, as well as you do. Let's move on.
You lead the way—the whole way. Have you got
a staff, a lopped stick, you could let me use
to put my weight on when I slip? This path
is hard going, they said."

                         Over his shoulders
he slung his patched-up knapsack, an old bundle   250
tied with twine. Eumaios found a stick for him,
the kind he wanted, and the two set out,
leaving the boys and dogs to guard the place.
In this way good Eumaios led his lord
down to the city.

                    And it seemed to him
he led an old outcast, a beggar man,
leaning most painfully upon a stick,
his poor cloak, all in tatters, looped about him.

Down by the stony trail they made their way   260
as far as Clearwater, not far from town—
a spring house where the people filled their jars.
Ithakos, Nêritos, and Polýktor built it,
and round it on the humid ground a grove,
a circular wood of poplars grew. Ice cold
in runnels from a high rock ran the spring,
and over it there stood an altar stone
to the cool nymphs, where all men going by
laid offerings.

                    Well, here the son of Dólios   270
crossed their path—Melánthios.

                         He was driving
a string of choice goats for the evening meal,
with two goatherds beside him; and no sooner

had he laid eyes upon the wayfarers
than he began to growl and taunt them both
so grossly that Odysseus' heart grew hot:

"Here comes one scurvy type leading another!
God pairs them off together, every time.
Swineherd, where are you taking your new pig,   280
that stinking beggar there, licker of pots?
How many doorposts has he rubbed his back on
whining for garbage, where a noble guest
would rate a cauldron or a sword?
                              Hand him
over to me, I'll make a farmhand of him,
a stall scraper, a fodder carrier! Whey
for drink will put good muscle on his shank!
No chance: he learned his dodges long ago—
no honest sweat. He'd rather tramp the country   290
begging, to keep his hoggish belly full.
Well, I can tell you this for sure:
in King Odysseus' hall, if he goes there,
footstools will fly around his head—good shots
from strong hands. Back and side, his ribs will catch it
on the way out!"

                              And like a drunken fool
he kicked at Odysseus' hip as he passed by.
Not even jogged off stride, or off the trail,
the Lord Odysseus walked along, debating   300
inwardly whether to whirl and beat
the life out of this fellow with his stick,
or toss him, brain him on the stony ground.
Then he controlled himself, and bore it quietly.
Not so the swineherd.
                              Seeing the man before him,
he raised his arms and cried:

                              "Nymphs of the spring,
daughters of Zeus, if ever Odysseus
burnt you a thighbone in rich fat—a ram's   310
or kid's thighbone, hear me, grant my prayer:
let our true lord come back, let heaven bring him

to rid the earth of these fine courtly ways
Melánthios picks up around the town—
all wine and wind! Bad shepherds ruin flocks!"

Melánthios the goatherd answered:

                    "Bless me!
The dog can snap: how he goes on! Some day
I'll take him in a slave ship overseas
and trade him for a herd!   320
                    Old Silverbow
Apollo, if he shot clean through Telémakhos
in hall today, what luck! Or let the suitors
cut him down!
                    Odysseus died at sea;
no coming home for him."

                    He flung this out
and left the two behind to come on slowly,
while he went hurrying to the king's hall.
There he slipped in, and sat among the suitors,   330
beside the one he doted on—Eurýmakhos.
Then working servants helped him to his meat
and the mistress of the larder gave him bread.

Reaching the gate, Odysseus and the forester
halted and stood outside, for harp notes came
around them rippling on the air
as Phémios picked out a song. Odysseus
caught his companion's arm and said:

                    "My friend,
here is the beautiful place—who could mistake it?   340
Here is Odysseus' hall: no hall like this!
See how one chamber grows out of another;
see how the court is tight with wall and coping;
no man at arms could break this gateway down!
Your banqueting young lords are here in force,
I gather, from the fumes of mutton roasting
and strum of harping—harping, which the gods
appoint sweet friend of feasts!"

And—O my swineherd!
you replied: 350

                    "That was quick recognition;
but you are no numbskull—in this or anything.
Now we must plan this action. Will you take
leave of me here, and go ahead alone
to make your entrance now among the suitors?
Or do you choose to wait?—Let me go forward
and go in first.

                    Do not delay too long;
someone might find you skulking here outside
and take a club to you, or heave a lance.   360
Bear this in mind, I say."

                    The patient hero
Odysseus answered:

                    "Just what I was thinking.
You go in first, and leave me here a little.
But as for blows and missiles,
I am no tyro at these things. I learned
to keep my head in hardship—years of war
and years at sea. Let this new trial come.
The cruel belly, can you hide its ache?   370
How many bitter days it brings! Long ships
with good stout planks athwart—would fighters rig them
to ride the barren sea, except for hunger?
Seawolves—woe to their enemies!"

                    While he spoke
an old hound, lying near, pricked up his ears
and lifted up his muzzle. This was Argos,
trained as a puppy by Odysseus,
but never taken on a hunt before
his master sailed for Troy. The young men, afterward,   380
hunted wild goats with him, and hare, and deer,
but he had grown old in his master's absence.
Treated as rubbish now, he lay at last
upon a mass of dung before the gates—
manure of mules and cows, piled there until

fieldhands could spread it on the king's estate.
Abandoned there, and half destroyed with flies,
old Argos lay.
                              But when he knew he heard
Odysseus' voice nearby, he did his best   390
to wag his tail, nose down, with flattened ears,
having no strength to move nearer his master.
And the man looked away,
wiping a salt tear from his cheek; but he
hid this from Eumaios. Then he said:

"I marvel that they leave this hound to lie
here on the dung pile;
he would have been a fine dog, from the look of him,
though I can't say as to his power and speed
when he was young. You find the same good build   400
in house dogs, table dogs landowners keep
all for style."

                              And you replied, Eumaios:

"A hunter owned him—but the man is dead
in some far place. If this old hound could show
the form he had when Lord Odysseus left him,
going to Troy, you'd see him swift and strong.
He never shrank from any savage thing
he'd brought to bay in the deep woods; on the scent
no other dog kept up with him. Now misery   410
has him in leash. His owner died abroad,
and here the women slaves will take no care of him.
You know how servants are: without a master
they have no will to labor, or excel.
For Zeus who views the wide world takes away
half the manhood of a man, that day
he goes into captivity and slavery."

Eumaios crossed the court and went straight forward
into the mégaron among the suitors;
but death and darkness in that instant closed   420
the eyes of Argos, who had seen his master,
Odysseus, after twenty years.

                    Long before anyone else
Telémakhos caught sight of the grey woodsman
coming from the door, and called him over
with a quick jerk of his head. Eumaios'
narrowed eyes made out an empty bench
beside the one the carver used—that servant
who had no respite, carving for the suitors.
This bench he took possession of, and placed it   430
across the table from Telémakhos
for his own use. Then the two men were served
cuts from a roast and bread from a bread basket.

At no long interval, Odysseus came
through his own doorway as a mendicant,
humped like a bundle of rags over his stick.
He settled on the inner ash wood sill,
leaning against the door jamb—cypress timber
the skilled carpenter planed years ago
and set up with a plumbline.   440

                    Now Telémakhos
took an entire loaf and a double handful
of roast meat; then he said to the forester:

"Give these to the stranger there. But tell him
to go among the suitors, on his own;
he may beg all he wants. This hanging back
is no asset to a hungry man."

The swineherd rose at once, crossed to the door,
and halted by Odysseus.

                    "Friend," he said,   450
"Telémakhos is pleased to give you these,
but he commands you to approach the suitors;
you may ask all you want from them. He adds,
your shyness is no asset to a beggar."

The great tactician, lifting up his eyes,
cried:

"Zeus aloft! A blessing on Telémakhos!
Let all things come to pass as he desires!"

Palms held out, in the beggar's gesture, he
received the bread and meat and put it down   460
before him on his knapsack—lowly table!—
then he fell to, devouring it. Meanwhile
the harper in the great room sang a song.
Not till the man was fed did the sweet harper
end his singing—whereupon the company
made the walls ring again with talk.

                                        Unseen,
Athena took her place beside Odysseus
whispering in his ear:

                              "Yes, try the suitors.   470
You may collect a few more loaves, and learn
who are the decent lads, and who are vicious—
although not one can be excused from death!"

So he appealed to them, one after another,
going from left to right, with open palm,
as though his life time had been spent in beggary.
And they gave bread, for pity—wondering, though,
at the strange man. Who could this beggar be,
where did he come from? each would ask his neighbor;
till in their midst the goatherd, Melánthios,   480
raised his voice:

                        "Hear just a word from me,
my lords who court our illustrious queen!
                        This man,
this foreigner, I saw him on the road;
the swineherd, here was leading him this way;
who, what, or whence he claims to be, I could not
say for sure."

                        At this, Antínoös
turned on the swineherd brutally, saying: 490

"You famous
breeder of pigs, why bring this fellow here?
Are we not plagued enough with beggars,
foragers and such rats?

                         You find the company
too slow at eating up your lord's estate—
is that it? So you call this scarecrow in?"

The forester replied:

                         "Antínoös,
well born you are, but that was not well said.   500
Who would call in a foreigner?—unless
an artisan with skill to serve the realm,
a healer, or a prophet, or a builder,
or one whose harp and song might give us joy.
All these are sought for on the endless earth,
but when have beggars come by invitation?
Who puts a field mouse in his granary? My lord,
you are a hard man, and you always were,
more so than others of this company—hard
on all Odysseus' people and on me.   510
But this I can forget
as long as Penélopê lives on, the wise and tender
mistress of this hall; as long
as Prince Telémakhos—"

                         But he broke off
at a look from Telémakhos, who said:

                         "Be still.
Spare me a long-drawn answer to this gentleman.
With his unpleasantness, he will forever make
strife where he can—and goad the others on."   520

He turned and spoke out clearly to Antínoös:

"What fatherly concern you show me! Frighten
this unknown fellow, would you, from my hall
with words that promise blows—may God forbid it!
Give him a loaf. Am I a niggard? No,
I call on you to give. And spare your qualms

as to my mother's loss, or anyone's—
not that in truth you have such care at heart:
your heart is all in feeding, not in giving."

Antínoös replied: 530

                              "What high and mighty
talk, Telémakhos! Control your temper.
If every suitor gave what I may give him,
he could be kept for months—kept out of sight!"

He reached under the table for the footstool
his shining feet had rested on—and this
he held up so that all could see his gift.

But all the rest gave alms,
enough to fill the beggar's pack with bread
and roast meat.   540
                              So it looked as though Odysseus
had had his taste of what these men were like
and could return scot free to his own doorway—
but halting now before Antínoös
he made a little speech to him. Said he:

"Give a mite, friend. I would not say, myself,
you are the worst man of the young Akhaians.
The noblest, rather; kingly, by your look;
therefore you'll give more bread than others do.
Let me speak well of you as I pass on   550
over the boundless earth!
                              I, too, you know,
had fortune once, lived well, stood well with men,
and gave alms, often, to poor wanderers
like this one that you see—aye, to all sorts,
no matter in what dire want. I owned
servants—many, god knows—and all the rest
that goes with being prosperous, as they say.
But Zeus the son of Kronos brought me down.

No telling   560
why he would have it, but he made me go
to Egypt with a company of rovers—

a long sail to the south—for my undoing.
Up the broad Nile and in to the river bank
I brought my dipping squadron. There, indeed,
I told the men to stand guard at the ships;
I sent patrols out—out to rising ground;
but reckless greed carried my crews away
to plunder the Egyptian farms; they bore off
wives and children, killed what men they found.   570
The news ran on the wind to the city, a night cry,
and sunrise brought both infantry and horsemen,
filling the river plain with dazzle of bronze;
then Zeus lord of lightning
threw my men into a blind panic; no one dared
stand against that host closing around us.
Their scything weapons left our dead in piles,
but some they took alive, into forced labor,
myself among them. And they gave me, then,
to one Dmêtor, a traveller, son of Iasos,   580
who ruled at Kypros. He conveyed me there.
From that place, working northward, miserably—"

But here Antínoös broke in, shouting:

                              "God!
What evil wind blew in this pest?
                              Get over,
stand in the passage! Nudge my table, will you?
Egyptian whips are sweet
to what you'll come to here, you nosing rat,
making your pitch to everyone!   590
These men have bread to throw away on you
because it is not theirs. Who cares? Who spares
another's food, when he has more than plenty?"

With guile Odysseus drew away, then said:

"A pity that you have more looks than heart.
You'd grudge a pinch of salt from your own larder
to your own handy man. You sit here, fat
on others' meat, and cannot bring yourself
to rummage out a crust of bread for me!"

Then anger made Antínoös' heart beat hard,   600
and, glowering under his brows, he answered:

                    "Now!
You think you'll shuffle off and get away
after that impudence? Oh, no you don't!"

The stool he let fly hit the man's right shoulder
on the packed muscle under the shoulder blade—
like solid rock, for all the effect one saw.
Odysseus only shook his head, containing
thoughts of bloody work, as he walked on,
then sat, and dropped his loaded bag again   610
upon the doorsill. Facing the whole crowd
he said, and eyed them all:

                            "One word only,
my lords, and suitors of the famous queen.
One thing I have to say.
There is no pain, no burden for the heart
when blows come to a man, and he defending
his own cattle—his own cows and lambs.
Here it was otherwise. Antínoös
hit me for being driven on by hunger—   620
how many bitter seas men cross for hunger!
If beggars interest the gods, if there are Furies
pent in the dark to avenge a poor man's wrong, then may
Antínoös meet his death before his wedding day!"

Then said Eupeithês' son, Antínoös:

                        "Enough.
Eat and be quiet where you are, or shamble elsewhere,
unless you want these lads to stop your mouth
pulling you by the heels, or hands and feet,
over the whole floor, till your back is peeled!"   630

But now the rest were mortified, and someone
spoke from the crowd of young bucks to rebuke him:

"A poor show, that—hitting this famished tramp—
bad business, if he happened to be a god.

You know they go in foreign guise, the gods do,
looking like strangers, turning up
in towns and settlements to keep an eye
on manners, good or bad."

                              But at this notion
Antínoös only shrugged.   640
                              Telémakhos,
after the blow his father bore, sat still
without a tear, though his heart felt the blow.
Slowly he shook his head from side to side,
containing murderous thoughts.
                              Penélopê
on the higher level of her room had heard
the blow, and knew who gave it. Now she murmured:

"Would god you could be hit yourself, Antínoös—
hit by Apollo's bowshot!"   650

                              And Eurýnomê
her housekeeper, put in:

                              "He and no other?
If all we pray for came to pass, not one
would live till dawn!"

                              Her gentle mistress said:

"Oh, Nan, they are a bad lot; they intend
ruin for all of us; but Antínoös
appears a blacker-hearted hound than any.
Here is a poor man come, a wanderer,   660
driven by want to beg his bread, and everyone
in hall gave bits, to cram his bag—only
Antínoös threw a stool, and banged his shoulder!"

So she described it, sitting in her chamber
among her maids—while her true lord was eating.
Then she called in the forester and said:

"Go to that man on my behalf, Eumaios,
and send him here, so I can greet and question him.

Abroad in the great world, he may have heard
rumors about Odysseus—may have known him!"   670

Then you replied—O swineherd!

                    "Ah, my queen,
if these Akhaian sprigs would hush their babble
the man could tell you tales to charm your heart.
Three days and nights I kept him in my hut;
he came straight off a ship, you know, to me.
There was no end to what he made me hear
of his hard roving; and I listened, eyes
upon him, as a man drinks in a tale
a minstrel sings—a minstrel taught by heaven   680
to touch the hearts of men. At such a song
the listener becomes rapt and still. Just so
I found myself enchanted by this man.
He claims an old tie with Odysseus, too—
in his home country, the Minoan land
of Krete. From Krete he came, a rolling stone
washed by the gales of life this way and that
to our own beach.
                    If he can be believed
he has news of Odysseus near at hand   690
alive, in the rich country of Thesprotia,
bringing a mass of treasure home."

Then wise Penélopê said again:

"Go call him, let him come here, let him tell
that tale again for my own ears.
                    Our friends
can drink their cups outside or stay in hall,
being so carefree. And why not? Their stores
lie intact in their homes, both food and drink,
with only servants left to take a little.   700
But these men spend their days around our house
killing our beeves, our fat goats and our sheep,
carousing, drinking up our good dark wine;
sparing nothing, squandering everything.
No champion like Odysseus takes our part.

Ah, if he comes again, no falcon ever
struck more suddenly than he will, with his son,
to avenge this outrage!"

                              The great hall below
at this point rang with a tremendous sneeze—   710
"kchaou!" from Telémakhos—like an acclamation.
And laughter seized Penélopê.
                              Then quickly,
lucidly she went on:

                              "Go call the stranger
straight to me. Did you hear that, Eumaios?
My son's thundering sneeze at what I said!
May death come of a sudden so; may death
relieve us, clean as that, of all the suitors!
Let me add one thing—do not overlook it—   720
if I can see this man has told the truth,
I promise him a warm new cloak and tunic."

With all this in his head, the forester
went down the hall, and halted near the beggar,
saying aloud:

                              "Good father, you are called
by the wise mother of Telémakhos,
Penélopê. The queen, despite her troubles,
is moved by a desire to hear your tales
about her lord—and if she finds them true,   730
she'll see you clothed in what you need, a cloak
and a fresh tunic.

                              You may have your belly
full each day you go about this realm
begging. For all may give, and all they wish."

Now said Odysseus, the old soldier:

"Friend,
I wish this instant I could tell my facts
to the wise daughter of Ikários, Penélopê—
and I have much to tell about her husband;   740
we went through much together.

But just now
this hard crowd worries me. They are, you said
infamous to the very rim of heaven
for violent acts: and here, just now, this fellow
gave me a bruise. What had I done to him?
But who would lift a hand for me? Telémakhos?
Anyone else?

No; bid the queen be patient.
Let her remain till sundown in her room,   750
and then—if she will seat me near the fire—
inquire tonight about her lord's return.
My rags are sorry cover; you know that;
I showed my sad condition first to you."

The woodsman heard him out, and then returned;
but the queen met him on her threshold, crying:

"Have you not brought him? Why? What is he thinking?
Has he some fear of overstepping? Shy
about these inner rooms? A hangdog beggar?"

To this you answered, friend Eumaios: 760

"No:
he reasons as another might, and well,
not to tempt any swordplay from these drunkards.
Be patient, wait—he says—till darkness falls.
And, O my queen, for you too that is better:
better to be alone with him, and question him,
and hear him out."

Penélopê replied:

"He is no fool; he sees how it could be.
Never were mortal men like these   770
for bullying and brainless arrogance!"

Thus she accepted what had been proposed,
so he went back into the crowd. He joined
Telémakhos, and said at once in whispers—
his head bent, so that no one else might hear:

"Dear prince, I must go home to keep good watch
on hut and swine, and look to my own affairs.
Everything here is in your hands. Consider
your own safety before the rest; take care
not to get hurt. Many are dangerous here.   780
May Zeus destroy them first, before we suffer!"

Telémakhos said:

                              "Your wish is mine, Uncle.
Go when your meal is finished. Then come back
at dawn, and bring good victims for a slaughter.
Everything here is in my hands indeed—
and in the disposition of the gods."

Taking his seat on the smooth bench again,
Eumaios ate and drank his fill, then rose
to climb the mountain trail back to his swine,   790
leaving the mégaron and court behind him
crowded with banqueters.
                              These had their joy
of dance and song, as day waned into evening.

BOOK EIGHTEEN

Blows and
a Queen's Beauty

LINES 1 – 14

Now a true scavenger came in—a public tramp   1
who begged around the town of Ithaka,
a by-word for his insatiable swag-belly,
feeding and drinking, dawn to dark. No pith
was in him, and no nerve, huge as he looked.
Arnaios, as his gentle mother called him,
he had been nicknamed "Iros" by the young
for being ready to take messages.
                              This fellow
thought he would rout Odysseus from his doorway,   10
growling at him:

                              "Clear out, grandfathei,
or else be hauled out by the ankle bone.
See them all giving me the wink? That means,
'Go on and drag him out!' I hate to do it.
Up with you! Or would you like a fist fight?"

Odysseus only frowned and looked him over,
taking account of everything, then said:

"Master, I am no trouble to you here.
I offer no remarks. I grudge you nothing.   20
Take all you get, and welcome. Here is room
for two on this doorslab—or do you own it?
You are a tramp, I think, like me. Patience:
a windfall from the gods will come. But drop
that talk of using fists; it could annoy me.
Old as I am, I might just crack a rib
or split a lip for you. My life would go
even more peacefully, after tomorrow,
looking for no more visits here from you."

Iros the tramp grew red and hooted: 30

"Ho,
listen to him! The swine can talk your arm off,
like an old oven woman! With two punches
I'd knock him snoring, if I had a mind to—
and not a tooth left in his head, the same
as an old sow caught in the corn! Belt up!
And let this company see the way I do it
when we square off. Can you fight a fresher man?"

Under the lofty doorway, on the door sill
of wide smooth ash, they held this rough exchange.   40
And the tall full-blooded suitor, Antínoös,
overhearing, broke into happy laughter.
Then he said to the others:

                              "Oh, my friends,
no luck like this ever turned up before!
What a farce heaven has brought this house!
                              The stranger
and Iros have had words, they brag of boxing!
Into the ring they go, and no more talk!"

All the young men got on their feet now, laughing,   50
to crowd around the ragged pair. Antínoös
called out:

                              "Gentlemen, quiet! One more thing:
here are goat stomachs ready on the fire
to stuff with blood and fat, good supper pudding.
The man who wins this gallant bout
may step up here and take the one he likes.
And let him feast with us from this day on:
no other beggar will be admitted here
when we are at our wine."   60

                              This pleased them all.
But now that wily man, Odysseus, muttered:

"An old man, an old hulk, has no business
fighting a young man, but my belly nags me;
nothing will do but I must take a beating.
Well, then, let every man here swear an oath
not to step in for Iros. No one throw
a punch for luck. I could be whipped that way."

So much the suitors were content to swear,
but after they reeled off their oaths, Telémakhos   70
put in a word to clinch it, saying:

                              "Friend,
if you will stand and fight, as pride requires,
don't worry about a foul blow from behind.
Whoever hits you will take on the crowd.
You have my word as host; you have the word
of these two kings, Antínoös and Eurýmakhos—
a pair of thinking men."

                              All shouted, "Aye!"
So now Odysseus made his shirt a belt   80
and roped his rags around his loins, baring
his hurdler's thighs and boxer's breadth of shoulder,
the dense rib-sheath and upper arms. Athena
stood nearby to give him bulk and power,
while the young suitors watched with narrowed eyes—
and comments went around:

"By god, old Iros now retiros."

                          "Aye,
he asked for it, he'll get it—bloody, too."

"The build this fellow had, under his rags!"   90

Panic made Iros' heart jump, but the yard-boys
hustled and got him belted by main force,
though all his blubber quivered now with dread.
Antínoös' angry voice rang in his ears:

"You sack of guts, you might as well be dead,
might as well never have seen the light of day,
if this man makes you tremble! Chicken-heart,
afraid of an old wreck, far gone in misery!
Well, here is what I say—and what I'll do.
If this ragpicker can outfight you, whip you,   100
I'll ship you out to that king in Epeíros,
Ékhetos—he skins everyone alive.
Let him just cut your nose off and your ears
and pull your privy parts out by the roots
to feed raw to his hunting dogs!"

                          Poor Iros
felt a new fit of shaking take his knees.
But the yard-boys pushed him out. Now both contenders
put their hands up. Royal Odysseus
pondered if he should hit him with all he had   110
and drop the man dead on the spot, or only
spar, with force enough to knock him down.
Better that way, he thought—a gentle blow,
else he might give himself away.
                          The two
were at close quarters now, and Iros lunged
hitting the shoulder. Then Odysseus hooked him
under the ear and shattered his jaw bone,
so bright red blood came bubbling from his mouth,
as down he pitched into the dust, bleating,   120
kicking against the ground, his teeth stove in.
The suitors whooped and swung their arms, half dead
with pangs of laughter.

Then, by the ankle bone,
Odysseus hauled the fallen one outside,
crossing the courtyard to the gate, and piled him
against the wall. In his right hand he stuck
his begging staff, and said:

      "Here, take your post.
Sit here to keep the dogs and pigs away.   130
You can give up your habit of command
over poor waifs and beggarmen—you swab.
Another time you may not know what hit you."

When he had slung his rucksack by the string
over his shoulder, like a wad of rags,
he sat down on the broad door sill again,
as laughing suitors came to flock inside;
and each young buck in passing gave him greeting,
saying, maybe,

     "Zeus fill your pouch for this! 140
May the gods grant your heart's desire!"

      "Well done
to put that walking famine out of business."

"We'll ship him out to that king in Epeíros,
Ékhetos—he skins everyone alive."

Odysseus found grim cheer in their good wishes—
his work had started well.
      Now from the fire
his fat blood pudding came, deposited
before him by Antínoös—then, to boot,   150
two brown loaves from the basket, and some wine
in a fine cup of gold. These gifts Amphínomos
gave him. Then he said:

     "Here's luck, grandfather;
a new day; may the worst be over now."

Odysseus answered, and his mind ranged far:

"Amphínomos, your head is clear, I'd say;
so was your father's—or at least I've heard
good things of Nísos the Doulíkhion,
whose son you are, they tell me—an easy man.   160
And you seem gently bred.

             In view of that,
I have a word to say to you, so listen.

Of mortal creatures, all that breathe and move,
earth bears none frailer than mankind. What man
believes in woe to come, so long as valor
and tough knees are supplied him by the gods?
But when the gods in bliss bring miseries on,
then willy-nilly, blindly, he endures.
Our minds are as the days are, dark or bright,   170
blown over by the father of gods and men.

So I, too, in my time thought to be happy;
but far and rash I ventured, counting on
my own right arm, my father, and my kin;
behold me now.

           No man should flout the law,
but keep in peace what gifts the gods may give.

I see you young blades living dangerously,
a household eaten up, a wife dishonored—
and yet the master will return, I tell you,   180
to his own place, and soon; for he is near.
So may some power take you out of this,
homeward, and softly, not to face that man
the hour he sets foot on his native ground.
Between him and the suitors I foretell
no quittance, no way out, unless by blood,
once he shall stand beneath his own roof-beam."

Gravely, when he had done, he made libation
and took a sip of honey-hearted wine,
giving the cup, then, back into the hands   190
of the young nobleman. Amphínomos, for his part,
shaking his head, with chill and burdened breast,
turned in the great hall.

Now his heart foreknew
the wrath to come, but he could not take flight,
being by Athena bound there.

Death would have him
broken by a spear thrown by Telémakhos.
So he sat down where he had sat before.

And now heart-prompting from the grey-eyed goddess   200
came to the quiet queen, Penélopê:
a wish to show herself before the suitors;
for thus by fanning their desire again
Athena meant to set her beauty high
before her husband's eyes, before her son.
Knowing no reason, laughing confusedly,
she said:

"Eurýnomê, I have a craving
I never had at all—I would be seen
among those ruffians, hateful as they are.   210
I might well say a word, then, to my son,
for his own good—tell him to shun that crowd;
for all their gay talk, they are bent on evil."

Mistress Eurýnomê replied:

"Well said, child,
now is the time. Go down, and make it clear,
hold nothing back from him.

But you must bathe
and put a shine upon your cheeks—not this way,
streaked under your eyes and stained with tears.   220
You make it worse, being forever sad,
and now your boy's a bearded man! Remember
you prayed the gods to let you see him so."

Penélopê replied:

"Eurýnomê,
it is a kind thought, but I will not hear it—
to bathe and sleek with perfumed oil. No, no,
the gods forever took my sheen away
when my lord sailed for Troy in the decked ships.

Only tell my Autonoë to come,   230
and Hippodameía; they should be attending me
in hall, if I appear there. I could not
enter alone into that crowd of men."

At this the good old woman left the chamber
to tell the maids her bidding. But now too
the grey-eyed goddess had her own designs.
Upon the quiet daughter of Ikários
she let clear drops of slumber fall, until
the queen lay back asleep, her limbs unstrung,
in her long chair. And while she slept the goddess   240
endowed her with immortal grace to hold
the eyes of the Akhaians. With ambrosia
she bathed her cheeks and throat and smoothed her brow—
ambrosia, used by flower-crowned Kythereia
when she would join the rose-lipped Graces dancing.
Grandeur she gave her, too, in height and form,
and made her whiter than carved ivory.
Touching her so, the perfect one was gone.
Now came the maids, bare-armed and lovely, voices
breaking into the room. The queen awoke   250
and as she rubbed her cheek she sighed:

                    "Ah, soft
that drowse I lay embraced in, pain forgot!
If only Artemis the Pure would give me
death as mild, and soon! No heart-ache more,
no wearing out my lifetime with desire
and sorrow, mindful of my lord, good man
in all ways that he was, best of the Akhaians!"

She rose and left her glowing upper room,
and down the stairs, with her two maids in train,   260
this beautiful lady went before the suitors.
Then by a pillar of the solid roof
she paused, her shining veil across her cheek,
the two girls close to her and still;
and in that instant weakness took those men
in the knee joints, their hearts grew faint with lust;

not one but swore to god to lie beside her.
But speaking for her dear son's ears alone
she said:

                                  "Telémakhos, what has come over you? 270
Lightminded you were not, in all your boyhood.
Now you are full grown, come of age; a man
from foreign parts might take you for the son
of royalty, to go by your good looks;
and have you no more thoughtfulness or manners?
How could it happen in our hall that you
permit the stranger to be so abused?
Here, in our house, a guest, can any man
suffer indignity, come by such injury?
What can this be for you but public shame?"   280

Telémakhos looked in her eyes and answered,
with his clear head and his discretion:

"Mother,
I cannot take it ill that you are angry.
I know the meaning of these actions now,
both good and bad. I had been young and blind.
How can I always keep to what is fair
while these sit here to put fear in me?—princes
from near and far whose interest is my ruin;
are any on my side?   290
                    But you should know
the suitors did not have their way, matching
the stranger here and Iros—for the stranger
beat him to the ground.
                   O Father Zeus!
Athena and Apollo! could I see
the suitors whipped like that! Courtyard and hall
strewn with our friends, too weak-kneed to get up,
chapfallen to their collarbones, the way
old Iros rolls his head there by the gate   300
as though he were pig-drunk! No energy
to stagger on his homeward path; no fight
left in his numb legs!"

Thus Penélopê
reproached her son, and he replied. Now, interrupting,
Eurýmakhos called out to her:

"Penélopê,
deep-minded queen, daughter of Ikários,
if all Akhaians in the land of Argos
only saw you now! What hundreds more   310
would join your suitors here to feast tomorrow!
Beauty like yours no woman had before,
or majesty, or mastery."

She answered:

"Eurýmakhos, my qualities—I know—
my face, my figure, all were lost or blighted
when the Akhaians crossed the sea to Troy,
Odysseus my lord among the rest.
If he returned, if he were here to care for me,
I might be happily renowned!   320
But grief instead heaven sent me—years of pain.
Can I forget?—the day he left this island,
enfolding my right hand and wrist in his,
he said:

'My lady, the Akhaian troops
will not easily make it home again
full strength, unhurt, from Troy. They say the Trojans
are fighters too; good lances and good bowmen,
horsemen, charioteers—and those can be
decisive when a battle hangs in doubt.   330
So whether God will send me back, or whether
I'll be a captive there, I cannot tell.
Here, then, you must attend to everything.
My parents in our house will be a care for you
as they are now, or more, while I am gone.
Wait for the beard to darken our boy's cheek;
then marry whom you will, and move away.'

The years he spoke of are now past; the night
comes when a bitter marriage overtakes me,

desolate as I am, deprived by Zeus   340
of all the sweets of life.

                              How galling, too,
to see newfangled manners in my suitors!
Others who go to court a gentlewoman,
daughter of a rich house, if they are rivals,
bring their own beeves and sheep along; her friends
ought to be feasted, gifts are due to her;
would any dare to live at her expense?"

Odysseus' heart laughed when he heard all this—
her sweet tones charming gifts out of the suitors   350
with talk of marriage, though she intended none.
Eupeíthês' son, Antínoös, now addressed her:

"Ikários' daughter, O deep-minded queen!
If someone cares to make you gifts, accept them!
It is no courtesy to turn gifts away.
But we go neither to our homes nor elsewhere
until of all Akhaians here you take
the best man for your lord."

                              Pleased at this answer,
every man sent a squire to fetch a gift—   360
Antínoös, a wide resplendent robe,
embroidered fine, and fastened with twelve brooches,
pins pressed into sheathing tubes of gold;
Eurýmakhos, a necklace, wrought in gold,
with sunray pieces of clear glinting amber.
Eurýdamas's men came back with pendants,
ear-drops in triple clusters of warm lights;
and from the hoard of Lord Polýktor's son,
Peisándros, came a band for her white throat,
jewelled adornment. Other wondrous things   370
were brought as gifts from the Akhaian princes.
Penélopê then mounted the stair again,
her maids behind, with treasure in their arms.

And now the suitors gave themselves to dancing,
to harp and haunting song, as night drew on;

black night indeed came on them at their pleasure.
But three torch fires were placed in the long hall
to give them light. On hand were stores of fuel,
dry seasoned chips of resinous wood, split up
by the bronze hatchet blade—these were mixed in   380
among the flames to keep them flaring bright;
each housemaid of Odysseus took her turn.

Now he himself, the shrewd and kingly man,
approached and told them:

                              "Housemaids of Odysseus,
your master so long absent in the world,
go to the women's chambers, to your queen.
Attend her, make the distaff whirl, divert her,
stay in her room, comb wool for her.
                         I stand here   390
ready to tend these flares and offer light
to everyone. They cannot tire me out,
even if they wish to drink till Dawn.
I am a patient man."

                         But the women giggled,
glancing back and forth—laughed in his face;
and one smooth girl, Melántho, spoke to him
most impudently. She was Dólios' daughter,
taken as ward in childhood by Penélopê
who gave her playthings to her heart's content   400
and raised her as her own. Yet the girl felt
nothing for her mistress, no compunction,
but slept and made love with Eurýmakhos.
Her bold voice rang now in Odysseus' ears:

"You must be crazy, punch drunk, you old goat.
Instead of going out to find a smithy
to sleep warm in—or a tavern bench—you stay
putting your oar in, amid all our men.
Numbskull, not to be scared! The wine you drank
has clogged your brain, or are you always this way,   410
boasting like a fool? Or have you lost
your mind because you beat that tramp, that Iros?

Look out, or someone better may get up
and give you a good knocking about the ears
to send you out all bloody."

                                    But Odysseus
glared at her under his brows and said:

                                    "One minute:
let me tell Telémakhos how you talk
in hall, you slut; he'll cut your arms and legs off!"   420

This hard shot took the women's breath away
and drove them quaking to their rooms, as though
knives were behind: they felt he spoke the truth.
So there he stood and kept the firelight high
and looked the suitors over, while his mind
roamed far ahead to what must be accomplished.

They, for their part, could not now be still
or drop their mockery—for Athena wished
Odysseus mortified still more.
                                    Eurýmakhos,   430
the son of Pólybos, took up the baiting,
angling for a laugh among his friends.

"Suitors of our distinguished queen," he said,
"hear what my heart would have me say.
                                    This man
comes with a certain aura of divinity
into Odysseus' hall. He shines.
                                    He shines
around the noggin, like a flashing light,
having no hair at all to dim his lustre."   440

Then turning to Odysseus, raider of cities,
he went on:

                                    "Friend, you have a mind to work,
do you? Could I hire you to clear stones
from wasteland for me—you'll be paid enough—
collecting boundary walls and planting trees?

I'd give you a bread ration every day,
a cloak to wrap in, sandals for your feet.
Oh no: you learned your dodges long ago—
no honest sweat. You'd rather tramp the country   450
begging, to keep your hoggish belly full."

The master of many crafts replied:

                              "Eurýmakhos,
we two might try our hands against each other
in early summer when the days are long,
in meadow grass, with one good scythe for me
and one as good for you: we'd cut our way
down a deep hayfield, fasting to late evening.
Or we could try our hands behind a plow,
driving the best of oxen—fat, well-fed,   460
well-matched for age and pulling power, and say
four strips apiece of loam the share could break:
you'd see then if I cleft you a straight furrow.
Competition in arms? If Zeus Kroníon
roused up a scuffle now, give me a shield,
two spears, a dogskin cap with plates of bronze
to fit my temples, and you'd see me go
where the first rank of fighters lock in battle.
There would be no more jeers about my belly.
You thick-skinned menace to all courtesy!   470
You think you are a great man and a champion,
but up against few men, poor stuff, at that.
Just let Odysseus return, those doors
wide open as they are, you'd find too narrow
to suit you on your sudden journey out."

Now fury mounted in Eurýmakhos,
who scowled and shot back:

                              "Bundle of rags and lice!
By god, I'll make you suffer for your gall,
your insolent gabble before all our men."   480

He had his foot-stool out: but now Odysseus
took to his haunches by Amphínomos' knees,

fearing Eurýmakhos' missile, as it flew.
It clipped a wine steward on the serving hand,
so that his pitcher dropped with a loud clang
while he fell backward, cursing, in the dust.
In the shadowy hall a low sound rose—of suitors
murmuring to one another.

                      "Ai!" they said.
"This vagabond would have done well to perish   490
somewhere else, and make us no such rumpus.
Here we are, quarreling over tramps; good meat
and wine forgotten; good sense gone by the board."

Telémakhos, his young heart high, put in:

"Bright souls, alight with wine, you can no longer
hide the cups you've taken. Aye, some god
is goading you. Why not go home to bed?—
I mean when you are moved to. No one jumps
at my command."

                    Struck by his blithe manner,   500
the young men's teeth grew fixed in their under lips,
but now the son of Nísos, Lord Amphínomos
of Aretíadês, addressed them all:

"O friends, no ruffling replies are called for;
that was fair counsel.
                  Hands off the stranger, now,
and hands off any other servant here
in the great house of King Odysseus. Come,
let my own herald wet our cups once more,
we'll make an offering, and then to bed.   510
The stranger can be left behind in hall;
Telémakhos may care for him; he came
to Telémakhos' door, not ours."

                  This won them over.
The soldier Moulios, Doulíkhion herald,
comrade in arms of Lord Amphínomos,
mixed the wine and served them all. They tipped out

drops for the blissful gods, and drank the rest,
and when they had drunk their thirst away
they trailed off homeward drowsily to bed.   520

BOOK NINETEEN

Recognitions and a Dream

LINES 1 – 13

Now by Athena's side in the quiet hall   1
studying the ground for slaughter, Lord Odysseus
turned to Telémakhos.

                              "The arms," he said.
"Harness and weapons must be out of sight
in the inner room. And if the suitors miss them,
be mild; just say 'I had a mind to move them
out of the smoke. They seemed no longer
the bright arms that Odysseus left at home
when he went off to Troy. Here where the fire's   10
hot breath came, they had grown black and drear.
One better reason struck me, too:
suppose a brawl starts up when you've been drinking—
you might in madness let each other's blood,
and that would stain your feast, your courtship.
                              Iron
itself can draw men's hands.'"

Then he fell silent,
and Telémakhos obeyed his father's word.
He called Eurýkleia, the nurse, and told her: 20

"Nurse, go shut the women in their quarters
while I shift Father's armor back
to the inner rooms—these beautiful arms unburnished,
caked with black soot in his years abroad.
I was a child then. Well, I am not now.
I want them shielded from the draught and smoke."

And the old woman answered:

"It is time, child,
you took an interest in such things. I wish
you'd put your mind on all your house and chattels.   30
But who will go along to hold a light?
You said no maids, no torch-bearers."

Telémakhos
looked at her and replied:

"Our friend here.
A man who shares my meat can bear a hand,
no matter how far he is from home."

He spoke so soldierly
her own speech halted on her tongue. Straight back
she went to lock the doors of the women's hall.   40
And now the two men sprang to work—father
and princely son, loaded with round helms
and studded bucklers, lifting the long spears,
while in their path Pallas Athena
held up a golden lamp of purest light.
Telémakhos at last burst out:

"Oh, Father,
here is a marvel! All around I see
the walls and roof beams, pedestals and pillars,
lighted as though by white fire blazing near.   50
One of the gods of heaven is in this place!"

Then said Odysseus, the great tactician,

"Be still: keep still about it: just remember it.
The gods who rule Olympos make this light.
You may go off to bed now. Here I stay
to test your mother and her maids again.
Out of her long grief she will question me."

Telémakhos went across the hall and out
under the light of torches—crossed the court
to the tower chamber where he had always slept.   60
Here now again he lay, waiting for dawn,
while in the great hall by Athena's side
Odysseus waited with his mind on slaughter.

Presently Penélopê from her chamber
stepped in her thoughtful beauty.
                              So might Artemis
or golden Aphroditê have descended;
and maids drew to the hearth her own smooth chair
inlaid with silver whorls and ivory. The artisan
Ikmálios had made it, long before,   70
with a footrest in a single piece, and soft
upon the seat a heavy fleece was thrown.
Here by the fire the queen sat down. Her maids,
leaving their quarters, came with white arms bare
to clear the wine cups and the bread, and move
the trestle boards where men had lingered drinking.
Fiery ashes out of the pine-chip flares
they tossed, and piled on fuel for light and heat.
And now a second time Melántho's voice
rang brazen in Odysseus' ears: 80

                    "Ah, stranger,
are you still here, so creepy, late at night
hanging about, looking the women over?
You old goat, go outside, cuddle your supper;
get out, or a torch may kindle you behind!"

At this Odysseus glared under his brows
and said:

"Little devil, why pitch into me again?
Because I go unwashed and wear these rags,
and make the rounds? But so I must, being needy;   90
that is the way a vagabond must live.
And do not overlook this: in my time
I too had luck, lived well, stood well with men,
and gave alms, often, to poor wanderers
like him you see before you—aye, to all sorts,
no matter in what dire want. I owned
servants—many, I say—and all the rest
that goes with what men call prosperity.
But Zeus the son of Krónos brought me down.
Mistress, mend your ways, or you may lose   100
all this vivacity of yours. What if her ladyship
were stirred to anger? What if Odysseus came?—
and I can tell you, there is hope of that—
or if the man is done for, still his son
lives to be reckoned with, by Apollo's will.
None of you can go wantoning on the sly
and fool him now. He is too old for that."

Penélopê, being near enough to hear him,
spoke out sharply to her maid:

                         "Oh, shameless,   110
through and through! And do you think me blind,
blind to your conquest? It will cost your life.
You knew I waited—for you heard me say it—
waited to see this man in hall and question him
about my lord; I am so hard beset."

She turned away and said to the housekeeper:

"Eurýnomê, a bench, a spread of sheepskin,
to put my guest at ease. Now he shall talk
and listen, and be questioned."

                         Willing hands   120
brought a smooth bench, and dropped a fleece upon it.
Here the adventurer and king sat down;
then carefully Penélopê began:

"Friend, let me ask you first of all:
who are you, where do you come from, of what nation
and parents were you born?"

                              And he replied:

"My lady, never a man in the wide world
should have a fault to find with you. Your name
has gone out under heaven like the sweet   130
honor of some god-fearing king, who rules
in equity over the strong: his black lands bear
both wheat and barley, fruit trees laden bright,
new lambs at lambing time—and the deep sea
gives great hauls of fish by his good strategy,
so that his folk fare well.

                              O my dear lady,
this being so, let it suffice to ask me
of other matters—not my blood, my homeland.
Do not enforce me to recall my pain.   140
My heart is sore; but I must not be found
sitting in tears here, in another's house:
it is not well forever to be grieving.
One of the maids might say—or you might think—
I had got maudlin over cups of wine."

And Penélopê replied:

                              "Stranger, my looks,
my face, my carriage, were soon lost or faded
when the Akhaians crossed the sea to Troy,
Odysseus my lord among the rest.   150
If he returned, if he were here to care for me,
I might be happily renowned!
But grief instead heaven sent me—years of pain.
Sons of the noblest families on the islands,
Doulíkhion, Samê, wooded Zakýnthos,
with native Ithakans, are here to court me,
against my wish; and they consume this house.
Can I give proper heed to guest or suppliant
or herald on the realm's affairs?

How could I?   160
wasted with longing for Odysseus, while here
they press for marriage.

Ruses served my turn
to draw the time out—first a close-grained web
I had the happy thought to set up weaving
on my big loom in hall. I said, that day:
'Young men—my suitors, now my lord is dead,
let me finish my weaving before I marry,
or else my thread will have been spun in vain.
It is a shroud I weave for Lord Laërtês   170
when cold Death comes to lay him on his bier.
The country wives would hold me in dishonor
if he, with all his fortune, lay unshrouded.'
I reached their hearts that way, and they agreed.
So every day I wove on the great loom,
but every night by torchlight I unwove it;
and so for three years I deceived the Akhaians.
But when the seasons brought a fourth year on,
as long months waned, and the long days were spent,
through impudent folly in the slinking maids   180
they caught me—clamored up to me at night;
I had no choice then but to finish it.
And now, as matters stand at last,
I have no strength left to evade a marriage,
cannot find any further way; my parents
urge it upon me, and my son
will not stand by while they eat up his property.
He comprehends it, being a man full grown,
able to oversee the kind of house
Zeus would endow with honor.   190

But you too
confide in me, tell me your ancestry.
You were not born of mythic oak or stone."

And the great master of invention answered:

"O honorable wife of Lord Odysseus,
must you go on asking about my family?
Then I will tell you, though my pain

be doubled by it: and whose pain would not
if he had been away as long as I have
and had hard roving in the world of men?   200
But I will tell you even so, my lady.

One of the great islands of the world
in midsea, in the winedark sea, is Krete:
spacious and rich and populous, with ninety
cities and a mingling of tongues.
Akhaians there are found, along with Kretan
hillmen of the old stock, and Kydonians,
Dorians in three blood-lines, Pelasgians—
and one among their ninety towns is Knossos.
Here lived King Minos whom great Zeus received   210
every ninth year in private council—Minos,
the father of my father, Deukálion.
Two sons Deukálion had: Idómeneus,
who went to join the Atreidai before Troy
in the beaked ships of war; and then myself,
Aithôn by name—a stripling next my brother.
But I saw with my own eyes at Knossos once
Odysseus.

                 Gales had caught him off Cape Malea,
driven him southward on the coast of Krete,   220
when he was bound for Troy. At Ámnisos,
hard by the holy cave of Eileithuía,
he lay to, and dropped anchor, in that open
and rough roadstead riding out the blow.
Meanwhile he came ashore, came inland, asking
after Idómeneus: dear friends he said they were;
but now ten mornings had already passed,
ten or eleven, since my brother sailed.
So I played host and took Odysseus home,
saw him well lodged and fed, for we had plenty;   230
then I made requisitions—barley, wine,
and beeves for sacrifice—to give his company
abundant fare along with him.

                Twelve days
they stayed with us, the Akhaians, while that wind
out of the north shut everyone inside—

even on land you could not keep your feet,
such fury was abroad. On the thirteenth,
when the gale dropped, they put to sea."

Now all these lies he made appear so truthful   240
she wept as she sat listening. The skin
of her pale face grew moist the way pure snow
softens and glistens on the mountains, thawed
by Southwind after powdering from the West,
and, as the snow melts, mountain streams run full:
so her white cheeks were wetted by these tears
shed for her lord—and he close by her side.
Imagine how his heart ached for his lady,
his wife in tears; and yet he never blinked;
his eyes might have been made of horn or iron   250
for all that she could see. He had this trick—
wept, if he willed to, inwardly.
                                        Well, then,
as soon as her relieving tears were shed
she spoke once more:

                              "I think that I shall say, friend,
give me some proof, it it is really true
that you were host in that place to my husband
with his brave men, as you declare. Come, tell me
the quality of his clothing, how he looked,   260
and some particular of his company."

Odysseus answered, and his mind ranged far:

"Lady, so long a time now lies between,
it is hard to speak of it. Here is the twentieth year
since that man left the island of my father.
But I shall tell what memory calls to mind.
A purple cloak, and fleecy, he had on—
a double thick one. Then, he wore a brooch
made of pure gold with twin tubes for the prongs,
and on the face a work of art: a hunting dog   270
pinning a spotted fawn in agony
between his forepaws—wonderful to see
how being gold, and nothing more, he bit

the golden deer convulsed, with wild hooves flying.
Odysseus' shirt I noticed, too—a fine
closefitting tunic like dry onion skin,
so soft it was, and shiny.
                       Women there,
many of them, would cast their eyes on it.
But I might add, for your consideration,   280
whether he brought these things from home, or whether
a shipmate gave them to him, coming aboard,
I have no notion: some regardful host
in another port perhaps it was. Affection
followed him—there were few Akhaians like him.
And I too made him gifts: a good bronze blade,
a cloak with lining and a broidered shirt,
and sent him off in his trim ship with honor.
A herald, somewhat older than himself,
he kept beside him; I'll describe this man: 290
round-shouldered, dusky, woolly-headed;
Eurýbatês, his name was—and Odysseus
gave him preferment over the officers.
He had a shrewd head, like the captain's own."

Now hearing these details—minutely true—
she felt more strangely moved, and tears flowed
until she had tasted her salt grief again.
Then she found words to answer:
                       "Before this
you won my sympathy, but now indeed   300
you shall be our respected guest and friend.
With my own hands I put that cloak and tunic
upon him—took them folded from their place—
and the bright brooch for ornament.
                       Gone now,
I will not meet the man again
returning to his own home fields. Unkind
the fate that sent him young in the long ship
to see that misery at Ilion, unspeakable!"

And the master improviser answered: 310

"Honorable
wife of Odysseus Laërtiadês,
you need not stain your beauty with these tears,
nor wear yourself out grieving for your husband.
Not that I can blame you. Any wife
grieves for the man she married in her girlhood,
lay with in love, bore children to—though he
may be no prince like this Odysseus,
whom they compare even to the gods. But listen:
weep no more, and listen: 320
I have a thing to tell you, something true.
I heard but lately of your lord's return,
heard that he is alive, not far away,
among Thesprótians in their green land
amassing fortune to bring home. His company
went down in shipwreck in the winedark sea
off the coast of Thrinákia. Zeus and Hêlios
held it against him that his men had killed
the kine of Hêlios. The crew drowned for this.
He rode the ship's keel. Big seas cast him up   330
on the island of Phaiákians, godlike men
who took him to their hearts. They honored him
with many gifts and a safe passage home,
or so they wished. Long since he should have been here,
but he thought better to restore his fortune
playing the vagabond about the world;
and no adventurer could beat Odysseus
at living by his wits—no man alive.
I had this from King Phaidôn of Thesprótia;
and, tipping wine out, Phaidôn swore to me   340
the ship was launched, the seamen standing by
to bring Odysseus to his land at last,
but I got out to sea ahead of him
by the king's order—as it chanced a freighter
left port for the grain bins of Doulíkhion.
Phaidôn, however, showed me Odysseus' treasure.
Ten generations of his heirs or more
could live on what lay piled in that great room.
The man himself had gone up to Dodona
to ask the spelling leaves of the old oak   350

what Zeus would have him do—how to return to Ithaka
after so many years—by stealth or openly.
You see, then, he is alive and well, and headed
homeward now, no more to be abroad
far from his island, his dear wife and son.
Here is my sworn word for it. Witness this,
god of the zenith, noblest of the gods,
and Lord Odysseus' hearthfire, now before me:
I swear these things shall turn out as I say.
Between this present dark and one day's ebb,   360
after the wane, before the crescent moon,
Odysseus will come.*

                                Penélopê,
the attentive queen, replied to him:

                                "Ah, stranger,
if what you say could ever happen!
You would soon know our love! Our bounty, too:
men would turn after you to call you blessed.
But my heart tells me what must be.
Odysseus will not come to me; no ship   370
will be prepared for you. We have no master
quick to receive and furnish out a guest
as Lord Odysseus was.
                          Or did I dream him?

Maids, maids: come wash him, make a bed for him,
bedstead and colored rugs and coverlets
to let him lie warm into the gold of Dawn.
In morning light you'll bathe him and anoint him
so that he'll take his place beside Telémakhos
feasting in hall. If there be one man there   380
to bully or annoy him, that man wins
no further triumph here, burn though he may.
How will you understand me, friend, how find in me,
more than in common women, any courage
or gentleness, if you are kept in rags
and filthy at our feast? Men's lives are short.
The hard man and his cruelties will be
cursed behind his back, and mocked in death.

But one whose heart and ways are kind—of him
strangers will bear report to the wide world,   390
and distant men will praise him."

                              Warily
Odysseus answered:

                              "Honorable lady,
wife of Odysseus Laërtiadês,
a weight of rugs and cover? Not for me.
I've had none since the day I saw the mountains
of Krete, white with snow, low on the sea line
fading behind me as the long oars drove me north.
Let me lie down tonight as I've lain often,   400
many a night unsleeping, many a time
afield on hard ground waiting for pure Dawn.
No: and I have no longing for a footbath
either; none of these maids will touch my feet,
unless there is an old one, old and wise,
one who has lived through suffering as I have:
I would not mind letting my feet be touched
by that old servant."

                              And Penélopê said:

"Dear guest, no foreign man so sympathetic   410
ever came to my house, no guest more likeable,
so wry and humble are the things you say.
I have an old maidservant ripe with years,
one who in her time nursed my lord. She took him
into her arms the hour his mother bore him.
Let her, then, wash your feet, though she is frail.
Come here, stand by me, faithful Eurýkleia,
and bathe—bathe your master, I almost said,
for they are of an age, and now Odysseus'
feet and hands would be enseamed like his.   420
Men grow old soon in hardship."

                              Hearing this,
the old nurse hid her face between her hands
and wept hot tears, and murmured:

                           "Oh, my child!
I can do nothing for you! How Zeus hated you,
no other man so much! No use, great heart,
O faithful heart, the rich thighbones you burnt
to Zeus who plays in lightning—and no man
ever gave more to Zeus—with all your prayers   430
for a green age, a tall son reared to manhood.
There is no day of homecoming for you.
Stranger, some women in some far off place
perhaps have mocked my lord when he'd be home
as now these strumpets mock you here. No wonder
you would keep clear of all their whorishness
and have no bath. But here am I. The queen
Penélopê, Ikários' daughter, bids me;
so let me bathe your feet to serve my lady—
to serve you, too.   440
                     My heart within me stirs,
mindful of something. Listen to what I say:
strangers have come here, many through the years,
but no one ever came, I swear, who seemed
so like Odysseus—body, voice and limbs—
as you do."

                          Ready for this, Odysseus answered:

"Old woman, that is what they say. All who have seen
the two of us remark how like we are,
as you yourself have said, and rightly, too."   450

Then he kept still, while the old nurse filled up
her basin glittering in firelight; she poured
cold water in, then hot.
                          But Lord Odysseus
whirled suddenly from the fire to face the dark.
The scar: he had forgotten that. She must not
handle his scarred thigh, or the game was up.
But when she bared her lord's leg, bending near,
she knew the groove at once.
                          An old wound   460
a boar's white tusk inflicted, on Parnassos
years ago. He had gone hunting there

in company with his uncles and Autólykos,
his mother's father—a great thief and swindler
by Hermès' favor, for Autólykos pleased him
with burnt offerings of sheep and kids. The god
acted as his accomplice. Well, Autólykos
on a trip to Ithaka
arrived just after his daughter's boy was born.
In fact, he had no sooner finished supper   470
than Nurse Euríkleia put the baby down
in his own lap and said:

                    "It is for you, now,
to choose a name for him, your child's dear baby;
the answer to her prayers."

                       Autólykos replied:

"My son-in-law, my daughter, call the boy
by the name I tell you. Well you know, my hand
has been against the world of men and women;
odium and distrust I've won. Odysseus   480
should be his given name. When he grows up,
when he comes visiting his mother's home
under Parnassos, where my treasures are,
I'll make him gifts and send him back rejoicing."

Odysseus in due course went for the gifts,
and old Autólykos and his sons embraced him
with welcoming sweet words; and Amphithéa,
his mother's mother, held him tight and kissed him,
kissed his head and his fine eyes.
                     The father   490
called on his noble sons to make a feast,
and going about it briskly they led in
an ox of five years, whom they killed and flayed
and cut in bits for roasting on the skewers
with skilled hands, with care; then shared it out.
So all the day until the sun went down
they feasted to their hearts' content. At evening,
after the sun was down and dusk had come,
they turned to bed and took the gift of sleep.

When the young Dawn spread in the eastern sky   500
her finger tips of rose, the men and dogs
went hunting, taking Odysseus. They climbed
Parnassos' rugged flank mantled in forest,
entering amid high windy folds at noon
when Hêlios beat upon the valley floor
and on the winding Ocean whence he came.
With hounds questing ahead, in open order,
the sons of Autólykos went down a glen,
Odysseus in the lead, behind the dogs,
pointing his long-shadowing spear.   510
                              Before them
a great boar lay hid in undergrowth,
in a green thicket proof against the wind
or sun's blaze, fine soever the needling sunlight,
impervious too to any rain, so dense
that cover was, heaped up with fallen leaves.
Patter of hounds' feet, men's feet, woke the boar
as they came up—and from his woody ambush
with razor back bristling and raging eyes
he trotted and stood at bay. Odysseus,   520
being on top of him, had the first shot,
lunging to stick him; but the boar
had already charged under the long spear.
He hooked aslant with one white tusk and ripped out
flesh above the knee, but missed the bone.
Odysseus' second thrust went home by luck,
his bright spear passing through the shoulder joint;
and the beast fell, moaning as life pulsed away.
Autólykos' tall sons took up the wounded,
working skillfully over the Prince Odysseus   530
to bind his gash, and with a rune they stanched
the dark flow of blood. Then downhill swiftly
they all repaired to the father's house, and there
tended him well—so well they soon could send him,
with Grandfather Autólykos' magnificent gifts,
rejoicing, over sea to Ithaka.
His father and the Lady Antikleía
welcomed him, and wanted all the news

of how he got his wound; so he spun out
his tale, recalling how the boar's white tusk   540
caught him when he was hunting on Parnassos.

This was the scar the old nurse recognized;
she traced it under her spread hands, then let go,
and into the basin fell the lower leg
making the bronze clang, sloshing the water out.
Then joy and anguish seized her heart; her eyes
filled up with tears; her throat closed, and she whispered,
with hand held out to touch his chin:

                          "Oh yes!
You are Odysseus! Ah, dear child! I could not   550
see you until now—not till I knew
my master's very body with my hands!"

Her eyes turned to Penélopê with desire
to make her lord, her husband, known—in vain,
because Athena had bemused the queen,
so that she took no notice, paid no heed.
At the same time Odysseus' right hand
gripped the old throat; his left hand pulled her near,
and in her ear he said:

                          "Will you destroy me,   560
nurse, who gave me milk at your own breast?
Now with a hard lifetime behind I've come
in the twentieth year home to my father's island.
You found me out, as the chance was given you.
Be quiet; keep it from the others, else
I warn you, and I mean it, too,
if by my hand god brings the suitors down
I'll kill you, nurse or not, when the time comes—
when the time comes to kill the other women."

Eurýkleia kept her wits and answered him: 570

"Oh, what mad words are these you let escape you!
Child, you know my blood, my bones are yours;
no one could whip this out of me. I'll be
a woman turned to stone, iron I'll be.

And let me tell you too—mind now—if god
cuts down the arrogant suitors by your hand,
I can report to you on all the maids,
those who dishonor you, and the innocent."

But in response the great tactician said:

"Nurse, no need to tell me tales of these.   580
I will have seen them, each one, for myself.
Trust in the gods, be quiet, hold your peace."

Silent, the old nurse went to fetch more water,
her basin being all spilt.
                   When she had washed
and rubbed his feet with golden oil, he turned,
dragging his bench again to the fire side
for warmth, and hid the scar under his rags.
Penélopê broke the silence, saying:

                   "Friend,   590
allow me one brief question more. You know,
the time for bed, sweet rest, is coming soon,
if only that warm luxury of slumber
would come to enfold us, in our trouble. But for me
my fate at night is anguish and no rest.
By day being busy, seeing to my work,
I find relief sometimes from loss and sorrow;
but when night comes and all the world's abed
I lie in mine alone, my heart thudding,
while bitter thoughts and fears crowd on my grief.   600
Think how Pandáreos' daughter, pale forever,
sings as the nightingale in the new leaves
through those long quiet hours of night,
on some thick-flowering orchard bough in spring;
how she rills out and tilts her note, high now, now low,
mourning for Itylos whom she killed in madness—
her child, and her lord Zêthos' only child.
My forlorn thought flows variable as her song,
wondering: shall I stay beside my son
and guard my own things here, my maids, my hall,   610
to honor my lord's bed and the common talk?

Or had I best join fortunes with a suitor,
the noblest one, most lavish in his gifts?
Is it now time for that?
My son being still a callow boy forbade
marriage, or absence from my lord's domain;
but now the child is grown, grown up, a man,
he, too, begins to pray for my departure,
aghast at all the suitors gorge on.

                Listen: 620
interpret me this dream: From a water's edge
twenty fat geese have come to feed on grain
beside my house. And I delight to see them.
But now a mountain eagle with great wings
and crooked beak storms in to break their necks
and strew their bodies here. Away he soars
into the bright sky; and I cry aloud—
all this in dream—I wail and round me gather
softly braided Akhaian women mourning
because the eagle killed my geese.   630
                  Then down
out of the sky he drops to a cornice beam
with mortal voice telling me not to weep.
'Be glad,' says he, 'renowned Ikários' daughter:
here is no dream but something real as day,
something about to happen. All those geese
were suitors, and the bird was I. See now,
I am no eagle but your lord come back
to bring inglorious death upon them all!'
As he said this, my honeyed slumber left me.   640
Peering through half-shut eyes, I saw the geese
in hall, still feeding at the self-same trough."

The master of subtle ways and straight replied:

"My dear, how can you choose to read the dream
differently? Has not Odysseus himself
shown you what is to come? Death to the suitors,
sure death, too. Not one escapes his doom."

Penélopê shook her head and answered:

"Friend,
many and many a dream is mere confusion,   650
a cobweb of no consequence at all.
Two gates for ghostly dreams there are: one gateway
of honest horn, and one of ivory.
Issuing by the ivory gate are dreams
of glimmering illusion, fantasies,
but those that come through solid polished horn
may be borne out, if mortals only know them.
I doubt it came by horn, my fearful dream—
too good to be true, that, for my son and me.
But one thing more I wish to tell you: listen   660
carefully. It is a black day, this that comes.
Odysseus' house and I are to be parted.
I shall decree a contest for the day.
We have twelve axe heads. In his time, my lord
could line them up, all twelve, at intervals
like a ship's ribbing; then he'd back away
a long way off and whip an arrow through.
Now I'll impose this trial on the suitors.
The one who easily handles and strings the bow
and shoots through all twelve axes I shall marry,   670
whoever he may be—then look my last
on this my first love's beautiful brimming house.
But I'll remember, though I dream it only."

Odysseus said:

                    "Dear honorable lady,
wife of Odysseus Laërtiadês,
let there be no postponement of the trial.
Odysseus, who knows the shifts of combat,
will be here: aye, he'll be here long before
one of these lads can stretch or string that bow   680
or shoot to thread the iron!"

                    Grave and wise,
Penélopê replied:

                    "If you were willing
to sit with me and comfort me, my friend,

no tide of sleep would ever close my eyes.
But mortals cannot go forever sleepless.
This the undying gods decree for all
who live and die on earth, kind furrowed earth.
Upstairs I go, then, to my single bed,   690
my sighing bed, wet with so many tears
after my Lord Odysseus took ship
to see that misery at Ilion, unspeakable.
Let me rest there, you here. You can stretch out
on the bare floor, or else command a bed."

So she went up to her chamber softly lit,
accompanied by her maids. Once there, she wept
for Odysseus, her husband, till Athena
cast sweet sleep upon her eyes.

BOOK TWENTY

Signs and a Vision

LINES 1 – 17

Outside in the entry way he made his bed—   1
raw oxhide spread on level ground, and heaped up
fleeces, left from sheep the Akhaians killed.
And when he had lain down, Eurýnomê
flung out a robe to cover him. Unsleeping
the Lord Odysseus lay, and roved in thought
to the undoing of his enemies.
                                        Now came a covey of women
laughing as they slipped out, arm in arm,
as many a night before, to the suitors' beds;   10
and anger took him like a wave to leap
into their midst and kill them, every one—
or should he let them all go hot to bed
one final night? His heart cried out within him
the way a brach with whelps between her legs
would howl and bristle at a stranger—so
the hackles of his heart rose at that laughter.
Knocking his breast he muttered to himself:

"Down; be steady. You've seen worse, that time
the Kyklops like a rockslide ate your men   20
while you looked on. Nobody, only guile,
got you out of that cave alive."

                              His rage
held hard in leash, submitted to his mind,
while he himself rocked, rolling from side to side,
as a cook turns a sausage, big with blood
and fat, at a scorching blaze, without a pause,
to broil it quick: so he rolled left and right,
casting about to see how he, alone,
against the false outrageous crowd of suitors   30
could press the fight.

                    And out of the night sky
Athena came to him; out of the nearby dark
in body like a woman; came and stood
over his head to chide him:

                              "Why so wakeful,
most forlorn of men? Here is your home,
there lies your lady; and your son is here,
as fine as one could wish a son to be."

Odysseus looked up and answered: 40

"Aye,
goddess, that much is true; but still
I have some cause to fret in this affair.
I am one man; how can I whip those dogs?
They are always here in force. Neither
is that the end of it, there's more to come.
If by the will of Zeus and by your will
I killed them all, where could I go for safety?
Tell me that!"

                    And the grey-eyed goddess said: 50

"Your touching faith! Another man would trust
some villainous mortal, with no brains—and what
am I? Your goddess-guardian to the end
in all your trials. Let it be plain as day:

if fifty bands of men surrounded us
and every sword sang for your blood,
you could make off still with their cows and sheep.
Now you, too, go to sleep. This all night vigil
wearies the flesh. You'll come out soon enough
on the other side of trouble."   60

                            Raining soft
sleep on his eyes, the beautiful one was gone
back to Olympos. Now at peace, the man
slumbered and lay still, but not his lady.
Wakeful again with all her cares, reclining
in the soft bed, she wept and cried aloud
until she had had her fill of tears, then spoke
in prayer first to Artemis:

                            "O gracious
divine lady Artemis, daughter of Zeus,   70
if you could only make an end now quickly,
let the arrow fly, stop my heart,
or if some wind could take me by the hair
up into running cloud, to plunge in tides of Ocean,
as hurricane winds took Pandareos' daughters
when they were left at home alone. The gods
had sapped their parents' lives. But Aphroditê
fed those children honey, cheese, and wine,
and Hêra gave them looks and wit, and Artemis,
pure Artemis, gave lovely height, and wise   80
Athena made them practised in her arts—
till Aphroditê in glory walked on Olympos,
begging for each a happy wedding day
from Zeus, the lightning's joyous king, who knows
all fate of mortals, fair and foul—
but even at that hour the cyclone winds
had ravished them away
to serve the loathsome Furies.
                            Let me be
blown out by the Olympians! Shot by Artemis,   90
I still might go and see amid the shades
Odysseus in the rot of underworld.
No coward's eye should light by my consenting!

Evil may be endured when our days pass
in mourning, heavy-hearted, hard beset,
if only sleep reign over nighttime, blanketing
the world's good and evil from our eyes.
But not for me: dreams too my demon sends me.
Tonight the image of my lord came by
as I remember him with troops. O strange   100
exultation! I thought him real, and not a dream."

Now as the Dawn appeared all stitched in gold,
the queen's cry reached Odysseus at his waking,
so that he wondered, half asleep: it seemed
she knew him, and stood near him! Then he woke
and picked his bedding up to stow away
on a chair in the mégaron. The oxhide pad
he took outdoors. There, spreading wide his arms,
he prayed:

                "O Father Zeus, if over land and water, 110
after adversity, you willed to bring me home,
let someone in the waking house give me good augury,
and a sign be shown, too, in the outer world."

He prayed thus, and the mind of Zeus in heaven
heard him. He thundered out of bright Olympos
down from above the cloudlands, in reply—
a rousing peal for Odysseus. Then a token
came to him from a woman grinding flour
in the court nearby. His own handmills were there,
and twelve maids had the job of grinding out   120
whole grain and barley meal, the pith of men.
Now all the rest, their bushels ground, were sleeping;
one only, frail and slow, kept at it still.
She stopped, stayed her hand, and her lord heard
the omen from her lips:

              "Ah, Father Zeus
almighty over gods and men!
A great bang of thunder that was, surely,
out of the starry sky, and not a cloud in sight.
It is your nod to someone. Hear me, then,   130

make what I say come true:
let this day be the last the suitors feed
so dainty in Odysseus' hall!
They've made me work my heart out till I drop,
grinding barley. May they feast no more!"

The servant's prayer, after the cloudless thunder
of Zeus, Odysseus heard with lifting heart,
sure in his bones that vengeance was at hand.
Then other servants, wakening, came down
to build and light a fresh fire at the hearth.   140
Telémakhos, clear-eyed as a god, awoke,
put on his shirt and belted on his sword,
bound rawhide sandals under his smooth feet,
and took his bronze-shod lance. He came and stood
on the broad sill of the doorway, calling Eurýkleia:

"Nurse, dear Nurse, how did you treat our guest?
Had he a supper and a good bed? Has he lain
uncared for still? My mother is like that,
perverse for all her cleverness:
she'd entertain some riff-raff, and turn out   150
a solid man."

                        The old nurse answered him:

"I would not be so quick to accuse her, child.
He sat and drank here while he had a mind to;
food he no longer hungered for, he said—
for she did ask him. When he thought of sleeping,
she ordered them to make a bed. Poor soul!
Poor gentleman! So humble and so miserable,
he would accept no bed with rugs to lie on,
but slept on sheepskins and a raw oxhide   160
in the entry way. We covered him ourselves."

Telémakhos left the hall, hefting his lance,
with two swift flickering hounds for company,
to face the island Akhaians in the square;
and gently born Eurýkleia, the daughter
of Ops Peisenóridès, called to the maids:

"Bestir yourselves! you have your brooms, go sprinkle
the rooms and sweep them, robe the chairs in red,
sponge off the tables till they shine.
Wash out the winebowls and two-handled cups.   170
You others go fetch water from the spring;
no loitering; come straight back. Our company
will be here soon; morning is sure to bring them;
everyone has a holiday today."

The women ran to obey her—twenty girls
off to the spring with jars for dusky water,
the rest at work inside. Then tall woodcutters
entered to split up logs for the hearth fire,
the water carriers returned; and on their heels
arrived the swineherd, driving three fat pigs,   180
chosen among his pens. In the wide court
he let them feed, and said to Odysseus kindly:

"Friend, are they more respectful of you now,
or still insulting you?"

                              Replied Odysseus:

"The young men, yes. And may the gods requite
those insolent puppies for the game they play
in a home not their own. They have no decency."

During this talk, Melánthios the goatherd
came in, driving goats for the suitors' feast,   190
with his two herdsmen. Under the portico
they tied the animals, and Melánthios
looked at Odysseus with a sneer. Said he:

                              "Stranger,
I see you mean to stay and turn our stomachs
begging in this hall. Clear out, why don't you?
Or will you have to taste a bloody beating
before you see the point? Your begging ways
nauseate everyone. There are feasts elsewhere."

Odysseus answered not a word, but grimly   200
shook his head over his murderous heart.

A third man came up now: Philoítios
the cattle foreman, with an ox behind him
and fat goats for the suitors. Ferrymen
had brought these from the mainland, as they bring
travellers, too—whoever comes along.
Philoítios tied the beasts under the portico
and joined the swineherd.

                          "Who is this," he said.
"Who is the new arrival at the manor?   210
Akhaian? or what else does he claim to be?
Where are his family and fields of home?
Down on his luck, all right: carries himself like a captain.
How the immortal gods can change and drag us down
once they begin to spin dark days for us!—
Kings and commanders, too."

                          Then he stepped over
and took Odysseus by the right hand, saying:

"Welcome, Sir. May good luck lie ahead
at the next turn. Hard times you're having, surely.   220
O Zeus! no god is more berserk in heaven
if gentle folk, whom you yourself begot,
you plunge in grief and hardship without mercy!
Sir, I began to sweat when I first saw you,
and tears came to my eyes, remembering
Odysseus: rags like these he may be wearing
somewhere on his wanderings now—
I mean, if he's alive still under the sun.
But if he's dead and in the house of Death,
I mourn Odysseus. He entrusted cows to me   230
in Kephallênia, when I was knee high,
and nów his herds are numberless, no man else
ever had cattle multiply like grain.
But new men tell me I must bring my beeves
to feed them, who care nothing for our prince,
fear nothing from the watchful gods. They crave
partition of our lost king's land and wealth.
My own feelings keep going round and round
upon this tether: can I desert the boy

by moving, herds and all, to another country,   240
a new life among strangers? Yet it's worse
to stay here, in my old post, herding cattle
for upstarts.

                I'd have gone long since,
gone, taken service with another king; this shame
is no more to be borne; but I keep thinking
my own lord, poor devil, still might come
and make a rout of suitors in his hall."

Odysseus, with his mind on action, answered:

"Herdsman, I make you out to be no coward   250
and no fool: I can see that for myself.
So let me tell you this. I swear by Zeus
all highest, by the table set for friends,
and by your king's hearthstone to which I've come,
Odysseus will return. You'll be on hand
to see, if you care to see it,
how those who lord it here will be cut down."

The cowman said:

                "Would god it all came true!
You'd see the fight that's in me!"   260

                Then Eumaios
echoed him, and invoked the gods, and prayed
that his great-minded master should return.
While these three talked, the suitors in the field
had come together plotting—what but death
for Telémakhos?—when from the left an eagle
crossed high with a rockdove in his claws.

Amphínomos got up. Said he, cutting them short:

"Friends, no luck lies in that plan for us,
no luck, knifing the lad. Let's think of feasting."   270

A grateful thought, they felt, and walking on
entered the great hall of the hero Odysseus,
where they all dropped their cloaks on chairs or couches

and made a ritual slaughter, knifing sheep,
fat goats and pigs, knifing the grass-fed steer.
Then tripes were broiled and eaten. Mixing bowls
were filled with wine. The swineherd passed out cups,
Philoítios, chief cowherd, dealt the loaves
into the panniers, Melánthios poured wine,
and all their hands went out upon the feast.   280

Telémakhos placed his father to advantage
just at the door sill of the pillared hall,
setting a stool there and a sawed-off table,
gave him a share of tripes, poured out his wine
in a golden cup, and said:

                              "Stay here, sit down
to drink with our young friends. I stand between you
and any cutting word or cuffing hand
from any suitor. Here is no public house
but the old home of Odysseus, my inheritance.   290
Hold your tongues then, gentlemen, and your blows,
and let no wrangling start, no scuffle either."

The others, disconcerted, bit their lips
at the ring in the young man's voice. Antínoös,
Eupeíthês' son, turned round to them and said:

"It goes against the grain, my lords, but still
I say we take this hectoring by Telémakhos.
You know Zeus balked at it, or else
we might have shut his mouth a long time past,
the silvery speaker."   300

                              But Telémakhos
paid no heed to what Antínoös said.

Now public heralds wound through Ithaka
leading a file of beasts for sacrifice, and islanders
gathered under the shade trees of Apollo,
in the precinct of the Archer—while in hall
the suitors roasted mutton and fat beef
on skewers, pulling off the fragrant cuts;

and those who did the roasting served Odysseus
a portion equal to their own, for so   310
Telémakhos commanded.

                    But Athena
had no desire now to let the suitors
restrain themselves from wounding words and acts.
Laërtês' son again must be offended.
There was a scapegrace fellow in the crowd
named Ktésippos, a Samian, rich beyond
all measure, arrogant with riches, early
and late a bidder for Odysseus' queen.
Now this one called attention to himself: 320

"Hear me, my lords, I have a thing to say.
Our friend has had his fair share from the start
and that's polite; it would be most improper
if we were cold to guests of Telémakhos—
no matter what tramp turns up. Well then, look here,
let me throw in my own small contribution.
He must have prizes to confer, himself,
on some brave bathman or another slave
here in Odysseus' house."

                    His hand went backward   330
and, fishing out a cow's foot from the basket,
he let it fly.

                 Odysseus rolled his head
to one side softly, ducking the blow, and smiled
a crooked smile with teeth clenched. On the wall
the cow's foot struck and fell. Telémakhos
blazed up:

                 "Ktésippos, lucky for you, by heaven,
not to have hit him! He took care of himself,
else you'd have had my lance-head in your belly;   340
no marriage, but a grave instead on Ithaka
for your father's pains.

               You others, let me see
no more contemptible conduct in my house!
I've been awake to it for a long time—by now
I know what is honorable and what is not.

Before, I was a child. I can endure it
while sheep are slaughtered, wine drunk up, and bread—
can one man check the greed of a hundred men?—
but I will suffer no more viciousness.   350
Granted you mean at last to cut me down:
I welcome that—better to die than have
humiliation always before my eyes,
the stranger buffeted, and the serving women
dragged about, abused in a noble house."

They quieted, grew still, under his lashing,
and after a long silence, Ageláos,
Damástor's son, spoke to them all:

                 "Friends, friends,
I hope no one will answer like a fishwife.   360
What has been said is true. Hands off this stranger,
he is no target, neither is any servant
here in the hall of King Odysseus.
Let me say a word, though, to Telémakhos
and to his mother, if it please them both:
as long as hope remained in you to see
Odysseus, that great gifted man, again,
you could not be reproached for obstinacy,
tying the suitors down here; better so,
if still your father fared the great sea homeward.   370
How plain it is, though, now, he'll come no more!
Go sit then by your mother, reason with her,
tell her to take the best man, highest bidder,
and you can have and hold your patrimony,
feed on it, drink it all, while she
adorns another's house."

                 Keeping his head,

Telémakhos replied:

               "By Zeus Almighty,
Ageláos, and by my father's sufferings,   380
far from Ithaka, whether he's dead or lost,
I make no impediment to Mother's marriage.
'Take whom you wish,' I say, 'I'll add my dowry.'

But can I pack her off against her will
from her own home? Heaven forbid!"

                    At this,
Pallas Athena touched off in the suitors
a fit of laughter, uncontrollable.
She drove them into nightmare, till they wheezed
and neighed as though with jaws no longer theirs,   390
while blood defiled their meat, and blurring tears
flooded their eyes, heart-sore with woe to come.
Then said the visionary, Theoklýmenos:

"O lost sad men, what terror is this you suffer?
Night shrouds you to the knees, your heads, your faces;
dry retch of death runs round like fire in sticks;
your cheeks are streaming; these fair walls and pedestals
are dripping crimson blood. And thick with shades
is the entry way, the courtyard thick with shades
passing a thirst toward Érebos, into the dark,   400
the sun is quenched in heaven, foul mist hems us in . . ."

The young men greeted this with shouts of laughter,
and Eurýmakhos, the son of Pólybos, crowed:

"The mind of our new guest has gone astray.
Hustle him out of doors, lads, into the sunlight;
he finds it dark as night inside!"

The man of vision looked at him and said:

"When I need help, I'll ask for it, Eurýmakhos.
I have my eyes and ears, a pair of legs,
and a straight mind, still with me. These will do   410
to take me out. Damnation and black night
I see arriving for yourselves: no shelter,
no defence for any in this crowd—
fools and vipers in the king's own hall."

With this he left that handsome room and went
home to Peiraios, who received him kindly.
The suitors made wide eyes at one another

and set to work provoking Telémakhos
with jokes about his friends. One said, for instance:

"Telémakhos, no man is a luckier host   420
when it comes to what the cat dragged in. What burning
eyes your beggar had for bread and wine!
But not for labor, not for a single heave—
he'd be a deadweight on a field. Then comes
this other, with his mumbo-jumbo. Boy,
for your own good, I tell you, toss them both
into a slave ship for the Sikels. That would pay you."

Telémakhos ignored the suitors' talk.
He kept his eyes in silence on his father,
awaiting the first blow. Meanwhile   430
the daughter of Ikários, Penélopê,
had placed her chair to look across and down
on father and son at bay; she heard the crowd,
and how they laughed as they resumed their dinner,
a fragrant feast, for many beasts were slain—
but as for supper, men supped never colder
than these, on what the goddess and the warrior
were even then preparing for the suitors,
whose treachery had filled that house with pain.

BOOK TWENTY-ONE

The Test of the Bow

LINES 1 – 17

Upon Penélopê, most worn in love and thought,   1
Athena cast a glance like a grey sea
lifting her. Now to bring the tough bow out and bring
the iron blades. Now try those dogs at archery
to usher bloody slaughter in.
                     So moving stairward
the queen took up a fine doorhook of bronze,
ivory-hafted, smooth in her clenched hand,
and led her maids down to a distant room,
a storeroom where the master's treasure lay: 10
bronze, bar gold, black iron forged and wrought.
In this place hung the double-torsion bow
and arrows in a quiver, a great sheaf—
quills of groaning.
                    In the old time in Lakedaímon
her lord had got these arms from Íphitos,
Eurýtos' son. The two met in Messenia
at Ortílokhos' table, on the day
Odysseus claimed a debt owed by that realm—

sheep stolen by Messenians out of Ithaka   20
in their long ships, three hundred head, and herdsmen.
Seniors of Ithaka and his father sent him
on that far embassy when he was young.
But Iphitos had come there tracking strays,
twelve shy mares, with mule colts yet unweaned.
And a fatal chase they led him over prairies
into the hands of Heraklês. That massive
son of toil and mortal son of Zeus
murdered his guest at wine in his own house—
inhuman, shameless in the sight of heaven—   30
to keep the mares and colts in his own grange.
Now Iphitos, when he knew Odysseus, gave him
the master bowman's arm; for old Eurýtos
had left it on his deathbed to his son.
In fellowship Odysseus gave a lance
and a sharp sword. But Heraklês killed Íphitos
before one friend could play host to the other.
And Lord Odysseus would not take the bow
in the black ships to the great war at Troy.
As a keepsake he put it by: 40
it served him well at home in Ithaka.

Now the queen reached the storeroom door and halted.
Here was an oaken sill, cut long ago
and sanded clean and bedded true. Foursquare
the doorjambs and the shining doors were set
by the careful builder. Penélopê untied the strap
around the curving handle, pushed her hook
into the slit, aimed at the bolts inside
and shot them back. Then came a rasping sound
as those bright doors the key had sprung gave way—   50
a bellow like a bull's vaunt in a meadow—
followed by her light footfall entering
over the plank floor. Herb-scented robes
lay there in chests, but the lady's milkwhite arms
went up to lift the bow down from a peg
in its own polished bowcase.
                              Now Penélopê
sank down, holding the weapon on her knees,

and drew her husband's great bow out, and sobbed
and bit her lip and let the salt tears flow.   60
Then back she went to face the crowded hall
tremendous bow in hand, and on her shoulder hung
the quiver spiked with coughing death. Behind her
maids bore a basket full of axeheads, bronze
and iron implements for the master's game.
Thus in her beauty she approached the suitors,
and near a pillar of the solid roof
she paused, her shining veil across her cheeks,
her maids on either hand and still,
then spoke to the banqueters: 70

                "My lords, hear me:
suitors indeed, you commandeered this house
to feast and drink in, day and night, my husband
being long gone, long out of mind. You found
no justification for yourselves—none
except your lust to marry me. Stand up, then:
we now declare a contest for that prize.
Here is my lord Odysseus' hunting bow.
Bend and string it if you can. Who sends an arrow
through iron axe-helve sockets, twelve in line?   80
I join my life with his, and leave this place, my home,
my rich and beautiful bridal house, forever
to be remembered, though I dream it only."

Then to Eumaios:

                "Carry the bow forward.
Carry the blades."

                Tears came to the swineherd's eyes
as he reached out for the big bow. He laid it
down at the suitors' feet. Across the room
the cowherd sobbed, knowing the master's weapon.   90
Antínoös growled, with a glance at both:

                "Clods.
They go to pieces over nothing.
                You two, there,
why are you sniveling? To upset the woman

even more? Has she not pain enough
over her lost husband? *Sit down.*
Get on with dinner quietly, or cry about it
outside, if you must. Leave us the bow.

A clean-cut game, it looks to me.　　　　　　　　　　100
Nobody bends that bowstave easily
in this company. Is there a man here
made like Odysseus? I remember him
from childhood: I can see him even now."

That was the way he played it, hoping inwardly
to span the great horn bow with corded gut
and drill the iron with his shot—he, Antínoös,
destined to be the first of all to savor
blood from a biting arrow at his throat,
a shaft drawn by the fingers of Odysseus　　　　　　110
whom he had mocked and plundered, leading on
the rest, his boon companions. Now they heard
a gay snort of laughter from Telémakhos,
who said then brilliantly:

　　　　　　　　　　　　　"A queer thing, that!
Has Zeus almighty made me a half-wit?
For all her spirit, Mother has given in,
promised to go off with someone—and
is that amusing? What am I cackling for?
Step up, my lords, contend now for your prize.　　　120
There is no woman like her in Akhaia,
not in old Argos, Pylos, or Mykênê,
neither in Ithaka nor on the mainland,
and you all know it without praise of mine.
Come on, no hanging back, no more delay
in getting the bow bent. Who's the winner?
I myself should like to try that bow.
Suppose I bend it and bring off the shot,
my heart will be less heavy, seeing the queen my mother
go for the last time from this house and hall,　　　130
if I who stay can do my father's feat."

He moved out quickly, dropping his crimson cloak,
and lifted sword and sword belt from his shoulders.
His preparation was to dig a trench,
heaping the earth in a long ridge beside it
to hold the blades half-bedded. A taut cord
aligned the socket rings. And no one there
but looked on wondering at his workmanship,
for the boy had never seen it done.

                He took his stand then   140
on the broad door sill to attempt the bow.
Three times he put his back into it and sprang it,
three times he had to slack off. Still he meant
to string that bow and pull for the needle shot.
A fourth try, and he had it all but strung—
when a stiffening in Odysseus made him check.
Abruptly then he stopped and turned and said:

"Blast and damn it, must I be a milksop
all my life? Half-grown, all thumbs,
no strength or knack at arms, to defend myself   150
if someone picks a fight with me.
                Take over,
O my elders and betters, try the bow,
run off the contest."

                And he stood the weapon
upright against the massy-timbered door
with one arrow across the horn aslant,
then went back to his chair. Antínoös
gave the word:

                "Now one man at a time   160
rise and go forward. Round the room in order;
left to right from where they dip the wine."

As this seemed fair enough, up stood Leódês
the son of Oinops. This man used to find
visions for them in the smoke of sacrifice.
He kept his chair well back, retired by the winebowl,
for he alone could not abide their manners
but sat in shame for all the rest. Now it was he

who had first to confront the bow,
standing up on the broad door sill. He failed.   170
The bow unbending made his thin hands yield,
no muscle in them. He gave up and said:

"Friends, I cannot. Let the next man handle it.
Here is a bow to break the heart and spirit
of many strong men. Aye. And death is less
bitter than to live on and never have
the beauty that we came here laying siege to
so many days. Resolute, are you still,
to win Odysseus' lady Penélopê?
Pit yourselves against the bow, and look   180
among Akhaians for another's daughter.
Gifts will be enough to court and take her.
Let the best offer win."

                     With this Leódês
thrust the bow away from him, and left it
upright against the massy-timbered door,
with one arrow aslant across the horn.
As he went down to his chair he heard Antínoös'
voice rising:

                         "What is that you say?   190
It makes me burn. You cannot string the weapon,
so 'Here is a bow to break the heart and spirit
of many strong men.' Crushing thought!
You were not born—you never had it in you—
to pull that bow or let an arrow fly.
But here are men who can and will."

He called out to the goatherd, Melánthios:

"Kindle a fire there, be quick about it,
draw up a big bench with a sheepskin on it,
and bring a cake of lard out of the stores.   200
Contenders from now on will heat and grease the bow.
We'll try it limber, and bring off the shot."

Melánthios darted out to light a blaze,
drew up a bench, threw a big sheepskin over it,

and brought a cake of lard. So one by one
the young men warmed and greased the bow for bending,
but not a man could string it. They were whipped.
Antínoös held off; so did Eurýmakhos,
suitors in chief, by far the ablest there.

Two men had meanwhile left the hall: 210
swineherd and cowherd, in companionship,
one downcast as the other. But Odysseus
followed them outdoors, outside the court,
and coming up said gently:

                              "You, herdsman,
and you, too, swineherd, I could say a thing to you,
or should I keep it dark?

                              No, no; speak,
my heart tells me. Would you be men enough
to stand by Odysseus if he came back?   220
Suppose he dropped out of a clear sky, as I did?
Suppose some god should bring him?
Would you bear arms for him, or for the suitors?"

The cowherd said:

                              "Ah, let the master come!
Father Zeus, grant our old wish! Some courier
guide him back! Then judge what stuff is in me
and how I manage arms!"

                              Likewise Eumaios
fell to praying all heaven for his return,   230
so that Odysseus, sure at least of these,
told them:

                              "I am at home, for I am he.
I bore adversities, but in the twentieth year
I am ashore in my own land. I find
the two of you, alone among my people,
longed for my coming. Prayers I never heard
except your own that I might come again.
So now what is in store for you I'll tell you:
If Zeus brings down the suitors by my hand   240

I promise marriages to both, and cattle,
and houses built near mine. And you shall be
brothers-in-arms of my Telémakhos.
Here, let me show you something else, a sign
that I am he, that you can trust me, look:
this old scar from the tusk wound that I got
boar hunting on Parnassos—
Autólykos' sons and I."

                          Shifting his rags
he bared the long gash. Both men looked, and knew,   250
and threw their arms around the old soldier, weeping,
kissing his head and shoulders. He as well
took each man's head and hands to kiss, then said—
to cut it short, else they might weep till dark—

"Break off, no more of this.
Anyone at the door could see and tell them.
Drift back in, but separately at intervals
after me.

                      Now listen to your orders:
when the time comes, those gentlemen, to a man,   260
will be dead against giving me bow or quiver.
Defy them. Eumaios, bring the bow
and put it in my hands there at the door.
Tell the women to lock their own door tight.
Tell them if someone hears the shock of arms
or groans of men, in hall or court, not one
must show her face, but keep still at her weaving.
Philoítios, run to the outer gate and lock it.
Throw the cross bar and lash it."

                    He turned back   270
into the courtyard and the beautiful house
and took the stool he had before. They followed
one by one, the two hands loyal to him.

Eurýmakhos had now picked up the bow.
He turned it round, and turned it round
before the licking flame to warm it up,

but could not, even so, put stress upon it
to jam the loop over the tip

     though his heart groaned to bursting.
Then he said grimly: 280

    "Curse this day.
What gloom I feel, not for myself alone,
and not only because we lose that bride.
Women are not lacking in Akhaia,
in other towns, or on Ithaka. No, the worst
is humiliation—to be shown up for children
measured against Odysseus—we who cannot
even hitch the string over his bow.
What shame to be repeated of us, after us!"

Antínoös said: 290

    "Come to yourself. You know
that is not the way this business ends.
Today the islanders held holiday, a holy day,
no day to sweat over a bowstring.
    Keep your head.
Postpone the bow. I say we leave the axes
planted where they are. No one will take them.
No one comes to Odysseus' hall tonight.
Break out good wine and brim our cups again,
we'll keep the crooked bow safe overnight,   300
order the fattest goats Melánthios has
brought down tomorrow noon, and offer thighbones burning
to Apollo, god of archers,
while we try out the bow and make the shot."

As this appealed to everyone, heralds came
pouring fresh water for their hands, and boys
filled up the winebowls. Joints of meat went round,
fresh cuts for all, while each man made his offering,
tilting the red wine to the gods, and drank his fill.
Then spoke Odysseus, all craft and gall: 310

"My lords, contenders for the queen, permit me:
a passion in me moves me to speak out.

I put it to Eurýmakhos above all
and to that brilliant prince, Antínoös. Just now
how wise his counsel was, to leave the trial
and turn your thoughts to the immortal gods! Apollo
will give power tomorrow to whom he wills.
But let me try my hand at the smooth bow!
Let me test my fingers and my pull
to see if any of the oldtime kick is there,   320
or if thin fare and roving took it out of me."

Now irritation beyond reason swept them all,
since they were nagged by fear that he could string it.
Antínoös answered, coldly and at length:

"You bleary vagabond, no rag of sense is left you.
Are you not coddled here enough, at table
taking meat with gentlemen, your betters,
denied nothing, and listening to our talk?
When have we let a tramp hear all our talk?
The sweet goad of wine has made you ravel   330
Here is the evil wine can do
to those who swig it down. Even the centaur
Eurýtion, in Peiríthoös' hall
among the Lapíthai, came to a bloody end
because of wine; wine ruined him: it crazed him,
drove him wild for rape in that great house.
The princes cornered him in fury, leaping on him
to drag him out and crop his ears and nose.
Drink had destroyed his mind, and so he ended
in that mutilation—fool that he was.   340
Centaurs and men made war for this,
but the drunkard first brought hurt upon himself.
The tale applies to you: I promise you
great trouble if you touch that bow. You'll come by
no indulgence in our house; kicked down
into a ship's bilge, out to sea you go,
and nothing saves you. Drink, but hold your tongue.
Make no contention here with younger men."

At this the watchful queen Penélopê
interposed: 350

"Antínoös, discourtesy
to a guest of Telémakhos—whatever guest—
that is not handsome. What are you afraid of?
Suppose this exile put his back into it
and drew the great bow of Odysseus—
could he then take me home to be his bride?
You know he does not imagine that! No one
need let that prospect weigh upon his dinner!
How very, very improbable it seems."

It was Eurýmakhos who answered her: 360

"Penélopê, O daughter of Ikários,
most subtle queen, we are not given to fantasy.
No, but our ears burn at what men might say
and women, too. We hear some jackal whispering:
'How far inferior to the great husband
her suitors are! Can't even budge his bow!
Think of it; and a beggar, out of nowhere,
strung it quick and made the needle shot!'
That kind of disrepute we would not care for."

Penélopê replied, steadfast and wary: 370

"Eurýmakhos, you have no good repute
in this realm, nor the faintest hope of it—
men who abused a prince's house for years,
consumed his wine and cattle. Shame enough.
Why hang your heads over a trifle now?
The stranger is a big man, well-compacted,
and claims to be of noble blood.
Ai!
Give him the bow, and let us have it out!
What I can promise him I will: 380
if by the kindness of Apollo he prevails
he shall be clothed well and equipped.
A fine shirt and a cloak I promise him;
a lance for keeping dogs at bay, or men;
a broadsword; sandals to protect his feet;
escort, and freedom to go where he will."

Telémakhos now faced her and said sharply:

"Mother, as to the bow and who may handle it
or not handle it, no man here
has more authority than I do—not one lord   390
of our own stony Ithaka nor the islands lying
east toward Elis: no one stops me if I choose
to give these weapons outright to my guest.
Return to your own hall. Tend your spindle.
Tend your loom. Direct your maids at work.
This question of the bow will be for men to settle,
most of all for me. I am master here."

She gazed in wonder, turned, and so withdrew,
her son's clearheaded bravery in her heart.
But when she had mounted to her rooms again   400
with all her women, then she fell to weeping
for Odysseus, her husband. Grey-eyed Athena
presently cast a sweet sleep on her eyes.

The swineherd had the horned bow in his hands
moving toward Odysseus, when the crowd
in the banquet hall broke into an ugly din,
shouts rising from the flushed young men:

                              "Ho! Where
do you think you are taking that, you smutty slave?"

"What is this dithering?"   410

                         "We'll toss you back alone
among the pigs, for your own dogs to eat,
if bright Apollo nods and the gods are kind!"

He faltered, all at once put down the bow, and stood
in panic, buffeted by waves of cries,
hearing Telémakhos from another quarter
shout:

"Go on, take him the bow!
                    Do you obey this pack?
You will be stoned back to your hills! Young as I am   420

my power is over you! I wish to God
I had as much the upper hand of these!
There would be suitors pitched like dead rats
through our gate, for the evil plotted here!"

Telémakhos' frenzy struck someone as funny,
and soon the whole room roared with laughter at him,
so that all tension passed. Eumaios picked up
bow and quiver, making for the door,
and there he placed them in Odysseus' hands.
Calling Eurýkleia to his side he said: 430

                "Telémakhos
trusts you to take care of the women's doorway.
Lock it tight. If anyone inside
should hear the shock of arms or groans of men
in hall or court, not one must show her face,
but go on with her weaving."

                    The old woman
nodded and kept still. She disappeared
into the women's hall, bolting the door behind her.
Philoítios left the house now at one bound,   440
catlike, running to bolt the courtyard gate.
A coil of deck-rope of papyrus fiber
lay in the gateway; this he used for lashing,
and ran back to the same stool as before,
fastening his eyes upon Odysseus.
                  And Odysseus took his time,
turning the bow, tapping it, every inch,
for borings that termites might have made
while the master of the weapon was abroad.
The suitors were now watching him, and some   450
jested among themselves:

                "A bow lover!"

"Dealer in old bows!"

               "Maybe he has one like it
at home!"

                    "Or has an itch to make one for himself."

"See how he handles it, the sly old buzzard!"

And one disdainful suitor added this:

"May his fortune grow an inch for every inch he bends it!"

But the man skilled in all ways of contending,   460
satisfied by the great bow's look and heft,
like a musician, like a harper, when
with quiet hand upon his instrument
he draws between his thumb and forefinger
a sweet new string upon a peg: so effortlessly
Odysseus in one motion strung the bow.
Then slid his right hand down the cord and plucked it,
so the taut gut vibrating hummed and sang
a swallow's note.

                    In the hushed hall it smote the suitors 470
and all their faces changed. Then Zeus thundered
overhead, one loud crack for a sign.
And Odysseus laughed within him that the son
of crooked-minded Kronos had flung that omen down.
He picked one ready arrow from his table
where it lay bare: the rest were waiting still
in the quiver for the young men's turn to come.
He nocked it, let it rest across the handgrip,
and drew the string and grooved butt of the arrow,
aiming from where he sat upon the stool.   480
                    Now flashed
arrow from twanging bow clean as a whistle
through every socket ring, and grazed not one,
to thud with heavy brazen head beyond.
                    Then quietly
Odysseus said:

                    "Telémakhos, the stranger
you welcomed in your hall has not disgraced you.
I did not miss, neither did I take all day
stringing the bow. My hand and eye are sound,   490

not so contemptible as the young men say.
The hour has come to cook their lordships' mutton—
supper by daylight. Other amusements later,
with song and harping that adorn a feast."

He dropped his eyes and nodded, and the prince
Telémakhos, true son of King Odysseus,
belted his sword on, clapped hand to his spear,
and with a clink and glitter of keen bronze
stood by his chair, in the forefront near his father.

BOOK TWENTY-TWO

Death in
the Great Hall

LINES 1 – 14

Now shrugging off his rags the wiliest fighter of the islands   1
leapt and stood on the broad door sill, his own bow in his hand.
He poured out at his feet a rain of arrows from the quiver
and spoke to the crowd:

                  "So much for that. Your clean-cut game is over.
Now watch me hit a target that no man has hit before,
if I can make this shot. Help me, Apollo."

He drew to his fist the cruel head of an arrow for Antínoös
just as the young man leaned to lift his beautiful drinking cup,
embossed, two-handled, golden: the cup was in his fingers: 10
the wine was even at his lips: and did he dream of death?
How could he? In that revelry amid his throng of friends
who would imagine a single foe—though a strong foe indeed—
could dare to bring death's pain on him and darkness on his eyes?

Odysseus' arrow hit him under the chin
and punched up to the feathers through his throat.

Backward and down he went, letting the winecup fall
from his shocked hand. Like pipes his nostrils jetted
crimson runnels, a river of mortal red,
and one last kick upset his table   20
knocking the bread and meat to soak in dusty blood.
Now as they craned to see their champion where he lay
the suitors jostled in uproar down the hall,
everyone on his feet. Wildly they turned and scanned
the walls in the long room for arms; but not a shield,
not a good ashen spear was there for a man to take and throw.
All they could do was yell in outrage at Odysseus:

"Foul! to shoot at a man! That was your last shot!"
"Your own throat will be slit for this!"

                                        "Our finest lad is down!   30
You killed the best on Ithaka."
                                        "Buzzards will tear your eyes out!"

For they imagined as they wished—that it was a wild shot,
an unintended killing—fools, not to comprehend
they were already in the grip of death.
But glaring under his brows Odysseus answered:

"You yellow dogs, you thought I'd never make it
home from the land of Troy. You took my house to plunder,
twisted my maids to serve your beds. You dared
bid for my wife while I was still alive.   40
Contempt was all you had for the gods who rule wide heaven,
contempt for what men say of you hereafter.
Your last hour has come. You die in blood."

As they all took this in, sickly green fear
pulled at their entrails, and their eyes flickered
looking for some hatch or hideaway from death.
Eurýmakhos alone could speak. He said:

"If you are Odysseus of Ithaka come back,
all that you say these men have done is true.
Rash actions, many here, more in the countryside.   50

But here he lies, the man who caused them all.
Antínoös was the ringleader, he whipped us on
to do these things. He cared less for a marriage
than for the power Kroníon has denied him
as king of Ithaka. For that
he tried to trap your son and would have killed him.
He is dead now and has his portion. Spare
your own people. As for ourselves, we'll make
restitution of wine and meat consumed,
and add, each one, a tithe of twenty oxen   60
with gifts of bronze and gold to warm your heart.
Meanwhile we cannot blame you for your anger."

Odysseus glowered under his black brows
and said:

                  "Not for the whole treasure of your fathers,
all you enjoy, lands, flocks, or any gold
put up by others, would I hold my hand.
There will be killing till the score is paid.
You forced yourselves upon this house. Fight your way out,
or run for it, if you think you'll escape death.   70
I doubt one man of you skins by."

They felt their knees fail, and their hearts—but heard
Eurýmakhos for the last time rallying them.

"Friends," he said, "the man is implacable.
Now that he's got his hands on bow and quiver
he'll shoot from the big door stone there
until he kills us to the last man.
                Fight, I say,
let's remember the joy of it. Swords out!
Hold up your tables to deflect his arrows.   80
After me, everyone: rush him where he stands.
If we can budge him from the door, if we can pass
into the town, we'll call out men to chase him.
This fellow with his bow will shoot no more."

He drew his own sword as he spoke, a broadsword of fine bronze,
honed like a razor on either edge. Then crying hoarse and loud

he hurled himself at Odysseus. But the kingly man let fly
an arrow at that instant, and the quivering feathered butt
sprang to the nipple of his breast as the barb stuck in his liver.
The bright broadsword clanged down. He lurched and fell aside, 90
pitching across his table. His cup, his bread and meat,
were spilt and scattered far and wide, and his head slammed on
    the ground.
Revulsion, anguish in his heart, with both feet kicking out,
he downed his chair, while the shrouding wave of mist closed on
    his eyes.

Amphínomos now came running at Odysseus,
broadsword naked in his hand. He thought to make
the great soldier give way at the door.
But with a spear throw from behind Telémakhos hit him   100
between the shoulders, and the lancehead drove
clear through his chest. He left his feet and fell
forward, thudding, forehead against the ground.
Telémakhos swerved around him, leaving the long dark spear
planted in Amphínomos. If he paused to yank it out
someone might jump him from behind or cut him down with a
    sword
at the moment he bent over. So he ran—ran from the tables
to his father's side and halted, panting, saying:

"Father let me bring you a shield and spear,   110
a pair of spears, a helmet.
I can arm on the run myself; I'll give
outfits to Eumaios and this cowherd.
Better to have equipment."

                    Said Odysseus:

"Run then, while I hold them off with arrows
as long as the arrows last. When all are gone
if I'm alone they can dislodge me."

                    Quick
upon his father's word Telémakhos   120
ran to the room where spears and armor lay.
He caught up four light shields, four pairs of spears,

four helms of war high-plumed with flowing manes,
and ran back, loaded down, to his father's side.
He was the first to pull a helmet on
and slide his bare arm in a buckler strap.
The servants armed themselves, and all three took their stand
beside the master of battle.

While he had arrows

he aimed and shot, and every shot brought down   130
one of his huddling enemies.
But when all barbs had flown from the bowman's fist,
he leaned his bow in the bright entry way
beside the door, and armed: a four-ply shield
hard on his shoulder, and a crested helm,
horsetailed, nodding stormy upon his head,
then took his tough and bronze-shod spears.

The suitors

who held their feet, no longer under bowshot,
could see a window high in a recess of the wall,   140
a vent, lighting the passage to the storeroom.
This passage had one entry, with a door,
at the edge of the great hall's threshold, just outside.

Odysseus told the swineherd to stand over
and guard this door and passage. As he did so,
a suitor named Ageláos asked the others:

"Who will get a leg up on that window
and run to alarm the town? One sharp attack
and this fellow will never shoot again."

His answer   150

came from the goatherd, Melánthios:

"No chance, my lord.

The exit into the courtyard is too near them,
too narrow. One good man could hold that portal
against a crowd. No: let me scale the wall
and bring you arms out of the storage chamber.
Odysseus and his son put them indoors,
I'm sure of it; not outside."

The goatish goatherd
clambered up the wall, toes in the chinks,   160
and slipped through to the storeroom. Twelve light shields,
twelve spears he took, and twelve thick-crested helms,
and handed all down quickly to the suitors.
Odysseus, when he saw his adversaries
girded and capped and long spears in their hands
shaken at him, felt his knees go slack,
his heart sink, for the fight was turning grim.
He spoke rapidly to his son:

"Telémakhos, one of the serving women
is tipping the scales against us in this fight,   170
or maybe Melánthios."

                         But sharp and clear
Telémakhos said:

                         "It is my own fault, Father,
mine alone. The storeroom door—I left it
wide open. They were more alert than I.
Eumaios, go and lock that door,
and bring back word if a woman is doing this
or Melánthios, Dólios' son. More likely he."

Even as they conferred, Melánthios   180
entered the storeroom for a second load,
and the swineherd at the passage entry saw him.
He cried out to his lord:

                         "Son of Laërtês,
Odysseus, master mariner and soldier,
there he goes, the monkey, as we thought,
there he goes into the storeroom.
                         Let me hear your will:
put a spear through him—I hope I am the stronger—
or drag him here to pay for his foul tricks   190
against your house?"

Odysseus said:
                         "Telémakhos and I
will keep these gentlemen in hall, for all their urge to leave.

You two go throw him into the storeroom, wrench his arms
and legs behind him, lash his hands and feet
to a plank, and hoist him up to the roof beams.
Let him live on there suffering at his leisure."

The two men heard him with appreciation
and ducked into the passage. Melánthios,   200
rummaging in the chamber, could not hear them
as they came up; nor could he see them freeze
like posts on either side the door.
He turned back with a handsome crested helmet
in one hand, in the other an old shield
coated with dust—a shield Laërtês bore
soldiering in his youth. It had lain there for years,
and the seams on strap and grip had rotted away.
As Melánthios came out the two men sprang,
jerked him backward by the hair, and threw him.   210
Hands and feet they tied with a cutting cord
behind him, so his bones ground in their sockets,
just as Laërtês' royal son commanded.
Then with a whip of rope they hoisted him
in agony up a pillar to the beams,
and—O my swineherd—you were the one to say:

"Watch through the night up there, Melánthios.
An airy bed is what you need.
You'll be awake to see the primrose Dawn
when she goes glowing from the streams of Ocean   220
to mount her golden throne.
                              No oversleeping
the hour for driving goats to feed the suitors."

They stooped for helm and shield and left him there
contorted, in his brutal sling,
and shut the doors, and went to join Odysseus,
whose mind moved through the combat now to come.
Breathing deep, and snorting hard, they stood
four at the entry, facing two score men.
But now into the gracious doorway stepped   230
Zeus's daughter Athena. She wore the guise of Mentor,
and Odysseus appealed to her in joy:

"O Mentor, join me in this fight! Remember
how all my life I've been devoted to you,
friend of my youth!"

For he guessed it was Athena,
Hope of Soldiers. Cries came from the suitors,
and Ageláos, Damástor's son, called out:

"Mentor, don't let Odysseus lead you astray
to fight against us on his side.   240
Think twice: we are resolved—and we will do it—
after we kill them, father and son,
you too will have your throat slit for your pains
if you make trouble for us here. It means your life.
Your life—and cutting throats will not be all.
Whatever wealth you have, at home, or elsewhere,
we'll mingle with Odysseus' wealth. Your sons
will be turned out, your wife and daughters
banished from the town of Ithaka."

Athena's anger grew like a storm wind as he spoke   250
until she flashed out at Odysseus:

"Ah, what a falling off!
Where is your valor, where is the iron hand
that fought at Troy for Helen, pearl of kings,
no respite and nine years of war? How many foes
your hand brought down in bloody play of spears?
What stratagem but yours took Priam's town?
How is it now that on your own door sill,
before the harriers of your wife, you curse your luck
not to be stronger?   260
Come here, cousin, stand by me,
and you'll see action! In the enemies' teeth
learn how Mentor, son of Álkimos,
repays fair dealing!"

For all her fighting words
she gave no overpowering aid—not yet;
father and son must prove their mettle still.
Into the smoky air under the roof

the goddess merely darted to perch on a blackened beam—
no figure to be seen now but a swallow.   270

Command of the suitors had fallen to Ageláos.
With him were Eurýnomos, Amphímedon,
Demoptólemos, Peisándros, Pólybos,
the best of the lot who stood to fight for their lives
after the streaking arrows downed the rest.
Ageláos rallied them with his plan of battle:

"Friends, our killer has come to the end of his rope,
and much good Mentor did him, that blowhard, dropping in.
Look, only four are left to fight, in the light there at the door.
No scattering of shots, men, no throwing away good spears;   280
we six will aim a volley at Odysseus alone,
and may Zeus grant us the glory of a hit.
If he goes down, the others are no problem."

At his command, then, "Ho!" they all let fly
as one man. But Athena spoiled their shots.
One hit the doorpost of the hall, another
stuck in the door's thick timbering, still others
rang on the stone wall, shivering hafts of ash.
Seeing his men unscathed, royal Odysseus
gave the word for action.   290

                    "Now I say, friends,
the time is overdue to let them have it.
Battlespoil they want from our dead bodies
to add to all they plundered here before."

Taking aim over the steadied lanceheads
they all let fly together. Odysseus killed
Demoptólemos, Telémakhos
killed Eurýadês, the swineherd, Élatos,
and Peisándros went down before the cowherd.
As these lay dying, biting the central floor,   300
their friends gave way and broke for the inner wall.
The four attackers followed up with a rush
to take spears from the fallen men.

Re-forming,
the suitors threw again with all their strength,
but Athena turned their shots, or all but two.
One hit a doorpost in the hall, another
stuck in the door's thick timbering, still others
rang on the stone wall, shivering hafts of ash.
Amphímedon's point bloodied Telémakhos'   310
wrist, a superficial wound, and Ktésippos'
long spear passing over Eumaios' shield
grazed his shoulder, hurtled on and fell.
No matter: with Odysseus the great soldier
the wounded threw again. And Odysseus raider of cities
struck Eurýdamas down. Telémakhos
hit Amphímedon, and the swineherd's shot
killed Pólybos. But Ktésippos, who had last evening thrown
a cow's hoof at Odysseus, got the cowherd's heavy cast
full in the chest—and dying heard him say: 320

"You arrogant joking bastard!
Clown, will you, like a fool, and parade your wit?
Leave jesting to the gods who do it better.
This will repay your cow's-foot courtesy
to a great wanderer come home."

The master
of the black herds had answered Ktésippos.
Odysseus, lunging at close quarters, put a spear
through Ageláos, Damástor's son. Telémakhos
hit Leókritos from behind and pierced him,   330
kidney to diaphragm. Speared off his feet,
he fell face downward on the ground.

At this moment that unmanning thunder cloud,
the aegis, Athena's shield,
took form aloft in the great hall.

And the suitors mad with fear
at her great sign stampeded like stung cattle by a river
when the dread shimmering gadfly strikes in summer,
in the flowering season, in the long-drawn days.

After them the attackers wheeled, as terrible as eagles   340
from eyries in the mountains veering over and diving down
with talons wide unsheathed on flights of birds,
who cower down the sky in chutes and bursts along the valley—
but the pouncing eagles grip their prey, no frantic wing avails,
and farmers love to watch those beakèd hunters.
So these now fell upon the suitors in that hall,
turning, turning to strike and strike again,
while torn men moaned at death, and blood ran smoking
over the whole floor.

       Now there was one   350
who turned and threw himself at Odysseus' knees—
Leódês, begging for his life:

       "Mercy,
mercy on a suppliant, Odysseus!
Never by word or act of mine, I swear,
was any woman troubled here. I told the rest
to put an end to it. They would not listen,
would not keep their hands from brutishness,
and now they are all dying like dogs for it.
I had no part in what they did: my part   360
was visionary—reading the smoke of sacrifice.
Scruples go unrewarded if I die."

The shrewd fighter frowned over him and said:

"You were diviner to this crowd? How often
you must have prayed my sweet day of return
would never come, or not for years!—and prayed
to have my dear wife, and beget children on her.
No plea like yours could save you
from this hard bed of death. Death it shall be!"

He picked up Ageláos' broadsword   370
from where it lay, flung by the slain man,
and gave Leódês' neck a lopping blow
so that his head went down to mouth in dust.

One more who had avoided furious death
was the son of Terpis, Phêmios, the minstrel,

singer by compulsion to the suitors.
He stood now with his harp, holy and clear,
in the wall's recess, under the window, wondering
if he should flee that way to the courtyard altar,
sanctuary of Zeus, the Enclosure God.　　　　　　380
Thighbones in hundreds had been offered there
by Laërtês and Odysseus. No, he thought;
the more direct way would be best—to go
humbly to his lord. But first to save
his murmuring instrument he laid it down
carefully between the winebowl and a chair,
then he betook himself to Lord Odysseus,
clung hard to his knees, and said:

　　　　　　　　　　　"Mercy,
mercy on a suppliant, Odysseus!　　　　　　390
My gift is song for men and for the gods undying.
My death will be remorse for you hereafter.
No one taught me: deep in my mind a god
shaped all the various ways of life in song.
And I am fit to make verse in your company
as in the gods'. Put aside lust for blood.
Your own dear son Telémakhos can tell you,
never by my own will or for love
did I feast here or sing amid the suitors.
They were too strong, too many; they compelled me."　　400

Telémakhos in the elation of battle
heard him. He at once called to his father:

"Wait: that one is innocent: don't hurt him.
And we should let our herald live—Medôn;
he cared for me from boyhood. Where is *he*?
Has he been killed already by Philoítios
or by the swineherd? Else he got an arrow
in that first gale of bowshots down the room."

Now this came to the ears of prudent Medôn
under the chair where he had gone to earth,　　410
pulling a new-flayed bull's hide over him.
Quiet he lay while blinding death passed by.

Now heaving out from under
he scrambled for Telémakhos' knees and said:

"Here I am, dear prince; but rest your spear!
Tell your great father not to see in me
a suitor for the sword's edge—one of those
who laughed at you and ruined his property!"

The lord of all the tricks of war surveyed
this fugitive and smiled. He said: 420

"Courage: my son has dug you out and saved you.
Take it to heart, and pass the word along:
fair dealing brings more profit in the end.
Now leave this room. Go and sit down outdoors
where there's no carnage, in the court,
you and the poet with his many voices,
while I attend to certain chores inside."

At this the two men stirred and picked their way
to the door and out, and sat down at the altar,
looking around with wincing eyes   430
as though the sword's edge hovered still.
And Odysseus looked around him, narrow-eyed,
for any others who had lain hidden
while death's black fury passed.

                          In blood and dust
he saw that crowd all fallen, many and many slain.

Think of a catch that fishermen haul in to a halfmoon bay
in a fine-meshed net from the white-caps of the sea:
how all are poured out on the sand, in throes for the salt sea,
twitching their cold lives away in Hêlios' fiery air: 440
so lay the suitors heaped on one another.

Odysseus at length said to his son:

"Go tell old Nurse I'll have a word with her.
What's to be done now weighs on my mind."

Telémakhos knocked at the women's door and called:

"Eurýkleia, come out here! Move, old woman.
You kept your eye on all our servant girls.
Jump, my father is here and wants to see you."

His call brought no reply, only the doors
were opened, and she came. Telémakhos   450
led her forward. In the shadowy hall
full of dead men she found his father
spattered and caked with blood like a mountain lion
when he has gorged upon an ox, his kill—
with hot blood glistening over his whole chest,
smeared on his jaws, baleful and terrifying—
even so encrimsoned was Odysseus
up to his thighs and armpits. As she gazed
from all the corpses to the bloody man
she raised her head to cry over his triumph,   460
but felt his grip upon her, checking her.
Said the great soldier then:

                              "Rejoice
inwardly. No crowing aloud, old woman.
To glory over slain men is no piety.
Destiny and the gods' will vanquished these,
and their own hardness. They respected no one,
good or bad, who came their way.
For this, and folly, a bad end befell them.
Your part is now to tell me of the women,   470
those who dishonored me, and the innocent."

His own old nurse Eurýkleia said:

                              "I will, then.
Child, you know you'll have the truth from me.
Fifty all told they are, your female slaves,
trained by your lady and myself in service,
wool carding and the rest of it, and taught
to be submissive. Twelve went bad,
flouting me, flouting Penélopê, too.
Telémakhos being barely grown, his mother   480
would never let him rule the serving women—
but you must let me go to her lighted rooms
and tell her. Some god sent her a drift of sleep."

But in reply the great tactician said:

"Not yet. Do not awake her. Tell those women
who were the suitors' harlots to come here."

She went back on this mission through his hall.
Then he called Telémakhos to his side
and the two herdsmen. Sharply Odysseus said:

"These dead must be disposed of first of all.   490
Direct the women. Tables and chairs will be
scrubbed with sponges, rinsed and rinsed again.
When our great room is fresh and put in order,
take them outside, these women,
between the roundhouse and the palisade,
and hack them with your swordblades till you cut
the life out of them, and every thought of sweet
Aphroditê under the rutting suitors,
when they lay down in secret."

                    As he spoke   500
here came the women in a bunch, all wailing,
soft tears on their cheeks. They fell to work
to lug the corpses out into the courtyard
under the gateway, propping one
against another as Odysseus ordered,
for he himself stood over them. In fear
these women bore the cold weight of the dead.
The next thing was to scrub off chairs and tables
and rinse them down. Telémakhos and the herdsmen
scraped the packed earth floor with hoes, but made   510
the women carry out all blood and mire.
When the great room was cleaned up once again,
at swordpoint they forced them out, between
the roundhouse and the palisade, pell-mell
to huddle in that dead end without exit.
Telémakhos, who knew his mind, said curtly:

"I would not give the clean death of a beast
to trulls who made a mockery of my mother
and of me too—you sluts, who lay with suitors."

He tied one end of a hawser to a pillar   520
and passed the other about the roundhouse top,
taking the slack up, so that no one's toes
could touch the ground. They would be hung like doves
or larks in springès triggered in a thicket,
where the birds think to rest—a cruel nesting.
So now in turn each woman thrust her head
into a noose and swung, yanked high in air,
to perish there most piteously.
Their feet danced for a little, but not long.

From storeroom to the court they brought Melánthios,   530
chopped with swords to cut his nose and ears off,
pulled off his genitals to feed the dogs
and raging hacked his hands and feet away.

As their own hands and feet called for a washing,
they went indoors to Odysseus again.
Their work was done. He told Eurýkleia:

                    "Bring me
brimstone and a brazier—medicinal
fumes to purify my hall. Then tell
Penélopê to come, and bring her maids.   540
All servants round the house must be called in."

His own old nurse Eurýkleia replied:

"Aye, surely that is well said, child. But let me
find you a good clean shirt and cloak and dress you.
You must not wrap your shoulders' breadth again
in rags in your own hall. That would be shameful."

Odysseus answered:

                    "Let me have the fire.
The first thing is to purify this place."

With no more chat Eurýkleia obeyed   550
and fetched out fire and brimstone. Cleansing fumes
he sent through court and hall and storage chamber.

Then the old woman hurried off again
to the women's quarters to announce her news,
and all the servants came now, bearing torches
in twilight, crowding to embrace Odysseus,
taking his hands to kiss, his head and shoulders,
while he stood there, nodding to every one,
and overcome by longing and by tears.

BOOK TWENTY-THREE

The Trunk of the Olive Tree

LINES 1 – 15

The old nurse went upstairs exulting,   1
with knees toiling, and patter of slapping feet,
to tell the mistress of her lord's return,
and cried out by the lady's pillow:

                                 "Wake,
wake up, dear child! Penélopê, come down,
see with your own eyes what all these years you longed for!
Odysseus is here! Oh, in the end, he came!
And he has killed your suitors, killed them all
who made his house a bordel and ate his cattle   10
and raised their hands against his son!"

                         Penélopê said:

"Dear nurse . . . the gods have touched you.
They can put chaos into the clearest head
or bring a lunatic down to earth. Good sense
you always had. They've touched you. What is this

mockery you wake me up to tell me,
breaking in on my sweet spell of sleep?
I had not dozed away so tranquilly
since my lord went to war, on that ill wind   20
to Ilion.

                  Oh, leave me! Back down stairs!
If any other of my women came in babbling
things like these to startle me, I'd see her
flogged out of the house! Your old age spares you that."

Eurýkleia said:

"Would I play such a trick on you, dear child?
It is true, true, as I tell you, he has come!
That stranger they were baiting was Odysseus.
Telémakhos knew it days ago—   30
cool head, never to give his father away,
till he paid off those swollen dogs!"

The lady in her heart's joy now sprang up
with sudden dazzling tears, and hugged the old one,
crying out:

                "But try to make it clear!
If he came home in secret, as you say,
could he engage them singlehanded? How?
They were all down there, still in the same crowd."

To this Eurýkleia said: 40

                "I did not see it,
I knew nothing; only I heard the groans
of men dying. We sat still in the inner rooms
holding our breath, and marvelling, shut in,
until Telémakhos came to the door and called me—
your own dear son, sent this time by his father!
So I went out, and found Odysseus
erect, with dead men littering the floor
this way and that. If you had only seen him!
It would have made your heart glow hot!—a lion   50
splashed with mire and blood.

But now the cold
corpses are all gathered at the gate,
and he has cleansed his hall with fire and brimstone,
a great blaze. Then he sent me here to you.
Come with me: you may both embark this time
for happiness together, after pain,
after long years. Here is your prayer, your passion,
granted: your own lord lives, he is at home,
he found you safe, he found his son. The suitors   60
abused his house, but he has brought them down."

The attentive lady said:

                       "Do not lose yourself
in this rejoicing: wait: you know
how splendid that return would be for us,
how dear to me, dear to his son and mine;
but no, it is not possible, your notion
must be wrong.
                 Some god has killed the suitors,
a god, sick of their arrogance and brutal   70
malice—for they honored no one living,
good or bad, who ever came their way.
Blind young fools, they've tasted death for it.
But the true person of Odysseus?
He lost his home, he died far from Akhaia."

The old nurse sighed:

                     "How queer, the way you talk!
Here he is, large as life, by his own fire,
and you deny he ever will get home!
Child, you always were mistrustful!   80
But there is one sure mark that I can tell you:
that scar left by the boar's tusk long ago.
I recognized it when I bathed his feet
and would have told you, but he stopped my mouth,
forbade me, in his craftiness.
                    Come down,
I stake my life on it, he's here!
Let me die in agony if I lie!"

Penélopê said:

"Nurse dear, though you have your wits about you,   90
still it is hard not to be taken in
by the immortals. Let us join my son, though,
and see the dead and that strange one who killed them."

She turned then to descend the stair, her heart
in tumult. Had she better keep her distance
and question him, her husband? Should she run
up to him, take his hands, kiss him now?
Crossing the door sill she sat down at once
in firelight, against the nearest wall,
across the room from the lord Odysseus.   100
                    There
leaning against a pillar, sat the man
and never lifted up his eyes, but only waited
for what his wife would say when she had seen him.
And she, for a long time, sat deathly still
in wonderment—for sometimes as she gazed
she found him—yes, clearly—like her husband,
but sometimes blood and rags were all she saw.
Telémakhos' voice came to her ears:

                    "Mother,   110
cruel mother, do you feel nothing,
drawing yourself apart this way from Father?
Will you not sit with him and talk and question him?
What other woman could remain so cold?
Who shuns her lord, and he come back to her
from wars and wandering, after twenty years?
Your heart is hard as flint and never changes!"

Penélopê answered:

                    "I am stunned, child.
I cannot speak to him. I cannot question him.   120
I cannot keep my eyes upon his face.
If really he is Odysseus, truly home,
beyond all doubt we two shall know each other

better than you or anyone. There are
secret signs we know, we two."

A smile
came now to the lips of the patient hero, Odysseus,
who turned to Telémakhos and said:

"Peace: let your mother test me at her leisure.
Before long she will see and know me best.   130
These tatters, dirt—all that I'm caked with now—
make her look hard at me and doubt me still.
As to this massacre, we must see the end.
Whoever kills one citizen, you know,
and has no force of armed men at his back,
had better take himself abroad by night
and leave his kin. Well, we cut down the flower of Ithaka,
the mainstay of the town. Consider that."

Telémakhos replied respectfully:

"Dear Father,   140
enough that you yourself study the danger,
foresighted in combat as you are,
they say you have no rival.

We three stand
ready to follow you and fight. I say
for what our strength avails, we have the courage."

And the great tactician, Odysseus, answered:

"Good.
Here is our best maneuver, as I see it:
bathe, you three, and put fresh clothing on,   150
order the women to adorn themselves,
and let our admirable harper choose a tune
for dancing, some lighthearted air, and strum it.
Anyone going by, or any neighbor,
will think it is a wedding feast he hears.
These deaths must not be cried about the town
till we can slip away to our own woods. We'll see
what weapon, then, Zeus puts into our hands."

They listened attentively, and did his bidding,
bathed and dressed afresh; and all the maids   160
adorned themselves. Then Phêmios the harper
took his polished shell and plucked the strings,
moving the company to desire
for singing, for the sway and beat of dancing,
until they made the manor hall resound
with gaiety of men and grace of women.
Anyone passing on the road would say:

"Married at last, I see—the queen so many courted.
Sly, cattish wife! She would not keep—not she!—
the lord's estate until he came."   170

                        So travellers'
thoughts might run—but no one guessed the truth.
Greathearted Odysseus, home at last,
was being bathed now by Eurýnomê
and rubbed with golden oil, and clothed again
in a fresh tunic and a cloak. Athena
lent him beauty, head to foot. She made him
taller, and massive, too, with crisping hair
in curls like petals of wild hyacinth
but all red-golden. Think of gold infused   180
on silver by a craftsman, whose fine art
Hephaistos taught him, or Athena: one
whose work moves to delight: just so she lavished
beauty over Odysseus' head and shoulders.
He sat then in the same chair by the pillar,
facing his silent wife, and said:

                        "Strange woman,
the immortals of Olympos made you hard,
harder than any. Who else in the world
would keep aloof as you do from her husband   190
if he returned to her from years of trouble,
cast on his own land in the twentieth year?

Nurse, make up a bed for me to sleep on.
Her heart is iron in her breast."

Penélopê
spoke to Odysseus now. She said:

"Strange man,
if man you are . . . This is no pride on my part
nor scorn for you—not even wonder, merely.
I know so well how you—how he—appeared   200
boarding the ship for Troy. But all the same . . .

Make up his bed for him, Eurýkleia.
Place it outside the bedchamber my lord
built with his own hands. Pile the big bed
with fleeces, rugs, and sheets of purest linen."

With this she tried him to the breaking point,
and he turned on her in a flash raging:

"Woman, by heaven you've stung me now!
Who dared to move my bed?
No builder had the skill for that—unless   210
a god came down to turn the trick. No mortal
in his best days could budge it with a crowbar.
There is our pact and pledge, our secret sign,
built into that bed—my handiwork
and no one else's!

An old trunk of olive
grew like a pillar on the building plot,
and I laid out our bedroom round that tree,
lined up the stone walls, built the walls and roof,
gave it a doorway and smooth-fitting doors.   220
Then I lopped off the silvery leaves and branches,
hewed and shaped that stump from the roots up
into a bedpost, drilled it, let it serve
as model for the rest. I planed them all,
inlaid them all with silver, gold and ivory,
and stretched a bed between—a pliant web
of oxhide thongs dyed crimson.

There's our sign!
I know no more. Could someone else's hand
have sawn that trunk and dragged the frame away?"   230

Their secret! as she heard it told, her knees
grew tremulous and weak, her heart failed her.
With eyes brimming tears she ran to him,
throwing her arms around his neck, and kissed him,
murmuring:

                        "Do not rage at me, Odysseus!
No one ever matched your caution! Think
what difficulty the gods gave: they denied us
life together in our prime and flowering years,
kept us from crossing into age together.   240
Forgive me, don't be angry. I could not
welcome you with love on sight! I armed myself
long ago against the frauds of men,
impostors who might come—and all those many
whose underhanded ways bring evil on!
Helen of Argos, daughter of Zeus and Leda,
would she have joined the stranger, lain with him,
if she had known her destiny? known the Akhaians
in arms would bring her back to her own country?
Surely a goddess moved her to adultery,   250
her blood unchilled by war and evil coming,
the years, the desolation; ours, too.
But here and now, what sign could be so clear
as this of our own bed?
No other man has ever laid eyes on it—
only my own slave, Aktoris, that my father
sent with me as a gift—she kept our door.
You make my stiff heart know that I am yours."

Now from his breast into his eyes the ache
of longing mounted, and he wept at last,   260
his dear wife, clear and faithful, in his arms,
longed for as the sunwarmed earth is longed for by a swimmer
spent in rough water where his ship went down
under Poseidon's blows, gale winds and tons of sea.
Few men can keep alive through a big surf
to crawl, clotted with brine, on kindly beaches
in joy, in joy, knowing the abyss behind:

and so she too rejoiced, her gaze upon her husband,
her white arms round him pressed as though forever.

The rose Dawn might have found them weeping still   270
had not grey-eyed Athena slowed the night
when night was most profound, and held the Dawn
under the Ocean of the East. That glossy team,
Firebright and Daybright, the Dawn's horses
that draw her heavenward for men—Athena
stayed their harnessing.

                    Then said Odysseus:

"My dear, we have not won through to the end.
One trial—I do not know how long—is left for me
to see fulfilled. Teirêsias' ghost forewarned me   280
the night I stood upon the shore of Death, asking
about my friends' homecoming and my own.

But now the hour grows late, it is bed time,
rest will be sweet for us; let us lie down."

To this Penélopê replied:

                   "That bed,
that rest is yours whenever desire moves you,
now the kind powers have brought you home at last.
But as your thought has dwelt upon it, tell me:
what is the trial you face? I must know soon;   290
what does it matter if I learn tonight?"

The teller of many stories said:

                    "My strange one,
must you again, and even now,
urge me to talk? Here is a plodding tale;
no charm in it, no relish in the telling.
Teirêsias told me I must take an oar
and trudge the mainland, going from town to town,
until I discover men who have never known
the salt blue sea, nor flavor of salt meat—   300
strangers to painted prows, to watercraft
and oars like wings, dipping across the water.

The moment of revelation he foretold
was this, for you may share the prophecy:
some traveller falling in with me will say:
'A winnowing fan, that on your shoulder, sir?'
There I must plant my oar, on the very spot,
with burnt offerings to Poseidon of the Waters:
a ram, a bull, a great buck boar. Thereafter
when I come home again, I am to slay   310
full hekatombs to the gods who own broad heaven,
one by one.

                     Then death will drift upon me
from seaward, mild as air, mild as your hand,
in my well-tended weariness of age,
contented folk around me on our island.
He said all this must come."

                  Penélopê said:

"If by the gods' grace age at least is kind,
we have that promise—trials will end in peace."   320

So he confided in her, and she answered.
Meanwhile Eurýnomê and the nurse together
laid soft coverlets on the master's bed,
working in haste by torchlight. Eurýkleia
retired to her quarters for the night,
and then Eurýnomê, as maid-in-waiting,
lighted her lord and lady to their chamber
with bright brands.
She vanished.

                  So they came   330
into that bed so steadfast, loved of old,
opening glad arms to one another.
Telémakhos by now had hushed the dancing,
hushed the women. In the darkened hall
he and the cowherd and the swineherd slept.

The royal pair mingled in love again
and afterward lay revelling in stories:
hers of the siege her beauty stood at home
from arrogant suitors, crowding on her sight,

and how they fed their courtship on his cattle,   340
oxen and fat sheep, and drank up rivers
of wine out of the vats.
                              Odysseus told
of what hard blows he had dealt out to others
and of what blows he had taken—all that story.
She could not close her eyes till all was told.

His raid on the Kikonês, first of all,
then how he visited the Lotos Eaters,
and what the Kyklops did, and how those shipmates,
pitilessly devoured, were avenged.   350
Then of his touching Aiolos's isle
and how that king refitted him for sailing
to Ithaka; all vain: gales blew him back
groaning over the fishcold sea. Then how
he reached the Laistrygonians' distant bay
and how they smashed his ships and his companions.
Kirkê, then: of her deceits and magic,
then of his voyage to the wide underworld
of dark, the house of Death, and questioning
Teirêsias, Theban spirit.   360
                              Dead companions,
many, he saw there, and his mother, too.
Of this he told his wife, and told how later
he heard the choir of maddening Seirênês,
coasted the Wandering Rocks, Kharybdis' pool
and the fiend Skylla who takes toll of men.
Then how his shipmates killed Lord Hêlios' cattle
and how Zeus thundering in towering heaven
split their fast ship with his fuming bolt,
so all hands perished.   370
                              He alone survived,
cast away on Kalypso's isle, Ogýgia.
He told, then, how that nymph detained him there
in her smooth caves, craving him for her husband,
and how in her devoted lust she swore
he should not die nor grow old, all his days,
but he held out against her.

                    Last of all
what sea-toil brought him to the Phaiákians;
their welcome; how they took him to their hearts   380
and gave him passage to his own dear island
with gifts of garments, gold and bronze . . .
                              Remembering,
he drowsed over the story's end. Sweet sleep
relaxed his limbs and his care-burdened breast.

Other affairs were in Athena's keeping.
Waiting until Odysseus had his pleasure
of love and sleep, the grey-eyed one bestirred
the fresh Dawn from her bed of paling Ocean
to bring up daylight to her golden chair,   390
and from his fleecy bed Odysseus
arose. He said to Penélopê:

                    "My lady,
what ordeals have we not endured! Here, waiting
you had your grief, while my return dragged out—
my hard adventures, pitting myself against
the gods' will, and Zeus, who pinned me down
far from home. But now our life resumes:
we've come together to our longed-for bed.
Take care of what is left me in our house;   400
as to the flocks that pack of wolves laid waste
they'll be replenished: scores I'll get on raids
and other scores our island friends will give me
till all the folds are full again.
                              This day
I'm off up country to the orchards. I must see
my noble father, for he missed me sorely.
And here is my command for you—a strict one,
though you may need none, clever as you are.
Word will get about as the sun goes higher   410
of how I killed those lads. Go to your rooms
on the upper floor, and take your women. Stay there
with never a glance outside or a word to anyone."

Fitting cuirass and swordbelt to his shoulders,
he woke his herdsmen, woke Telémakhos,

ordering all in arms. They dressed quickly,
and all in war gear sallied from the gate,
led by Odysseus.

                              Now it was broad day
but these three men Athena hid in darkness,   420
going before them swiftly from the town.

BOOK
TWENTY-FOUR

Warriors, Farewell

LINES 1 – 18

Meanwhile the suitors' ghosts were called away   1
by Hermês of Kyllênê, bearing the golden wand
with which he charms the eyes of men or wakens
whom he wills.
                 He waved them on, all squeaking
as bats will in a cavern's underworld,
all flitting, flitting criss-cross in the dark
if one falls and the rock-hung chain is broken.
So with faint cries the shades trailed after Hermês,
pure Deliverer.   10
                 He led them down dank ways,
over grey Ocean tides, the Snowy Rock,
past shores of Dream and narrows of the sunset,
in swift flight to where the Dead inhabit
wastes of asphodel at the world's end.

Crossing the plain they met Akhilleus' ghost,
Patróklos and Antílokhos, then Aias,
noblest of Danaans after Akhilleus

in strength and beauty. Here the newly dead
drifted together, whispering. Then came   20
the soul of Agamémnon, son of Atreus,
in black pain forever, surrounded by men-at-arms
who perished with him in Aigísthos' hall.
Akhilleus greeted him:

                     "My lord Atreidês,
we held that Zeus who loves the play of lightning
would give you length of glory, you were king
over so great a host of soldiery
before Troy, where we suffered, we Akhaians.
But in the morning of your life   30
you met that doom that no man born avoids.
It should have found you in your day of victory,
marshal of the army, in Troy country;
then all Akhaia would have heaped your tomb
and saved your honor for your son. Instead
piteous death awaited you at home."

And Atreus' son replied:

                     "Fortunate hero,
son of Pêleus, godlike and glorious,
at Troy you died, across the sea from Argos,   40
and round you Trojan and Akhaian peers
fought for your corpse and died. A dustcloud wrought
by a whirlwind hid the greatness of you slain,
minding no more the mastery of horses.
All that day we might have toiled in battle
had not a storm from Zeus broken it off.
We carried you out of the field of war
down to the ships and bathed your comely body
with warm water and scented oil. We laid you
upon your long bed, and our officers   50
wept hot tears like rain and cropped their hair.
Then hearing of it in the sea, your mother, Thetis,
came with nereids of the grey wave crying
unearthly lamentation over the water,
and trembling gripped the Akhaians to the bone.
They would have boarded ship that night and fled
except for one man's wisdom—venerable

Nestor, proven counselor in the past.
He stood and spoke to allay their fear: 'Hold fast,
sons of the Akhaians, lads of Argos.   60
His mother it must be, with nymphs her sisters,
come from the sea to mourn her son in death.'

Veteran hearts at this contained their dread
while at your side the daughters of the ancient
seagod wailed and wrapped ambrosial shrouding
around you.
                    Then we heard the Muses sing
a threnody in nine immortal voices.
No Argive there but wept, such keening rose
from that one Muse who led the song.   70
                              Now seven
days and ten, seven nights and ten, we mourned you,
we mortal men, with nymphs who know no death,
before we gave you to the flame, slaughtering
longhorned steers and fat sheep on your pyre.

Dressed by the nereids and embalmed with honey,
honey and unguent in the seething blaze,
you turned to ash. And past the pyre Akhaia's
captains paraded in review, in arms,
clattering chariot teams and infantry.   80
Like a forest fire the flame roared on, and burned
your flesh away. Next day at dawn, Akhilleus,
we picked your pale bones from the char to keep
in wine and oil. A golden ámphora
your mother gave for this—Hephaistos' work,
a gift from Dionysos. In that vase,
Akhilleus, hero, lie your pale bones mixed
with mild Patróklos' bones, who died before you,
and nearby lie the bones of Antílokhos,
the one you cared for most of all companions   90
after Patróklos.
                    We of the Old Army,
we who were spearmen, heaped a tomb for these
upon a foreland over Hellê's waters,
to be a mark against the sky for voyagers
in this generation and those to come.

Your mother sought from the gods magnificent trophies
and set them down midfield for our champions. Often
at funeral games after the death of kings
when you yourself contended, you've seen athletes   100
cinch their belts when trophies went on view.
But these things would have made you stare—the treasures
Thetis on her silver-slippered feet
brought to your games—for the gods held you dear.
You perished, but your name will never die.
It lives to keep all men in mind of honor
forever, Akhilleus.

                   As for myself, what joy
is this, to have brought off the war? Foul death
Zeus held in store for me at my coming home;   110
Aigísthos and my vixen cut me down."

While they conversed, the Wayfinder came near,
leading the shades of suitors overthrown
by Lord Odysseus. The two souls of heroes
advanced together, scrutinizing these.
Then Agamémnon recognized Amphímedon,
son of Meláneus—friends of his on Ithaka—
and called out to him:

                   "Amphímedon,
what ruin brought you into this undergloom?   120
All in a body, picked men, and so young?
One could not better choose the kingdom's pride.
Were you at sea, aboard ship, and Poseidon
blew up a dire wind and foundering waves,
or cattle-raiding, were you, on the mainland,
or in a fight for some stronghold, or women,
when the foe hit you to your mortal hurt?
Tell me, answer my question. Guest and friend
I say I am of yours—or do you not remember
I visited your family there? I came   130
with Prince Meneláos, urging Odysseus
to join us in the great sea raid on Troy.
One solid month we beat our way, breasting

south sea and west, resolved to bring him round,
the wily raider of cities."

                    The new shade said:

"O glory of commanders, Agamémnon,
all that you bring to mind I remember well.
As for the sudden manner of our death
I'll tell you of it clearly, first to last.   140
After Odysseus had been gone for years
we were all suitors of his queen. She never
quite refused, nor went through with a marriage,
hating it, ever bent on our defeat.
Here is one of her tricks: she placed her loom,
her big loom, out for weaving in her hall,
and the fine warp of some vast fabric on it.
We were attending her, and she said to us:
'Young men, my suitors, now my lord is dead,
let me finish my weaving before I marry,   150
or else my thread will have been spun in vain.
This is a shroud I weave for Lord Laërtês
when cold Death comes to lay him on his bier.
The country wives would hold me in dishonor
if he, with all his fortune, lay unshrouded.'
We had men's hearts; she touched them; we agreed.
So every day she wove on the great loom—
but every night by torchlight she unwove it,
and so for three years she deceived the Akhaians.
But when the seasons brought the fourth around,   160
as long months waned, and the slow days were spent,
one of her maids, who knew the secret, told us.
We found her unraveling the splendid shroud,
and then she had to finish, willy nilly—
finish, and show the big loom woven tight
from beam to beam with cloth. She washed the shrouding
clean as sun or moonlight.
                    Then, heaven knows
from what quarter of the world, fatality
brought in Odysseus to the swineherd's wood   170
far up the island. There his son went too
when the black ship put him ashore from Pylos.

The two together planned our death-trap. Down
they came to the famous town—Telémakhos
long in advance: we had to wait for Odysseus.
The swineherd led him to the manor later
in rags like a foul beggar, old and broken,
propped on a stick. These tatters that he wore
hid him so well that none of us could know him
when he turned up, not even the older men.   180
We jeered at him, took potshots at him, cursed him.
Daylight and evening in his own great hall
he bore it, patient as a stone. That night
the mind of Zeus beyond the stormcloud stirred him
with Telémakhos at hand to shift his arms
from mégaron to storage room and lock it.
Then he assigned his wife her part: next day
she brought his bow and iron axeheads out
to make a contest. Contest there was none;
that move doomed us to slaughter. Not a man   190
could bend the stiff bow to his will or string it,
until it reached Odysseus. We shouted,
'Keep the royal bow from the beggar's hands
no matter how he begs!' Only Telémakhos
would not be denied.

                So the great soldier
took his bow and bent it for the bowstring
effortlessly. He drilled the axeheads clean,
sprang, and decanted arrows on the door sill,
glared, and drew again. This time he killed   200
Antínoös.

                There facing us he crouched
and shot his bolts of groaning at us, brought us
down like sheep. Then some god, his familiar,
went into action with him round the hall,
after us in a massacre. Men lay groaning,
mortally wounded, and the floor smoked with blood.

That was the way our death came, Agamémnon.
Now in Odysseus' hall untended still
our bodies lie, unknown to friends or kinsmen   210
who should have laid us out and washed our wounds

free of the clotted blood, and mourned our passing.
So much is due the dead."

                              But Agamémnon's
tall shade when he heard this cried aloud:

"O fortunate Odysseus, master mariner
and soldier, blessed son of old Laërtês!
The girl you brought home made a valiant wife!
True to her husband's honor and her own,
Penélopê, Ikários' faithful daughter!   220
The very gods themselves will sing her story
for men on earth—mistress of her own heart,
Penélopê!
Tyndáreus' daughter waited, too—how differently!
Klytaimnéstra, the adulteress,
waited to stab her lord and king. That song
will be forever hateful. A bad name
she gave to womankind, even the best."

These were the things they said to one another
under the rim of earth where Death is lord.   230

Leaving the town, Odysseus and his men
that morning reached Laërtês' garden lands,
long since won by his toil from wilderness—
his homestead, and the row of huts around it
where fieldhands rested, ate and slept. Indoors
he had an old slave woman, a Sikel, keeping
house for him in his secluded age.

Odysseus here took leave of his companions.

"Go make yourselves at home inside," he said.
"Roast the best porker and prepare a meal.   240
I'll go to try my father. Will he know me?
Can he imagine it, after twenty years?"

He handed spear and shield to the two herdsmen,
and in they went, Telémakhos too. Alone
Odysseus walked the orchard rows and vines.

He found no trace of Dólios and his sons
nor the other slaves—all being gone that day
to clear a distant field, and drag the stones
for a boundary wall.

                              But on a well-banked plot   250
Odysseus found his father in solitude
spading the earth around a young fruit tree.

He wore a tunic, patched and soiled, and leggings—
oxhide patches, bound below his knees
against the brambles; gauntlets on his hands
and on his head a goatskin cowl of sorrow.
This was the figure Prince Odysseus found—
wasted by years, racked, bowed under grief.
The son paused by a tall pear tree and wept,
then inwardly debated: should he run   260
forward and kiss his father, and pour out
his tale of war, adventure, and return,
or should he first interrogate him, test him?
Better that way, he thought—
first draw him out with sharp words, trouble him.
His mind made up, he walked ahead. Laërtês
went on digging, head down, by the sapling,
stamping the spade in. At his elbow then
his son spoke out:

                              "Old man, the orchard keeper   270
you work for is no townsman. A good eye
for growing things he has; there's not a nurseling,
fig tree, vine stock, olive tree or pear tree
or garden bed uncared for on this farm.
But I might add—don't take offense—your own
appearance could be tidier. Old age
yes—but why the squalor, and rags to boot?
It would not be for sloth, now, that your master
leaves you in this condition; neither at all
because there's any baseness in your self.   280
No, by your features, by the frame you have,
a man might call you kingly,
one who should bathe warm, sup well, and rest easy
in age's privilege. But tell me:

who are your masters? whose fruit trees are these
you tend here? Tell me if it's true this island
is Ithaka, as that fellow I fell in with
told me on the road just now? He had
a peg loose, that one: couldn't say a word
or listen when I asked about my friend,   290
my Ithakan friend. I asked if he were alive
or gone long since into the underworld.
I can describe him if you care to hear it:
I entertained the man in my own land
when he turned up there on a journey; never
had I a guest more welcome in my house.
He claimed his stock was Ithakan: Laërtês
Arkeísiadês, he said his father was.
I took him home, treated him well, grew fond of him—
though we had many guests—and gave him   300
gifts in keeping with his quality: seven
bars of measured gold, a silver winebowl
filigreed with flowers, twelve light cloaks,
twelve rugs, robes and tunics—not to mention
his own choice of women trained in service,
the four well-favored ones he wished to take."

His father's eyes had filled with tears. He said:

"You've come to that man's island, right enough,
but dangerous men and fools hold power now.
You gave your gifts in vain. If you could find him   310
here in Ithaka alive, he'd make
return of gifts and hospitality,
as custom is, when someone has been generous.
But tell me accurately—how many years
have now gone by since that man was your guest?
your guest, my son—if he indeed existed—
born to ill fortune as he was. Ah, far
from those who loved him, far from his native land,
in some sea-dingle fish have picked his bones,
or else he made the vultures and wild beasts   320
a trove ashore! His mother at his bier
never bewailed him, nor did I, his father,

nor did his admirable wife, Penélopê,
who should have closed her husband's eyes in death
and cried aloud upon him as he lay.
So much is due the dead.

                 But speak out, tell me further:
who are you, of what city and family?
where have you moored the ship that brought you here,
where is your admirable crew? Are you a peddler   330
put ashore by the foreign ship you came on?"

Again Odysseus had a fable ready.

"Yes," he said, "I can tell you all those things.
I come from Rover's Passage where my home is,
and I'm King Allwoes' only son. My name
is Quarrelman.

                 Heaven's power in the westwind
drove me this way from Sikania,
off my course. My ship lies in a barren
cove beyond the town there. As for Odysseus,   340
now is the fifth year since he put to sea
and left my homeland—bound for death, you say.
Yet landbirds flying from starboard crossed his bow—
a lucky augury. So we parted joyously,
in hope of friendly days and gifts to come."

A cloud of pain had fallen on Laërtês.
Scooping up handfuls of the sunburnt dust
he sifted it over his grey head, and groaned,
and the groan went to the son's heart. A twinge
prickling up through his nostrils warned Odysseus   350
he could not watch this any longer.
He leaped and threw his arms around his father,
kissed him, and said:

                 "Oh, Father, I am he!
Twenty years gone, and here I've come again
to my own land!

                 Hold back your tears! No grieving!
I bring good news—though still we cannot rest.
I killed the suitors to the last man!
Outrage and injury have been avenged!"   360

Laërtês turned and found his voice to murmur:

"If you are Odysseus, my son, come back,
give me some proof, a sign to make me sure."

His son replied:

                              "The scar then, first of all.
Look, here the wild boar's flashing tusk
wounded me on Parnassos; do you see it?
You and my mother made me go, that time,
to visit Lord Autólykos, her father,
for gifts he promised years before on Ithaka.   370
Again—more proof—let's say the trees you gave me
on this revetted plot of orchard once.
I was a small boy at your heels, wheedling
amid the young trees, while you named each one.
You gave me thirteen pear, ten apple trees,
and forty fig trees. Fifty rows of vines
were promised too, each one to bear in turn.
Bunches of every hue would hang there ripening,
weighed down by the god of summer days."

The old man's knees failed him, his heart grew faint,   380
recalling all that Odysseus calmly told.
He clutched his son. Odysseus held him swooning
until he got his breath back and his spirit
and spoke again:

                              "Zeus, Father! Gods above!—
you still hold pure Olympos, if the suitors
paid for their crimes indeed, and paid in blood!
But now the fear is in me that all Ithaka
will be upon us. They'll send messengers
to stir up every city of the islands."   390

Odysseus the great tactician answered:

"Courage, and leave the worrying to me.
We'll turn back to your homestead by the orchard.
I sent the cowherd, swineherd, and Telémakhos
ahead to make our noonday meal."

                    Conversing
in this vein they went home, the two together,
into the stone farmhouse. There Telémakhos
and the two herdsmen were already carving
roast young pork, and mixing amber wine.   400
During these preparations the Sikel woman
bathed Laërtês and anointed him,
and dressed him in a new cloak. Then Athena,
standing by, filled out his limbs again,
gave girth and stature to the old field captain
fresh from the bathing place. His son looked on
in wonder at the godlike bloom upon him,
and called out happily:

                    "Oh, Father,
surely one of the gods who are young forever   410
has made you magnificent before my eyes!"

Clearheaded Laërtês faced him, saying:

"By Father Zeus, Athena and Apollo,
I wish I could be now as once I was,
commander of Kephallenians, when I took
the walled town, Nérikos, on the promontory!
Would god I had been young again last night
with armor on me, standing in our hall
to fight the suitors at your side! How many
knees I could have crumpled, to your joy!"   420

While son and father spoke, cowherd and swineherd
attended, waiting, for the meal was ready.
Soon they were all seated, and their hands
picked up the meat and bread.

                    But now old Dólios
appeared in the bright doorway with his sons,
work-stained from the field. Laërtês' housekeeper,
who reared the boys and tended Dólios
in his bent age, had gone to fetch them in.
When it came over them who the stranger was   430

they halted in astonishment. Odysseus
hit an easy tone with them. Said he:

"Sit down and help yourselves. Shake off your wonder.
Here we've been waiting for you all this time,
and our mouths watering for good roast pig!"

But Dólios came forward, arms outstretched,
and kissed Odysseus' hand at the wrist bone,
crying out:

              "Dear master, you returned!
You came to us again! How we had missed you!   440
We thought you lost. The gods themselves have brought you!
Welcome, welcome; health and blessings on you!
And tell me, now, just one thing more: Penélopê,
does she know yet that you are on the island?
or should we send a messenger?"

Odysseus gruffly said,

              "Old man, she knows.
Is it for you to think of her?"

             So Dólios
quietly took a smooth bench at the table   450
and in their turn his sons welcomed Odysseus,
kissing his hands; then each went to his chair
beside his father. Thus our friends
were occupied in Laërtês house at noon.

Meanwhile to the four quarters of the town
the news ran: bloody death had caught the suitors;
and men and women in a murmuring crowd
gathered before Odysseus' hall. They gave
burial to the piteous dead, or bore
the bodies of young men from other islands   460
down to the port, thence to be ferried home.
Then all the men went grieving to assembly
and being seated, rank by rank, grew still,
as old Eupeíthês rose to address them. Pain
lay in him like a brand for Antínoös,

the first man that Odysseus brought down,
and tears flowed for his son as he began:

"Heroic feats that fellow did for us
Akhaians, friends! Good spearmen by the shipload
he led to war and lost—lost ships and men,   470
and once ashore again killed these, who were
the islands' pride.

                    Up with you! After him!—
before he can take flight to Pylos town
or hide at Elis, under Epeian law!
We'd be disgraced forever! Mocked for generations
if we cannot avenge our sons' blood, and our brothers!
Life would turn to ashes—at least for me;
rather be dead and join the dead!

                    I say   480
we ought to follow now, or they'll gain time
and make the crossing."

                    His appeal, his tears,
moved all the gentry listening there;
but now they saw the crier and the minstrel
come from Odysseus' hall, where they had slept.
The two men stood before the curious crowd,
and Medôn said:

                    "Now hear me, men of Ithaka.
When these hard deeds were done by Lord Odysseus   490
the immortal gods were not far off. I saw
with my own eyes someone divine who fought
beside him, in the shape and dress of Mentor;
it was a god who shone before Odysseus,
a god who swept the suitors down the hall
dying in droves."

                    At this pale fear assailed them,
and next they heard again the old forecaster,
Halithérsês Mastóridês. Alone
he saw the field of time, past and to come.   500
In his anxiety for them he said:

"Ithakans, now listen to what I say.
Friends, by your own fault these deaths came to pass.

You would not heed me nor the captain, Mentor;
would not put down the riot of your sons.
Heroic feats they did!—all wantonly
raiding a great man's flocks, dishonoring
his queen, because they thought he'd come no more.
Let matters rest; do as I urge; no chase,
or he who wants a bloody end will find it."   510

The greater number stood up shouting "Aye!"
But many held fast, sitting all together
in no mind to agree with him. Eupeíthês
had won them to his side. They ran for arms,
clapped on their bronze, and mustered
under Eupeíthês at the town gate
for his mad foray.

      Vengeance would be his,
he thought, for his son's murder; but that day
held bloody death for him and no return.   520

At this point, querying Zeus, Athena said:

"O Father of us all and king of kings,
enlighten me. What is your secret will?
War and battle, worse and more of it,
or can you not impose a pact on both?"

The summoner of cloud replied:

      "My child,
why this formality of inquiry?
Did you not plan that action by yourself—
see to it that Odysseus, on his homecoming,   530
should have their blood?

      Conclude it as you will.
There is one proper way, if I may say so:
Odysseus' honor being satisfied,
let him be king by a sworn pact forever,
and we, for our part, will blot out the memory
of sons and brothers slain. As in the old time
let men of Ithaka henceforth be friends;
prosperity enough, and peace attend them."

Athena needed no command, but down   540
in one spring she descended from Olympos
just as the company of Odysseus finished
wheat crust and honeyed wine, and heard him say:

"Go out, someone, and see if they are coming."

One of the boys went to the door as ordered
and saw the townsmen in the lane. He turned
swiftly to Odysseus.

                              "Here they come,"
he said, "best arm ourselves, and quickly."

All up at once, the men took helm and shield—   550
four fighting men, counting Odysseus,
with Dólios' half dozen sons. Laërtês
armed as well, and so did Dólios—
greybeards, they could be fighters in a pinch.
Fitting their plated helmets on their heads
they sallied out, Odysseus in the lead.

Now from the air Athena, Zeus's daughter,
appeared in Mentor's guise, with Mentor's voice,
making Odysseus' heart grow light. He said
to put cheer in his son: 560

                              "Telémakhos,
you are going into battle against pikemen
where hearts of men are tried. I count on you
to bring no shame upon your forefathers.
In fighting power we have excelled this lot
in every generation."

                    Said his son:

"If you are curious, Father, watch and see
the stuff that's in me. No more talk of shame."

And old Laërtês cried aloud: 570

"Ah, what a day for me, dear gods!
to see my son and grandson vie in courage!"

Athena halted near him, and her eyes
shone like the sea. She said:

                              "Arkeísiadês,
dearest of all my old brothers-in-arms,
invoke the grey-eyed one and Zeus her father,
heft your spear and make your throw."

Power flowed into him from Pallas Athena,
whom he invoked as Zeus's virgin child,   580
and he let fly his heavy spear.
                              It struck
Eupeíthês on the cheek plate of his helmet,
and undeflected the bronze head punched through.
He toppled, and his armor clanged upon him.
Odysseus and his son now furiously
closed, laying on with broadswords, hand to hand,
and pikes: they would have cut the enemy down
to the last man, leaving not one survivor,
had not Athena raised a shout   590
that stopped all fighters in their tracks.

                    "Now hold!"
she cried. "Break off this bitter skirmish;
end your bloodshed, Ithakans, and make peace."

Their faces paled with dread before Athena,
and swords dropped from their hands unnerved, to lie
strewing the ground, at the great voice of the goddess.
Those from the town turned fleeing for their lives.
But with a cry to freeze their hearts
and ruffling like an eagle on the pounce,   600
the lord Odysseus reared himself to follow—
at which the son of Kronos dropped a thunderbolt
smoking at his daughter's feet.
                              Athena
cast a grey glance at her friend and said:

"Son of Laërtês and the gods of old,
Odysseus, master of land ways and sea ways,

command yourself. Call off this battle now,
or Zeus who views the wide world may be angry."

He yielded to her, and his heart was glad.   610
Both parties later swore to terms of peace
set by their arbiter, Athena, daughter
of Zeus who bears the stormcloud as a shield—
though still she kept the form and voice of Mentor.

NOTE

Line numbers at the head of each page throughout this book refer to the Greek text. A few lines thought spurious or out of place in antiquity, and later, have been omitted from the translation. These are:

Book I, lines 275 through 278 and 356 through 359.
Book IX, line 483.
Book XI, line 245.
Book XIII, lines 320 and 321.
Book XIV, line 154, lines 161 and 162, lines 504 through 506.
Book XVI, line 101.
Book XVII, line 402.
Book XXIII, line 320.

The translator wishes to record his gratitude for aid of various kinds. A Guggenheim Fellowship helped him to begin; a Ford grant helped him to finish. Dudley Fitts and Sally Fitzgerald read and commented invaluably on the entire work in the course of writing. About half of the poem benefited from close readings by Andrew Chiappe, Jason Epstein, and John F. Nims. Valuable corrections and suggestions were given on shorter sections by John Berryman, Colin G. Hardie, Michael Jameson, Randall Jarrell, Priscilla Jenkins, and John Crowe Ransom. One salutary blast came from Ezra Pound. For the patient publisher, Anne Freedgood gave the manuscript a discerning reading.

POSTSCRIPT

SOME DETAILS OF SCENE AND ACTION

I

The ship on which I sailed from Piraeus one summer night approached Odysseus' kingdom from the south in the early morning. Emerging on deck of the occasion, I saw a mile or so to the west the bright flank of a high island, broadside to the rising sun. This was Kephallenia, identified by tradition with Samê of *The Odyssey;* in fact the port where we presently put in is called Samê. Beyond it to the north and dead ahead rose another island mass, lying from northwest to southeast and therefore visible only on its western side, all shadow, a dark silhouette. This was Thiaki or Ithaka.

Now, one of the innumerable questions never quite settled by students of Homer is the intended meaning of these two lines, concerning Ithaka and neighboring islands, in Book IX of *The Odyssey* (lines 25 and 26):

αὐτὴ δὲ χθαμαλὴ πανυπερτάτη εἰν ἁλὶ κεῖται
πρὸς ζόφον, αἱ δέ τ᾽ ἄνευθε πρὸς ἠῶ τ᾽ ἠέλιόν τε.

Uncertainties ramify handsomely in the first line, but let me confine myself here to the second, which literally means, or appears to mean, that Ithaka lies "toward the gloom, while the other islands lie apart toward the Dawn and the Sun." Long before my Ithakan landfall I knew that this line has been thought simply inaccurate. But when I saw the islands with my own eyes in the morning light I felt at once that I had discovered the image behind Homer's words. He, too, I felt sure, had looked ahead over a ship's bow at that hour and had seen those land masses, one sunny and one in gloom, just as I saw them. An overnight sail from Pylos would have brought him there at the right time.

This notion was, of course, highly exhilarating. I am sorry that further consideration has more or less deflated it. One trouble with it was that Homer (or Odysseus, the speaker in this passage) did not describe Ithaka as being itself shadowy or gloomy but as lying in a certain direction, "toward" the "gloom." If the contrast between Ithaka and Samê at sunrise had been in his mind, he could have put it more distinctly. Not that Homer is always lucid grammatically, but "toward the gloom" for "in gloom" is not his kind of vagueness. Then, too, the word ζόφος in Homer does not mean simply gloom; it means the gloom of one end of the world, one quarter of the compass, generally held by the ancients to be the west. ἤδη γὰρ φάος οἴχεθ᾽ ὑπὸ ζόφον says Athena in Book III, 335, "The sun has gone down already under the gloom [of the west]," and Odysseus asks Elpênor in Book XI, 57, πῶς ἦλθες ὑπὸ ζόφον ἠερόεντα, "How did you come down under the cloudy gloom [of the world's end]?"

It would be excellent if these clear instances were also conclusive, and πρὸς ζόφον were to be translated "toward the west" or "toward the western gloom." But here precisely is the difficulty. Ithaka does not in fact lie "west" of the other islands in the group. Neither does Leukas, the more northerly island that some students have believed to be Homer's Ithaka. So far as Ithaka itself is concerned, the fact is that the northern horn of Kephallenia, across a channel a mile or so wide, reaches up along the length of the island to the west. How now?

Well, it must be recalled that Homer knew no other west than the direction of sunset, and in midsummer, in that latitude, the sun goes down at a spot on the horizon far north of true west. Whether the poet was an Ionian or an Athenian, he is unlikely to have visited the islands except in the sailing season. Homer's sunset quarter could have been roughly northwest by west. This very nearly solves the difficulty, but perhaps not quite. If we are still a few points off, so to speak, I am glad to say that recourse may be had to the Greek geographer, Strabo.

According to Lord Rennell of Rodd, in the Annual of the British School in Athens, No. xxxiii, Session 1932-33, Strabo "entertained no doubt" that in the line I have quoted, ζόφος "indicated the north, as the Sun does the south." That is to say, Strabo and Lord Rennell pass lightly over the antithesis between ζόφος and Dawn in that line of Homer in order to embrace the antithesis between ζόφος and the Sun, whose usual path in north latitudes passes south of the zenith. Most of Kephallenia does indeed lie to the south of Ithaka, and so does the island now called Zante, very likely the Zakynthos of *The Odyssey*. As for Doulikhion, Rennell and others rather desperately identify it with one of the small Ekhinades to the east.

Pondering this argument, I asked myself why each of the antitheses noted in the phrase should not be given equal value, or half of full value. Granted that Ithaka is "west" with respect to Doulikhion and "north" with respect to Zakynthos and Samê-Kephallenia, then πρὸς ζόφον could be briefly rendered "to the northwest," and the other islands πρὸς ἠῶ τ' ἠέλιόν τε could be said to "lie east and south." Here I left this question.

II

If you will do an hour or two of hard climbing on Ithaka you can reach the spinal ridge of the island and there, while you cool off, you can look across the blue channel to the west at the steep side of Samê a mile away. Close in to the other shore you will see a tiny islet known as Daskalion. This, with no great satisfaction, the commentators identify with Asteris, the small island behind which the suitors in their long boat lay in wait for Telémakhos at the end of Book IV. This identification in turn depends on another, that of a small round cove on the west side of Ithaka, somewhat north of the islet, as the harbor from which Telémakhos put out on his evening voyage. The longer I looked at this setting the more quarrelsome I felt with received opinion. It is true that at first glance all the requisites are there: the channel, the islet, the harbor. I am afraid, of course, that received opinion may be right. But on this point I have remained cranky and fond of my private reasons for dissent.

It appears that Polis Bay, as the round cove is tendentiously named, was once larger, and that it was a port of call in the classical period for Greek ships passing up the channel, outward bound for Italy. This fact of itself seems to me irrelevant if we are concerned to find the port of Ithaka at the time of the Trojan War, long before colonization or commerce with Italy, or even in Homer's time, late in the eighth century, when voyages to the western Mediterranean had just begun. The harbor described in

The Odyssey serves, above all, ships that ply to and from Elis, the mainland of the Peloponnesus to the southeast, and Thesprotia, or Acarnania, to the east. It was from the southeast that my ship, the S. S. Miaoulis, arrived, and the Miaoulis put me ashore at Vathy on the deep harbor of the same name (it means "deep"). This is the longest and best sheltered of three bays opening southward off the wide Gulf of Molos, which runs inward from east to west and almost cuts Ithaka in two. Along the quay of Vathy in the evening I saw open caïques from the mainland unloading cattle in slings. From pasture land to the stony island, pastureless, the caïques had brought these cows to be slaughtered for Ithakan markets. Here was a ferry service exactly like the one alluded to in Book XX, 187, of *The Odyssey*. As the Gulf of Molos is the roadstead of Ithaka, Vathy is its natural harbor—or at least so it seems to the ferrymen, to the Greek steamship company, and to me.

But how could Vathy have been the port from which Telémakhos sailed, if on leaving it he would have had to issue eastward by the Gulf of Molos into the open sea, passing through no channel between Ithaka and Samê? This objection would be insuperable if Homer had been an Ithakan. Since he surely was not, but was a visitor like myself, I think it worth reporting that on the day after my arrival I had another visual revelation. From high ground on the north part of Ithaka I saw a small island, perfectly satisfying Homer's description of Asteris, that seemed to lie between Ithaka and Samê to the south. I said to my guide, "What island is that?" "Oh, that is Attako," he said. I looked at my map, which showed Attako lying in the sea to the east of Itahaka. "Are you sure?" said I. "Of course, I'm sure, I've been fishing there many times." No one would have guessed from the map that from the northeast height of Ithaka, looking south, you see this islet against the background of what appears to be another island mass but is in fact the southern part of Ithaka. What looks like a "channel" is the mouth of the Gulf of Molos.

My surmise is that Homer on his peregrination over Odysseus' island made mistakes like mine, that he confused the Gulf of Molos with the channel between Ithaka and Samê, and that his islet "Asteris" is the island Attako, not the tiny rock called Daskalion. Do not suppose that my theory lacks textual support. Attako has high ground from which the suitors could have kept their watch (XVI, 365); Daskalion has not. Moreover, to bear out my identification of Vathy with Telémakhos' harbor, I can refer to at least one detail of his embarkation. Athena is said to have moored his ship "at the harbor's edge," in Book II, 391 ἐπ' ἐσχατιῇ λιμένος, and once he had shoved off she sent him a following wind that took him out to sea. From what quarter blew this wind? From the west, for it is expressly called Ζέφυρος, the west wind, in II, 420–21. This is just the wind you would need astern if you wanted to put out from the mouth of Vathy Bay, but if you were putting out from Polis Bay it would blow you right back in.

It can be urged against me that the stern wind supplied by Athena lasted all night and took Telémakhos' ship all the way to Pylos. A steady wind from the west would have taken him not south to Pylos, but east, let us say, to Missolonghi. Perhaps, as I have myself argued that Homer's west lay in a more northerly quarter, his Zephyr also blew from that quarter and would serve a ship sailing from Polis Bay down the channel between Ithaka and Samê. I do not, of course, see why it could not have been the west wind at the start and have changed direction during the night, but in the end I compromised in deference to the established view. It is a northwest wind in my text. I may add that on my second evening at Vathy the wind freshened from that direction and, blowing over open water, made a fluttering and percussive effect in my eardrums—not entirely agreeable—like the noise of Homer's line for it:

ἀκραῆ Ζέφυρον, κελάδοντ' ἐπὶ οἴνοπα πόντον.

III

The notes may suggest some of the pleasures and complexities of going to see for yourself. I would be a fool to plume myself on my dip into those studies on ancient sites that have occupied good men and women for years. But I am forever grateful for my days on Ithaka as I am for other days, few but moving, in Athens and elsewhere in Greece. A rendering for the opening of Book III,

Ἥλιος δ' ἀνόρουσε, λιπὼν περικαλλέα λίμνην

came into my head in the Saronic Gulf, and a week later at sunrise in Heraklion I found words for the next phrase, οὐρανὸν ἐς πολύχαλκον. By these and other keepsakes I am reminded that if I had never listened to the cicadas and drunk the resined wine I would have done the job differently, if I had done it at all. But most of it was what all writing is, a sedentary labor, or joy, sustained at a worktable. At one elbow, in this case, there were always those lines and parts of lines that have been pored over by so many for centuries. Of the puzzling ones I will give a few more examples, two at least of them notorious, with some account of the elucidation I think they demand. Multiply these cases by a thousand, and you will see what the preliminary or incidental work was like. As befits a dramatic poem, the first case is a tiny detail of action.

In Book XI Odysseus hears the shade of Agamémnon tell how Aigísthos and Klytaimnestra murdered him on his return from Troy, and with him his companions. They were all butchered, he says bitterly, like swine. I take it that he means what he says. The way you butcher a pig is by piercing or cutting its throat, and it does not seem unreasonable to imagine here, and to bear in mind elsewhere, that this is what happened to Agamémnon. He describes the banquet scene, the laden tables, and the floor fuming with blood where the victims lay. Then, in line 421, he says he heard a most piteous cry from his royal slave and mistress, Kassandra,

> τὴν κτεῖνε Κλυταιμνήστη δολόμητις
> ἀμφ᾽ ἐμοί, αὐτὰρ ἐγώ ποτὶ γαίῃ χεῖρας ἀείρων
> βάλλον ἀποθνῄσκων περὶ φασγάνῳ

and great difficulty has been found in grasping precisely what action this passage was meant to convey. Klytaimnestra was in the act of killing Kassandra, so much is clear, and Kassandra was close beside the fallen Agamémnon. But what does he say he himself was doing? Consider it word for word in the order in which it appears: "but I upon (or against) the ground lifting my hands / was throwing [them] while dying around the swordblade." Half the problem is to divide or punctuate this.

On one prevailing interpretation we should divide or punctuate after βάλλον and must therefore take ἀποθνῄσκων περὶ φασγάνῳ to mean "dying around the swordblade," that is, with a blade left in his body. This is contrary to slaughtering procedure, but Professor W. B. Stanford in his annotated edition of *The Odyssey* tells us that there are many precedents for taking it so.

He refers to four passages in *The Iliad* and to one in Sophocles'
Ajax. With all respect I must say that none of these makes a good
precedent for Stanford's reading, because in none of them does
anyone die "around a swordblade" left in him by anyone else.
Ajax has, of course, impaled himself on his own sword. Of the
cases cited in *The Iliad*, one is concerned with an arrow and two
with spears, weapons often left sticking in tenacious parts of the
foe. It is otherwise with a sword; a sword in these poems was
something a killer held onto if he could. The fourth case in *The
Iliad* might be a better precedent, not for Stanford's notion of
Agamémnon's wound but for mine (since it is an allusion to
slaughtering), if the preposition used were not ἀμφὶ instead of
περί. In short, the evidence is inconclusive.

Moreover, if you adopt this awkward reading, you are left with
a clause that represents Agamémnon as lifting his hands and
throwing them. With what purpose? Or perhaps I should ask,
with what aim? Victor Bérard imagined that he meant to shield
Kassandra. A. T. Murray, the Loeb translator, thought he tried
to hit Klytaimnestra. Butcher and Lang, W. H. D. Rouse, and
T. E. Lawrence accepted "let fall" as a translation of βάλλον: he
lifted his hands and helplessly let them fall. Others, including
Stanford, take ποτὶ γαίῃ as "against the ground" with βάλλον
and suggest that he beat his hands against the ground to invoke
vengeance from infernal powers.

I cannot myself hear the shade of the hero saying any of these
things, except possibly what Murray has him say. But it is quite
possible to punctuate the lines in another way, like this: "But I
upon the ground, lifting my hands, was throwing them—while
dying—around the swordblade." Or to put it in English, "As I
lay on the ground I heaved up my hands and flung them with a
dying effort around the swordblade." There is a scholion in which
the lines are so understood, but the scholiast adds πρὸς ἐκσπάσαι
τὸ ξίφος, "to pull out the sword"—no doubt in order to die more
quickly. G. H. Palmer, one of the few translators to follow the
scholiast, settled for "clutched" as a rendering for βάλλον. This
was logical, since Palmer, like the Alexandrian and like Stanford,
conceived the blade as embedded in Agamémnon. A man with a
blade in his midriff would not "fling" his hands around it when
all he had to do was, precisely, to clutch it. But βάλλον is stronger
than "clutch," and the sword was not in Agamémnon, in any case.

He would have had to heave up and fling his hands around the blade if the blade were a short distance away, within reach but still requiring an effort. This is where the sword of Klytaimnestra must have been while she slashed or poked at Kassandra. Therefore I prefer to think that as Klytaimnestra used the sword, Agamémnon, reckless of his hands, tried to get it away from her. Alone among modern translators, so far as I can discover, E. V. Rieu adopted this reading. It not only satisfies all the conditions, syntactical and verbal, but it makes all possible dramatic sense of the line.

IV

If you think of the poem as a play or a cinema—inevitable if not irresistible thoughts—you will find many problems for the set designer and the property man. There are two fine ones in the big closing scenes. How precisely are we to visualize the contest with Odysseus' hunting bow, announced by Penélopê in Book XIX and carried out in Book XXI? And in Book XXII what precisely is the layout of the great hall and adjoining passage by which the suitors, for the moment out of sight of Odysseus, are given throwing spears at a crucial point in the fight? The Greek is ambiguous or sketchy.

In XIX Penélopê tells her interesting new confidant of a sudden decision: next day her suitors will be challenged to perform an old feat of her husband's, and she will be the prize. It is a feat (line 573) with πελέκεας, axes,

τοὺς πελέκεας, τοὺς κεῖνος ἐνὶ μεγάροισιν ἑοῖσιν

ἵστασχ' ἑξείης, δρυόχους ὥς, δώδεκα πάντας.

στὰς δ' ὅ γε πολλὸν ἄνευθε διαρρίπτασκεν ὀιστόν.

"those axes that he used to set up in his hall all twelve in line like a ship's ribs (or props), then he would take his stand far off and shoot an arrow through." The prize will go to that suitor who most easily strings her husband's bow and "shoots through all twelve axes." To this Odysseus replies in effect that tomorrow is not too soon; her husband will be there before any of the younger men can string the bow διοϊστεῦσαί τε σιδήρον "and shoot through the iron." It need not escape us that this phrase is rather an addition. We might imagine shooting through twelve axes if they were arranged in a line slightly staggered, leaving an interval of an inch or so for the arrow to pass. The alternative is to imagine apertures in the axeheads, and the phrase of Odysseus, repeated by Telémakhos in Book XXI, inclines us to that. He speaks with familiarity, not to mention his remarkable confidence. It is not the speech of a man still interested in concealing from his wife how well he knows her husband.

If the arrow is to pass "through the iron" and we interpret this to mean through apertures in the axeheads, then what apertures are meant? D. B. Monro in his edition of *The Odyssey*, Books XIII–XXIV, printed drawings of two perforated ancient axeheads, one from a Mycenean excavation, another from an early classical metope, and a third drawing of the very late classical *bipennis*, a double axe whose crescent blades form by their inner edges two circular openings, the one above the haft open and unobstructed. An arrow could pass through any one of these types of axeheads. With archaelogical backing, then, we may imagine twelve pervious axes in alignment for the contest. Penélopê's phrase, "like a ship's ribs (or props)," in fact makes us see twelve axes stuck in the ground by their helves.

Oddly enough, there are quite serious objections to this reading. When we say "axe" we mean axehead and helve together. But it seems more likely that the word πέλεκυς to Penélopê meant "axehead" alone. In Book V when Kalypso gives Odysseus a πέλεκυς for cutting timber, she must complete the gift with a στειλειόν, or helve of olive wood (line 236). In all the references to the gauntlet Odysseus' arrow had to run, there is no allusion to a στειλειόν though a closely related word appears. On the contrary, when Penélopê brings the bow back from the storeroom in XXI, 58, her maids bring along a basket full of iron and bronze "accessories of the contest," certainly axeheads without helves. Any normal axehead, then as now, had an aperture: it had the socket hole where a helve could be fitted. Is there positive evidence that this was the aperture in question: There is indeed.

When Odysseus finally makes his prize-winning shot in XXI, 420 sqq., we hear that

πελέκεων δ' οὐκ ἤμβροτε πάντων
πρώτης στειλειῆς, διὰ δ' ἀμπερὲς ἦλθε θύραζε.

"he didn't miss the πρώτης στειλειῆς of all the axeheads, and the arrow went clean through and out." Confusion about the word στειλειή appears to be ancient and inexhaustible; it was taken very early to mean "helve" or "haft"—that is, to be a synonym for στειλειόν—and translators in torment have tried to make sense of a shot that did not miss the first axe helve. But if Homer had meant that, if he had meant πρώτου στειλειοῦ, he could have said it. It is metrically equivalent and phonetically a little better. Professor Stanford thinks, and with excellent reason, that the difference in gender may be significant. He agrees with the twelfth century Archbishop of Thessalonica, Eustathius, that the feminine form, στειλειή, meant "socket" as στειλειόν meant "helve." What Homer intended to say was very simple: that Odysseus didn't miss his bull's eye, the first socket hole in the line of twelve.

It is a perfect conclusion, but it lets us in for other difficulties. If the axeheads were without helves, if each was turned so that its socket hole faced the archer, how were they set up and supported? In what respect was the line of axeheads comparable to "a ship's ribs (or props)"? The second question is easier to answer: the point of similarity could have been merely that in both cases there were equal intervals between one and another. As to the way of setting up the axeheads, all we have to go on are two lines and a half, XXI, 120 sqq., in which Telémakhos prepares the contest:

πρῶτον μὲν πελέκεας στῆσεν, διὰ τάφρον ὀρύξας
πᾶσι μίαν μακρήν, καὶ ἐπὶ στάθμην ἴθυνεν,
ἀμφὶ δὲ γαῖαν ἔναξε

Literally, "first he set up the axeheads, after digging a trench through for all, a single trench, a long one, and he trued [it or them] to the line, and he pressed earth on both sides." It is pertinent to remember that in Homer's "additive" style items are not always given in any particular order. That is, the pressing of the earth could have preceded or accompanied the truing, and we may understand that he trued the axeheads, not the trench. If we held the theory that axeheads fitted on helves were being set up, a trench would bed the helves, around which earth could then be pressed to hold them upright. I have given the evidence against that. On the other and better theory that axeheads alone were used, is there anything in the context to suggest how they were held up?

Well, a byproduct of a trench is a long pile of loose earth. If the loose earth beside the trench were "pressed" up in a narrow ridge, with peaks at equal distances, the axeheads could be stuck in these, one blade in the earth and one out, since the πέλεκυς was double-bladed. The verb νάσσω that appears here in the aorist active, ἔναξε, "pressed," had the sense "be piled" in the passive in later Greek. The very point of digging a trench could have been to supply enough earth for this purpose; if it had been a matter of embedding axe helves, they could have been planted in a line of holes like fence posts or fruit trees. It is a good deal to read into these lines, but I am willing to risk it because I see nothing else for it. Telémakhos made a bedding of earth for the axeblades and trued them ἐπὶ στάθμην, "to the line," by the wall builder's immemorial technique, a stretched cord. One more question: if set up in this way, could the axeheads have been high enough for the bowshot from the door? Odysseus made the bowshot while seated on his stool. He held the bow horizontally in the usual ancient style. If he shot from the hip just above knee level in a flat trajectory, the axeheads as I see them could have been at the right height.

v

If those passages needed unfolding, more unfolding still must be done to render with clarity the several lines beginning at 126 of Book XXII—a sketch for a ground plan or a stage set. Odysseus has been doing execution with his bow while Telémakhos has brought arms from the storeroom; now all the arrows are gone, and father and son and the two herdsmen arm themselves for combat with spears. The narrative continues:

ὀρσοθύρη δέ τις ἔσκεν ἐϋδμήτῳ ἐνὶ τοίχῳ
ἀκρότατον δὲ παρ' οὐδὸν ἐϋσταθέος μεγάροιο
ἦν ὁδὸς ἐς λαύρην, σανίδες δ' ἔχον εὖ ἀραρυῖαι

"There was a certain ὀρσοθύρη in the well-built wall. And at the edge [or along the top] of the threshold of the hall there was an entry way into the passage, and well-fitted folding doors kept it closed." This is all baffling, and the editors have left it so. We wish to know what the ὀρσοθύρη was and in which wall it was located. We also wish to know what if anything the ὀρσοθύρη had to do with the passage, where the passage ran, and where precisely the "entry way" opened into it. These lines do not tell us. But we can learn some of the answers from the action that now takes place.

First, Odysseus tells the swineherd to stand over near the "entry way" and guard it, μία δ᾽ οἴη γίγνετ᾽ ἐφορμή, "for there was only one way in." Why guard it? Because it must be a possible exit for the suitors who have been under fire at the other end of the hall—the only possible exit, we gather, besides the main door where Odysseus and Telémakhos have taken their stand. Now one of the surviving suitors, Ageláos, says to the others,

 Ὦ φίλοι, οὐκ ἂν δή τις ἀν᾽ ὀρσοθύρην ἀναβαίη
 καὶ εἴποι λαοῖσι

"Friends, why doesn't someone climb up by the ὀρσοθύρη and tell the townsmen?" From this it is clear that by climbing through the ὀρσοθύρη you could get into the passage and out by the door where the swineherd has been posted. Out where? If ἀκρότατον δὲ παρ᾽ οὐδὸν is taken to mean "along the top" of the threshold inside the main door, any man issuing at that point would run into the arms of Odysseus and company. It must mean "at the edge" of the threshold outside the entrance. If this were not the meaning, the swineherd would not have had to move to be in a position to guard the "entry way." His movement, incidentally, seems to have escaped notice by Ageláos, who has also failed to see that Odysseus has no more arrows. The goatherd, Melánthios, answers him:

 οὔ πως ἔστ᾽, Ἀγέλαε διοτρεφές. ἄγχι γὰρ αἰνῶς
 αὐλῆς καλὰ θύρετρα καὶ ἀργαλέον στόμα λαύρης.
 καί χ᾽ εἷς πάντας ἐρύκοι ἀνήρ, ὅς τ᾽ ἄλκιμος εἴη.

"It can't be done. The fair door of the courtyard is terribly near [or the fair door is terribly near the courtyard] and the mouth of the passage is hard [to force]; one man alone if he were strong could hold off all of us." If the mouth of the passage is hard to force, it must be a narrow passage, narrow as a catwalk. Melánthios' remark that one strong man could hold it suggests that he has seen Odysseus order the swineherd outside. All this is fairly clear. But precisely what is "terribly near" to what? That is not so clear.

Monro and Stanford thought Melánthios meant that the gate into the courtyard from the road was near—near to Odysseus, or near to the exit from the passage. Since the gate is in fact on the other side of the courtyard, these editors thought it could be called "terribly near" only from the point of view of a man in fear of archery as he crossed the courtyard. I find this interpretation strange. A man thinking of making a run under fire would complain of how far the gate seemed, not how near. It may be irrelevant that there can be no more archery, anyway, for Odysseus is out of arrows; Melánthios, like Ageláos, may not have noticed this (neither Monro nor Stanford appears to have noticed it, either). But I doubt that αὐλῆς θύρετρα necessarily or even possibly means the gate from the road into the courtyard. The word θύραι has been used for this. Here is a different word whose proper meaning is certainly "door" and not "gate." It could mean the door from the passageway into the courtyard, and I think it does. To what or whom is that door terribly near? To Odysseus, who has already posted a guard there. On this interpretation these lines cohere.

Melánthios proposes to bring the suitors arms from the storeroom, and he climbs

ἐς θαλάμους Ὀδυσῆος ἀνὰ ῥῶγας μεγάροιο

"up the breaks of the hall and into the storeroom of Odysseus." The ῥῶγας or "breaks" have been thought to be steps, but steps are κλίμακες. A closer reading would be "fissures" or chinks in the wall, toe holds for a goatherd. Although it is not expressly mentioned at this point, there is no doubt that the aperture to which he climbs is the ὀρσοθύρη, and I should now note that etymologically this word almost certainly means a "raised door" or window. Since his destination is the storeroom, it follows not only that this window-opening gives on the passage by which Ageláos thought someone might get out, but that the passage itself leads to the storeroom at the back of the house. It is the same passage by which at the beginning of the slaughter Telémakhos ran to get arms for his father and friends. From the passage, through the window, Melánthios can hand out arms to the suitors.

Where is the ὀρσοθύρη? At the far end of the hall from the entrance, as stands to reason and as we learn explicitly later on in line 333 from the position of Phêmios, the harper, when the fight is over. It must be a window in one of the side walls, for two reasons. First, the passage that it lights and ventilates runs along the side of the hall from front to rear. Second, one of the side walls could have a recessed part like a shallow transept, not visible from the entrance. The context requires this. The ὀρσοθύρη and all that happens there are out of sight of Odysseus. The young men harried by his shooting would have huddled on the other side of any angle in the wall that offered shelter, and there the ὀρσοθύρη would have come to their attention. Odysseus may well have had this in mind when he ordered the passage guarded. But why didn't one of the suitors use the ὀρσοθύρη instead of letting the goatherd work for them? The question as framed almost answers itself: they were accustomed to service. There may be another reason, too. One of the scholia on the ὀρσοθύρη informs us that

ὑψηλοτέρα ἦν ἐφ᾽ ᾗ ἦν ὀροῦσαι καὶ ἀναθορεῖν

"it was quite high; you had to make a jump to get up to it." Perhaps jumping for a hole in the wall was beneath the dignity of Akhaian gentlemen with flowing hair.

VI

Details like these may turn out to be self-consistent, but what of the poem as a whole? Does it hang together? Did a single composer hold it all in his mind? Whatever opinion we may hold on the famous Question, we may accept at least one modest principle: When proof to the contrary is lacking, any given passage should be interpreted in consonance with the rest. Take the eagles.

During the assembly scene in Book II, Zeus launches two eagles from a ridge, either τῷ δ᾽ or τώ δ᾽ according to the alternative readings. The Oxford editor, T. W. Allen, reasonably chose the first, meaning "for him," that is, for the last speaker, Telémakhos. The eagles are to be an omen for him. When in their gliding flight they reach a point over the center of the agora they wheel and beat their wings, and then we have two more alternative readings, ἐς δ᾽ ἰδέτην πάντων κεφαλάς or ἐς δ᾽ ἱκέτην πάντων κεφαλάς, that is, either the pair "looked at the heads of all [below]" or they "came down on" all the heads. Again Allen chose the reading more charged with life and sense: "came down on." In the next clause, ὄσσοντο δ᾽ ὄλεθρον, the verb has changed from the dual form, used when the pair of birds was the subject, to a plural form. Does this mean a change of subject? Not necessarily; Homer often uses plural verb forms for dual subjects;

indeed he has already done so once in this passage, though not in this sentence. If it does mean a change of subject, then the "heads," or men in the crowd, are said to behold death or doom in the diving eagles; if it does not mean a change of subject, the diving eagles are said to make doom visible to the men, or in a word to menace them with doom. "Death was in their glare," as Murray ingeniously puts it, making perhaps the best of both alternatives. Perhaps, but wait. The next line presents us again with a dual form, this time in a middle participle. It goes:

δρυψαμένω δ' ὀνύχεσσι παρειὰς ἀμφί τε δειρὰς

"tearing, this pair, with talons, cheeks and all around necks (or throats)."

Now, the received interpretation of this, cited by Liddell & Scott and followed by Murray and practically everyone, takes the middle voice of the verb as reflexive here, meaning they tore *each other's* cheeks and throats. But first let me observe that the middle may or may not have this shade of meaning. It is the voice you would use in Greek if you wanted to say, "We cut ourselves a slice," and you would not be referring to a knife fight. Second, if the two eagles are a sign, what after all do they signify? What future event do they portend? The old augur Halithersês has no doubt, and neither have we: they stand for the return of Odysseus and the doom of the suitors. Why two eagles? In order that the sign, a sign for Telémakhos, may give him, or at any rate ourselves, to understand that he and Odysseus together will attack the suitors. The two eagles correspond to the two royal assailants. Why then should they assail one another? What would any intelligent augur make of that? No, no, surely; they assail the suitors, who have been arraigned by Telémakhos in the assembly, and if this were not the case there would be no point in their having "come down on the heads of all," for an eagle fight would have been as well or better conducted high in the air. A scholiast says, τὸ δὲ καταδρύψαι τὰς παρειὰς τὸν τῶν μνηστήρων ἐσήμανε φόνον, and *he* does not use the middle but the active voice: "that business of tearing the [suitors'] cheeks signified the suitors' violent death." We are to see the eagles' portent not merely "in their glare" but in their ripping talons.

Between Book II and Book XV no eagles fly, or at any rate no significant ones, but in Book XV, 160, as Telémakhos is taking leave of Meneláos and Helen, just as he is saying how fine it

would be to meet his father on Ithaka so that he could tell him
of their hospitality, ἐπέπτατο δεξιὸς ὄρνις, αἰετὸς ἀργὴν χῆνα
φέρων "a bird, an eagle, flew up on the right, lugging a white
goose." This portent is quickly interpreted by Helen. It means,
she says, that just as the eagle flew from the wild mountain of his
birth to pounce on the domestic bird, so Odysseus will appear
out of the rough world of his wanderings to avenge the wrongs
done him at home. Near the end of the same Book (525 sqq.) the
motif is repeated. Again the omen appears as if in comment on a
speech by Telémakhos, who has just been wondering aloud
whether anything will prevent his mother's marriage to Eurý-
makhos. This time the portentous bird is not an eagle, αἰετός,
but a hawk, κίρκος, carrying a captured dove. And this time the
interpretation is not given immediately; it is given to Penélopê
in Book XVII (152 sqq.) by the diviner, Theoklýmenos, who tells
her it meant that Odysseus had already landed on Ithaka. Again
there is an interval of two Books, and in XIX (535 sqq.) the motif
comes to a kind of flowering when Penélopê recounts her "dream"
to the beggar, who is Odysseus. This time there is a more exact
correspondence between the terms of the equation; Penélopê was
in a position to be exact. Upon the geese feeding at her house

ἐλθὼν δ᾽ ἐξ ὄρεος μέγας αἰετὸς ἀγκυλοχείλης

πᾶσι κατ᾽ αὐχένας ἧξε καὶ ἔκτανεν

"coming from the mountain a great eagle with crooked beak broke
their necks and killed them all."

Thus in four passages the descent of Odysseus on the suitors
has been foreboded or foreseen in strikes made by birds of prey.
In three cases the attacking birds are eagles; once it is a hawk.
The appearance of the motif twice in Book XVII and once again
in Book XIX harks back to its introduction in Book II. It also
anticipates the climax of the flight in Odysseus' hall in Book XXII.
At that point Athena unfurls her storm cloud, the aegis, overhead,
and the surviving suitors break and run like cattle stung by
gadflies. Now (302) comes the simile:

οἱ δ᾽ ὥς τ᾽ αἰγυπιοὶ γαμψώνυχες ἀγκυλοχεῖλαι

ἐξ ὀρέων ἐλθόντες ἐπ᾽ ὀρνίθεσσι θόρωσι, κτλ

"But the pursuers, like αἰγυπιοί with hooked talons and crooked
beak issuing from the mountains to dive on flights of birds, etc."
We had expected eagles, αἰετοί, or hawks, κίρκοι, but the word
is αἰγυπιοί, and I am distressed to say that the usual translation

of that is "vultures." Liddell & Scott give "vulture" for αἰγυπιός. But let us consider the case patiently. We have not met the word before in *The Odyssey*. Liddell & Scott and the Homeric lexicographer, Autenrieth, cite three occurrences in *The Iliad*. In Book VII, 59, when Athena and Apollo are represented as taking their seats on the oak of Zeus as Hektor challenges the Akhaians,

ἑζέσθην ὄρνισιν ἐοικότες αἰγυπιοῖσι

"They perched like birds, like αἰγυπιοί." In Book XVII, 460, Automedon making chariot forays among the Trojans is likened to an αἰγυπιός among geese. Most interesting of all is the case in Book XVI, 428, when Patroklos and Sarpedon clash in battle— for here the first line of the simile is the very same line that we find represented in *The Odyssey:*

οἱ δ᾽ ὥς τ᾽ αἰγυπιοὶ γαμψώνυχες ἀγκυλοχεῖλαι

πέτρῃ ἐφ᾽ ὑψηλῇ μεγάλα κλάζοντε μάχωνται

"like αἰγυπιοί with hooked talons and crooked beak / on a high rock, crying loud, they fought."

Now, it seems to me that on the Homeric evidence there is something wrong with translating this word as "vulture." A vulture as we understand the term is a carrion bird rather than a hunting bird, and in every context of both *Iliad* and *Odyssey* where a vulture in our sense is clearly indicated Homer uses the word γύψ. In no instance, as we have seen, is αἰγυπιός used of a carrion bird; on the contrary, in two cases, one in *The Iliad* and one our climactic simile in *The Odyssey,* it is used of a hunting bird, and in one of the two remaining cases it supplies a simile for two gods at rest on a bough. If Homer had meant γύψ he could have used γύψ, a handy word and one he used often enough elsewhere. But he used another word, and used it because he unquestionably meant another thing. He meant a bird like a hawk or an eagle, a killer, a treat to geese, a hunter of small birds in general. He did not mean the stinking buzzard that feeds on corpses left by others.

In the first edition of my *Odyssey* I translated αἰγυπιοί in Book XXII as "eagles" to go with the eagle passages that lead up to it. I went too far. If the poet had wished to say "eagles" he could have used the word for eagles, αἰετοί. Instead, he lifted a line from *The Iliad*, as he often did, presumably because it would suit his purpose here. How, then, should αἰγυπιοί be rendered? Well, I see that John Moore, in his recent excellent version of Sophocles' *Ajax*, (The Complete Greek Tragedies, ed. Lattimore

& Grene, Chicago), encountering this problem in line 169,
μέγαν αἰγυπιὸν δ᾽ ὑποδείσαντες, κτλ
translates

> *But fear of the huge falcon, etc.*

possibly in view of considerations like those I have been expounding. In reviewing I have followed his example. I hope Homer would be better pleased. No doubt the four attackers in Book XXII are more justly likened to falcons than to eagles if, as I suspect, falcons more often hunt in company; the wild eagle, unless paired by Zeus, I imagine hunts alone.

SOME GENERAL CONSIDERATIONS

I

An artist in narrative as we know it will have been interested in his art through reading, and he will expect to be read. It is difficult for us to realize what it means that the man who made *The Odyssey* may never have read anything at all. Five or six centuries before his time, in the heroic age of his poem, there had been a Greek syllabary at Mykenai and elsewhere, apparently used mainly for keeping accounts and lists. A memory of this may have survived in a line of *The Iliad*, but the syllabary itself had long gone out of use, and the world of Homer was illiterate. During the eighth century B.C. the people of the Greek mainland and islands imported a Semitic alphabet and began using it, at least for brief inscriptions. If Homer lived to see this, he probably thought of it as a new magic or amusement, almost certainly not as the medium of his work. We can surmise that we owe our text of *Iliad* and *Odyssey* not to Homer but to the importunity of some technician who "took them down," as nowadays a man would do with a tape recorder. Even in the unlikely event that Homer himself wrote out versions of one or both poems, the fact would remain that he and his audience were not readers but auditors of stories in verse.

Dozens of these stories had been told, or sung, among Aegean people for generations before Homer, forming a tradition possibly as old as English literature is now. We may imagine small communities of a feudal sort whose gentry found in the recitation or performance of these tales all history, all theatre, and all that we think of as literary entertainment. The performers were no doubt sometimes amateurs, but more often as time went on they were professionals who spent a lifetime in a hard craft. Our poet came late and had had supremely gifted predecessors. He inherited a traditional art comparable in range and refinement to the art of the musical virtuoso in our day, but more creative and fluid, for in some degree it remained an art of improvisation.

Thirty years ago my teacher and friend Milman Parry showed how many Homeric lines were constructed out of metrical formulas, out of a vocabulary of metrical parts that with slight modification or none would serve in the context of various actions or descriptions. This vocabulary of phrases was like an Erector or Mecanno set for making verse as you went along. Parry and Albert Lord, who has continued his work, studied the similar technique of oral epic still practised in our day in Jugoslavia. Professor Lord's important book, *The Singer of Tales* (Harvard, 1960), is an account of their researches and conclusions, and it is indicated reading for anyone who wants to understand the kind of art that Homer practised. We appear to know more about this art than Plato did. It is a technique rather simply described: many formulas ready in the memory give the storyteller or singer a means of developing action and dialogue as the spirit moves him, with formulaic lines or passages to buoy him up when invention fails. A stringed instrument is indispensable. Meter is indispensable. What Lord calls the "phonological context," the alliterative and voweling pattern, to a certain extent determines invention.

I cannot refer to these studies without making one or two reservations. Parry thought Homer's vocabulary of formulas almost wholly traditional and conventional, but I could never see why originality in detail should be denied a poet to whom it was impossible to deny originality in the large—in conception and organization. I should suppose, too, that although his medium was suited to improvisation, it was no less suited to composition and rehearsal beforehand—an aspect of the matter rather slighted in Parry and Lord. Finally, while statements of the theory sometimes give us to understand that formulaic structure was all-pervasive in both *Iliad* and *Odyssey*, I have yet to see this proved.

My own reading of both poems has left me with the impression that while there are many recurrences and reshapings, there are also many passages without echo or precedent—as we might infer from the fact that many Homeric words occur once and once only.

Our understanding of the Homeric poems, however, has been permanently altered and improved by Parry's work and Lord's, and the famous Homeric Question, the question of single or multiple authorship of *Iliad* and *Odyssey*, will never be the same again. There is little doubt now that from the singers before him Homer had learned not only a rich metrical language but a large repertory of themes. Old themes, like that of the return of heroes, he handled again with joyous elaboration and cunning. It is likely that his compositions, from the nature of the case, varied from one performance to another. No doubt a tale might be told either briefly and broadly or at length and with subtlety, depending on audience and occasion. There was no canonical version.

As Professor Lord puts it: "The theme is in reality protean; in the singer's mind it has many shapes, all the forms in which he has ever sung it, although his latest rendering of it will naturally be freshest in his mind . . . And the shapes that it has taken in the past have been suitable for the song of the moment. In a traditional poem, therefore, there is a pull in two directions: one is toward the song being sung and the other is toward the previous use of the same theme. The result is that characteristic of oral poetry which literary scholars have found hardest to understand and accept, namely, an occasional inconsistency, the famous nod of a Homer."

Our versions of *Iliad* and *Odyssey* must have originated in those versions that at the moment of dictation or recording the performer, whether Homer or a follower of Homer, happened to sing. He may have been more inspired on other occasions, but it is fair to assume that when it came to recording he did his best, and did well. Perhaps on this occasion he chose to record the "long songs" and to restore, so to speak, many cuts often made in performance. Neither poem as we have it could have been recorded at one sitting, and it is possible that long intervals elapsed between the recording of one part and that of another. Given the conditions, and given what Professor Lord calls the protean nature of the themes, we can no longer take inconsistencies in the poems as proof of multiple authorship.

Artist and writer know that any work, ancient or modern, even any masterwork, could easily have been very different from what it is. If you are curious about these matters, you can often see, in drafts and sketches, part at least of the sheaf or spectrum of possible forms of which the "final" version of a story or poem or picture represents a selection—not necessarily or invariably the best—or simply a terminus at which effort stopped. An element of the composite remains in all but the most perfect composition. Of this general truth the Homeric poems are special instances. It is not difficult to see in each poem traces of other stories, or of other versions in which the same stories were handled differently. For more than a century Homeric criticism devoted itself to spotting logical and linguistic discrepancies, discovering one or the other poem to be a "wretched patchwork," in the words of one eminent scholar. While I was engaged on this translation, Professor Denys Page's Bryn Mawr lectues, published as *The Homeric Odyssey* (Oxford, 1955), argued, or reargued, the case against "unity" with asperity and flourish. But many of his points were debater's points, and I doubt that Page realized all the implications of Parry's work or Lord's.

To sum up, *The Odyssey* could well have been composed by one singer, working with themes he had heard from others, in a medium developed by others; if single in one sense, the authorship was certainly multiple in another. There is no way of proving it single in any sense. An admirer, a son, an apprentice, a collaborator, may have contributed passages or sections—a final section perhaps, as many critics have thought—to the "long song" as we have it. But the contrary is also possible. The truth, I think, is that we are too remote in time and language to decide. These, roughly, are the considerations that ought to be present to our minds when we think of Homer. But it is not necessary to put the name in quotation marks.

II

A living voice in firelight or in the open air, a living presence bringing into life his great company of imagined persons, a master performer at his ease, touching the strings, disposing of many voices, many tones and tempos, tragedy, comedy, and glory, holding his auditors in the palm of his hand: was Homer all of this? We can only suppose that he was. If what we imagine is true, Homer must himself have been his poems, in a physical sense unequalled in the case of any poet since. Imagine *Henry IV* and *The Tempest* composed not for production by a company of actors but as solo performances by Shakespeare himself. Or imagine it in the case of either, not both. The notion is still astonishing, and it is difficult to believe it.

I learn from W. S. Merwin, in the introduction to his translations of *Spanish Ballads* (Anchor, 1961), that the wandering *juglares* of medieval Spain, who sang and recited the epic *cantares,* "might be accompanied in their performance by mimes, known as *remendadores,* and *cazarros*—a name which included clowns and most varieties of stunt man." Well, stunt men, or tumblers, are mentioned as performing along with a poet or singer at Meneláos' court in Book IV of *The Odyssey.* But no mimes assist any ἀοιδός in the Homeric poems. This of itself would not prove that Homer did his own impersonations. The ἀοιδός, as Homer presented him was a figure of the heroic age, four or five centuries before his time. But so far as I know there is no evidence whatever that Homer himself, or the ἀοιδοί in his immediate tradition, or their successors, the rhapsodes, were accompanied by mimes or actors.

We have no perfect word for ἀοιδός, for the kind of artist Homer was. "Bard" was fairly exact but has become a joke. "Skald" takes us too far into druidical regions. "Minstrel" is better but still too slight, too trammeled with doublet and hose, and faintly raffish after Gilbert & Sullivan. The Italian compound word *cantastore* is at least neutral and is a definition of sorts. Lord did well to adopt the English equivalent, "singer of tales." But I am not satisfied. The term does not do justice to the creative and inventive power of the ἀοιδός. It does not suggest his mimetic art. And there is a difficulty about "singer" as a term for the poet and performer of these things.

That the telling of a story, and the incidental acting of roles, should be called "singing"—this will strike us first as affected or strange. We may indeed think of opera, disciplined and expressive opera like the *Orfeo* of Gluck, true lyric theatre as the Italians call it; but the orchestra and the stage, the whole convention, are alien to Homer. Perhaps it is enough to recall certain fine acting voices. As a child I sat aloft in the second balcony of an old theatre in Illinois while a traveling company played *Sancho Panza,* and I remember the beautiful voice of the late Otis Skinner rising effortless, malleable and pure, or falling to a crystalline whisper, far off there below, in unhurried declamation, while the whole theatre sat spellbound by that human instrument alone. There is no doubt that the master ἀοιδός had a gift like that, a trained voice of great expressive and melodic range.

By all accounts, too, the Homeric performer used a second instrument and depended on it: the κίθαρις, an affair of a few gut strings with some kind of resonator, possibly a tortoise shell, like the later lyre. It would be anachronistic to think of it as a guitar or lute, so I call it a "gittern harp" and sometimes refer to the performer as a harper. Homer describes him more than once as plucking or strumming an overture to a given tale or song, and he must have used the instrument not only for accompaniment but for pitch, and to fill pauses while he took thought for the next turn. No doubt the instrument marked rhythm, too.

We need not delude ourselves as to how far these generalities really take us. How in particular the voice, the metered verse, and the stringed instrument were related in these performances, and in the recital of poetry throughout antiquity, I do not well understand, and I do not think anyone does perfectly. In our own tradition the "music of verse" is one thing and "music" proper is another. A song is a song, not necessarily a poem. *The Peaceful Western Wind* and *Mistress Mine* indeed happen to be both, and I have heard Christopher Casson lean to a small Irish harp and sing *Oft in the Stilly Night* so attentively that it seemed twice the poem I had known before. But this is exceptional. Who would set to music the great lyrics of Yeats? Who could improve on *Lear* by scoring it? Here all is in the shape and movement of metered language. But we find the verse of Homer—and this is my point—as beautiful in itself as the verse of Yeats or Shakespeare. What we call a "musical arrangement" would disperse or confuse the effect of it. We can be sure, I think, that harp or κίθαρις played a very subdued part, however essential, in the original Homeric performance.

III

One of our first discoveries in reading Homer will be that he was a poet in our sense of the word, a man gifted at making verse.

All the learning that we may later assemble, all we can know or guess of the artist as an improviser and entertainer, even our fugitive sense of him as the demiurge of a world transfigured, all this cannot supersede—indeed it is founded on—our pleasure in him line by line, the way we hear or read him. I will never forget how unexpectedly moved I was years ago when for the first time I heard Telémakhos in Book I speak of his father as

ἀνέρος οὗ δή που λεύκ' ὀστέα πύθεται ὄμβρῳ

Looking up, I said to myself, in effect, "Why, this really is poetry!" and I meant poetry as good as "Call for the robin redbreast and the wren." Many times afterward, in reading or translating Homer, I have again paused over a line or a pair of lines in recognition and homage.

Parry thought this incomparable medium, the formulaic hexameter, had been shaped through centuries of trial and error, a testing and refining process conducted on many occasions before generations of auditors, so that in the end only the fittest language survived and the virtuoso had at his command the best words in the best order for anything he cared to relate or invent. I used at first to feel that the recurrent epithets and formula lines were a mere convention and a bore. In time I realized that they were musical phrases, brief incantations, of which the miserable renderings gave little or no idea. These formulas entered the repertory not only because they were useful but because they were memorable, I mean because nobody who had once heard them could easily forget them; and that is true to this day.

Ἦμος δ' ἠριγένεια φάνη ῥοδοδάκτυλος Ἠώς

It is possible that by Homer's time even he could not have said precisely what the two epithets in this line meant—and there are a number of others of which the same is true—but the line had been kept for its fragrance, a fragrance of Dawn, inimitable and unsurpassable, no more boring in its recurrence than Dawn itself. Because there are hundreds of lines like this and more hundreds of half lines and phrases, the very medium of Homer is pervaded by lyric quality. The simplest phrases have it. Hear Hektor saying (*Iliad* VI, 264), "Don't offer me any sweet wine, dear mother:"

Μή μοι οἶνον ἄειρε μελίφρονα πότνια μῆτερ

How could you render that? Consider the voweling, and consider how the first epithet, after the ghost of a pause, hovers between "wine" and "mother." There is, besides, a peculiar cleanliness and lightness of movement, as often in Homer, and there is something else that I call the cut or sculpture of words. It is easiest to be aware of this in the last two feet of certain hexameters: νόστον ἑταίρων and ἔνδον ἐόντων. These are rounded shapes.

I am not being what Professor Irving Babbitt used to call "fanciful." If you will make the effort to imagine this Greek as still virgin of any visual signs at all, associated with no letters, no Greek characters, no script, no print—as purely and simply expressive sound, you will be able to perceive it in the air, its true medium, and to hear how it shapes and tempers the air by virtue of stops and tones. I will quote two more lines, one for consonants, and one for vowels. The first is Aphroditê saying in *Iliad* V, 359,

φίλε κασίγνητε κόμισαί τέ με δός τέ μοι ἵππους

in which we hear the light tongue of the goddess of love herself in three coquettish particles, τε . . . τε . . . τε. . . . My second example is the first line sung by those temptresses of the sea, known to Homer as Seirênês, and it is a typical triumph of formulary art since it is a modified version of a line that occurs in *The Iliad* in quite a different context, and in the mouth of quite a different personage. Here it is, XII, 184:

Δεῦρ' ἄγ' ἰών, πολύαιν' Ὀδυσεῦ, μέγα κῦδος Ἀχαιῶν

There is a rhythm of anapests, and intricate rhyming: Δεῦ and σεῦ on the beat, λύ on the off beat and κῦ on the beat, αἰν' and αι on the beat, ών on the beat and ῶν on the off beat, and ἄγ' turned round widdershins on μέγα: this is a conjuring kind of echolalia. But more: the crooning vowels are for low seductive voices, rising in mid-line with αιν' and then rising and opening with a savage shout in Ἀχαιῶν at the end.

You might call this sort of thing "phonetic wit"—though it may have come to the artist without calculation. Along with it, in Homer, there is a lot of verbal wit enjoyed for its own sake and also syntactical wit, a quality of style that Chapman and Pope could appreciate. Chiastic order is a favorite form, and *The Iliad* especially teems with it. Book IV, 125:

λίγξε βιός, νευρὴ δὲ μέγ' ἴαχεν, ἆλτο δ' ὀϊστὸς

I could go on indefinitely, but I should cut this short and say that we are not meant very often to stop and consider so curiously. The narrative pace does not encourage it. You can be a connoisseur of the single line if you like, but this is only the beginning of appreciation. Homer is lyric but rarely indulges the lyric, he keeps his surface alive but keeps it moving; the line is only the medium, as I began by calling it, and as such it is subordinate to practically everything else. It is subordinate in the first place to the passage, to the effect created by the placement of lines in succession. Continuous prose cannot achieve the switches and surprises that you get by playing on a regular meter, a measured base. Of these effects Homer, formulas and all, was a master. We have often heard how the movement of the hexameter line itself could be varied by pauses, lightened by dactyls, retarded by spondees; but we have heard less of what could happen in the movement from line to line and in the course of action or speeches. A change of pace, a change of mood, an ironic aside, a quick look into the past or into the distance—we find all these between one line and the next.

Homer's humor, too, in *The Iliad* rather grim or slapstick, for in *The Odyssey* more subtly comic, often dawns on us at the unexpected swerve of a new line. In *Iliad* VIII there is a crash of lightning against the Akhaians and the best charioteers give way. Idómeneus retreats, Agamémnon retreats, big Aias and little Aias retreat, but Nestor? Nestor alone stood fast, we hear, and just as we begin to admire the veteran the next line says (81),

οὔ τι ἑκών, ἀλλ' ἵππος ἐτείρετο

"Not that he wanted to in the least, but one of his horses was disabled." In *Odyssey* IV, after Helen's story of how virtuously she kept Odysseus' secret when she had recognized him spying in Troy, Meneláos cannot refrain from a pointed story to keep the record straight. There is a march of hexameters extolling Odysseus' courage when he and the Akhaian captains were waiting in the wooden horse to bring death upon the Trojans. Then abruptly, in 274, ἦλθες ἔπειτα σὺ κεῖσε. The words make a trochee and two amphibrachs: "Who should come by there but *you* then"—and he goest on to tell of the peril she put them all in by mimicking the voices of their wives. You can see this trick of the sudden change of movement and tone played by Eurýmakhos in *Odyssey* I, 405, when after several lines of hearty assurance to Telémakhos he looks at him harder, ἀλλ' ἐθέλω σε, φέριστε, περὶ ξείνοιο ἐρέσθαι and the sneer becomes, yes, audible.

Another thing, more highly dramatic, is of course the calculated and gradated heightening of tone or energy throughout a longer passage. For a crescendo of passion, I suppose Akhilleus' great tirade in *Iliad* IX, 307 sqq., cannot be matched, but Odysseus, among his other gifts of gab, has a way of beginning mild and ending deadly. In XVIII there are two examples, a relatively brief one in his reply to Iros, 15 sqq., and a longer one to Eurýmakhos, 366 sqq.

Now all these that I have mentioned are tiny applications of a principle everywhere at work over the expanse of both poems. Narrative art lives as a river lives, first by grace of tributaries—in Homer by the continual refreshment of invention and unlooked-for turns—and second by the direction of flow. If in the line and passage the poems are interesting, as they are, heaven knows they are even more interesting, in the ways they take as their currents widen. Not that Homer is free of *longueurs:* Phoinix' tale of Meleagros in *Iliad* IX strikes me as windy, and in the slow movement of *The Odyssey* at least one of the digressions and retards—the pedigree of Theoklýmenos—was too much even for this virtuoso to bring off. He nods, and we nod with him. But almost always the attention of the audience is courted and held. The earliest critics noticed how Homer varied his effects: for an offhand example, Telémakhos arrives off Pylos by sea at dawn, arrives at Sparta by land at nightfall. The battle scenes in *The Iliad* are sometimes thought monotonous; in fact they are prodigiously inventive and differ one from another not only in general shape but in detail: time after time, it is true, a man falls and his armor clangs upon him, but either he or the man next to him has just been killed in an entirely new way. The formulas give the narrative musical consistency; the innovations keep it alive. The more it is the same, the more it changes. In the very use of the formulas themselves, remarkable effects are got by slight additions or modifications. Penélopê's visits to the banquet hall in *The Odyssey* are formulary: she appears with her maids, she draws her veil down and across her face, she speaks, she retires, weeps, and goes to sleep. The first time (I, 365) after she is gone the suitors make a din, they all swear they will have her; the second time (XVI, 413) she appears and retires as before but there is no din, no swearing; the third time (XVIII, 212) there is no din, but on her appearance (not on her withdrawal) a new line is added to the formula, telling us that the suitors knees were weakened with lust for her; then comes the swearing line from Book I. Someone has called this trick of style "incremental repetition." It can be, as it is in this case, very powerful.

IV

A probable rate of Homeric performance was about five hundred lines an hour. So far as I know, nobody has gone very far with deductions from this fact. The first four books of *The Odyssey* are obviously a narrative and dramatic unit, so are the next four, and so are the next four. These are three successive waves of action, and each runs to about two thousand lines or about four hours of performance. There is no reason for not regarding this as the duration of a formal recital. If we look again at the second half of the poem we will see that these twelve Books, too, fall into three divisions of about the same length. XIII through XVI, XVII through XX, and XXI through XXIV. These six divisions could well be considered the true Books of *The Odyssey*, within which the traditional Books are like chapters or cantos. Please understand that I have no positive authority for this suggestion; it merely accords with units of probable performance and with the organization of the poem. I would not discard the traditional twenty-four sections, made by Alexandrians who were perhaps following a still earlier tradition.

My six divisions, at any rate, will help us to see the entire poem in outline. In the first performance (I through IV) the last is of course foreshadowed if not determined, Olympian decisions are taken, we are introduced on the scene to the situation that is to be remedied, the conflict to be decided, and we are prepared to meet the famous man who has it all to cope with. In the second (V-VIII) we find him in a distant setting and see him in action, facing other situations, other challenges, making his way back toward the big one that awaits him. In the third (IX-XII) he himself takes over the narration and interests us directly in his past adventures, as though he were now the poet before us. In the fourth or "slow movement" as I call it (XIII-XVI) we see him at last near to his home and battleground, gathering information, testing a likely helper, and reunited with his son. In the fifth (XVII-XX) he enters the scene itself, comes to grip with his situation, suffers it, and sizes up the persons involved in it at close hand. In the sixth (XXI-XXIV) he fights and wins, remedies and recomposes everything.

That is an outline in the most general terms. If I tried to follow and comment on the narrative in detail I would never finish. But there are a few matters. . . . One is this: the universe of *The Odyssey* is subject to moral law, and in the first few lines briefly, or amply in the first few hundred, we are informed of this law, of how it may be violated, and how badly, sooner or later, the offenders come off. The poet was not Plato, Augustine, or Immanuel Kant, and we need not bother to pick flaws in his thinking. He tells us that Odysseus' crew perished for their ἀτασθαλίῃσιν, and then Zeus remarks that Aigísthos in particular and mortals in general have aggravated their lot by the same misdemeanor. What is this misdemeanor? Presumption, impious and reckless: a folly of greed. It is more than taking what belongs to a vague "someone else"—for you are permitted some raids and wars of conquest; it is claiming and taking more than your share in your own commonwealth, without a decent respect for the views of heaven or the opinions of mankind. Wife-stealing and murder, usurpation and insolence: these are the crimes against private and public order that the Olympians meditate as the poem opens. Specific objects of meditation are two Akhaian kingdoms left masterless by the war. Mykênai succumbed, now Ithaka is threatened. The two casts of characters are parallel, as they will be often again, openly or by implication, throughout the poem: Aigísthos and the suitors, Klytaimnéstra and Penélopê, Agamémnon and Odysseus, Orestês and Telémakhos. The present action will stand out more sharply by contrast with the dark action in Mykênai years before.

A very learned and close student of literature, Erich Auerbach, was led by the argument he was making at the time to assert that "the Homeric style knows only a foreground, only a uniformly illuminated, uniformly objective present." It would be better to remove the word "only" and to add that the Homeric style knows a constant background of retrospect and allusion to the past. It is so in *The Iliad*, and more so in *The Odyssey*. In fact, that past of which the events of *The Iliad* form a part stands everywhere behind the events of *The Odyssey*, the perspective in which *The Odyssey* takes place.

The relationship between the two poems is fascinating. Clearly, both are drawn from the same great fund of stories about the heroes of the expedition against Troy, both are composed in the same formulary tradition, and *The Odyssey* was second in order of composition. Besides a great many lines of *The Iliad* adapted or even playfully parodied in *The Odyssey*, there is one curious bit of evidence that I do not remember seeing noticed. The audience of *The Iliad* had to be kept straight at every point as to which of the two armies was being referred to, hence a great number of formula lines ending with the Greek for "Akhaians," a short syllable and two longs in any of the plural cases. These line endings were so convenient metrically that they were kept throughout *The Odyssey*, even in contexts where they were no longer functional, where it was unnecessary to distinguish Akhaians from anyone else. But no single incident or event of *The Iliad* is so much as referred to in *The Odyssey*, and this is so striking (there are also a few odd differences of vocabulary) that it has been possible to argue that the composer of *The Odyssey* did not even know *The Iliad*. We will be sensible to conclude that he not only knew but leaned on it familiarly; that he, like Odysseus, did not hold with twice-told tales; and that he wanted to complete and complement *The Iliad* by working into his background events that took place after the funeral of Hektor, the close of that poem.

Of these events, the fate of Agamémnon, as I have said, is from first to last the pattern of tragedy against which *The Odyssey* is played to a happy ending. In the successive appearances of the Mykênai theme, something is added each time—here is incremental repetition for you—until the climax in Book XI when Agamémnon himself tells his story. There is also a coda, in Book XXIV. But of course Mykênai is only a part of the background richly given in the first four Books and kept in view later, a background not only of depth in time but of the wide world beyond Ithaka. To make clearer the disorder of that realm there is first the order of Nestor's kingdom, where sacrifice and prayer are duly offered before meat (the suitors in Books I and II neither sacrifice nor pray) and then the splendor of Meneláos' court. In the discourse of the two great gentlemen there are echoes of battles long ago, and there are also images of other seas and lands far to the east and south. Most important of all, from one Book to another in the "Telémakheia" the figure of the absent Odysseus grows more vivid in what is said about him. We are being prepared for an entrance. We are even prepared thematically, in Meneláos' story of seafaring, of detention on an island, of the nymph Eidothea and the Ancient of the Sea, for the adventures of Odysseus.

V

The Odyssey is about a man who cared for his wife and wanted to rejoin her. In the resonance of this affection, and by way of setting it off, the poem touches on a vast diversity of relationships between men and women: love maternal and filial, love connubial and adulterous, seduction and concubinage, infatuation super-human and human, chance encounters lyric and prosaic. There are many women, young and old, enchantresses and queens and serving maids. In the "society," as we say, of *The Odyssey*, women can be very distinguished: Athena is powerful in the highest circles, Arêtê holds equal power with her husband in Phaiakia, Helen has been reestablished in the power of her beauty, which if I am not mistaken she makes Telémakhos feel. The honor roll of lovely dead ladies in Book XI is fully appropriate to this poem. Three of the principal adventures of Odysseus are with exquisite young women of great charm and spirit, and during each of these episodes the audience must wonder how he can possibly move on. He wants to regain his home and kingdom, it is true. But besides that, as Kalypso inquires, what is it about Penélopê that draws him homeward? Her distinction is often mentioned, but do we ever see it overwhelmingly demonstrated?

I believe we do, or should. The demonstration, however, is dramatic and has been missed by many people, though not by all, through a failure to grasp the nature of *The Odyssey* as performance. Let me again insist upon it. More than half of this poem is dialogue. We know that in the first centuries after the Homeric poems were written down, they were presented as performances by rhapsodes who had them by heart, and we know from the *Ion* of Plato that such performances could be histrionic, highly and effectively so. There must have existed among these professionals a tradition of interpretation, nuance, gesture, and "business" in general that may easily have descended from the ἀοιδοί, the inventors, from Homer himself. Into later and literary ages none of this survived. The French Homerist Victor Bérard

noticed years ago that our text of *The Odyssey* often resembles
an acting script. But no stage directions are included, and if we
ask how to play any particular scene we find that there has been
no Harley Granville-Barker of Homeric studies.

Well, let us at our leisure look into one situation and one big
scene that will answer Kalypso's question.

The purpose of Odysseus, determining the action of the poem,
is to get home and to prevail there. Once he lands on Ithaka his
problem is a tactical one: how, with his son and two fieldhands,
to take on more than one hundred able-bodied young men and
kill them all. By the end of Book XVI he has thought his problem
through to a certain point: Telémakhos is to precede him to the
manor, he is able to follow as a beggar, and at a signal from him
the young man is to remove all shields, helmets, and throwing
spears from those racks in the banquet hall where, as we
remember, they were located in Book I. To be exact, not all are
to be removed; a few are to be put aside for use against the
suitors. My first observation is that this is as far as Odysseus ever
goes, by himself, in planning the final combat. He goes no farther
in the course of Book XVII and Book XVIII, and as if to fix this
in our minds the poet at the beginning of Book XIX has him
repeat his previous instructions about removing the arms; in fact
he and Telémakhos do the job together. (This repetition used to
be thought an interpolation; the arms, at any rate, are removed.)

Let us now consider what *does* happen in Books XVII and
XVIII. If I am right in dividing the poem into six performances,
these Books with XIX and XX make up the fifth. Early in XVII
Telémakhos leaves the swineherd's hut, goes home to the manor
hall, and passes on to his mother the news given him by Meneláos
at Sparta—that Odysseus is not dead but alive. The words are
barely out of his mouth before his supercargo, the diviner, swears
to Penélopê that her husband is not only alive but on the island
at that very moment. Since the first piece of news is certainly
authentic, the second—though it may seem fantastic—must at
least quicken her interest in any stranger who appears. The only
stranger about to appear is Odysseus in his rags. We may or may
not recall Helen's boast of having recognized him through a similar
disguise in a similar situation at Troy; if we do—and after all we
heard the story only the other evening—our feeling of suspense
may be heightened. Presently, strange to relate, Odysseus is in

fact recognized just outside the manor. A dying old hunting dog who hasn't seen him for twenty years knows him by the sound of his voice.

Odysseus now enters the hall, begging, and one of the suitors banqueting there hits him with a footstool. Penélopê has heard the scene from her room. She orders the swineherd to fetch the beggar in case he has news of Odysseus, and the swineherd tells her the beggar does indeed have news, at least he has sworn that Odysseus is nearby on the mainland and will soon be home. "If Odysseus comes, he will repay the violence of the suitors," she says, using the future tense for that eventuality in the most hopeful speech she has yet made. At this point Telémakhos, downstairs in hall, sneezes, and Penélopê laughs at the good omen—the first time she has laughed in *The Odyssey*. She goes eagerly to the door, but Eumaios returns without the beggar, who wishes to put off a meeting until the young men have left the hall for the night. In spite of her impatience, the lady concedes that the stranger is right and is no fool.

Are we to suppose here, at the end of XVII, that it has even crossed her mind who the stranger might be? For the audience, this is already a very interesting question. The answer is, probably not—though it is clear how excited she has become.

In the next Book, XVIII, Penélopê feels impelled for reasons she cannot analyze to go downstairs among the suitors, to dazzle the young men with her beauty and to be solicitous of the beggar, who has come off well in a fist fight. She is now in the beggar's presence. Is it his presence that prompts her to a rather gratuitous speech, a speech with an air of being "to whom it may concern," recalling her husband's instructions when he left for the Trojan War? Her point is that she cannot hold out much longer against marriage with one of her suitors. She induces the young men to give her some gifts (to the amusement of Odysseus) and then withdraws until the evening is over and the suitors have left the place. We come to Book XIX. It is after dark. From the empty banquet hall Odysseus and his son remove the arms and put them back in a storeroom. Before they do this, however, Telémakhos has the old servant, Eurýkleia, temporarily lock all the maids in the women's quarters? Why? Because among these women there are a dozen mistresses and accomplices of the suitors, who are only waiting until the house is quiet to slip out and join their lovers in the town. We already know one of these girls, Melántho, mistress of Eurýmakhos. When Penélopê comes down to interview the beggar by firelight, this girl is with her, as the poet carefully makes us see. The whole interview is conducted in her presence. If she should suspect the identity of the beggar, Odysseus' tactical plan—to catch the suitors in hall without spears and trust to Athena—will miscarry, to say the least.

As the interview begins, Penélopê follows the usual formula and asks the stranger who he is. His reply is evasive, though it is moving if we remember that these are the first words he has spoken to her in twenty years. She proceeds to explain to him— to him, a stranger and vagabond—what her predicament is. She tells him of the famous feat of weaving and unweaving by which she had kept her suitors waiting for more than three years. It is as if she were justifying herself aloud for being, as she tells him she is now, at the end of her resources. Justifying herself to her husband? That is the fact, but it may still be something of which we are meant to be aware while she is not. In return for her confidence, Odysseus confides that he is a grandson of King Minos of Crete and that he once entertained Odysseus at Knossos. The lady weeps. She dries her eyes and asks him to prove it by recalling how Odysseus looked. He does so, very accurately, describing a brooch and tunic that Penélopê had given him. He adds, with a typical Odyssean touch, that the Cretan women had found him a fine sight in his tunic. The lady weeps a second time and remarks that *she* will never lay eyes on Odysseus again.

The beggar now contradicts her. He now ventures a speech that, taken along with all that has led up to it, looks like a serious effort to impart information. He not only repeats what he has already told the swineherd and the swineherd has relayed to her—that Odysseus is on the mainland and coming home—but he swears very solemnly that Odysseus will arrive (306)

τοῦδ' αὐτοῦ λυκάβαντος

"this very λυκάβας" and "between the waning and the new moon." Nobody can be sure what λυκάβας means, but it may well mean "the going of daylight" and the phrase could have the sense "before another day passes." As to the phrase about the new moon, there is very little doubt that this is precise. The next day, as we will hear in Book XX, is a feast day to Apollo, and that would be the festival of the new moon awaited in the evening.

So he is telling her twice, cryptically and elliptically for the benefit of the maids in earshot, that her husband will be home tomorrow.

Now we, the audience, must suppose that this lady, who has been represented often as extremely intelligent, will be asking herself with some urgency how the vagabond before her could possibly swear to anything so definite. She is controlled, as usual. She answers that if he were right he would soon know her love, but no, he can't be right. Odysseus cannot return. She offers him a footbath and he declines it unless there is an old maid-servant to give it to him. Penélopê says there is in fact an old woman who nursed Odysseus in infancy, and she tells Eurýkleia to bathe him. Here is an actor's line (358).

νίψον σοῖο ἄνακτος

"Bathe your master's—" the line begins, and a shiver runs through the audience. The next word, however, is not πόδας "feet" but ὁμήλικα "coeval" or "contemporary." (I think that Sophocles, for one, noted this feat of brinkmanship in a single line.) Now we have the well-known episode of the footbath during which Eurýkleia recognizes Odysseus by his scar, but he throttles her and keeps her quiet. This has been generally held to be the only recognition that takes place in Book XIX. At the climax when the old woman glances toward Penélopê as if to reveal Odysseus, the poet tells us that Athena has turned the lady's mind elsewhere so that she doesn't notice. Penélopê, in other words, is lost in thought, and we are aware of all that she has to think about. I find the outcome of her thinking very impressive.

When Penélopê speaks again, she tells the beggar that she has a dream for him to interpret—the dream of her pet geese killed by an eagle who professed to be Odysseus. In this there is a remarkable little confession that she had grown fond, in a way, of having the suitors about her, but there is more to it than that. When she says that on waking she saw the dream geese still there, what can she possibly mean except, "It is a dream to think that you can kill them; they are so many, they will survive and you will not." This at any rate is what the beggar answers. He assures her that there is no other way to interpret the dream than as Odysseus, in the dream, has already done: the suitors will be killed. Assuming the presence of the unfaithful maid—or maids— he takes a serious risk here in order to make it clear to her that he is ready for battle. She now remarks that dreams are not to be counted on, but that she has one more thing to tell him: listen carefully. She has made up her mind that *tomorrow* will be the day of decision as to whom she will marry, and the decision will be reached through the test of the bow. In reply to this the beggar says in effect that that will be excellent and tomorrow will not be too soon.

I agree with the late Philip Whaley Harsh, of Stanford, that this is one of the most interesting recognition scenes ever devised. Part of my argument was anticipated by Professor Harsh in the *American Journal of Philology*, Vol. 71 (1950). It is possible—though I think barely possible—to read the scene in the previously accepted way as involving no more communication between the man and woman than is compatible with their respective roles of lady and beggar, the roles they stick to, though so precariously. On this reading all evidence of understanding between them is coincidence and irony. But that is simply not consistent with the situation as a whole—a situation built up for the audience in the course of this performance. During the day, before the evening, Penélopê has been told first that her husband is alive, second that he is on the island, and third that he is coming soon. She has been waiting for ten years with no such authentic news and no such startling expectations and had made the suitors wait for nearly four. Are we, the audience, to believe that she wouldn't wait a few days longer to see if her husband turns up? Is it conceivable that, instead of waiting, the woman so distinguished for tenacity would this very evening give up the waiting game and seriously propose to marry the next day? How could she come to this abrupt decision in the course of her evening scene with Odysseus unless she realized that the stranger before her was indeed her husband?

Why in short, underrrate the high and beautiful tension of the scene and the nerve, the magnificence of Penélopê? Not Kalypso, not Nausikaa, not Kirkê could have played this scene. Consider what she bestows on Odysseus. Up to now his plan of action, as I have noticed, has been fairly desperate. Now it is she, not he, who remembers the big hunting bow that has hung in an inner room since he left Ithaka. Archery against men who have no missiles is in fact the only practical way of beating the numerical odds. Penélope supplies the weapon for the suitors' downfall, and she does so for that purpose and no other. At the opening of Book

XXI when Athena sends her for the bow, the goddess is said to prompt her to this as "the contest and start of slaughter"—a phrase that goes naturally by the syntax with what is in Penélopê's mind. In the course of that Book it is Penélopê who insists at the crucial moment that the beggar be given a try at the bow; she all but literally places it in his hands. I conclude that for the last and greatest of Odysseus' feats of arms his wife is as responsible as he is. The reasons for his affection should now be clear.

VI

If in other Books, especially in XXIII, there are details inconsistent with the interpretation I have given, we may regard these as instances of what Professor Lord has called the varying "pulls" of previous versions. But I am not sure there are any real inconsistencies. There is a certain mystery, if you like, but so is there mystery in *Daisy Miller.* Harsh explained Penélopê's affected incredulity and hesitation in XXIII as due to emotional exhaustion (she had been terribly afraid that Odysseus couldn't do it) and to the need to collect herself before resuming a marriage interrupted for twenty years. Twenty years is no trifle. If you left home to take part in the Second World War, imagine yourself lost to view afterward and only now returning; or if your father went to the war, imagine it of him. One difference between Homer and many of his commentators is that Homer could imagine people in situations. Some commentators even call it an "inconsistency" that the shade of Amphímedon in Book XXIV credits Odysseus with having thought up the archery contest—as though Amphímedon could have known any better, or make any better assumption.

As I noted earlier, Book XXIV has often been regarded as a later addition to the poem. This is mainly because two early critics, Aristophanes and Aristarchus, are said to have called line 296 of XXIII the "goal" or "end" of *The Odyssey.* This line, on which Odysseus and Penélopê retire to bed, could have been the conclusion of an old-fashioned movie but not of a poem like this. It is true that there are also some linguistic grounds, but they do not appear to be probative. Even if they were, I could only say that in substance Book XXIV is fully "Homeric" and that whoever

composed it knew what he was doing. The many references to
Laërtês throughout the poem require Book XXIV; so do at least
two previous allusions by Odysseus to the aftermath of the fight
with the suitors. In this Book the comparison between Penélopê
and Klytaimnéstra, recurrent throughout the poem, is rounded
off by Agamémnon himself. But there is another artistic reason
for Book XXIV, and a great one. If Homer's incidental purpose
in *The Odyssey* was to complete and complement *The Iliad*, XXIV
in effect completes both poems at once. The Akhaian antagonists
of *The Iliad*, Agamémnon and Akhilleus, are here reconciled
among the dead, and as *The Iliad* closed with Hektor's funeral,
The Odyssey does not come to a close until the funeral of Akhilleus
has been described.

A page or so more and I will have done with my reflections. I
have named Professor Lord's book and Professor Harsh's article,
each illuminating in its way. Two more books that I have valued
are *Homer and the Monuments*, by H. L. Lorimer (Macmillan,
London, 1950) and *The Poetry of Homer* by S. E. Bassett
(University of California Press, 1938). Rhys Carpenter on *Folk
Tale, Fiction and Saga in the Homeric Epics* (University of
California Press, 1946) is full of interesting arguments. So, as I
have said, is Denys Page's book on *The Odyssey*, though I read
it rather as a brief than as a judgment. His later book, *History
and the Homeric Iliad* (University of California Press, 1959) is
more brilliant still. The most recent good annotated edition is W.
B. Stanford's (Macmillan, London, 1947). D. B. Monro's annotated
edition of Books XIII-XIV with its long Appendix (Oxford, 1901),
is a superb monument of scholarship and good sense in its time.
I am indebted to it for my excision of lines 275-278 in Book I, an
excision that obviates one of Page's chief criticisms. I like Monro's
statement about the "Telémakheia": "It secures that gradual
heightening of interest which is the chief secret of dramatic art."
I also owe to Monro, and to J. D. Denniston's wonderful book,
The Greek Particles (Oxford, 1954), confirmation of my sense that
the colloquial entered into Homer's style in *The Odyssey*.[1]

1 When this was written I had not yet discovered T. B. M. Webster's *From Mycenae
to Homer*, a work of scholarship that I admire. I should have been glad, too, to know
Ulysses Found, by Ernle Bradford, the most recent and the best study by an
experienced seaman of the Mediterranean routes and landfalls of Odysseus. R.F.,
September 1969.

A word about "translation." *The Odyssey,* considered strictly as an aesthetic object, is to be appreciated only in Greek. It can no more be translated into English than rhododendron can be translated into dogwood. You must learn Greek if you want to experience Homer, just as you must go to the Acropolis and look at it if you want to experience the Parthenon. There is a sense, however, in which the Greek poem was itself a translation. It was a translation into Homer's metered language, into his narrative and dramatic style, of an action invented and elaborated in the imagination. This action and the personages involved in it were what mattered most to poet and audience.

It might be possible to translate, or retranslate, this action into our language. We may assume that Homer used all the Greek he knew, all the resources of the language available to him and amenable to his meter. Three or more Greek dialects and perhaps half a millennium of Greek hexameter poetry contributed to Homer's language; so did a wide spectrum of idiom from the hieratic to the colloquial. Anglo-Irish-American provides comparable linquistic and poetic resources, a spectrum of idiom comparably wide. If you can grasp the situation and action rendered by the Greek poem, every line of it, and by the living performer that it demands, and if you will not betray Homer with prose or poor verse, you may hope to make an equivalent that he himself would not disavow.

Why care about an old work in a dead language that no one reads, or at least no one of those who, glancing at their Rolex watches, guide us into the future? Well, I love the future myself and expect everything of it: better artists than Homer, better works of art than *The Odyssey.* The prospect of looking back at our planet from the moon seems to me to promise a marvelous enlargement of our views.[2] But let us hold fast to what is good, hoping that if we do anything any good those who come after us will pay us the same compliment. If the world was given to us to explore and master, here is a tale, a play, a song about that endeavor long ago, by no means neglecting self-mastery, which in a sense is the whole point. Electronic brains may help us to

2 This enlargement has now occurred making everyone realize with a new pang not only the beauty of our blue planet but, by contrast with lunar and extralunar desolations, its bounty and fantasy of life. R.F., September 1969.

use our heads but will not excuse us from that duty, and as to our hearts—cardiograms cannot diagnose what may be most ill about them, or confirm what may be best. The faithful woman and the versatile brave man, the wakeful intelligence open to inspiration or grace—these are still exemplary for our kind, as they always were and always will be. Nor do I suppose that the pleasure of hearing a story in words has quite gone out. Even movies and TV make use of words. *The Odyssey* at all events was made for your pleasure, in Homer's words and in mine.

Robert Fitzgerald

Perugia, June 1962